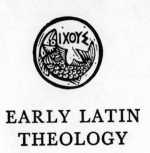

EARLY LATIN
THEOLOGY

THE LIBRARY OF CHRISTIAN CLASSICS

ICHTHUS EDITION

EARLY LATIN THEOLOGY

Selections from
Tertullian, Cyprian, Ambrose
and Jerome

Translated and edited by

S. L. GREENSLADE, D.D. Oxon., Hon. D.D. Edin.

Canon of Durham
Van Mildert Professor of Divinity
University of Durham

PHILADELPHIA
THE WESTMINSTER PRESS

Published simultaneously in Great Britain and the United States of America
by the S.C.M. Press Ltd, London, and The Westminster Press, Philadelphia.

First published MCMLVI

Library of Congress Catalog Card Number 56-5229

9 8 7 6 5 4 3 2 1

Typeset in Great Britain
Printed in the United States of America

GENERAL EDITORS' PREFACE

The Christian Church possesses in its literature an abundant and incomparable treasure. But it is an inheritance that must be reclaimed by each generation. THE LIBRARY OF CHRISTIAN CLASSICS is designed to present in the English language, and in twenty-six volumes of convenient size, a selection of the most indispensable Christian treatises written prior to the end of the sixteenth century.

The practice of giving circulation to writings selected for superior worth or special interest was adopted at the beginning of Christian history. The canonical Scriptures were themselves a selection from a much wider literature. In the Patristic era there began to appear a class of works of compilation (often designed for ready reference in controversy) of the opinions of well-reputed predecessors, and in the Middle Ages many such works were produced. These medieval anthologies actually preserve some noteworthy materials from works otherwise lost.

In modern times, with the increasing inability even of those trained in universities and theological colleges to read Latin and Greek texts with ease and familiarity, the translation of selected portions of earlier Christian literature into modern languages has become more necessary than ever; while the wide range of distinguished books written in vernaculars such as English makes selection there also needful. The efforts that have been made to meet this need are too numerous to be noted here, but none of these collections serves the purpose of the reader who desires a library of representative treatises spanning the Christian centuries as a whole. Most of them embrace only the age of the Church Fathers, and some of them have long been out of print. A fresh translation of a work already

9

translated may shed much new light upon its meaning. This is true even of Bible translations despite the work of many experts through the centuries. In some instances old translations have been adopted in this series, but wherever necessary or desirable, new ones have been made. Notes have been supplied where these were needed to explain the author's meaning. The introductions provided for the several treatises and extracts will, we believe, furnish welcome guidance.

JOHN BAILLIE
JOHN T. MCNEILL
HENRY P. VAN DUSEN

CONTENTS

AMBROSE

JEROME

PREFACE

The choice of works to illustrate the theology of the early Latin Fathers—understood as those before Augustine—was not easy. There is no lack of western writing on such central doctrines of the Christian faith as the Trinity and the Person of Christ. One thinks at once of Tertullian against Praxeas, Novatian and Hilary of Poitiers on the Trinity, Ambrose on the Faith and on the Holy Spirit. But the Greek Fathers are much the more important in this field, and they are amply covered in this series. Again there are classics like Tertullian's *Apology*, the *Octavius* of Minucius Felix and Ambrose's *De Mysteriis*; but these can be found in recent and good English versions, readily obtainable. It seemed wise, therefore, even though it meant the exclusion of so great a man as Hilary of Poitiers, to choose from the works of the four most eminent of the earlier Latin Fathers, Tertullian, Cyprian, Ambrose and Jerome, and to give some unity and individuality to the present volume by taking a theme which does not figure so largely in the writings of the Greek Fathers published in the Library of Christian Classics and which received considerable attention from the Latins, namely, the Church.

I have not limited myself, however, to the Doctrine of the Church in the narrow sense, preferring to illustrate Latin thought on the life of the Church as well as its nature and constitution. Thus the *De Praescriptionibus Haereticorum* of Tertullian and the *De Catholicae Ecclesiae Unitate* of Cyprian provide the fundamental western theory of the Church, Tertullian's *De Idololatria* and some of Jerome's letters portray its relation to society in general (the theme of the Church and the World), and letters have been selected from the correspondence of Ambrose primarily to show how he conceived the relation of the Church to the State and how he put his thoughts into practice. Other letters of Jerome and Ambrose tell of the training and duties of the clergy. I had at one time wished to include the *De Officiis* of Ambrose, the first "manual" of Christian ethics, but the work is so long that it would have taken up

far too much of the available space. Perhaps I should have
found room for something from Optatus, whose teaching on the
problems raised by the Baptismal Controversy anticipated and
influenced much of Augustine's.

One result of my choice is that some of the material is not,
despite the general title, directly theological, but would rather
be classed as historical; but I believe it all deserves to be ranked
among the Christian classics. While the number of separate
items has called for a considerable amount of introduction,
my notes are not, of course, intended as a full commentary. I
have appended to Tertullian's *De Praescriptionibus* a selection
of the chief passages in Irenaeus which underlay western
thought on the Church, and also a little of his *De Pudicitia* to
define his position as a Montanist, the trend of thought against
which the catholic doctrine is most sharply defined.

My four writers are not easy to translate, and in Tertullian's
case the original text has been quite imperfectly preserved.
They are all highly rhetorical, most or all of the time, and
modern taste, at any rate in England, does not favour grandilo-
quence. I doubt whether anything but a very free paraphrase
could give the authentic flavour of Tertullian in English. I
have thought it my duty to keep closer to the Latin, and while
I have tried to write idiomatic modern English, avoiding both
the horrid literalism of the Ante-Nicene Christian Library and
the exaggeratedly biblical or "religious" style of some other
versions, I am conscious that many passages would have read
less stiffly had I allowed myself more freedom; and I regret
my inability to reproduce the majority of Tertullian's puns
and plays on words. Cyprian's rhetoric is of a different kind:
diffuse, exuberant, repetitive. He prefers two words to one, and
I have sometimes omitted one of a pair of synonyms. I have
consulted several other translations of Tertullian, Cyprian,
and Ambrose. Some are good, some—I must say—very bad.
When I liked their renderings, I have used them unblushingly.
The version of Jerome, however, is essentially that of Dean
Fremantle in the series, *Nicene and Post-Nicene Fathers*. This
strikes me as an excellent translation of its kind, rather more
wordy, rather more formal, than would probably be written
today, but vigorous and imaginative. But, besides points of
detail which needed correction, he was inclined to incorporate
explanatory glosses into his text, he translated from the Vallarsi
–Migne text, and he nearly always substituted the English
Version of the Scriptures (usually Authorized Version,

occasionally the Revised) for the text quoted by Jerome. I have removed most glosses, brought the version into line with Hilberg's text (with a few exceptions where I could not accept Hilberg) and have substituted translations of Jerome's own biblical citations, however different from the present English Versions. Throughout the volume it should be remembered that the biblical citations are, except for a few of Jerome's, pre-Vulgate; and that where they are from the Old Testament, they are usually derived from the Septuagint Greek, and not from the Hebrew original.

S. L. Greenslade

Tertullian

Tertullian

GENERAL INTRODUCTION

I

O F TERTULLIAN'S LIFE-STORY THERE IS NOT MUCH
to be said. He was born in Carthage, according to
Jerome, and was the son of a centurion. He was evidently given a good education in grammar and rhetoric, and
he was a trained lawyer. In middle life he was converted to
Christianity, lived and wrote in Carthage, presumably as a
presbyter of the church there (though this cannot be proved
beyond question), gradually moved towards Montanism, eventually broke with the catholics of Carthage to join that body,
and died in old age, not before A.D. 220. His Christian writings
cover the period from A.D. 197 to the papacy of Callistus,
218–222.

After a brief exhortation to Christians facing martyrdom,
Tertullian launched out as an apologist with the *Ad Nationes*,
followed by the magnificent *Apology*, in which he is principally
anxious to remove the political and social charges commonly
brought against Christianity. These three works date from
197. The apologetic interest continues in *The Testimony of the
Soul*, the witness of natural instinct to the existence of the one
God, and in the later *Ad Scapulam* (212). Another main group
consists of the attacks on Gnostics: the *De Praescriptionibus
Haereticorum*, an early work which disposes of all heresy in
principle, removing the necessity of arguing against each in
particular; the large work against Marcion; books against
Hermogenes and the Valentinians; the treatises *On the Flesh of
Christ* and *On the Resurrection of the Flesh*, the *Scorpiace* (Serpent's
Bite) and the *De Anima*, though the last is also a positive presen-
tation of Tertullian's doctrine of the soul. His most influential
work of controversial theology was not directed against a

21

Gnostic; this is the book against the modalist Praxeas, a major source of western Trinitarian doctrine. Most of his other extant writings are moral and disciplinary. From his early period, that is, up to about 206 and before there are any traces of Montanism, come *On the (Lord's) Prayer, On Baptism, On Patience, On Penance, On Women's Dress, To his Wife, On the Virgin's Veil.* Of these the *De Baptismo* is important liturgically, as is the *De Oratione* to a less extent, while the *De Paenitentia* is of great, though occasionally baffling, significance for the history of the penitential discipline. Some years later came *The Soldier's Crown* (211), a repudiation of military service for Christians, and *De Idololatria* ("The Church and the World"). The *Exhortation to Chastity* also dates from this period. Fully Montanist are *On Flight in Persecution* (213), *On Monogamy, On Fasting, On Chastity (De Pudicitia). Adversus Praxeam* was also written in the Montanist phase, though it is not determined by Montanism. Tertullian wrote in Greek as well as Latin. *De Spectaculis* was certainly issued also in Greek, and he wrote in Greek on Baptism, not the extant work. Thirty-one works are extant, the two not mentioned above being *De Pallio*, a *jeu d'esprit* on the philosopher's cloak, and the unfinished *Against the Jews.* Tertullian was probably also the editor (some say the author) of the beautiful *Passion of St. Perpetua.* Not all his works have survived. Lost treatises include one against Hermogenes on the *Origin of the Soul,* one against the sect of Apelles, and books on *Fate, Paradise,* the *Christian's Hope,* and *Ecstasy.* The last might have told us much about Montanism.

II

Tertullian's style is the despair of the translator. He is passionate, vivacious, full of puns and plays on words, decorating his material with all manner of rhetorical devices. Again and again his ingenuity over-reaches itself, and he becomes tortuous and obscure, especially when he compresses the material of a sentence into two or three pregnant words. He must sometimes have had his tongue in his cheek, but there are other times when he cannot have known how wearisome his quibbling could become. At his best, however, he is forceful and brilliant. He used words as he thought he would, made them say what he wanted, and invented them if they did not already exist. If his substance is less original than his form (so far as that distinction is valid), the reader can never doubt that he is in contact with a powerful and original mind. It is conventional to call him the "Father of Latin Theology." The title is deserved, but needs to be understood. Take, for example, the *De Praescriptionibus*. This undoubtedly exercised a great influence on the doctrine of the Church in the West—notably on and through Cyprian—but the fundamental notions came from Irenaeus, who, even if he wrote in the Greek tongue, was a western bishop and was presumably read in the West. Tertullian's debt to him for his material against the Gnostics is equally obvious, and he does not conceal it. He had read the Greek Apologists also, and was well acquainted with their Logos doctrine. Nevertheless Tertullian's own contribution to the doctrine of the Trinity in *Adversus Praxeam* is real and important. He certainly prepared the way for the serious, pessimistic, doctrine of the Fall which came to characterize the West; and in this respect he broke away from his Greek masters. If his rigorism in morals and discipline was not accepted, the books were there—and even the Montanist ones were copied and read—to be used by any who wanted support for a stern view of the Christian life. His legalistic concepts of sin as debt and of reward and punishment were unfortunate legacies, only too real.

When he is described as the father of *Latin* theology, attention is drawn also to his contribution to the making of a Latin theological terminology, and it is unquestionably true that much of the language of later days can be traced back to him. But even here a *caveat* must be entered. "To him we owe a great part of the Christian Latin vocabulary," said Souter. True, but just how much depends on the date of the earliest Latin versions of the Bible, and perhaps of a few other Latin translations of Greek works such as the Letter of Clement to Corinth and the *Shepherd* of Hermas. As long as it was believed that these were all later than Tertullian, or even that he himself made the first Latin translations of Scripture, it could be said that he *created*, in large part, Latin theological terminology. Today it is more commonly held that he had at least a Latin Bible to help him.

Qualifications made, he stands out as one of the most influential men of the early Church. "Hand me the Master," Cyprian used to say to his secretary. Novatian's work on the Trinity rests on Tertullian's, the *Commonitorium* of Vincent of Lerins and its criterion of catholicity owe much to the *De Praescriptionibus*, Leo's *Tome* draws on Tertullian for its

Christological conceptions and terms. There will be many who prefer the subtler and, at the same time, more humane, more generous, more reasonable, Alexandrians. Tertullian did not like philosophy, though he could not quite get rid of his own Stoic notion of matter. Apart from that, he genuinely tried to understand Christianity as *divinum negotium*, as Revelation, as something that God has done. With all his exaggerations and perversions of detail, he was yet a major force in keeping the West steady and sensible, historical and biblical, against the much more fundamental perversions of theosophical and—shall we say, premature?—philosophical speculation.

The Prescriptions against the Heretics

INTRODUCTION

I

THE TWENTIETH CENTURY HAS SEEN A PREDOMIN-
ant concern with the problem of Revelation, and, in
close connexion, with the nature and authority of the
Church which is constituted by the Revelation in Christ.
Something similar was taking place in the second century.
The Gnostics, while claiming to be Christians, looked partly
to reason and partly to mysticism and special revelations for
their teachings. They used some of the books which now form
the New Testament, but they treated them in a very high-
handed fashion, as regards both text and interpretation; and
they used other books which the Church has subsequently
repudiated. Yet there were genuine Christian elements in
or behind their teaching, and to many they must have seemed
the most up-to-date religious teachers of the time, interpreting
the Christian revelation in the light of the best contemporary
thought. To the ordinary bishop or presbyter, responsible for
the instruction of simple people, they would be at best a nuis-
ance and at worst a serious danger—if they were not actually
an attraction to him—unless he could find something firm and
clear to hold on to and to teach.

The theologians of the second and early third century,
Justin to some extent, Irenaeus in particular, Clement of Alexandria and Tertullian, were prepared to argue against Gnostic
notions or teachers *seriatim*, and did so. But some of them recognized that the over-riding question raised by Gnosticism was,
What is authentic Christianity? It was necessary to determine
the authoritative sources of the faith (that is primarily, to
delimit the sacred books, to form a Canon), and it was expedient, if it could be done, to show where authentic Christianity

was to be found in the contemporary world. The clue to the answers was the one word, *apostolic*. The saving revelation, it was argued, had been given once and for all in the historical Christ through historical events at a point in history, events which had been prophesied and prepared for in the Old Testament. The revelation had been communicated as a *corpus* of teaching, "the faith," by Christ to the apostles, and by the apostles to the churches which they founded.

This communication took shape in three principal ways. First, in the writings of the apostles themselves or their immediate associates. Therefore it is these books, and these alone, which can and must be added to the Old Testament as canonical scripture, and these books will be binding in authority. In practice there was some division of opinion about a few books, but, in contrast to Marcion's brief canon of Luke's Gospel plus Paul, the core of the present New Testament was received as a New Testament (individually the books had long been used) by the end of the second century. Secondly, the essence of the apostolic missionary preaching, the *kerygma* with which modern scholarship has been so much concerned, could never be forgotten, for it remained essential to straightforward evangelism. Thus the local churches were always conscious of an apostolic Rule of Faith or Rule of Truth, which might also be embodied in a baptismal profession of faith, a creed. These were very short, and gave theologians plenty of scope for argument and error. However, faithfulness to the Rule provided a first test of fundamental Christianity, and departure from it was a danger signal. The Rule also laid down the guiding lines of biblical exegesis. Thirdly, the original revelation was preserved by the responsible teaching of a regular, authorized, approved ministry, especially in those churches which had been founded and instructed by the apostles themselves and could prove their continuity since apostolic times. In these the ministers, primarily the bishops, were in the first place the outward witness to, and in the second place the divinely assisted organs of, this continuity. In such churches, then, using the apostolic books, faithful to the apostolic Rule of Faith, watched over by responsible bishops, having an unbroken continuity of faith and worship and discipline since the days of the apostles, you can confidently look to find authentic Christianity. Here is Christian tradition, and here is the Christian Church. If you are doubtful about the teaching of any one local church, you can find the truth in the agreement of many.

The argument was built up gradually, though much of it was instinctive in the life of the Church from very early times. At the beginning of the second century Ignatius, already conscious of Gnostic perversions and the threat of schism, emphasized the need to hold by the bishop. Later on Hegesippus saw the importance of the episcopal successions as witnesses to historic continuity, and he reported that the churches which had long lists taught the same thing. It was Irenaeus who worked the position out with massive theological understanding. But who would read Irenaeus? Only the scholar, then and now. He is the great mind behind Tertullian, and the Church is profoundly indebted to him for his understanding of the historical character of redemption and the central place which he gave to the theology of Paul. As theology everyone will prefer his sobriety of statement to Tertullian's quips and paradoxes. But it was Tertullian's brilliance and audacity which found readers, and in this clever pamphlet many later theologians saw, for good or ill, the essence of "the catholic position" and a short way with all dissenters.

This book has been called the "most plausible and the most mischievous" of all Tertullian's writings, and even harder things have been said of it. What is the value of the argument? We must, of course, distinguish between the essential drift of it and its frills. In many ways it was sound in its own day, and in some ways it remains sound. The Gnostics were a strange breed, even if one has more sympathy than Tertullian for Marcion's strugglings with the difficulties of the Old Testament and with the Pauline antitheses of law and liberty, works and grace. Retrospectively, however, it is obvious that the Gnostics did not teach what we mean by Christianity, and they are rejected because they sat loose to the crucial historic Revelation, because they had no continuity of Christian faith and life, and, in short, because they could not stand the test of universality in time or space. This begs some questions, but seems sound in the main, and it is what Tertullian's argument comes to. On the other hand it is obvious that he assumes far too much about the clarity and fixity of the original revelation, which he thinks of in propositional form, as modern critics would say. He does not allow enough for human error in transmission locally, nor for such a rapid spread of error as was shown to be possible in the fourth century. Time has not facilitated the application of his principles. What remains true is that Christianity is a religion of revelation,

anchored in an historic event, and that the significance of that
event, recorded in and interpreted by the Bible, is grasped by
the individual within the life of a concrete, historical, Church.

II

The precise form which the argument takes in this work is a
tour de force, though fundamentally serious. The closing words
show that Tertullian was prepared to argue with Gnostics
about particular doctrines, and he produced a long series of
works of this kind. But here he claims that the Church need not
so argue; it can simply stand on its own authority. In so far as
the Gnostics appeal to and argue from Scripture, the Church
need not listen to them. It must simply stand on its right to the
possession of the true Scriptures and of a long and open tradition of interpretation. If the Gnostics want to be Christians
within the Church, they will accept these books and this tradition of interpretation, based on the Rule of Faith. If they will
not—and their mutilation of Scripture and rejection of some
apostolic writings give them away—they put themselves outside the Church, and the Church need take no notice of their
teaching. But they must not be allowed to claim the Church's
Scriptures. The only way they could prove any claim would be
to show that their communities—if any are stable enough—are
churches with an historical continuity from the apostles. If the
Gnostics do not appeal to Scripture, they put themselves out of
court automatically.

Tertullian is, of course, confident that the Gnostic groups will
not be able to prove their historic continuity in the way which
he regards as decisive, the unbroken line of bishops in each
local church. Here is one of the difficulties in his position. It
was perfectly sensible to suggest that authentic Christianity is
likely to be found where there is concrete, historical continuity,
and that a regular ministry is an element in, and a help to,
such continuity. It is a very different thing to say that authentic
Christianity cannot exist where the succession of ministry is
broken, or that it always does exist where the succession is
found. This cannot be argued out in a brief introduction. However, some aspects of the teaching of Irenaeus and Tertullian
should be made clear. Above all, their concern is always for
the preservation of true doctrine, the faith. They are only
secondarily concerned with the means by which the institutional
Church is maintained in being, though they are concerned

with that, as a means to the main object. Secondly, the apostolic succession in question consists in the line of bishops in each local church, not a chain of consecrator and consecrated, which would give quite a different list. Apostolic succession always means the former in the early Church. Thirdly, there is no particular stress on their being bishops. The argument does not stand or fall by episcopacy, though certainly Tertullian takes it for granted. Irenaeus sometimes calls the successions successions of presbyters. The essential point is that there should be an orderly succession of responsible ministers in each local church.

This understanding of the Church of the apostolic succession lent itself to something which was not, it seems, predominantly in the mind of Tertullian, and certainly not of Irenaeus, namely an institutionalism in which the notes of authority, fixity, and good churchmanship are emphasized at the expense of other, and perhaps more important, features of the Christian life. And it became fatally easy to test membership of the Church simply in terms of adherence to a bishop in apostolic succession. Tertullian was to abandon all this in favour of Montanism, largely, it is probable, because of its moral and disciplinary rigorism (whereas the average Christian was content to think himself guaranteed salvation by loyalty to the institutional Church), but also because he ceased to hold the doctrine of authority which he expounds in the *De Praescriptionibus*. For the Montanist there can be new revelation through the Spirit; authority lies in the present and immediate work of the Spirit and, in human terms, in spiritual men or women, not in a collection of bishops. Tertullian's chief source, Irenaeus, and his eventual position are illustrated briefly in the appendices.

III

There is no need to worry about the technical meaning of *praescriptio*. Tertullian had been trained in the law; he knew what *praescriptiones* were still in use, and very likely he knew the obsolete ones as well. But he is not proposing that the Church shall actually go to law with the Gnostics, and he has not to be minutely accurate in his legal forms. He has more than one *praescriptio* in mind, and uses the plural in c. 45 and in the reference to this work in *De Carne Christi* 2, "Sed plenius eiusmodi praescriptionibus adversus omnes haereses alibi iam usi sumus." The two oldest manuscripts have *De Praescriptione* as the title, which has become the commoner form in modern times. Other manuscripts and the earliest editors give *De Praescriptionibus*, which may well be correct. One *praescriptio* is that of possession, *longae possessionis* or *longi temporis*. This must be in Tertullian's mind in c. 38, and no doubt is valid all through, for the Church, historically continuous, has always possessed the Scriptures. But the main *praescriptio* is that which distinguishes at the outset a prior issue, and limits discussion to that issue. The Church will not need to argue with Gnostics about the meaning of Scripture if the prior point is settled, that the Gnostics have no right to use Scripture. The Church may possess it by a prescriptive right, as we would say, but the principal *praescriptio* is the plea that this point should be decided first. Modern legal terms sometimes used, such as demurrer, exception, limitation, are all rather misleading, and it seems best to transliterate it as prescription.

It is astonishing that some older scholars should have thought this tract a work of Tertullian's Montanist period. So far from having anything Montanist in it, it is completely contradictory to the principles of that movement. The misconception arose from an allusion at the beginning of *Adversus Marcionem* to another book which *sustinebit* against heretics a refutation on the ground of a *praescriptio novitatis*, that is, the *praescriptio longi temporis*. But *sustinebit* means that the argument will hold good, not that the book has still to be written. It precedes the works which reveal Montanist influence (from c. 206 onwards) and the books against individual Gnostics, and may be placed about A.D. 200.

For the text we have the chief manuscript of Tertullian, *Codex Agobardinus (Parisinus* 1622), of the ninth century, as far as chapter 40. The other important one is of the eleventh century, *Seletstadiensis* or *Paterniacensis* 439. There are two fifteenth-century MSS. of it at Florence, and another at Leyden. The latest full critical edition is that by Kroymann in the Vienna *Corpus*, 1942. It has the advantage of modern scientific processes for the examination of the much-damaged *Agobardinus*, and certainly improves the text in places, but Kroymann's many conjectures and his constant resort to *lacunae* are not convincing. The basis of the present translation is therefore still eclectic. For details of editions and translations consult the bibliography. The edition by R. F. Refoulé in *Corpus Christianorum* was not available when the translation was made. He uses also the fifteenth-century *Codex Luxemburgensis* 75; and, like me, he rejects many of Kroymann's emendations.

The Prescriptions against the Heretics

THE TEXT

1. The times we live in provoke me to remark that we ought not to be surprised either at the occurrence of the heresies, since they were foretold, or at their occasional subversion of faith, since they occur precisely in order to prove faith by testing it.[1] To be scandalized, as many are, by the great power of heresy is groundless and unthinking. What power could it have if it never occurred? When something is unquestionably destined to come into existence, it receives, together with the purpose of its existence, the force by which it comes to exist and which precludes its non-existence.

2. Fever, for example, we are not surprised to find in its appointed place among the fatal and excruciating issues which destroy human life, since it does in fact exist; and we are not surprised to find it destroying life, since that is why it exists. Similarly, if we are alarmed that heresies which have been produced in order to weaken and kill faith can actually do so, we ought first to be alarmed at their very existence. Existence and power are inseparable.

Faced with fever, which we know to be evil in its purpose and power, it is not surprise we feel, but loathing; and as it is not in our power to abolish it, we take what precautions we can against it. But when it comes to heresies, which bring eternal death and the heat of a keener fire with them, there are men who prefer to be surprised at their power rather than avoid it, although they have the power to avoid it. But heresy will lose its strength if we are not surprised that it is strong. It happens either that we expose ourselves to occasions of stumbling by being surprised, or else that in being made to stumble we come to be surprised, supposing the power of heresy to spring

<hr/>

[1] Matt. 7:15; 24:4, 11, 24; I Cor. 11:19, the foundation text for this introduction, cf. c. 4.

from some inherent truth. It is surprising, to be sure, that evil should have any strength of its own—though heresy is strongest with those who are not strong in faith! When boxers and gladiators fight, it is very often not because he is strong or invincible that the victor wins, but because the loser is weak. Matched subsequently against a man of real strength, your victor goes off beaten. Just so, heresy draws its strength from men's weakness and has none when it meets a really strong faith.

3. Those who are surprised into admiration are not infrequently edified by the captives of heresy—edified to their downfall.[2] Why, they ask, have so-and-so and so-and-so gone over to that party, the most faithful and wisest and most experienced members of the Church? Surely such a question carries its own answer. If heresy could pervert them, they cannot be counted wise or faithful or experienced. And is it surprising that a person hitherto of good repute should afterwards fall? Saul, though good beyond all others, was afterwards overthrown by jealousy. David, a good man after the Lord's heart, was afterwards guilty of murder and adultery. Solomon, whom the Lord had endowed with all grace and wisdom, was led by women into idolatry. To remain without sin was reserved for the Son of God alone. If then a bishop or deacon, a widow, a virgin or a teacher, or even a martyr, has lapsed from the Rule of Faith, must we conclude that heresy possesses the truth? Do we test the faith by persons or persons by the faith? No one is wise, no one is faithful, no one worthy of honour unless he is a Christian, and no one is a Christian unless he perseveres to the end.

You are human, and so you know other people only from the outside. You think as you see, and you see only what your eyes let you see. But "the eyes of the Lord are lofty."[3] "Man looketh on the outward appearance, God looketh on the heart."[4] So "the Lord knoweth them that are his"[5] and roots up the plant which he has not planted. He shows the last to

---

[2] A cryptic sentence, and clumsy in my translation. The text is uncertain. I read *miriones*, the *lectio difficilior*, not *infirmiores*; and I link it with the frequent "surprise" of c. 2. Perhaps it should be rendered more bluntly, "some gaping fools". *Aedificari in ruinam* is a play on words, with allusions to Matt. 7:26; I Cor. 8:10.

[3] IV Esdras 8:20, *elevati* in Vulgate. Perhaps Tertullian understands *alti* as "going deep" into men's hearts.

[4] I Sam. 16:7.

[5] II Tim. 2:19.

be first, he carries a fan in his hand to purge his floor. Let the chaff of light faith fly away as it pleases before every wind of temptation. So much the purer is the heap of wheat which the Lord will gather into his garner.

Some of the disciples were offended and turned away from the Lord himself. Did the rest at once suppose that they too must leave his footsteps? No, convinced that he is the word of life, come down from God, they persevered in his company to the end, although he had gently asked them whether they also wished to go. It is of less consequence if some, like Phygelus and Hermogenes, Philetus and Hymenaeus, deserted his apostle.[6] It was an apostle that betrayed Christ. Are we surprised that some desert the Church when it is our sufferings after Christ's example that show us to be Christians? "They went out from us," the Bible says, "but they were not of us; for if they had been of us, they would no doubt have continued with us."[7]

4. Instead of dwelling on such things let us keep in mind the Lord's sayings and the apostles' letters, which warned us that heresies would come and ordered us to shun them. Feeling, as we do, no alarm at their occurrence, we need not be surprised at their ability to perform that which compels us to shun them. The Lord teaches that many ravening wolves will come in sheep's clothing. What is this sheep's clothing but the outward profession of the name "Christian"? The ravening wolves are the crafty thoughts and impulses lurking within to attack Christ's flock. The false prophets are the false preachers, the false apostles the spurious evangelists, the antichrists, now as ever, the rebels against Christ. Today heresy plays this part. The assaults of its perverse teaching upon the Church are no whit less severe than the dreadful persecutions which the antichrist will carry out in his day. In fact they are worse. Persecution at least makes martyrs: heresy only apostates.

There had to be heresies so that those who are approved might be made manifest, those who did not stray into heresy as well as those who stood firm in persecution, in case anyone should want those who change their faith into heresy to be counted as approved simply because he says somewhere else: "Prove all things, hold fast that which is good,"[8] words which they misinterpret to suit themselves. As if it were not possible to "prove all things" wrongly, and so fasten erroneously upon some evil choice!

[6] II Tim. 1:15; 2:17. [7] I John 2:19. [8] I Thess. 5:21.

5. Again, when he blames party strife and schism, which are unquestionably evils, he at once adds heresy.[9] What he links with evils, he is of course proclaiming to be itself an evil. Indeed in saying that he had believed in their schisms and parties just because he knew that heresies must come, he makes heresy the greater evil, showing that it was in view of the greater evil that he readily believed in the lesser ones. He cannot have meant that he believed in the evil things because heresy is good. He was warning them not to be surprised at temptations of an even worse character, which were intended, he said, to "make manifest those who are approved," that is, those whom heresy failed to corrupt. In short, as the whole passage aims at the preservation of unity and the restraint of faction, while heresy is just as destructive of unity as schism and party strife, it must be that he is setting heresy in the same reprehensible category as schism and party. So he is not approving those who have turned aside to heresy. On the contrary, he urges us with strong words to turn aside from them, and teaches us all to speak and think alike.[10] That is what heresy will not allow.

6. I need say no more on that point, for it is the same Paul who elsewhere, when writing to the Galatians,[11] classes heresy among the sins of the flesh, and who counsels Titus to shun a heretic after the first reproof[12] because such a man is perverted and sinful, standing self-condemned. Besides, he censures heresy in almost every letter when he presses the duty of avoiding false doctrine, which is in fact the product of heresy. This is a Greek word meaning choice, the choice which anyone exercises when he teaches heresy or adopts it. That is why he calls a heretic self-condemned; he chooses for himself the cause of his condemnation. We Christians are forbidden to introduce anything on our own authority or to choose what someone else introduces on his own authority. Our authorities are the Lord's apostles, and they in turn chose to introduce nothing on their own authority. They faithfully passed on to the nations the teaching which they had received from Christ. So we should anathematize even an angel from heaven if he were to preach a different gospel.[13] The Holy Ghost had already at that time foreseen that an angel of deceit would come in a virgin called Philumene, transforming himself into an angel of

9 I Cor. 11:18–9.　　　　　　　　10 I Cor. 1:10.
11 Gal. 5:20.
12 Titus 3:10. Tertullian's text omits "and second," cf. c. 16, n. 33.
13 Gal. 1:8.

light, by whose miracles and tricks Apelles was deceived into introducing a new heresy.[14]

7. These are human and demonic doctrines, engendered for itching ears by the ingenuity of that worldly wisdom which the Lord called foolishness, choosing the foolish things of the world to put philosophy to shame. For worldly wisdom culminates in philosophy with its rash interpretation of God's nature and purpose. It is philosophy that supplies the heresies with their equipment. From philosophy come the aeons and those infinite forms—whatever they are—and Valentinus's human trinity. He had been a Platonist.[15] From philosophy came Marcion's God, the better for his inactivity. He had come from the Stoics.[16] The idea of a mortal soul[17] was picked up from the Epicureans, and the denial of the restitution of the flesh was taken over from the common tradition of the philosophical schools. Zeno taught them to equate God and matter, and Heracleitus comes on the scene when anything is being laid down about a god of fire. Heretics and philosophers perpend the same themes and are caught up in the same discussions. What is the origin of evil, and why? The origin of man, and how? And—Valentinus's latest subject—what is the origin of God? No doubt in Desire and Abortion![18] A plague on Aristotle, who taught them dialectic, the art which destroys as much as it builds, which changes its opinions like a coat, forces its conjectures, is stubborn in argument, works hard at being contentious and is a burden even to itself. For it reconsiders every point to make sure it never finishes a discussion.

From philosophy come those fables and endless genealogies and fruitless questionings, those "words that creep like as doth a canker." To hold us back from such things, the Apostle testifies expressly in his letter to the Colossians that we should beware of philosophy. "Take heed lest any man circumvent

14 For Philumene and Apelles see c. 30. He was Marcion's chief disciple.
15 Most Gnostics spoke of aeons, emanations of deity. On Valentinus see c. 33, and for his human trinity, man's threefold constitution as *materialis*, *animalis*, and *spiritalis*, see Tert., *Adv. Valent.*, 17, 25, 26, itself based on Irenaeus, *Adversus Haereses*, I, i, 11 (ed. Harvey).
16 In his *Adv. Marcionem*, Tertullian taunts Marcion because his good God had cared nothing about the world before the sending of Christ. But Marcion's teaching about God had nothing to do with Stoic *apatheia*.
17 Marcion's disciple, Lucanus, taught this, cf. Tert., *Res. Carn.*, 2.
18 *De enthymesi et ectromate*, Greek Gnostic terms. Desire was cast forth shapeless from the Pleroma and afterwards gave birth to the Demiurge, the creator God, cf. *Adv. Valent.*, 17, 18. Kroymann reads *ektenoma*. *Arte inserunt Aristotelem*. I translate the received *Miserum Aristotelem*.

you through philosophy or vain deceit, after the tradition of men," against the providence of the Holy Ghost.[19] He had been at Athens where he had come to grips with the human wisdom which attacks and perverts truth, being itself divided up into its own swarm of heresies by the variety of its mutually antagonistic sects. What has Jerusalem to do with Athens, the Church with the Academy, the Christian with the heretic? Our principles come from the Porch of Solomon,[20] who had himself taught that the Lord is to be sought in simplicity of heart. I have no use for a Stoic or a Platonic or a dialectic Christianity. After Jesus Christ we have no need of speculation, after the Gospel no need of research. When we come to believe, we have no desire to believe anything else; for we begin by believing that there is nothing else which we have to believe.

8. I come then to the point which members of the Church adduce to justify speculation and which heretics press in order to import scruple and hesitation. It is written, they say: "Seek, and ye shall find."[21] But we must not forget *when* the Lord said these words. It was surely at the very beginning of his teaching when everyone was still doubtful whether he was the Christ. Peter had not yet pronounced him to be the Son of God, and even John had lost his conviction about him. It was right to say: "Seek, and ye shall find," at the time when, being still unrecognized, he had still to be sought. Besides, it applied only to the Jews. Every word in that criticism was pointed at those who had the means of seeking Christ. "They have Moses and Elijah," it says; that is, the law and the prophets which preach Christ. Similarly he says elsewhere, and plainly: "Search the Scriptures, in which ye hope for salvation, for they speak of me."[22] That will be what he meant by "Seek, and ye shall find."

The following words, "Knock, and it shall be opened unto you," obviously apply to the Jews. At one time inside the house of God, the Jews found themselves outside when they were thrown out because of their sins. The Gentiles, however, were never in God's house. They were but a drop from the bucket, dust from the threshing-floor,[23] always outside. How can anyone who has always been outside knock where he has

19 I Tim. 1:4, etc.; II Tim. 2:17; Col. 2:8.
20 Cf. II Cor. 6:14. Solomon's Porch (John 10:23; Acts 3:11; 5:12) is contrasted with the Porch (Stoa) of the Stoic Zeno. The allusion to Wisdom 1:1 (simplicity) strengthens the link with Solomon.
21 Matt. 7:7; Luke 11:9.   22 Luke 16:29; John 5:39.   23 Isa. 40:15.

never been? How can he recognize the door if he has never been taken in or thrown out by it? Surely it is the man who knows that he was once inside and was turned out, who recognizes the door and knocks? Again, the words, "Ask, and ye shall receive," [24] fit those who know whom to ask and by whom something has been promised, namely the God of Abraham, of Isaac, and of Jacob, of whose person and promises the Gentiles were equally ignorant. Accordingly he said to Israel: "I am not sent but unto the lost sheep of the house of Israel." [25] He had not yet begun to cast the children's bread to the dogs nor yet told the apostles to go into the way of the Gentiles. If at the end he ordered them to go and teach and baptize the Gentiles, it was only because they were soon to receive the Holy Spirit, the Paraclete, who would guide them into all truth. This also supports our conclusion. If the apostles, the appointed teachers of the Gentiles, were themselves to receive the Paraclete as their teacher, then the words, "Seek, and ye shall find," were much less applicable to us than to the Jews. For we were to be taught by the apostles without any effort of our own, as they were taught by the Holy Spirit. All the Lord's sayings, I admit, were set down for all men. They have come through the ears of the Jews to us Christians. Still, many were aimed at particular people and constitute for us an example rather than a command immediately applicable to ourselves.

9. However, I shall now make you a present of that point. Suppose that "Seek, and ye shall find" was said to us all. Even then it would be wrong to determine the sense without reference to the guiding principles of exegesis. No word of God is so unqualified or so unrestricted in application that the mere words can be pleaded without respect to their underlying meaning.

My first principle is this. Christ laid down one definite system of truth [26] which the world must believe without qualification, and which we must seek precisely in order to believe it when we find it. Now you cannot search indefinitely for a single definite truth. You must seek until you find, and when you find, you must believe. Then you have simply to keep what you have come to believe, since you also believe that there is nothing else to believe, and therefore nothing else to seek, once you have found and believed what he taught who bids you seek nothing

24 John 16:24, used as an equivalent to Matt. 7:7.
25 Matt. 15:24.
26 A great deal of Tertullian's argument depends on this.

beyond what he taught. If you feel any doubt as to what this truth is, I undertake to establish that Christ's teaching is to be found with us. For the moment, my confidence in my proof allows me to anticipate it, and I warn certain people not to seek for anything beyond what they came to believe, for that was all they needed to seek for. They must not interpret, "Seek, and ye shall find," without regard to reasonable methods of exegesis.

10. The reasonable exegesis of this saying turns on three points: matter, time, and limitation. As to matter, you are to consider what is to be sought; as to time, when; and as to limitation, how far. What you must seek is what Christ taught, and precisely as long as you are not finding it, precisely until you do find it. And you did find it when you came to believe. You would not have believed if you had not found, just as you would not have sought except in order to find. Since finding was the object of your search and belief of your finding, your acceptance of the faith debars any prolongation of seeking and finding. The very success of your seeking has set up this limitation for you. Your boundary has been marked out by him who would not have you believe, and so would not have you seek, outside the limits of his teaching.

But if we are bound to go on seeking as long as there is any possibility of finding, simply because so much has been taught by others as well, we shall be always seeking and never believing. What end will there be to seeking? What point of rest for belief? Where the fruition of finding? With Marcion? But Valentinus also propounds: "Seek, and ye shall find." With Valentinus? But Apelles also will knock at my door with the same pronouncement, and Ebion and Simon [27] and the whole row of them can find no other way to ingratiate themselves with me and bring me over to their side. There will be no end, as long as I meet everywhere with, "Seek and ye shall find," and I shall wish I had never begun to seek, if I never grasp what Christ taught, what should be sought, what must be believed.

11. We may go astray without harm if we do not go wrong —though to go astray is to go wrong; we may wander without harm, I mean, if no desertion is intended. However, if I once believed what I ought to believe and now think I must seek something else afresh, presumably I am hoping that there is

---

[27] From the Ebionite sect ("the Poor") Tertullian wrongly supposes a personal founder called Ebion. Simon Magus (Acts 8) is the conventional "founder" of Gnosticism. For both cf. c. 33.

something else to be found. But I should never have hoped that, unless I had either never believed, though I seemed to, or else had stopped believing. So in deserting my faith I am shown up as an apostate. Let me say once for all, no one seeks unless there is something he did not possess or something he has lost. The old woman in the parable had lost one of her ten pieces of silver, and so she began to seek it. When she found it, she stopped seeking. The neighbour had no bread, so he began to knock. When the door was opened and he was given the bread, he stopped knocking. The widow kept asking to be heard by the judge because she was not being granted an audience. When she was heard, she insisted no longer.[28] So clear is it that there is an end to seeking and knocking and asking. For to him that asketh, it shall be given, it says, and to him that knocketh, it shall be opened, and by him that seeketh, it shall be found. I have no patience with the man who is always seeking, for he will never find. He is seeking where there will be no finding. I have no patience with the man who is always knocking, for the door will never be opened. He is knocking at an empty house. I have no patience with the man who is always asking, for he will never be heard. He is asking one who does not hear.

12. Even if we ought to be seeking now and always, where should we seek? Among the heretics, where everything is strange and hostile to our truth, men we are forbidden to approach? What slave expects his food from a stranger, let alone his master's enemy? What soldier hopes to get bounty or pay from neutral, let alone hostile, kings? Unless of course he is a deserter or a runaway or a rebel! Even the old woman was seeking the piece of silver inside her own house. Even the man who was knocking hammered at his neighbour's door. Even the widow was appealing to a judge who, though hard, was not hostile. Instruction and destruction never reach us from the same quarter. Light and darkness never come from the same source. So let us seek in our own territory, from our own friends and on our own business, and let us seek only what can come into question without disloyalty to the Rule of Faith.

13. The Rule of Faith[29]—to state here and now what we

---

[28] Luke 15:8; 11:5; 18:3.

[29] *Regula Fidei*, a summary of the apostolic preaching, preserved—one might almost say, instinctively—in the tradition of the churches and used as a test of all teaching. It is similar to baptismal creeds, but not used liturgically nor fixed verbally. Irenaeus gives it in two forms, *Haer.*, I, ii (see

maintain—is of course that by which we believe that there is but one God, who is none other than the Creator of the world, who produced everything from nothing through his Word, sent forth before all things; that this Word is called his Son, and in the Name of God was seen in divers ways by the patriarchs, was ever heard in the prophets and finally was brought down by the Spirit and Power of God the Father into the Virgin Mary, was made flesh in her womb, was born of her and lived as Jesus Christ; who thereafter proclaimed a new law and a new promise of the kingdom of heaven, worked miracles, was crucified, on the third day rose again, was caught up into heaven and sat down at the right hand of the Father; that he sent in his place the power of the Holy Spirit to guide believers; that he will come with glory to take the saints up into the fruition of the life eternal and the heavenly promises and to judge the wicked to everlasting fire, after the resurrection of both good and evil with the restoration of their flesh.

This Rule, taught (as will be proved) by Christ, allows of no questions among us, except those which heresies introduce and which make heretics.

14. Provided the essence of the Rule is not disturbed, you may seek and discuss as much as you like. You may give full rein to your itching curiosity where any point seems unsettled and ambiguous or dark and obscure. There must surely be some brother endowed with the gift of knowledge who can teach you, someone who moves among the learned who will share your curiosity and your inquiry. In the last resort, however, it is better for you to remain ignorant, for fear that you come to know what you should not know.[30] For you do know what you should know. "Thy faith hath saved thee,"[31] it says; not thy biblical learning. Faith is established in the Rule. There it has its law, and it wins salvation by keeping the law. Learning derives from curiosity and wins glory only from its zealous pursuit of scholarship. Let curiosity give place to faith, and glory to salvation. Let them at least be no hindrance, or let them keep quiet. To know nothing against the Rule is to know everything.

---

p. 65) and *Epideixis*, 6; Tertullian in three, here and in *Virg. Vel.*, 1 and *Prax.*, 2. For Tertullian's forms see E. Evans, *Tertullian's Treatise against Praxeas* (S.P.C.K., 1948), and for the subject in general, D. van den Eynde, *Les normes de l'enseignement chrétien* (Paris, 1933) and J. N. D. Kelly, *Early Christian Creeds* (Longmans, 1950).

[30] The text is corrupt here.   [31] Luke 18:42.

Grant that heretics are not enemies of the truth, grant that we were not warned to avoid them, what is the good of conferring with men who themselves profess that they are still seeking? If they are indeed still seeking, they have still found nothing certain. Whatever they hold is only provisional. Their continual searching shows up their hesitation. And so when you, a seeker like them, look to men who are seekers themselves, the doubter to the doubters, the uncertain to the uncertain, then, blind yourself, you must needs be led by the blind into the ditch.[32] But, in fact, it is only for the sake of deceiving us that they pretend to be still seeking. By first filling us with anxiety, they hope to commend their own views to us. The moment they get near us they begin to defend the very propositions which, they had been saying, need investigation. We must be as quick to refute them, making them understand that it is not Christ we deny, but themselves. In that they are still seeking, they do not yet hold any convictions. In that they possess no convictions, they have not yet come to believe. In that they have not yet come to believe, they are not Christians.

An objection is raised. "They do hold convictions and believe, but assert the necessity of 'seeking' in order to defend their faith." Yes, but before they defend it they deny it, confessing by their seeking that they have not yet believed. Not Christians even to themselves, how can they be to us? What sort of faith are they arguing when they come with deceit? What truth are they vindicating when they introduce it with a lie? Another objection. "They discuss and persuade on the basis of Scripture." Naturally. From what other source than the literature of the faith could they talk about the things of the faith?

15. So I reach the position I had planned. I was steering in this direction, laying the foundations by my introductory remarks. From this point onwards I shall contest the ground of my opponents' appeal. They plead Scripture, and some people are influenced from the outset by this audacious plea. Then, as the contest goes on, they weary even the strong, they capture the weak and send the waverers off torn with anxiety. Therefore I take my stand above all on this point: they are not to be admitted to any discussion of Scripture at all. If the Scriptures are to be their strong point (supposing they can get hold of them), we must first discover who are the rightful owners of the Scriptures, in case anyone is given access to them without any kind of right to them.

[32] Matt. 15:14.

16. Do not suspect me of raising this objection from want of confidence or from a desire to enter upon the issues in some other way. My reason is primarily the obedience which our faith owes to the Apostle when he forbids us to enter upon questionings, to lend our ears to novel sayings, to associate with a heretic after one correction[33]—not, observe, after one *discussion*. In designating correction as the reason for meeting a heretic, he forbade discussion, and he says *one* correction because the heretic is not a Christian. He is to have no right to a second censure, like a Christian, before two or three witnesses,[34] since he is to be censured for the very reason that forbids discussion with him. Besides, arguments about Scripture achieve nothing but a stomach-ache or a headache.

17. Any given heresy rejects one or another book of the Bible. What it accepts, it perverts with both additions and subtractions to suit its own teaching, and if, in some cases, it keeps books unmaimed, it none the less alters them by inventing different interpretations from ours.[35] False exegesis injures truth just as much as a corrupt text. Baseless assumptions naturally refuse to acknowledge the instrument of their own refutation. They rely on passages which they have put together in a false context or fastened on because of their ambiguity. What will you accomplish, most learned of biblical scholars, if the other side denies what you affirmed and affirms what you denied? True, you will lose nothing in the dispute but your voice; and you will get nothing from their blasphemy but bile.

18. You submit yourself to a biblical disputation in order to strengthen some waverer. Will he in fact incline to the truth any more than to heresy? He sees that you have accomplished nothing, the rival party being allowed equal rights of denial and affirmation and an equal status. As a result he will go away from the argument even more uncertain than before, not knowing which he is to count as heresy. The heretics too can retort these charges upon us. Maintaining equally that the truth is with them, they are compelled to say that it is we who introduce the falsifications of Scripture and the lying interpretations.

19. It follows that we must not appeal to Scripture[36] and we

---

33 Titus 3:10. The true text is certainly "first and second," but many Old Latin MSS. and Latin Fathers omit "and second," e.g., Cyprian, *Ep.* 59:20.
34 As in Matt. 18:16—thy ⟨Christian⟩ brother.
35 On this subject see c. 38.
36 That is, in dealing with *heretics* one must not argue about Scripture. In general, Tertullian does, of course, appeal to Scripture as the final authority in doctrine.

must not contend on ground where victory is impossible or uncertain or not certain enough. Even if a biblical dispute did not leave the parties on a par, the natural order of things would demand that one point should be decided first, the point which alone calls for discussion now, namely, who hold the faith to which the Bible belongs, and from whom, through whom, when and to whom was the teaching delivered by which men become Christians? For only where the true Christian teaching and faith are evident will the true Scriptures, the true interpretations, and all the true Christian traditions be found.

20. Our Lord Jesus Christ, whoever[37] he is—if he will permit me to speak in this way for the moment—of whatever God he is Son, of whatever matter Man and God, whatever faith he taught, whatever reward he promised, himself declared, while he lived on earth, what he was, what he had been, how he was fulfilling his Father's will, what he was laying down as man's duty. He declared all this either openly to the people or privately to the disciples, twelve of whom he had specially attached to his person and destined to be the teachers of the nations. One of them was struck off. The remaining eleven, on his return to his Father after the resurrection, he ordered to go and teach the nations, baptizing them into the Father and into the Son and into the Holy Ghost.

At once, therefore, the apostles (whose name means "sent") cast lots and added a twelfth, Matthias, in the place of Judas, on the authority of the prophecy in a psalm of David; and having obtained the promised power of the Holy Spirit to work miracles and to speak boldly, they set out through Judaea first, bearing witness to their faith in Jesus Christ and founding churches, and then out into the world, proclaiming the same doctrine of the same faith to the nations. Again they set up churches in every city, from which the other churches afterwards borrowed the transmission of the faith and the seeds of doctrine and continue to borrow them every day, in order to become churches.[38] By this they are themselves reckoned apostolic as being the offspring of apostolic churches. Things of every kind must be

---

[37] That is, *whatever* the truth turns out to be, it can only be found in the teaching of Christ, given openly to the apostles and transmitted by them to the churches.

[38] Observe that they become churches by receiving the apostolic faith and doctrine, not by receiving a ministry in apostolic succession by ordination. Not that the two are incompatible, but Tertullian's emphasis, as with Irenaeus, is on the faith, even though both lay stress on apostolic succession of ministry, as then conceived. For the latter see c. 32.

classed according to their origin. These churches, then, numerous as they are, are identical with that one primitive apostolic Church from which they all come. All are primitive and all apostolic. Their common unity is proved by fellowship in communion, by the name of brother and the mutual pledge of hospitality—rights which are governed by no other principle than the single tradition of a common creed.[39]

21. On this ground, therefore, we rule our prescription.[40] If the Lord Christ Jesus sent the apostles to preach, none should be received as preachers except in accordance with Christ's institution. For no one knows the Father save the Son and he to whom the Son has revealed him, nor is the Son known to have revealed him to any but the apostles whom he sent to preach—and of course to preach what he revealed to them. And I shall prescribe now that what they preached (that is, what Christ revealed to them) should be proved only through the identical churches which the apostles themselves established by preaching to them both *viva voce*, as one says, and afterwards by letters. If this is so, it follows that all doctrine which is in agreement with those apostolic churches, the wombs and sources of the faith, is to be deemed true on the ground that it indubitably preserves what the churches received from the apostles, the apostles from Christ, and Christ from God. It follows, on the other hand, that all doctrine which smacks of anything contrary to the truth of the churches and apostles of Christ and God must be condemned out of hand as originating in falsehood.

It remains for me to show whether this doctrine of ours, the Rule of which I have set out above, does originate in the tradition of the apostles and whether, in consequence, the other doctrines come from falsehood. We are in communion with the apostolic churches. That is not true of any other doctrine. This is evidence of truth.

22. But since the proof is so short and simple that, if it were brought forward at once, there would be nothing further to discuss, let us give place for a moment to the other side, as if we had not produced our proof. Perhaps they think they can set something in motion to weaken this prescription. Sometimes they say that the apostles did not know everything. Then they change their ground and say that while the apostles indeed knew everything, they did not hand everything on to

39 *Sacramenti*, meaning here a system of religion.
40 For the principles of this central chapter see the *Introduction*.

everybody.[41] Both suggestions are the product of the same demented state of mind, and in both they are exposing Christ to blame for sending out apostles who were either inadequately instructed or not sufficiently straightforward.

Who in his senses can believe that the men whom the Lord gave to be teachers were ignorant of anything? For he kept them in his company, taught them, and lived with them inseparably. He used to explain all difficulties to them privately, saying that they were permitted to know secrets which the people were not allowed to understand. Was anything hidden from Peter, the rock[42] on which the Church was to be built, Peter who was given the keys of the kingdom of heaven and authority to bind and loose in heaven and on earth? Was anything hidden from John, most beloved of the Lord, who lay on his breast, to whom he pointed out the traitor Judas in advance, and whom he commended to Mary as a son in his own place? What could he wish to keep from the knowledge of those to whom he showed even his own glory, and Moses and Elijah and the voice of his Father from heaven as well—not rejecting the others, but because "by three witnesses shall every word be established."[43] So those also were ignorant to whom after the resurrection he deigned to expound all the Scriptures in the way!

At one time, it is true, he did say: "I have yet many things to say unto you, but ye cannot bear them now." But by adding: "When he, the Spirit of truth, is come, he will guide you into all the truth,"[44] he showed that they who would receive the whole truth through the Spirit of truth, as he promised, were ignorant of nothing. That promise he certainly fulfilled. The Acts of the Apostles proves the descent of the Holy Spirit. Those who reject this book as scripture cannot be of the Holy Spirit since they cannot yet recognize that the Holy Spirit was sent to the disciples. Nor can they maintain that they are the Church, since they cannot prove when and in what cradle this body of theirs had its beginning. It is of considerable importance to them to have no proof of their own position, for in that way they stop the refutation of their own lies from the same source.[45]

---

[41] Compare Irenaeus in Appendix I, B (p. 67).

[42] Here the rock is Peter himself, as in Tert., *Monog.*, 8 and *Pudic.*, 21 (Appendix II, p. 76). In *Adv. Marc.*, IV, 13, it is Christ.

[43] Deut. 19:15; Matt. 18:16; II Cor. 13:1.   [44] John 16: 12–13.

[45] Marcion and his followers rejected Acts. Thus they reject their continuity with the apostolic Church. But at least they have secured that they cannot be refuted from a book which they *themselves* recognize as authoritative.

23. To scoff at some measure of ignorance in the apostles, they urge that Peter and his companions were reproved by Paul.[46] That proves that something was lacking, they say. Thus they hope to build up their argument that a fuller knowledge could have supervened later on, such as came to Paul when he reproved his predecessors. At this point I can say to those who repudiate the Acts of the Apostles: "You have first to show who this Paul is, what he was before he became an apostle, and how he became an apostle." For they make a great deal of use of him on other occasions in matters of dispute. Now to the critical mind which demands evidence, it is not good enough that Paul should himself profess to have been changed from persecutor to apostle. Even the Lord did not bear witness of himself.

However, let them believe without the Scriptures, so that they can believe against the Scriptures. Even so, how can their point that Peter was reproved by Paul prove that Paul introduced a new form of Gospel, different from that which Peter and the rest put out before him? No, when he was converted from persecutor to preacher, he was taken to the brethren by brethren as one of the brethren, to men and by men who had "put on" faith at the apostles' hands.[47] After that, as he tells us himself, he went up to Jerusalem to meet Peter. Their common faith and preaching made this both a duty and a right. Had he preached some contrary faith, they would not have marvelled that the persecutor had turned preacher. They would not have glorified the Lord that his enemy Paul had arrived. So they gave him their right hands, the sign of fellowship and agreement, and they arranged among themselves a distribution of their spheres of work—not a division of the Gospel.[48] It was not that each should preach something different, but that each should preach to different people, Peter to the Circumcision, Paul to the Gentiles. But if Peter was reproved for dissociating himself from the Gentiles out of respect of persons after he had once eaten with them, that was surely a fault of conduct, not of preaching. It did not announce a God other than the Creator, another Christ not born of Mary, a hope other than the resurrection.

24. It is not my good fortune (or rather, my misfortune)

[46] Gal. 2:11.
[47] Acts 9:17, 27. "Put on," *fidem induerant*, cf. Gal. 3:27, "put on Christ" in baptism.
[48] Gal. 1:18–24; 2:9.

to set the apostles on one another. However, since these sons of perversity bring that reproof up in order to cast suspicion upon the earlier teaching, I will reply, as it were, for Peter. Paul himself said that he became all things to all men, to the Jews a Jew, to the Gentiles a Gentile, that he might gain all. At particular times, in particular persons and cases, they would blame actions which at other times, in other persons and cases, they would be just as ready to sanction. Peter, for instance, might well reprove Paul for himself circumcising Timothy though he forbade circumcision. It is folly to pronounce judgment on an apostle.[49] How fortunate that Peter is made equal to Paul in his martyrdom!

No doubt Paul was caught up to the third heaven and borne to paradise, and there heard certain things. But they were things which could not possibly equip him to preach a different doctrine, since by their nature they must not be communicated to any human being.[50] But if any heresy claims to be following something which did leak out and come to someone's knowledge, then either Paul is guilty of betraying the secret or else they must show that someone else was caught up into paradise after Paul, someone who was permitted to utter what Paul was not allowed to mutter.

25. But, as I said before, it is just as demented to allow that the apostles were in no respect ignorant and did not differ in their preaching, and yet to have it that they did not reveal everything to all alike but entrusted some things openly to all and some things secretly to a few. This is because Paul said to Timothy: "O Timothy, guard the deposit," and again: "Keep the good deposit"! What is this deposit? A secret one, to be reckoned part of another doctrine? Or was it part of that charge of which he says: "This charge I commit unto thee, son Timothy"? Or of that commandment of which he says: "I charge thee in the sight of God, who quickeneth all things, and of Jesus Christ, who before Pontius Pilate witnessed the good confession, that thou guard the commandment"? What commandment and what charge? The context makes it clear that in these words there is no hinting at a hidden doctrine, but a command not to admit any but the teaching which he had heard from Paul himself, and (I think) openly—"before many witnesses," as he says. It makes no difference if they will

49 It is interesting to recall the discussion of the Galatians incident in the correspondence between Jerome and Augustine.
50 II Cor. 12:2 ff.

not have these many witnesses to be the Church. Nothing that
was proclaimed before many witnesses could be kept secret.
Nor can they interpret as evidence of some hidden gospel
Paul's desire that Timothy should entrust "these things to
faithful men, fit to teach others." "*These* things" meant the
things of which he was then writing. To refer to things hidden
in their minds he would have said *those*, as of something absent,
not *these*.[51]

26. When he was entrusting the ministry of the Gospel to
anyone—a ministry not to be carried out indiscriminately or
carelessly—it was natural to add, in accordance with the Lord's
words, that the minister should not cast pearls before swine
or give that which is holy to the dogs. The Lord spoke openly
without hint of any hidden mystery.[52] He had himself commanded them to preach in the light and on the house-tops
whatever they had heard in the darkness and in secret. In a
figure of their ministry, he had himself instructed them by a
parable not to keep one pound (that is, one word of his) hidden
and fruitless. He himself taught that a lamp is not usually
pushed away under a bushel, but set up on a lampstand to
give light to all in the house. These commands the apostles
either neglected or failed to understand if, by hiding any of
the light (that is, of the word of God and the mystery of Christ),
they did not fulfil them. I cannot suppose they were afraid of
anyone; they feared neither Jewish nor Gentile violence. The
men who did not keep silence in synagogues and public places
would preach all the more freely in church. No, they could not
have converted Jew or Gentile unless they had systematically
set out what they wanted them to believe. Much less would
they have withheld something from churches already believing,
to entrust it to a few other individuals separately. Even if they
discussed a few matters within the family-circle, so to speak,
it is incredible that they were such things as would introduce
a new Rule of Faith different from and contrary to the one
which they gave to all the world. They would not speak of
one God in church and another at home, describe one kind of
Christ openly and another secretly, announce one hope of
resurrection to all, another to the few. Their own letters
beseech all "to speak the same thing, and that there be no
divisions" and schisms in the Church, because they preached

51 The citations are: I Tim. 6:20; II Tim. 1:14; I Tim. 1:18; 6:13f.; II
Tim. 2:2. These, those=*haec, illa.*
52 *Tecti sacramenti*, and "mystery of Christ" below is *sacramentum.*

the same message, whether it be Paul or any of the others. Besides, they remembered: "Let your speech be, Yea, yea; Nay, nay: for whatsoever is more is of evil," words which forbade them to handle the Gospel in contradictory ways.[53]

27. If we cannot believe either that the apostles did not know the full scope of their message or that they did not publish to all the whole content of the Rule, we have to consider whether perhaps, while the apostles preached straightforwardly and fully, the churches through their own fault altered what the apostles offered them. You will find the heretics putting forward all these incitements to doubt. They instance churches reproved by the apostle: "O foolish Galatians, who hath bewitched you?" and "Ye were running well; who did hinder you?" and, right at the beginning: "I marvel that ye are so quickly removed from him that called you in grace unto another gospel." Again, they quote the Epistle to the Corinthians, that they were still carnal, having to be fed with milk, not yet able to bear meat, the Corinthians who thought they knew something when they did not yet know anything as they ought to know it.[54] Since they object that the churches were reproved, let them be sure that they mended their faults. At all events let them recognize the churches for whose faith and knowledge and manner of life the Apostle rejoices and gives thanks to God.[55] And today these churches are one with the churches then reproved in the privileges of a single tradition of teaching.

28. Suppose all have erred. Suppose even the Apostle was deceived when he gave his testimony. Suppose the Holy Spirit had no regard for any church, to guide it into the truth, although it was for this purpose that Christ sent him and asked him of the Father to be the teacher of the truth. Suppose the steward of God, the vicar of Christ, neglected his office, allowing the churches for a time to understand and believe other than as he himself preached through the apostles. Even so, is it likely that so many churches would have erred into one faith?[56] With so many chances you do not get a uniform result. Doctrinal error in the churches must have shown variations.

[53] I Cor. 1:10; Matt. 5:37.
[54] Gal. 3:1; 5:7; 1:6; I Cor. 3:1 f; 8:2.
[55] The opening verses of Rom., Eph., Phil., Col., I and II Thess. contain praise, mostly of faith; these are *all* the other churches.
[56] For the argument compare Irenaeus in Appendix I, A (p. 66). This kind of appeal to catholicity remains important, but time has weakened it. Even in the fourth century "the whole world groaned to find itself Arian."

Where uniformity is found among many, it is not error but tradition. Will anyone venture to affirm that the error lay in the authors of the tradition?

29. However the error arose, it reigned, I suppose, as long as there were no heresies! Truth was waiting for a Marcionite or a Valentinian to set her free. Meanwhile, everything was done wrong—the preaching of the Gospel, the acceptance of the creed, the thousands upon thousands of baptisms, the works of faith, the miracles, the gifts of grace, the priesthoods and the ministries, all wrong, and even the martyrs wrongly crowned. Or if they were not done wrongly and ineffectually, how do you explain that the things of God were taking their course before it was known what God they belonged to? That there were Christians before Christ was discovered? Or heresy before true doctrine? The real thing always exists before the representation of it; the copy comes later. It would be quite absurd that heresy should be taken for the earlier doctrine, if for no other reason than that the earlier doctrine itself prophesied that heresies would come and would have to be watched. To the Church of this doctrine was it written— indeed, Doctrine herself was writing to her own Church— "Though an angel from heaven preach any other gospel than that which we have preached, let him be anathema." [57]

30. Where was Marcion then, the ship-owner of Pontus, the student of Stoicism? Where was Valentinus then, the disciple of Plato? It is well known that they lived not so long ago, about the reign of Antoninus, and at first accepted the doctrine of the catholic Church at Rome under Bishop Eleutherus of blessed memory, until, on account of the ever-restless speculation with which they were infecting the brethren also, they were expelled once and again (Marcion indeed together with the £2,000 which he had given to the Church) and, when they were finally banished into permanent excommunication, scattered the poisonous seeds of their peculiar doctrines abroad. Later, when Marcion professed penitence, the terms laid down for his reconciliation were that he should restore to the Church all whom he had instructed in the way of perdition. He accepted the condition, but was first overtaken by death. [58] For "there

[57] Gal. 1:8.
[58] On Marcion see E. C. Blackman, *Marcion and his Teaching* (London, 1948), and on Valentinus, F. Sagnard, *La Gnose Valentinienne* (Paris, 1947). Tertullian refuted Marcion seriously and at length, but his tract against Valentinus is more of a caricature. The dates here are muddled.

must be heresies." That does not make heresy a good thing.
Evil also must be. The Lord must be betrayed. But woe to the
traitor—in case anyone wants to defend heresy on this ground!
Look next at Apelles' pedigree. [59] It goes back no farther than
Marcion. It was Marcion who taught and moulded him, but
he fell with a woman, deserting Marcion's continence, and
withdrew to Alexandria, away from the eyes of his most holy
master. Returning a few years later, no better except that he
was no longer a Marcionite, he fastened on another woman, the
same virgin Philumene whom I mentioned earlier. She afterwards became a horrible prostitute, and it was under her
malign influence that he wrote the *Revelations* which he learned
from her. There are still people living who remember them, in
fact their own disciples and successors, who can scarcely deny
that they were late-comers. Besides, they are convicted by their
own works, as the Lord said. If Marcion separated the New
Testament from the Old, he is later than what he separated.
He could only separate what was united. And if it was united
before it was separated, its subsequent separation shows that
the separator came later. Again, when Valentinus reinterprets
and corrects whatever he corrected precisely as having been
faulty before, he proves that it had belonged to someone else.

I mention these as the more outstanding and more
familiar corrupters of the truth. I could add a certain Nigidius
and Hermogenes and many others who go about today pervert-
ing the ways of the Lord. [60] Let them show me on what authority

Antoninus Pius reigned 138–161, Eleutherus was Bishop of Rome 174–189.
Marcion went to Rome *c.* 140 and was excommunicated in 144. Valentinus went from Alexandria to Rome about the same time, but was there
somewhat longer. Some editors (e.g., Preuschen, Rauschen) reject the
sentences "Later, when Marcion . . . death," since there is no other
evidence of this repentance. Willingness to make disciplinary concession
to schismatics who can bring their flocks with them into the catholic
Church (returning *cum suis*) is found elsewhere, e.g., in Cyprian, *Ep.*, 55
(Rome), and in fourth century African canon law dealing with Donatism.

[59] *Stemma*, pedigree, seems right here, though C. Agobardinus has *stigma*,
which Kroymann keeps. Apelles is not mentioned by Irenaeus but was
known, as an old man, to Rhodo, late in the second century (ap. Eus.,
H.E., V, 13). Tertullian wrote an *Adversus Apelleiacos*, now lost, and often
mentions him and Philumene. Most later information seems to have
come from him. Marcion himself was a strict ascetic, whose orthodox
opponents acknowledge his personal sanctity.

[60] Nigidius is not otherwise known. Hermogenes came from the East,
where Theophilus of Antioch wrote against him. He settled in Carthage
and was living there when Tertullian wrote his *Adversus Hermogenem*
c. 205–206. This is extant, but Tertullian's other work against him, *De*

they have come forward. If they preach a different God,
why do they make use of the creatures and books and names
of the God they preach against? If it is the same God, why
preach him differently? Let them prove that they are the new
apostles, let them tell us that Christ has come down a second
time, taught a second time, was crucified a second time, dead
a second time, raised a second time. It was on that basis that
he used to make apostles [61] and give them the power to perform
the same signs as himself. I want to see their miracles produced,
though I must admit that their greatest miracle is the topsy-
turvy way they imitate the apostles. They brought the dead to
life. These heretics put the living to death.

31. But this is a digression. I will return to my argument
that truth comes first [62] and falsification afterwards. This finds
additional support in the parable where the Lord sows the
good wheat-seed first and the enemy, the devil, afterwards
adulterates the crop with barren tares. Properly interpreted,
this represents the different doctrines, since seed is used as a
figure of the word of God in other places as well. So the order
established in the parable makes it clear that what was first
handed down is dominical and true, while what was introduced
later is foreign and false. This verdict will hold good against
all later heresies which have no firm vantage-point from which
to claim the faith for themselves with complete conviction.

32. But if any heresies venture to plant themselves in the
apostolic age, so that they may be thought to have been handed
down by the apostles because they existed in their time, we can
say, Let them exhibit the origins of their churches, let them
unroll the list of their bishops, coming down from the beginning
by succession in such a way that their first bishop had for his
originator and predecessor one of the apostles or apostolic
men; one, I mean, who continued with the apostles. For this
is how the apostolic churches record their origins. [63] The

censu animae, is lost. Tertullian frequently refers to this work and to Hermogenes in his *De Anima*. See the introduction to J. H. Waszink's commentary on that work (Amsterdam, 1947).

[61] The text is corrupt here. Christ did not make apostles without giving
them the power to work miracles.

[62] *Principalitas veritatis*. This sense of *principalitas* as temporal priority must
be kept in mind for the interpretation of passages in Irenaeus
(Appendix I, B) and Cyprian.

[63] For the argument in general see the Introduction. The succession is that
of all the bishops in a see, not a chain of consecrations. Did Tertullian
suppose that the apostolic men had been ordained by apostles, or was
he content if churches could trace their historic continuity back to

church of Smyrna, for example, reports that Polycarp was placed there by John,[64] the church of Rome that Clement was ordained by Peter.[65] In just the same way the other churches produced men who were appointed to the office of bishop by the apostles and so transmitted the apostolic seed to them.

Let the heretics invent something of the sort for themselves. Blasphemers already, they will have no scruples. But even if they do invent something, it will be useless to them. If their teaching is compared with the teaching of the apostles, the differences and contradictions between them will cry out that theirs is not the work of any apostle or apostolic man. For the apostles would not have differed from each other in their teaching and the apostolic men would not have contradicted the apostles. Or are we to believe that the men who learned from the apostles preached something different? Consequently they will be challenged according to this standard by those churches which, though they can produce no apostle or apostolic man as their direct founder, since they are much later foundations (churches are being founded every day), yet, because they agree in the same faith, are reckoned to be no less apostolic through their kinship in doctrine.[66] So, when the heresies are challenged by our churches according to these two standards,[67] let them one and all show how they regard themselves as apostolic. But they are not, and they cannot prove themselves to be what they are not. Nor can they be received into peace and communion by churches which are in any way apostolic when they are in no way apostolic on account of their disagreement in creed.[68]

33. In addition, I enter an examination of the actual teachings which then, in the time of the apostles, were brought to light and rejected by those same apostles. For they will be

companions of the apostles, whose teaching could be trusted? For a similar problem compare the "other distinguished men" of *I Clement*, 44.

[64] Irenaeus, who had known Polycarp, says that he was appointed by the apostles (*Haer.*, III, iii). He was already Bishop of Smyrna when Ignatius wrote to him (*c.* 115), but still young; he was martyred in 156.

[65] The early succession lists of Rome give the order as Linus, Anacletus, Clement, e.g., Irenaeus in Appendix I, B. Clement was the first of any eminence, and wrote the important letter to the church of Corinth, *c.* A.D. 95. On these succession problems see Lightfoot's great commentaries on Clement, Ignatius, and Polycarp, and A. Ehrhardt, *The Apostolic Succession*, 1953.

[66] That is, Carthage will be able to deal with heretics!

[67] *Utramque formam*, apostolic succession and apostolic doctrine.

[68] *Sacramenti*, as at the end of c. 20.

more easily refuted when they are discovered either to have
been already in existence at that time or to have taken their
seeds from those which then existed.

In the First Epistle to the Corinthians Paul reproves those
who deny or doubt the resurrection. That opinion belonged to
the Sadducees. Part of it has been taken up by Marcion,
Apelles, and Valentinus, and any others who impugn the
resurrection of the flesh.[69] Then, writing to the Galatians, he
inveighs against those who observe and defend circumcision
and the Law. That is Ebion's heresy.[70] Instructing Timothy,
he attacks those who forbid marriage. That is taught by Marcion and his follower Apelles.[71] Similarly he touches those who
said that the resurrection had already happened. The Valentinians affirm this of themselves.[72] And when he mentions
endless genealogies,[73] we recognize Valentinus, in whose teaching some Aeon or other with a novel name, and not always
the same name, begets, from his own Grace, Sense and Truth,
who also procreate from themselves Word and Life, who in their
turn generate Man and Church. Then from this first Ogdoad
of Aeons come ten others, and a dozen more Aeons with marvellous names are born to make up the whole story of the Thirty.
When the same apostle blames those who are "in bondage to the
elements," he gives us a glimpse of Hermogenes, who, introducing an unoriginate Matter, makes it equal with the unoriginate
God, and having thus made a goddess of the Mother of the elements, can be in bondage to her whom he makes equal to God.[74]

In the Apocalypse John is told to chastise those who eat things
sacrificed to idols and commit fornication. Today we have a
new kind of Nicolaitan,[75] called the Gaian heresy.[76] In the

---

[69] Only part because, according to Tertullian, *Res. Carn.*, 36, the Sadducees
did not admit the salvation of body or soul, while the Gnostics taught
the immortality of the soul.

[70] Gal. 5:2. For Ebion cf. n. 27. The Ebionites were "Judaizers," cf. Iren., I,
26.

[71] I Tim. 4:3. Marcion made marriage a bar to baptism. The growth of his
sect depended on converts and unbaptized adherents.

[72] II Tim. 2:18. The suggestion was that the resurrection happened in
baptism (*Res. Carn.*, 19) or in the acquisition of truth (Iren., II, xlviii, 2).

[73] I Tim. 1:4. On what follows see Irenaeus *passim* and Sagnard, *op. cit.*
in n. 58.

[74] Gal. 4:3, 9, cf. n. 60. Tertullian puns on *materia, mater*.

[75] Rev. 2:14–15. The Nicolaitans are obscure, but were always included in
the old lists of Gnostic sects.

[76] *Gaiana*, apparently the Cainites, libertinists like the Nicolaitans and
Ophites.

epistle, however, he gives the name of Antichrist above all to those who denied that "Christ is come in the flesh" and to those who did not believe that "Jesus is the Son of God." [77] The former position was maintained by Marcion, the latter by Ebion. As for the Simonian system of angel-worshipping sorcery, that of course ranked as idolatry and was condemned by the apostle Peter in the person of Simon himself. [78]

34. These, I believe, are the types of spurious doctrine which, as we learn from the apostles, existed in their day. Yet among so many different perversions of the truth we come across no teaching to arouse controversy about God as Creator of the universe. No one dared to conjecture a second God. [79] They were more likely to feel doubt about the Son than the Father until Marcion introduced another God of sheer goodness besides the Creator; until Apelles turned some glorious creator angel of the higher God into the God of the Law and of Israel, declaring him to be of fire; [80] until Valentinus scattered his Aeons about and derived the origin of the Creator God from the fault of one Aeon. [81] To these men alone and to these men first was true divinity revealed! Doubtless they obtained greater consideration and fuller grace from the devil, who saw a fresh opportunity here to outdo God and, by his poisonous doctrines, achieve what the Lord said was impossible, namely, set the disciples above their master. [82]

So these heresies may date their beginnings as they choose. The date makes no difference if they are not grounded in the truth. Certainly they did not exist in the apostles' time; they cannot have done. If they had existed then, they too would have

[77] I John 2:22; 4:3. Marcion could not admit an Incarnation, flesh being the source of evil; the Ebionites did not believe in the Deity of Christ at all. Note that Tertullian does not need to say which Epistle of John he quotes. He only recognized one; cf. *Pudic.*, 19.

[78] Acts 8, Iren., I, xvi. Cf. c. 10. Tertullian's argument requires him to make the most of the earliest forms of Gnosticism, traced to founders condemned in the New Testament. It is odd that he says so little anywhere of Basilides; he is mentioned in *Res. Carn.*, 2.

[79] A second God, the position which the more biblical Gnostics like Marcion were driven to adopt, primarily because they could not identify the God portrayed in the Old Testament with the God of the New, revealed in Jesus, secondarily because they (and with them the more philosophical Gnostics) would not attribute creation and contact with matter to the absolute God.

[80] For this fiery angel-god see *Res. Carn.*, 5 and *De Anima*, 23, with Waszink's note.

[81] The fall of "Desire for Wisdom" from the Pleroma, cf. c. 7.

[82] Matt. 10:24.

been expressly named, so that they too could be suppressed. Those which did exist under the apostles are condemned at the time they are named. Either, then, the present heresies are the same as existed in the apostles' time, rudimentary then and somewhat refined by now, in which case their condemnation is carried on from that time; or else different heresies have come into being, different but later in origin, which have taken over some opinions from the older ones, in which case they must share their condemnation as they share their preaching. This follows from the principle of "later date" mentioned above,[83] according to which, even if they had no part in the doctrines condemned, they would be prejudged solely on the ground of their age as all the more spurious in that they were not even named by the apostles. This makes it doubly sure that they are the heresies which were then foretold.

35. By these rules we have challenged and convicted all the heresies. Whether they are later than or contemporary with the apostles, provided they differ from them, and whether they were censured by the apostles in general or specifically, provided they were condemned beforehand, let them for their part venture to reply with similar prescriptions against our teaching. If they deny its truth, they must prove it a heresy, convicting it by the same standard by which they are themselves convicted; and at the same time they must show where to look for that truth which, as we have now proved, is not to be found with them. Our teaching is not later; it is earlier than them all. In this lies the evidence of its truth, which everywhere has the first place. It is nowhere condemned by the apostles; they defend it. This is the proof that it belongs to them. For seeing that they condemn all foreign teaching, what they do not condemn is manifestly their own property; and that is why they defend it.

36. Come now, if you are ready to exercise your curiosity better in the business of your own salvation, run through the apostolic churches, where the very thrones of the apostles preside to this day over their districts, where the authentic letters of the apostles are still recited, bringing the voice and face of each one of them to mind.[84] If Achaea is nearest to you,

[83] *Posteritas*; cf. c. 31 and n. 62.
[84] Eusebius, *H.E.*, VII, 19, believed that the actual throne of James still existed at Jerusalem. Some think that Tertullian means by *cathedrae* here the physical objects. That is unnecessary, and on the whole unlikely, but not impossible. But "authentic" will scarcely mean autograph; he means unmutilated texts.

you have Corinth. If you are not far from Macedonia, you have Philippi and Thessalonica. If you can go to Asia, you have Ephesus. If you are close to Italy, you have Rome, the nearest authority for us also.[85] How fortunate is that church upon which the apostles poured their whole teaching together with their blood, where Peter suffered like his Lord, where Paul was crowned with John's death, where the apostle John, after he had been immersed in boiling oil without harm, was banished to an island.[86]

Let us see what she learned, what she taught, what bond of friendship[87] she had with the churches of Africa. She knows one Lord God, Creator of the universe, and Christ Jesus, born of the Virgin Mary, Son of God the Creator, and the resurrection of the flesh; she unites the Law and the Prophets with the writings of the evangelists and the apostles; from that source she drinks[88] her faith, and that faith she seals with water, clothes with the Holy Spirit,[89] feeds with the eucharist, encourages to martyrdom; and against that teaching she receives no one. This is the teaching, I will not say now, which foretold heresies, but from which heresies have sprung. But they are not of it, ever since they came to be against it. Even from the kernel of the smooth, rich, and useful olive comes the rough wild

---

[85] Cf. *Adv. Marc.*, IV, 5, a very similar passage. "Us" means Carthage and the Latin African church which, whether or not it was founded or received its ministry from Rome, certainly looked to that apostolic see for doctrinal authority. *Auctoritas* may have the double sense of origin and authority. It does not imply jurisdiction and sovereignty. I do not feel convinced that it should be taken here as a technical term of Roman law, meaning "title deed to possession," as by T. G. Jalland, *The Church and the Papacy* (1944), p. 147. It is uncertain whether "and Thessalonica" stood in the original text.

[86] This is the first mention of Peter's crucifixion, but cf. John 21:18 and Tacitus, *Annals*, XV, 44, which speaks of the victims of Nero as *crucibus adfixi*. Origen adds head downwards (*ap.* Eus., *H.E.*, III, 1). Paul was decapitated, according to tradition, like John the Baptist; this would be his right as a Roman citizen. This is the first appearance of the story of John and the boiling oil.

[87] Reading *contesserarit*, cf. *contesseratio hospitalitatis* in c. 20, *ad fin*. Breaking a *tessera* and taking a half each was a pledge of friendship. But in this context there is much to be said for the other reading *contestetur*, "what common witness to the faith is shared by Rome and Africa," as in the next sentence; and *contesserarit*, if correct, implies that the friendship is based on a common faith, with Rome as the giver. In the parallel passage, *Adv. Marc.*, IV, 5, *sonent* perhaps supports *contestetur*.

[88] *Potat*, which could be transitive, "gives her children to drink."

[89] *Aqua signat, sancto spiritu vestit*. On sealing, and the connexion between the parts of baptism, see G. W. H. Lampe, *The Seal of the Spirit* (1951).

olive. Even from the seed of the most pleasant and sweetest of figs springs the empty and useless wild fig. Just so have heresies come from our stock, but not of our kind; they spring from the seed of truth, but in their falsehood they are wild growths.

37. If therefore truth must be adjudged to us "as many as walk according to this rule" [90] which the Church has handed down from the apostles, the apostles from Christ, and Christ from God, the principle which we propounded is established, the principle which ruled that heretics are not to be allowed to enter an appeal to Scripture, since, without using Scripture, we prove that they have nothing to do with Scripture. If they are heretics, they cannot be Christians, since the names which they accept come not from Christ but from the heretics whom they follow of their own choice. So, not being Christians, they acquire no right to Christian literature, and we have every right to say to them: "Who are you? When did you arrive, and where from? You are not my people; what are you doing on my land? By what right are you cutting down my timber, Marcion? By whose leave are you diverting my waters, Valentinus? By what authority are you moving my boundaries, Apelles? [91] This property belongs to me. And all the rest of you, why are you sowing and grazing here at your will? It is my property. I have been in possession for a long time, I came into possession before you appeared. [92] I have good title-deeds from the original owners of the estate. I am heir to the apostles. As they provided in their will, as they bequeathed it in trust and confirmed it under oath, so, on their terms, I hold it. You they permanently disinherited and disowned as strangers and enemies." And how can heretics be strangers and enemies to the apostles except through their difference in doctrine, which each of them, on his own judgment, has either produced or received against the apostles?

38. Corruption of the Scriptures and of their interpretation is to be expected wherever difference in doctrine is discovered. Those who proposed to teach differently were of necessity driven to tamper with the literature of doctrine, for they could not have taught differently had they not possessed different sources of teaching. Just as their corruption of doctrine would

[90] Gal. 6:16.
[91] Marcion and Apelles removed awkward passages from the Bible, Valentinus perverted their interpretation. See next chapter.
[92] Here is an allusion to the *praescriptio longae possessionis* or *longi temporis*, but surely as an addition to the main argument, though bound up with it.

not have been successful without their corruption of its literature, so our doctrinal integrity would have failed us without
the integrity of the sources by which doctrine is dealt with.

Now, in our sources, what is there to contradict our teaching?
What have we imported of our own making, that we should
find it contradicted in Scripture, and remedy the defect by
subtraction or addition or alteration? What we are, that the
Scriptures have been from their beginning. We are of them,
before there was any change, before you mutilated them.
Mutilation [93] must always be later than the original. It springs
from hostility, which is neither earlier than, nor at home
with, what it opposes. Consequently no man of sense can believe
that it is we who introduced the textual corruptions into
Scripture, we who have existed from the beginning and are the
first, any more than he can help believing that it is they, who
are later and hostile, who were the culprits. One man perverts
Scripture with his hand, another with his exegesis. If Valentinus seems to have used the whole Bible, he laid violent hands
on the truth with just as much cunning as Marcion. Marcion
openly and nakedly used the knife, not the pen, massacring
Scripture to suit his own material. Valentinus spared the text,
since he did not invent scriptures to suit his matter, but matter
to suit the Scriptures. Yet he took more away, and added more,
by taking away the proper meanings of particular words and
by adding fantastic arrangements. [94]

39. These were the inventions of "spiritual wickedness
against which is our wrestling," brethren, inventions we had
to look into, necessary to faith, so that "they which are elect
may be made manifest" and the reprobate be discovered. [95]
To that end they possess a power and a facility in devising and
teaching error which need not be wondered at as something
difficult and inexplicable, since an example of a similar facility
is ready to hand in secular literature. You can see today a
completely different story put together out of Virgil, the
matter being adapted to the lines and the lines to the matter.

---

93 *Interpolatio*, but this is wider than our "interpolation," which was not
the principal abuse.
94 Marcion rejected the Old Testament, and his New Testament Canon
consisted of Luke's Gospel and ten Pauline Epistles (not the Pastorals
or Hebrews). From these many passages connecting Christ with the Old
Testament or with flesh, and many passages about the Law, had to be
excised. Irenaeus gives examples of Valentinian perversions in *Haer.*,
I, i, 6; I, xiii, 1.
95 Eph. 6:12; I Cor. 11:19.

Hosidius Geta, for example, sucked a whole tragedy of *Medea* out of Virgil.[96] A relative of mine, among other pastimes of his pen, extracted the *Table of Cebes* from the same poet.[97] We give the name "Homerocentons" to those who make their centos, like patchwork, out of the poems of Homer, stitching together into one piece scraps picked up here, there, and everywhere. And the Bible is indubitably richer in its resources for every conceivable subject. Indeed, when I read that heresies must be, I think I may say without fear of contradiction that by the will of God the Scriptures themselves were so arranged as to furnish matter for the heretics. For without Scripture there can be no heresy.

40. I shall be asked next, Who interprets the meaning of those passages which make for heresy? The devil, of course, whose business it is to pervert truth, who apes even the divine sacraments in the idol-mysteries.[98] Some he baptizes—his own believers, his own faithful. He promises the removal of sins by his washing, and, if my memory serves, in this rite seals his soldiers on their foreheads. He celebrates the oblation of bread, brings on a representation of the resurrection, and buys a wreath at the point of the sword. Why, he actually restricts his High Priest to one marriage.[99] He has his virgins, he has his continents.[1] If we turn over the religious legislation of Numa Pompilius,[2] if we look at his priestly functions and his badges

[96] This Hosidius Geta is otherwise unknown, but the cento *Medea* is extant, ed. Baehrens, *Poet. Lat. Min.* (Teubner), IV, 219ff.

[97] Cebes was a Pythagorean and a pupil of Socrates, but this dialogue is very much later. The *Pinax* (*Tabula*) was a picture in a temple, showing the course of human life. The dialogue allegorizes it. It is extant, ed. Praechter, Teubner, 1893.

[98] The standard explanation of the resemblance between some Christian rites and those of pagan cults, especially some of the mystery religions. Justin and Tertullian often use it. The following instances come from the rites of Mithraism (for which see the writings of Cumont), but I think Kroymann is right in removing the word *Mithra*, before *signat* (seals), from the text as a gloss. The grammatical and logical subject throughout the sentence is the devil.

[99] *Pontifex Maximus*. So Tert., *ad Uxor.*, I, 7, and elsewhere. Was it true? Not in his own day, when the emperor was *Pontifex Maximus*. There is reference, of course, to I Tim. 3:2. For Christian ideas see Ambrose, *Letter* 63 (p. 274).

[1] E.g., Vestals. *Continentes* may mean celibates, but can refer to discipline or renunciation within marriage, cf. Tert., *ad Uxor.*, I, 8.

[2] Traditionally the second King of Rome, 715–673 B.C. Advised by the nymph Egeria, he reformed Roman religion and organized the colleges of priests. But, as with Moses, much that is later has gathered round his name.

and his privileges, the sacrificial ministrations[3] and instruments and vessels, the niceties of vows and expiations, will it not be evident that the devil has imitated the scrupulosity[4] of the Jewish Law?

If he was so eager to copy and express in the affairs of idolatry the very things by which the sacraments of Christ are administered, we may be sure that he has had an equal longing and an equal ability to adapt the literature of sacred history and the Christian religion to his profane and emulous faith with the same ingenuity, sentence by sentence, word by word, parable by parable. We must not doubt, therefore, that the spiritual wickednesses from which heresy comes were sent by the devil, or that heresy is not far from idolatry, since both are of the same author and handiwork. Either they invent another God against the Creator or, if they confess one Creator, their teaching about him is false. Every falsehood about God is a kind of idolatry.[5]

41. I must not leave out a description of the heretics' way of life—futile, earthly, all too human, lacking in gravity, in authority, in discipline, as suits their faith.[6] To begin with, one cannot tell who is a catechumen and who is baptized. They come in together, listen together, pray together. Even if any of the heathen arrive, they are quite willing to cast that which is holy[7] to the dogs and their pearls (false ones!) before swine. The destruction of discipline is to them simplicity, and our attention to it they call affectation. They are in communion with everyone everywhere. Differences of theology are of no concern to them as long as they are all agreed in attacking

---

[3] At the word "ministrations" we lose the chief manuscript, *Agobardinus*, and there are several places in the remaining chapters where the text is very uncertain.

[4] *Morositatem*, cf. *Adv. Marc.*, IV, 35, *morositatem legis* and *ibid.*, II, 18, *sacrificiorum . . . scrupulositates.*

[5] Cf. Tert., *Idol.*, 1, *tota substantia (idololatriae) mendax.*

[6] This interesting chapter needs fuller annotation than is possible here. Tertullian may have been thinking as much of the Montanists, whom he afterwards joined, as of the Marcionites and other Gnostics. Women played an important part in Montanism as prophetesses. Something of Tertullian's Montanist ideas about the ministry may be seen in *De Pudicitia*, 21 (App. II); another important chapter in a work of his Montanist period is *De Exhortatione Castitatis*, 7, where he speaks of the priesthood of the laity. Marcion did not exclude catechumens from attendance at the eucharist proper, as the Church did (Jerome, *Comm. in Gal.*, 6:6).

[7] *Sanctum*, meaning the eucharist, as in Jerome, *Letter* 15 (p. 308).

the truth. They are all puffed up, they all promise knowledge. Their catechumens are perfect [8] before they are fully instructed. As for the women of the heretics, how forward they are! They have the impudence to teach, to argue, to perform exorcisms, to promise cures, perhaps even to baptize. [9] Their ordinations are hasty, irresponsible and unstable. Sometimes they appoint novices, [10] sometimes men tied to secular office, sometimes renegades from us, hoping to bind them by ambition as they cannot bind them by the truth. Nowhere can you get quicker promotion than in the camp of the rebels, where your mere presence is a merit. So one man is bishop today, another tomorrow. The deacon of today is tomorrow's reader, [11] the priest of today is tomorrow a layman. For they impose priestly [12] functions even upon laymen.

42. What am I to say about the ministry of the word? Their concern is not to convert the heathen, but to subvert our folk. The glory they seek comes from bringing the upright down, not raising the fallen up. Since their work results from no constructive operations of their own, but from the destruction of the truth, they undermine our constructions to build their own. Take their complaints against the Law of Moses and the prophets and God the Creator away from them, and they have nothing to say. So it comes about that they find it easier to pull down standing buildings than to build up fallen ruins. In such labour only do they show themselves humble and suave and respectful. But they have no reverence for their own leaders. The reason why there are practically no schisms among the heretics is that when they occur they are not noticed, for their very unity is schism. I am much mistaken if among themselves they do not make alterations in their own rules of faith, each of them adapting what he has received to suit himself, just as the man who handed it down had put it together to suit himself. Its development does not belie its nature and the character

---

[8] *Perfecti*, Greek *teleioi*, a favourite Gnostic and mystery term for full initiation. Here, baptized without adequate instruction on the Creed.

[9] Cf. *Virg. Vel.*, 9, "A woman is not allowed to speak in church, nor to teach or baptize (*tingere*, as here) or offer (the sacrifice) or to claim a share in any masculine function, much less in the priestly (*sacerdotalis*) office."

[10] *Neophytos*, I Tim. 3:6, cf. Ambrose, *Letter* 63 (p. 276).

[11] *Lector*, the first mention of this minor order.

[12] *Sacerdotalia munera*. In Tertullian and Cyprian *sacerdos* usually, if not always, means bishop; and so commonly, but less exclusively, in the fourth century. The adjective may cover presbyters. For the laity see *Exhort. Cast.*, 7.

of its origin. The Valentinians and Marcionites have taken the
same liberty as Valentinus and Marcion themselves to make
innovations in faith at their pleasure. In short, when heresies
are closely examined, they are all found to be in disagreement
on many points with their own founders. A great number of
them even have no churches. Motherless and homeless, they
wander about bereft of faith and banished from the truth.[13]

43. Notorious, too, are the dealings of heretics with swarms of
magicians and charlatans and astrologers and philosophers—
all, of course, devotees of speculation. "Seek, and ye shall find,"
they keep reminding us. You can judge the quality of their
faith from the way they behave. Discipline is an index to doctrine. They say that God is not to be feared. So everything is
free to them and unrestrained. But where is God not feared,
except where he is not present? Where God is not present,
there is no truth either; and where there is no truth, discipline
like theirs is natural. But where God is present, there is the fear
of God, which is the beginning of wisdom.[14] Where there is
the fear of God, there are decent gravity, vigilant care and
anxious solicitude, well-tested selection, well-weighed communion and deserved promotion, religious obedience, devoted
service, modest appearance, a united Church, and all things
godly.

44. By the same argument, the evidences of a stricter
discipline among us are additional proofs of truth. To abandon
the truth ill befits anyone who is mindful of the judgment to
come, when we must all stand before the judgment-seat of
Christ,[15] rendering an account above all of our faith. And what
will they say whose adulterous heresy has defiled the faith, the
virgin committed to them by Christ? They will allege, I suppose,
that nothing was ever said to them by him or his apostles about
the baneful and perverse doctrines to come, no command ever
given to beware of them and loathe them. No, *they*[16] will
acknowledge their own fault, in that they did not prepare us
in advance! They will add much more about the authority
of all the heretical teachers, how wonderfully they confirmed
faith in their own doctrines with miracles, how they raised the

---

13 I accept provisionally Kroymann's *extorres quasi veritate vagantur*. There
are numerous emendations of the corrupt text, including *sibilati*, hissed
off the stage, which Refoulé retains.
14 Ps. 111:10; Prov. 9:10.   15 II Cor. 5:10.
16 *They*, that is, Christ and the apostles, a striking sense if the change of
subject is not too harsh. Those who think it is emend the text variously.

dead, restored the sick, predicted the future, so that they might properly be accepted as apostles. As if it were not written that many should come and perform the greatest of miracles to fortify the deceptiveness of a corrupt preaching!

So they will deserve forgiveness. But if some, mindful of the writings and pronouncements of the Lord and the apostles, have stood firm in the integrity of the faith, these, I suppose, will risk losing forgiveness when the Lord replies: "Certainly I had told you beforehand that false teachers would arise in my name and in the name of the prophets and apostles, and I had commanded my disciples to tell you this; but you were not expected to believe it.[17] I had entrusted the Gospel and the teaching of the same Rule to my apostles once for all; but afterwards it pleased me to make a few changes in it. I had promised resurrection, even of the flesh; but that I reconsidered, in case I should not be able to implement it. I had declared myself born of a Virgin; but afterwards I was ashamed of that. I had called him Father who makes the sun and the rain; but another and better Father adopted me. I had forbidden you to lend your ears to heretics; but I was wrong." Such opinions may well be entertained by those who wander from the right path and take no precautions against the dangers which imperil the true faith.

45. There, for the present, is my case against all heresies in general. I claim that by definite, just and inescapable prescriptions[18] they are to be disallowed any discussion of Scripture. At some future time, if the grace of God permits me, I shall reply to some of them in particular.

[17] Again the text, and in this case the order of the phrases, is not certain. Some put this phrase later, viz., since you did not believe it (my Gospel, etc.), I made some changes.
[18] Note the plural *praescriptionibus*.

APPENDIX I: IRENAEUS

Tertullian derived much of his fundamental material from the treatise of Irenaeus, Bishop of Lyons, against the heretics, written about A.D. 185. This has survived in an early Latin version and in other translations. The original Greek is only extant in quotations. A few of the passages most relevant to the understanding of Tertullian are printed here without comment, though they need much. Since the methods of referring to Irenaeus are not uniform, a table is given here. Migne, *P.G.*, VII, follows the enumeration of Massuet, 1710. Many English scholars cite from W. W. Harvey's edition, Cambridge, 1857. Now we have also F. Sagnard's in *Sources Chrétiennes*, but so far only Book III. My extracts are:

Massuet-Migne	Harvey	Sagnard
A. I, x, 1–2	I, ii, iii	
B. III, i, ii, iii, iv	III, pref., i, ii, iii, iv	pp. 94–122.
C. III, xxiv	III, xxxviii	pp. 398–400.
D. IV, xxvi, 2–3;	IV, xl, 2; xli, 1; xlii, 1	
xxvii, 1		
E. IV, xxxiii, 7–8	IV, liii	

Passages from Adversus Haereses *to illustrate Tertullian*[1]

(A)

The Church, though dispersed throughout the whole world to the ends of the earth, received from the apostles and their disciples the faith in one God, the Father almighty, "who made heaven and earth, the sea, and all that in them is," and in one Christ Jesus, the Son of God, incarnate for our salvation, and in the Holy Ghost, who preached through the prophets the dispensations of God and the comings and the

[1] Selections from Irenaeus, *Adversus Haereses*, are also to be found in *Early Christian Fathers*, Ed. Cyril C. Richardson (Library of Christian Classics, Vol. I).

birth of the Virgin and the passion and the resurrection from the dead, and the reception into heaven of the beloved, Christ Jesus our Lord, in the flesh, and his coming from heaven in the glory of the Father to sum up all things and to raise up all flesh of all mankind, that unto Christ Jesus our Lord and God and Saviour and King, according to the good pleasure of the invisible Father, "every knee should bow, of things in heaven, and things on earth, and things under the earth, and that every tongue should confess" him, and to execute just judgment upon all; to send "spiritual wickedness" and the angels who transgressed and became apostate, and the impious and unrighteous and unjust and blasphemous among men, into eternal fire, but upon the righteous and the holy and those who keep his commandments and persevere in his love—some from the beginning, some from repentance—to bestow the gift of life and incorruption, surrounding them with eternal glory.

Having received this preaching and this faith, as I said before, the Church, though dispersed throughout the whole world, keeps it carefully, as dwelling in one house; and she believes these doctrines as though she had one soul and one heart, and preaches and teaches them, and hands them down, as if she had one mouth. For although there are different languages in the world, the force of the tradition is one and the same. The churches planted in Germany neither believe nor hand down anything different; nor do those in Spain or among the Celts or in the East or Egypt or Libya, nor those established in the middle of the world. As God's creature, the sun, is one and the same throughout the whole world, so the preaching of the truth shines everywhere and enlightens all who are willing to come to a knowledge of the truth. The most eloquent of the rulers of the churches will say nothing different (for no one is above the Master), nor will the poor speaker detract from the tradition. Since the faith is one and the same, nothing is added to it by one who can speak at length about it, and nothing is taken from it by one who has little to say.

(B)

Remember, then, what I have said in the first two books. If you add what follows, you will have a complete refutation of all the heresies and you will fight against them confidently and unremittingly on behalf of the one, true, and life-giving faith which the Church received from the apostles and distributed to her children.

For the Lord of all gave the power of the Gospel to his apostles, through whom we have come to know the truth, that is, the teaching of the Son of God. It was to them that the Lord said, "He that heareth you, heareth me: and he that despiseth you, despiseth me, and him that sent me." For we have not come to know the plan of our salvation through any but those through whom the Gospel came to us. This Gospel they at first preached. Afterwards, by the will of God, they handed it down to us in the Scriptures, to be "the pillar and ground" of our faith. It is wrong to say that they preached before they had "perfect knowledge," as some persons dare to say, boasting that they improve on the apostles. For after our Lord rose from the dead and they were "clothed with power from on high when the Holy Ghost came upon them," they were filled with all gifts and had "perfect knowledge." They went out "unto the uttermost part of the earth," bringing glad tidings of good things from God and announcing the peace of heaven to men. And they who did this possessed each and all the Gospel of God.

Thus Matthew, among the Hebrews, produced a written gospel in their language, while Peter and Paul were preaching at Rome and founding the Church. After their departure, Mark, the disciple and interpreter of Peter, himself handed on to us in writing what Peter had preached. Luke, the companion of Paul, set down in a book the gospel preached by him. Afterwards John also, the disciple of the Lord, "which also leaned on his breast," himself published the gospel during his stay at Ephesus in Asia. All these handed down to us belief in one God, maker of heaven and earth, announced by the Law and the prophets, and in one Christ, the Son of God. Whoever does not agree with them despises those who had part in the Lord, despises the Lord himself, despises the Father also; and he is self-condemned because he resists and opposes his own salvation, as all heretics do.

When they are refuted from Scripture, they turn to accuse the Scriptures themselves—the text is not good, they are not authentic, they contradict each other, one cannot discover the truth from Scripture if one does not know the tradition. For the truth, they say, has not been handed down in writing but orally, and that is why Paul said, "Howbeit we speak wisdom among the perfect: yet a wisdom not of this world." This wisdom each of them says is the wisdom which he has found for himself, a pure fiction, of course. That explains how they can believe that the truth is now in Valentinus, now in Marcion, now in Cerinthus. And afterwards it was in Basilides and whoever disputes against the Church without being able to say a word in the way of salvation. For everyone of them is in every way so perverted that he corrupts the Rule of Truth and is not ashamed to preach himself.

But again, when we challenge them by the tradition which comes from the apostles and is guarded in the churches through the successions of the presbyters, they oppose tradition, saying that they, being wiser not only than the presbyters but even than the apostles, have discovered the unadulterated truth. The apostles, they say, mingled matters of the Law with the words of the Saviour. And not the apostles only, but even the Lord himself, they say, made speeches which came now from the Demiurge, now from the Intermediary, and sometimes from the Summit, while they themselves know the hidden mystery without doubt, without contamination, without adulteration. What an utterly impudent blasphemy against their Maker!

So it has come about that they are not now in agreement either with Scripture or with Tradition. It is against enemies like this that we have to fight, dear friend, slippery creatures who try to escape you on all sides, like snakes. Therefore we must resist them on all sides, in the hope that our blows may put some of them to shame and bring them to turn towards the truth. Difficult though it is for a mind once possessed by error to recover its senses, it is not altogether impossible to escape error when confronted with truth.

So all who wish to see the truth can in every church look at the tradition of the apostles manifested throughout the world. And we can enumerate those who were appointed bishops in the churches by the apostles and their successions up to our own day. They neither taught nor knew anything resembling the ravings of these folk. Even if the apostles had known hidden mysteries which they taught the perfect separately and without the knowledge of the rest, they would hand them on above all to the men to whom they were committing the churches themselves. For they wanted those whom they were leaving as their successors, handing on to them their own office of teaching, to be very perfect and blameless in all things, since from their faultless behaviour would come great advantage, while their fall would be the greatest calamity.

But since it would be very tedious in a volume like this to enumerate the successions of all the churches, we single out the very great and very ancient and universally known church founded and established at Rome by the two apostles Peter and Paul. By pointing to its tradition from the apostles and its "faith proclaimed to men" which reach us through the successions of bishops, we confound all those who in any way, whether through self-satisfaction or vainglory or blindness and evil thoughts, assemble otherwise than is proper. For with this church, on account of its more weighty origin, every church, that is, the faithful from all quarters, must necessarily agree, since in it the tradition from the apostles has always been preserved by those who come to it from all quarters.

[Then Irenaeus gives the episcopal list of Rome from Linus to Eleutherus, followed by the words:]

By the same order and the same succession the tradition in the Church from the apostles and the preaching of the truth have reached us. And this is complete proof that there is one and the same life-giving faith which has been preserved in the Church from the apostles up till now and has been handed on in truth.

[He then speaks of the apostolic tradition and succession of the church of Smyrna, alludes to John at Ephesus, and concludes:]

Therefore, with so many proofs at hand, we must no longer search elsewhere for the truth which can so easily be taken from the Church, to which, as to a rich storehouse, the apostles most plentifully brought all that belongs to the truth, that "whosoever will may take the water of life from it." This is the door of life, but all the rest are thieves and robbers. Therefore we must avoid them, but love deeply the things of the Church and lay hold on the tradition of truth. Surely, even if some quite small matter were in dispute, we ought to have recourse to the oldest churches, in which the apostles lived, and take from them a definite and clear answer to the question in hand? And if the apostles themselves had not left us the Scriptures, should we not have been obliged to follow the order of tradition which they handed down to those to whom they committed the churches?

This ordinance has won the assent of many barbarian peoples who believe in Christ. They have salvation written on their hearts by the Spirit without paper and ink. They diligently keep the ancient tradition, believing in one God, Maker of heaven and earth and of all things in them, through Christ Jesus, the Son of God, who, on account of his surpassing love for his creation, endured to be born of the Virgin, himself in himself uniting man with God, who suffered under Pontius Pilate and rose again and was received up in splendour, who will come in glory as the Saviour of those who are saved and the Judge of those who are judged, sending into eternal fire those who distort the truth and despise his Father and his coming.

Those who have come to believe this faith without letters are barbarians so far as concerns our language, but in thought and habit and manner of life, by reason of their faith, they are exceedingly wise and pleasing to God, walking as they do in all righteousness and purity and wisdom. If anyone preaches the inventions of the heretics to them in their own language, they will at once stop their ears and run off to a distance, refusing to listen to this blasphemous discourse. So by means of the ancient apostolic tradition they keep their minds from entertaining any word of their monstrous talk.

For among the heretics no congregation and no doctrine has been established. There were no Valentinians before Valentinus, no Marcionites before Marcion. Not one of all the wicked opinions already enumerated was in existence before the authors and inventors of their perversity. Valentinus went to Rome under Hyginus, flourished under Pius, and lasted till the time of Anicetus. Cerdon, Marcion's predecessor, also appeared under Hyginus, the eighth bishop. He went on to the end coming frequently into church and making his confession, sometimes teaching secretly, sometimes again making his confession, sometimes convicted in his evil teaching and separated from the assembly of the brethren. Marcion, who succeeded him, flourished under Anicetus, the tenth bishop. The rest of those called Gnostics took their origin from Menander, the disciple of Simon, as I have shown. Each of these became the father and head of the opinion which he adopted.

All these people, then, rose up in their apostasy much later, in the middle of the Church's history.

Such is the apostolic tradition in the Church, which remains with us. Let us now return to the scriptural proof furnished by the apostles who wrote down the gospel, where they wrote down the teaching about God, proving that our Lord Jesus

Christ is the Truth and that in him is no lying at all. So David, prophesying his birth from a Virgin and his resurrection from the dead, says: "Truth has sprung out of the earth." The apostles also, being disciples of the Truth, are beyond lying; there can be no fellowship between truth and lying, as there is none between light and darkness; the presence of the one excludes the other.

(C)

So we have refuted all who introduce wicked opinions about our Maker and Creator, who also fashioned this world, above whom there is no other God. With our proofs we have overthrown those who teach falsely concerning the substance of our Lord and the dispensation which he fulfilled for the sake of man, his creature. On the other hand, the preaching of the Church is everywhere constant, persisting without change and resting, as I have shown, on the testimony of the prophets and the apostles and all the disciples, through the beginning, the middle, and the end, and through the whole dispensation of God and that habitual operation which effects man's salvation, residing in our faith—faith which we received from the Church and keep safe, faith which continually, by the Spirit of God, like something precious stored in a good vessel, renews its youth and rejuvenates the vessel also.

This gift of God has been entrusted to the Church, like breath to the man he formed, so that all the members may be given life as they receive it, and in this gift has been dispensed the means of communion with Christ, namely the Holy Spirit, the earnest of incorruption, the confirmation of our faith, the ladder by which we mount to God. For "in the Church," it says, " God hath set apostles, prophets, teachers," and all the other workings of the Spirit, no part in which is enjoyed by all those who do not resort to the Church, but cheat themselves of life through their evil opinions and wicked actions.

For where the Church is, there also is the Spirit of God; and where the Spirit of God is, there is the Church and all grace. And the Spirit is truth. Therefore those who have no part in him are not nourished to life at the breasts of their mother, and receive nothing of the fountain "clear as crystal," proceeding out of the body of Christ, but they "hew them out broken cisterns" from earthy ditches and drink putrid, muddy water. They fly from the faith of the Church for fear of being refuted; they reject the Spirit in order not to be instructed. Estranged

from the truth, they fitly wallow in every error, tossed to and
fro by it, changing their minds at every moment, never achiev-
ing an established conviction. They would rather be sophists
of words than disciples of the truth. For they have not been
founded upon the one rock, but upon sand, a sand full of
pebbles.

(D)

Therefore it is right to obey the presbyters in the Church,
those, that is, who possess the succession from the apostles, as
I have shown, who, together with their succession in the episcopate, received the sure gift of truth according to the good pleasure of the Father. The others, however, who stand apart from
the original succession and assemble wherever it may be, should
be held in suspicion, either as heretics with perverse opinions
or as schismatics, puffed-up and complacent, or again as hypo-
crites, acting for the sake of gain and vainglory. All these have
fallen away from the truth. The heretics, indeed, who bring
strange fire, that is, strange doctrine, to the altar of God, will be
burned up by fire from heaven, like Nadab and Abihu. Those
who rise up against the truth and encourage others against
the Church of God remain in hell, swallowed up by an earthquake, like Korah, Dathan, and Abiram, and their company.
Those who rend and divide the unity of the Church receive
from God the same punishment as Jeroboam.

[Irenaeus then speaks of "those who are believed by many
to be presbyters," but whose conduct is unworthy. "From such
it is right to hold apart, but to adhere to those who keep the
apostles' teaching and, together with their presbyteral order,
display sound speech and a blameless manner of life for the
instruction and correction of the others." He refers to the good
conduct of Moses (Num. 16:15), Samuel (I Sam. 12:3) and
Paul (II Cor. 2:17; 7:2), continuing: "Such presbyters the
Church nourishes, concerning whom the prophet says, 'I will
give thy princes in peace, and thy bishops in rightousness.'"]

Teaching us where to find such men, Paul says: "God hath
set in the Church first apostles, secondly prophets, thirdly
teachers." Where, then, the gifts of God have been set, there
must we learn the truth, that is, from those who possess the
Church's succession from the apostles and with whom is the
sound and blameless way of life and unadulterated and incor-
ruptible speech. For they preserve our faith in the one God

who made all things, and they increase the love which we bear to the Son of God, who made such great dispensations for us, and they expound the Scriptures to us without danger, neither blaspheming God nor dishonouring the patriarchs nor despising the prophets.

(E)

[Gnostic teaching about the spiritual man is false. The true spiritual man, of whom Paul says: "He that is spiritual judgeth all things, and he himself is judged of no man" is the man who truly receives that Spirit of God who from the beginning was present to mankind in all God's dispensations, who announced the future, revealed the present, and narrates the past. This spiritual man will judge heathen, Jews, Marcion, and all Gnostics, etc.]

He will judge also those who work schisms, being empty of the love of God, seeking their own advantage rather than the unity of the Church, rending and dividing, and, so far as they can, killing the great and glorious Body of Christ for trifling and haphazard reasons, speaking peace and working war, truly straining out the gnat but swallowing the camel. No reform they bring about can compare with the harm of schism. He will judge also all who are outside the truth, that is, outside the Church; but he himself will be judged by no man. For to him everything holds together—a complete faith in one God almighty, from whom are all things, a firm belief in the Son of God, Christ Jesus our Lord, through whom are all things, and his dispensations, through which the Son of God was made man, and in the Spirit of God, who furnishes knowledge of the truth and produces the dispensations of Father and Son among men in every generation, as the Father wills.

True knowledge is the teaching of the apostles, the ancient constitution of the Church in the whole world, the proper character of the Body of Christ according to the successions of the bishops to whom the apostles handed on the Church in every place. It has come down to us, kept safe and sound without any forging of scriptures, a complete statement, without addition or subtraction. It is reading without falsification, lawful and scrupulous exposition according to the Scriptures, without danger or blasphemy. It is the supreme gift of love, more precious than knowledge, more glorious than prophecy, more excellent than all other gifts.

APPENDIX II:

TERTULLIAN, *DE PUDICITIA*

In his catholic days Tertullian wrote a treatise, *De Paenitentia*, on the disciplinary system of the Church. His more rigid views, after he became a Montanist, are given in the late work, *De Pudicitia*, generally placed about A.D. 220. It appears to have been provoked by the "laxer" pentitential discipline of Callistus, Bishop of Rome, A.D. 218–222. Most scholars think that the work is directly addressed to him, but some believe that it attacks the Bishop of Carthage, who, on this hypothesis, will have adopted Callistus's policy. The passages given here are not intended to illustrate the Roman primacy, which is not the subject of this volume, but the doctrine of the Church. It will be observed that I translate *ecclesiae* in the fourth paragraph of c. 21 as a dative, not a genitive, and suppose that Callistus is attacked as a representative of the "catholic-psychic" church, not as one who is robbing that church for himself. All scholarly books on the early history of the papacy discuss this passage; for the contents of the "edict" consult A. D'Alès, *L'Édit de Calliste*, Paris, 1914, and the books (e.g., of Galtier, Poschmann, Mortimer) on early penitential discipline.

De Pudicitia

c. 1. I hear that an edict has been issued, and that a peremptory one. The Sovereign Pontiff, indeed, the bishop of bishops, puts forth his edict: "To those who have done penance, I remit the sins of adultery and fornication." What an edict! Who is going to endorse that with a "Well done"? And where will this bounteous gift be posted up? On the spot, I suppose, on the very doors of the brothels, just by the advertisements of lust. Penance like that must surely be promulgated exactly where the offence is going to be committed. We must read about the pardon where we go in hoping for it. But this is read in the Church, proclaimed in the Church—and the Church is a virgin!

c. 21. If the apostles understood these figures better, they naturally paid more attention to them. But I will proceed to my point by distinguishing between the teaching of the apostles and their power. Discipline governs a man, power marks him with a special character. But again, what is the power? The Spirit, and the Spirit is God. What did he teach? That we should have no fellowship with the works of darkness. Mark what he commands. And who could pardon sins? That is his prerogative. "For who remits sins, save God alone?" That means, mortal sins committed against himself and his temple. As for offences against yourself, you are commanded, in the person of Peter, to forgive them seventy times seven. So if it were established that the blessed apostles had in fact granted such forgiveness in cases where pardon depended on God, not man, they would have done it not in virtue of discipline but of power. For they raised the dead, which God alone can do; they restored the sick, which none but Christ can do; and they went so far as to inflict chastisement, a thing which Christ was unwilling to do. For to inflict suffering was not fitting for him who came to suffer. Ananias was struck dead, Elymas was struck blind, to prove that Christ *could* have done this also.

Similarly the prophets had forgiven the penitent both murder and adultery, because they gave proof of their severity as well. Show me now, apostolic sir, some evidence that you are a prophet, and I will acknowledge your divine authority; and make good your claim to the power of remitting sins of that kind. But if you have obtained only a disciplinary office, and do not preside with absolute sovereignty, but as a minister, who are you to grant forgiveness, and by what right? Unable to prove yourself prophet or apostle, you lack the quality by virtue of which forgiveness can be granted.

But (you say) the Church has the power to pardon sins. I acknowledge this and mean it even more than you do, for in the new prophets I have the Paraclete himself saying, "The Church can pardon sins, but I will not do it, lest they commit other sins." What if it was a spirit of false prophecy that made this pronouncement? But surely it would have suited a subverter better to commend himself by clemency, and so to tempt others to sin? Or if he was eager to make his claim accord with the Spirit of truth, then the Spirit of truth can indeed grant pardon to fornicators, but will not do so at the peril of a great number of people.

As for your present decision, I want to ask on what grounds

you assume this right for the Church. Is it because the Lord said to Peter: "Upon this rock I will build my Church, to thee I have given the keys of the kingdom of heaven," or: "Whatsoever thou shalt bind or loose on earth shall be bound or loosed in heaven," that you therefore presume that the power of binding and loosing has come down to yourself also, that is, to the whole Church akin to Peter? Who are you to alter and subvert the plain intention of the Lord when he conferred this upon Peter personally? "Upon thee," he says, "I will build my Church," and "To thee I will give the keys," not to the Church. And he said, "Whatsoever *thou* shalt bind or loose," not what *they* bind or loose.

This teaching is confirmed in the event. The Church was built up in Peter, that is, through him. He inserted the key, and you see how. "Ye men of Israel, hear these words: Jesus of Nazareth, a man destined for you by God," etc. He was the first, for instance, to unlock, by Christian baptism, the entrance to the kingdom of heaven where sins formerly bound are loosed and sins which have not been loosed are bound, in accordance with true salvation. He bound Ananias with the bonds of death and loosed the lame man from the harm of his infirmity. In the discussion about keeping the Law, it was Peter, inspired by the Spirit, who first spoke of the calling of the Gentiles: "And now why have ye tempted the Lord, putting a yoke upon the brethren which neither we nor our fathers were able to bear? But we believe that through the grace of Jesus we shall be saved in like manner as they." This decision both loosed those parts of the Law which were abrogated and also bound what was kept of it. So, in respect of the capital offences of Christians, the power to loose and bind was by no means made over to Peter. If the Lord had instructed him to pardon his brother until seventy times seven when he sinned against him, he would certainly have commanded him to bind, or retain, nothing afterwards, except perhaps sins committed not against a brother, but against the Lord. For the forgiving of sins committed against a man creates a presumption that sins against God are not to be remitted.

Now what of all that concerns the Church—your church, I mean, sir Psychic? For following Peter's person, that power will belong to spiritual men, apostle or prophet. For the Church itself is properly and fundamentally spirit, in which is the Trinity of one Divinity, Father, Son, and Holy Spirit. It is the Spirit who gathers together the Church which the Lord made to consist in three. From that beginning, the whole number of those who agree in this faith takes its being as the Church from its founder and consecrator. Therefore the Church will indeed pardon sins, but the Church which is spirit, through a spiritual man, not the Church which is a collection of bishops. Law and judgment belong to the Lord, not the servant, to God, not the priest.

On Idolatry

INTRODUCTION

I

WHEN TERTULLIAN ADDRESSED HIS *Apology* FOR Christianity to the magistrates of the Roman Empire, he was concerned to prove that Christians were loyal and valuable citizens. They prayed for the Emperor and those in authority under him, for the peace and security of the State; they did not cheat their neighbours, not even the tax-collector; they took a full part in the business of everyday life. "We are not Brahmans, naked sages of India, dwellers in forests, exiles from life. We reject no fruit of God's labours. Not without your forum, your meat-market, your baths, shops, factories, inns, market-days and all kinds of business, we live together with you in this world. We go to sea with you, serve in the army with you, work in the country, buy and sell. Our crafts and our labour are at your disposal." And in a different context: "We have filled everything of yours, cities, tenements, villages, towns, exchanges, even the camp, tribes, town-councils, the palace, the senate, the law-court."

No doubt this was true enough in fact, and he had a right to state the facts against the common charge that Christians were enemies of the human race. But in writings addressed to Christians Tertullian takes a very different line. The two-sidedness may be somewhat disingenuous, or it may be due to disappointment with the results of his apologetic writings. The State gave no recognition to the Church, and any idea of a Christian State was beyond his horizon. If Caesars could be Christians—but that is impossible. The end of the world will come before that! So far, then, from having any expectation of permeating society with Christian institutions, he does not look for tolerance of Christian peculiarities. The Christian must face the fact that he is going to live in a pagan society, with all its forms and institutions riddled with idolatry, and that the State or his neighbours will expect or compel him to do things which involve him in that idolatry, the worst of all sins. How can the Church live in the world?

Tertullian's answer is to urge Christians to make as clean a break as possible with the world. If the greater part of the world is not to be saved, let the faithful make sure of their own salvation. At the same time, the missionary power of the Church will be enhanced when it becomes clear that Christians possess the secret of a better life. The contrast between the Church and the world must be made to stand out with all possible sharpness. There can be no compromise with paganism in any form. So he will open the eyes of those of his brethren who have not perceived the idolatry lurking behind such apparently innocent pleasures as decking one's front door with laurels to greet the Emperor; and he will show up the pitiful attempts made by some Christians to have the best of both worlds.

That there must have been many problems is obvious. They had arisen in Corinth, and Tertullian has Paul's letters much in mind. The *Epistle to Diognetus* had indicated the paradoxes of Christian life in the world, without giving advice on specific issues. The Jews had their own difficulties. It is interesting to compare with Tertullian the almost contemporary tractate of the Mishnah, *Abodah Zarah* (Idolatry).[1] Another comparison worth making is with Clement of Alexandria, who in some ways is more liberal and humanistic than Tertullian, but has his own fundamental preference for the life of contemplation over the practical life. Tertullian began with a book *On the Shows*, in which he argued that Christians must keep away from theatre, arena, circus, and so forth, partly because they are generally immoral, but primarily because of their connexion with idolatry. Again, in *On the Soldier's Crown*, he repudiated the military service which he had brought forward in the *Apology*, partly because of the moral issue, but essentially because the soldier cannot easily escape participation in idolatry. Another work, *On Women's Dress*, attacks the moral offences of vanity and luxury, but also points out the pagan associations of so many of the details of fashionable costume.

On Idolatry tackles the subject more broadly. Every Christian knows that he must not worship idols. But what does that

[1] Edited with notes by W. A. L. Elmslie in *Texts and Studies*, VIII, 2 (Cambridge, 1911).

principle entail? Many points are clear to Tertullian. A Christian cannot serve as a magistrate, a soldier, a schoolmaster, or in any profession which involves him directly in idolatrous ceremonies. The Christian craftsman must not build temples, make images or anything else explicitly for use in the pagan cultus. The Christian business man must not sell wares, incense for example, for such a purpose. Further, the Christian must not allow the pagan to think that he admits the existence of the heathen gods, for instance by taking oaths by them; and he must avoid anything which would minister to the demons— and for Tertullian these are very real—who stand behind the idols. This excludes dabbling in magic and astrology. But Tertullian presses very hard. The craftsman and the merchant and the tradesman must take care that they do not *indirectly* minister to idolatry. Push this to the extreme limit, and there will be few things that they can sell. It will be practically impossible for a Christian to be a carpenter or a farmer. Tertullian does not in fact insist on the extreme logic of his position, as a number of writers have too glibly asserted of him. Often he is mocking at excuses, and has his tongue in his cheek. He does maintain that in the last resort one must be prepared to suffer the loss of everything for one's faith. There is more than one kind of martyrdom, and the blood of the martyrs is the seed of the Church.

The book largely speaks for itself. There may be more than one view about the practicability of its ethic and discipline. Its author does not envisage a society which, though still pagan, is prepared to make allowances for Christian difficulties. Yet this happened more and more as the third century went on. Already the pagans who tried to respect Christian consciences and yet wanted firm contracts (chap. 23) are an instance of this. The discussions about public office and military service turned on the possibility of avoiding idolatry, and evidently some thought this could be done. As the Church grew, it was to be expected that, except in the sporadic times of persecution, society would find ways for Christians to partake more fully in public and social life. With that would come dangers which Tertullian was not prepared to risk. On the other hand, if the danger of dropping Christian standards could be overcome, increasing involvement in the world might increase opportunities of converting the world. But Tertullian had no hope of baptizing the customs and institutions of the Roman world.

The problems which he forced upon his contemporaries

cannot be evaded, even if they can be handled rather more temperately. They arise every day where Christians live in a professedly non-Christian society, and they arise no less, if sometimes unrealized—which was one of his concerns—in nominally Christian surroundings. How many Christians even now make objects for heathen cults without thinking what they are doing? In what ways should we "respect other people's opinions" in matters of religion? And what is not a matter of religion? This is Tertullian's fundamental point. He wanted Christians to search for the religious implications of everything they did. In detail he was too scrupulous, most of us would probably say, but the challenge is sound in principle. One has but to think of a few sayings which imply autonomies—art for art's sake, business is business, political necessity, reasons of State.

II

Some would group *De Idololatria* with *De Spectaculis*, to which it refers, and place it about A.D. 200. Others associate it with *De Corona Militis*, which can be dated to A.D. 211. Monceaux regarded this as proved by what he took to be a reference to *De Corona* in c. 19: "The question is now being discussed" (cf. *De Corona*, 11), and he suggested that the public joys of c. 15 were those upon Caracalla's accession in 211. This is likely enough, though the words in chapter 19 do not prove that *De Corona* had actually been written. If the book is thus dated, it was written when Tertullian was well on the way to Montanism. It contains none of the out-and-out Montanist terms which would prove this later date, such as *psychicus* for the non-Montanist Christian; but neither does *De Corona*, which is certainly of A.D. 211. There are several references to the Holy Spirit, but none such as to prove the Montanism, and there are two or three other phrases (cf. notes 19, 63) which might be held to show Montanist leanings, though they are not demonstrative.

Even if the work was written at this stage in Tertullian's life, we should not too quickly conclude that its severity is merely the product of Montanism. *De Spectaculis*, for instance, is an early work. It might rather be that it was the rejection of his uncompromising views and the refusal to enforce them by the disciplinary system of the Church which drove him to the final break; for this must have occurred soon afterwards. The book itself is written as from within the Church.

III

The only known manuscript of *De Idololatria* is the ninth century *Codex Agobardinus*, and even this fails us just before the end of chapter 18. Not included in the first collection of Tertullian's works, edited by Beatus Rhenanus at Basel in 1521, it appeared in print for the first time in the collected edition of Gagnaeus, Paris, 1545, which was really edited by Mesnart, and again in the edition of Gelenius, Basel, 1550. Mesnart and Gelenius each had a manuscript other than the Agobardinus, both now lost. The text from chapter 19 onwards depends on them. The modern critical text is that of Reifferscheid and Wissowa in the Vienna *Corpus*, volume 20, (1890); this has been followed almost exactly in the present translation. For other editions see the bibliography at the end.

On Idolatry

1. The principal charge against the human race, the world's deepest guilt, the all-inclusive cause of judgment, is idolatry. Although each particular fault keeps its own characteristic features and will certainly be condemned under its own name, it is listed under the count of idolatry. Forget the terms on the charge-sheet and look at what they do. An idolater is also a murderer. You ask who he has killed? No stranger, no enemy, but—if it adds at all to the scope of the indictment—himself. By what inducement? His own error. What weapon? God's wrath. How many blows? One for every act of idolatry. You can only deny that an idolater has committed murder if you deny that he has gone to perdition. Again, in idolatry you are to see adultery and fornication. Every servant of false gods commits adultery against the truth, since all falsehood is adulteration. In the same way he is sunk in fornication. Can anyone co-operate with unclean spirits without polluting himself with the filth of fornication? Holy Scripture, you will allow, uses the word fornication when it attacks idolatry. Then fraud. Fraud, I take it, consists essentially in seizing another's property or denying him what is owed, and to defraud a fellow human being is certainly reckoned a major crime. But idolatry defrauds God, denying him his proper honours and conferring them upon others. It adds insult to injury. If fraud, no less than adultery and fornication, entails death, then idolatry, which partakes of all three, cannot escape the guilt of murder.

After offences so fatal and destructive of salvation, any others, as we go down the list, are seen to be essentially present in idolatry in one way or another. The lusts of the world are there. What idolatrous ceremony takes place without a display of dress and decoration? Wantonness and drunkenness are there, since pagan festivities are mostly frequented for the sake of food and drink and lust. Injustice is there, for what could be more unjust than the idolatry which fails to acknowledge the Father of justice? Vanity is there, for its whole principle is vain. Lying is there, for its whole being is a lie. So all sins are discovered in idolatry, and idolatry in all of them. The same point can be made another way. All offences are against God, and everything which is against him must be put down to the demons and unclean spirits who are in possession of the idols.[1] It follows that every offender commits idolatry, for what he does belongs to the owners of the idols.

2. However, let us leave all the crimes we can name to their own special business. We will keep to idolatry proper. Enough for idolatry to have its own name, a name so hostile to God; enough to have its own rich material of crime, with ramifications and proliferations so far-reaching that we have abundant cause to see what a variety of precautions have to be taken against it, so wide is its scope. It overthrows the servants of God in countless ways, both when they do not recognize it and when they shut their eyes to it. Most men limit idolatry to its simplest forms, such as burning incense, offering a sacrifice, giving a sacred banquet, accepting a priesthood or some religious obligation. One might as well limit adultery to kisses, embraces and physical intercourse, or murder to bloodshed and taking life. Surely we Christians must know how the Lord widened their scope, by pointing to the adultery present even in desire, whenever there is a lustful glance of the eye or a shameless impulse of the soul, and by condemning the murder present even in a curse or an insult, in every movement of anger, every neglect of charity towards a brother. John teaches similarly that he who hates his brother is a murderer.[2] If that were not so, and if we were to be judged only on the ground of those offences which even the heathen world has decided to punish, the devil's ingenuity in malice would have but small compass; and so would God's moral rule by which he fortifies us against "the depths[3] of the devil." How will our righteousness abound over the scribes and Pharisees,[4] as the Lord commanded, if we do not perceive the abundance of its opposite, unrighteous-

---

[1] For Tertullian's views on demons and gods see *Apology*, 22–23.

[2] Matt. 5:28, 22; I John 3:15.

[3] *Altitudines*, as in *Agobardinus*, cf. Rev. 2:24. Most editors change to *latitudines*, presumably to conform with *idololatriae latitudo* earlier in the chapter; this may be right as Tertullian does not elsewhere quote Rev. 2:24, and *latitudines* occurs in c. 8.

[4] Matt. 5:20, *abundabit super*. Elsewhere in Tertullian, *redundare*.

ness? But if unrighteousness is summed up in idolatry, it is important to guard ourselves in advance against its abundance by recognizing idolatry even where it is not at once evident.

3. Once, for a time, there were no idols. Before the makers of these monstrosities shot up, the temples were solitary and the shrines empty, as you may see today in spots where traces of antiquity survive.[5] Of course idolatry was practised, in fact if not in name. Even today it can go on without temple or idol. But when the devil brought into the world the makers of statues and portraits and every kind of image, the practice, untaught as yet but fraught with disaster to mankind, took its name and its development from the idols. From that moment every craft which in any way produces an idol has become a source of idolatry, no matter whether it is the modeller making his statue, the sculptor carving, or the embroiderer sewing. The material used to form the idol makes no difference either—plaster, paint, stone, bronze, silver, thread. As there is idolatry even without idols, it certainly cannot matter what an idol is like when there is one, what it is made of, or in what shape. It must not be supposed that only effigies consecrated in human form count as idols.[6] To make my point, I must translate the word. In Greek εἶδος means form. It has a diminutive εἴδωλον, like our *formula* from *form*. So every "form" or "formula" has a claim to be called "idol." Thus every attendance upon any idol, every service rendered to one, is idolatry; and thus every maker of an idol is guilty of one and the same offence—unless the People of God were not guilty of idolatry because it was not the image of a man, but only of a calf,[7] that they consecrated!

4. God forbids the making of idols no less than the worshipping of them. Just as any object of worship must first be made, so what must not be worshipped must not be made. That is the prior obligation. For this reason, in order to root out the materials of idolatry, God's law proclaims: "Thou shalt not make an idol"; and by adding: "Nor the likeness of any thing that is in heaven or in the earth or in the sea," it utterly forbade such crafts to the servants of God.[8] Enoch had anticipated

---

[5] Cf. H. J. Rose, *Ancient Roman Religion*, p. 26: "The gods lived in their holy places, and as time went on, it became the custom (it had not originally been so) to build them houses. . . . The deities' presence was commonly made known to worshippers by signs or emblems."

[6] *Ibid.*, 27: "Later, again, the foreign fashion of having images in human shapes in the temples was adopted, though not universally approved."

[7] Ex. 32.

[8] Lev. 26:1; Ex. 20:3–4: Deut. 5:7–8.

this law when he prophesied that the demons and the spirits of the rebellious angels would turn to idolatry every element and property of the universe, everything which heaven and sea and earth contain, to be consecrated as a god against God.[9] So it is that human error worships everything but the very Creator of everything. Their images are idols, the consecration of images is idolatry. Whatever sin idolatry commits must be put down to all the makers of all the idols.

Enoch, for instance, threatens idol-worshippers and idol makers alike, and predicts their damnation. And again: "I swear unto you, ye sinners, that the gloom of destruction is made ready for the day of blood. Ye that serve stones and that make images of gold and silver and wood and stone and clay, and that serve phantoms and demons and infamous spirits and every error not according to knowledge, ye shall find no help in them."[10] Isaiah says: "Ye are witnesses, whether there be a God beside me. And there were not any then. They that fashion and carve are all of them vanity, doing what they lust; which shall not profit them." Continuing, the whole passage testifies against the makers as much as the worshippers, ending with the words: "Know that their heart is ashes, and they do err, and no man can deliver his own soul." David also includes the makers, saying: "Let them that make them be like unto them."[11] Need I, with my poor memory, suggest anything more? Need I quote more from Scripture? When the Holy Spirit has spoken,[12] that is surely enough, and we have no need to discuss further whether the Lord has first cursed and condemned the makers of those idols whose worshippers he curses and condemns.

5. Of course I shall reply with all care to the excuses of such craftsmen, men who should never be admitted into the house of God by anyone who knows the Christian rule of life. The words they so often put forward, "I have nothing else to live by", can be retorted immediately and sharply: "You can live then? If you are living on your own terms, why do you come to God?" Then there is the argument which they

9 Tertullian argues that Enoch is scripture in *Cult. Fem.*, I, 3, and quotes or alludes to him in *Apol.*, 22; *Cult. Fem.*, I, 2; II, 10; *Idol.*, 4, 9, 15; *Res. Carn.* 32; *Virg. Vel.*, 7. The first passage here is Enoch 19:1.
10 Enoch 99:6, 7. For the text, R. H. Charles, *Apocrypha and Pseudepigrapha of the Old Testament*, Oxford, 1913, II, 270, and *id.*, *The Book of Enoch*, Oxford, 1912. It seems to be Tertullian himself who introduces "makers."
11 Isa. 44:8–9, 20; Ps. 115:8.
12 In Scripture, therefore no proof of Montanism.

impudently produce from the Bible itself. The Apostle said (so they argue): "Let each man continue as he was found."[13] On that interpretation we can all continue in our sins. We were all without exception sinners when we were found. Christ came down for no other reason than to set sinners free. Again, they say the Apostle taught that, after his own example, every man should work with his own hands for his living.[14] If *all* hands can plead this instruction, the thieves at the baths live by their hands, I suppose, and burglars get their living with their hands, and forgers produce their false documents with their hands (not their feet!), while the actors in the pantomime toil for their living with their hands and every limb in their bodies besides. If we are not to exclude the crafts which God's discipline does not admit, we shall have to throw the Church open to everyone who supports himself by his hands and his own work.[15]

An objection is raised against my affirmation that likenesses are forbidden. Why then did Moses in the desert make the likeness of a serpent from brass?[16] My answer is that figures which were designed for some hidden purpose, not to set the law aside, but to be types,[17] are in a separate category. Otherwise, if we understand them to be against the Law, are we not ascribing inconstancy to God, like the Marcionites who destroy his deity by making him mutable on the ground that he orders in one place what he forbids in another?[18] If anyone refuses to see that the effigy of a brazen serpent, shaped like one who is hung, displayed a figure of the Lord's cross which was to free us from the serpents (that is, from the devil's angels) in that it hangs the devil (the serpent) dead by its means—or you may accept any other explanation of the figure which has been

---

13 I. Cor. 7:20.

14 I Thess. 4:11.

15 In the *Egyptian Church Order* actors are not accepted as Christians unless they give up their profession; so also *pantomimi* in the canons of C. Elvira. For further detail see Brightman in Swete, *Essays on the Early History of the Church and the Ministry*, pp. 320–330.

16 This argument appears also in *Adv. Marc.*, III, 18 = *Adv. Jud.*, 10, and in *Adv. Marc.*, II, 22. The brazen serpent as a type of the cross occurs already in the *Epistle of Barnabas*, c. 12.

17 *Ad exemplarium causae suae.* Figure in this passage is *figura*.

18 Marcion rejected the God of the Old Testament because of the difference of character between him and the Father of Jesus, but also because within the Old Testament he contradicts himself. True Deity is impassible and immutable. Marcion took the text literally, and without any sense of progressive revelation; the Church interpreted it allegorically, when necessary, and with a sense of history moving towards Christ.

revealed[19] to better men than I, provided you remember the Apostle's declaration that whatever happened to the People then was by way of figure.[20] Fortunately it was one and the same God who both, in the Law, forbade the making of a likeness, and also, by an extraordinary command, enjoined the likeness of the serpent. If you pay heed to this same God, you have his law, "Thou shalt not make a likeness." If you are thinking of the subsequent command to make a likeness, take Moses as your model and do not make any likeness contrary to the Law unless God gives you also a direct command.

6. Suppose there were no law of God forbidding us to make idols, and no word of the Holy Spirit[21] threatening their manufacturers no less than their worshippers, even so, a Christian who understood his baptismal profession[22] would see for himself that such crafts are at odds with the faith. How have we renounced the devil and his angels if we are making them? What sort of divorce have we declared when we go on living, if not with them, then on them? Have we really broken away from them, as we undertook to do, if we are still tied to them by gratitude for our maintenance? Can your tongue deny what your hand confesses, your words demolish what your work constructs? Can you proclaim the one God while you fabricate many, the true God while you make false ones? "I make them," (someone is saying) "but I do not worship them." As if what frightens him off worshipping them were not the very thing that should have kept him off making them, fear of God's wrath, in both cases! But you do worship when you make them such as can be worshipped. You worship them, not with the breath of some cheap smoke, but with the breath of your own spirit, not at the cost of some beast's soul, but your own. You sacrifice your talents to them, pour out your sweat to them, light for them the candle of your skill. You are more than a priest to them, since it is through you that they have a priest. Your diligence is their deity. If you yourself deny that you worship what you make, they at least do not deny it, they for whom you kill the fatter and larger and more golden[23] victim, your own salvation, every day.

19 A touch of Montanism? Not necessarily.
20 I Cor. 10:11.
21 Cf. n. 12. Again, it does not seem that *lex* and *spiritus* are contrasted.
22 *Sacramentum nostrum*, oath of allegiance in the sacrament of baptism. Note the ancient formula following, several times mentioned by Tertullian.
23 *Auratiorem*, cf. Pliny, *Nat. Hist.*, XXXIII, 3; Verg., *Aen.*, V, 366; IX, 627.

7. On this score a zealous faith will raise its voice, lamenting that the Christian comes into church from the idols, comes from the enemy workshop into the house of God, raises to God the Father hands that have mothered idols, adores with hands which outside are adored in opposition to God, touches the Body of the Lord with hands which give the demons their bodies. And worse. Small matter, maybe, if they receive from other hands something to contaminate. But they hand to others what they have contaminated, for idol-makers are accepted into the ranks of the clergy. For shame! The Jews laid their hand upon Christ once only, these men harass his Body every day. Off with those hands! Now let them mark how the words of Scripture fit them: "If thy hand offend thee, cut it off." [24] What hands are more fit to be cut off than those which offend the Body of the Lord?

8. Crafts of many other kinds, while they may not involve the manufacture of idols, are equally blameworthy when they provide the idols with the indispensable instruments of their power. If you furnish a temple, an altar, a shrine, if you work the gilding, fashion the emblems or even make a niche, decorating is as bad as building. To confer authority in that way is a greater service than to give form.

If the necessity of maintaining oneself is pressed to such an extent, there are other kinds of handicraft to provide a living, without departing from Christian discipline by making idols. The plasterer knows how to mend roofs, lay on stuccoes, polish a cistern, trace mouldings and pattern walls with a variety of decorations other than images. The painter, the marbler, the bronze-worker, any sculptor, can easily extend his scope. Anyone who can paint a picture can daub a sideboard. Anyone who can carve a Mars from a plank can quickly knock up a cupboard. Every craft is the mother of another, or near akin; none is entirely independent. There are as many branches of the arts as there are human desires. You object that the profits and the price of your work are different? Yes, but there is a corresponding difference in the labour. The smaller profits are balanced by the continual employment. How many walls want pictures? How many temples and shrines are built for the idols? But houses and mansions and baths and blocks of flats are always in demand. Shoes and slippers you can gild every day, but rarely a Mercury or a Serapis. That should yield ample profit for the handicrafts. Extravagance and

[24] Matt. 18:8.

ostentation are more common than all religion. Ostentation
will require more plates and cups than religion, extravagance
gets through more wreaths than ceremonial.

So we encourage men to practise the kind of craft which
does not touch idols or what belongs to idols. But since
many things are common to men and idols, we must also take
care that no one asks anything at our hands for the use of an
idol without our knowledge. If we allow it and do not take the
normal precautions, we shall not, I think, be clear of the infection of idolatry when our hands, with our knowledge, are caught
in attendance upon demons or ministering to their glory and
their needs.

9. Among the arts and crafts we notice some occupations
which are intrinsically idolatrous. I ought not to have to speak
about astrology; but I will say a few words about it, since
someone has recently appealed in defence of his persistence in
that profession. I do not allege that he is honouring the idols
when he writes their names on the heavens, or when he assigns
the whole power of God to them, in that men are led to think
they need not call upon God, on the assumption that we are
driven by the immutable will of the stars. I have only one
proposition to make. The angels who deserted God in their
love of women were also the inventors of this curious art,
and God condemned them on that account as well. God's
insistent sentence has reached even to the earth, and men
bear witness to it without knowing what they are doing. The
astrologers are being expelled like their angels. Rome and
Italy are forbidden to the astrologers, as heaven is to their
angels. Pupils and masters suffer the same penalty of exile.[25]

But the Magi came from the East, you say.[26] We know that
magic and astrology are connected. So it was interpreters of
the stars who first proclaimed the birth of Christ and were the
first to bring him presents. I suppose that put Christ under an
obligation to them! Well, does it follow that the religion of those
Magi will protect the astrologers now? Today, no doubt, their
lore is of Christ. It is the stars of Christ that they observe and
predict, not the stars of Saturn or Mars or any other of the

[25] The *Egyptian Church Order* rejects magicians and star-gazers as catechumens, unless they desist. The idea that the fallen angels of Gen. 6 invented
astrology is a patristic commonplace. There is probably reference to
Enoch 6 as well as Gen. 6, and, in "God's sentence," etc., to Enoch 14:5:
"the decree has gone forth to bind you." For the expulsion from Rome
see, for example, Tacitus, *Annals*, II, 31.
[26] Matt. 2:1–12.

departed in that company. No, their science was allowed only until the Gospel came, with the intention that, once Christ was born, no one should thereafter read any nativity in the heavens. The incense, myrrh, and gold were offered to the infant Lord then to mark the end of sacrificing and of worldly glory, which Christ was to take away. It was not to prevent Herod pursuing them that the Magi were warned in a dream (undoubtedly sent by God) to return to their own country another way, not that by which they had come. The true meaning was that they should not walk in their former way of life. For Herod did not pursue them. He was unaware that they had departed another way, since he did not know by what way they had come. We must take "way" to mean way of life and thought. So the Magi were ordered to walk henceforth another way.[27]

Similarly God in his patience allowed that other form of magic which works by miracles—even emulating Moses[28]— to drag on until the Gospel. Once the Gospel had come, the apostles cursed and excommunicated Simon Magus, newly baptized, because his thoughts still lingered with his charlatan way of life, planning, among the miracles of his profession, to traffic in the Holy Spirit through the laying on of hands.[29] The other magician, the one with Sergius Paulus, was punished with the loss of his sight because he withstood the apostles.[30] If any astrologers had fallen in with the apostles, they would doubtless have suffered the same fate. Astrology is a species of magic, and when magic is punished, the species is condemned in the genus. After the Gospel, you will nowhere find sophist, Chaldaean, soothsayer, diviner or magician, except of course under punishment. "Where is the wise? where is the scribe? where is the inquirer of this age? hath not God made foolish the wisdom of this world?"[31] A fine astrologer[32] you are, if you did not know you would become a Christian! If you did know it, you ought also to have known that you would have no more to do with that profession of yours. If it predicts the climacterics of others, it should inform you of the danger threatening itself. "Thou hast neither part nor lot in this matter."[33] One whose

---

[27] This spiritual interpretation is common later, e.g., Hilary, Ambrose, Augustine, Leo.
[28] Ex. 7:11.
[29] Acts 8:18–19.   [30] Acts 13:6–11.
[31] I Cor. 1:20. One is tempted to translate *conquisitor* "research scientist."
[32] *Mathematice.*
[33] Acts 8:21, said to Simon. For Simon as the founder of Gnosticism see *Praescr. Haer.*, 33 (p. 55).

finger and rod abuse heaven cannot hope for the kingdom of heaven.

10. We must also ask about schoolmasters and the other teachers of letters, though their affinity with all manner of idolatry is really beyond question.[34] In the first place, they are bound to praise the gods of the heathen, rehearse their names, genealogies, stories, and all their ornaments and attributes. Next, they must keep their feasts and celebrations, since it is by them that they compute their income.[35] What schoolmaster will attend the *Quinquatria* without his Table of the Seven Idols? He consecrates the very first payment of a new pupil to the honour and name of Minerva, so that, even if he does not nominally "eat of that which is sacrificed to idols"—not being dedicated to any idol—he is to be shunned as an idolater. Is he any less defiled? Is gain expressly dedicated to the honour of an idol any better than plain idolatry? Minerva has as much claim on the Minerval gifts as Saturn upon the Saturnal, which

[34] Here Tertullian faces a difficult situation, for there were no Christian schools. He is sterner than some Christians in refusing to allow Christians to teach, partly because the content of the teaching was the pagan classics (at a time when people believed in the gods), and partly because the schoolmaster cannot evade the pagan festivals associated with his profession. However, the *Egyptian Church Order* allows a schoolmaster to go on teaching if he has no other occupation by which to live, though "it is good that he should leave off"; and the later *Canons of Hippolytus* adds that he must vituperate the gods and explain that they are demons. Tertullian's concession about children is perhaps unexpected from him, and suggests that most Christian parents could not have taken their children very far. He wants them to be able to read the Bible for themselves, a motive of Christian education familiar ever since.

[35] A number of the allusions are explained by the following passage from Rose, *op. cit.*, pp. 63–64: "The Roman year was ushered in by Mars' own month. . . . The next lucky date, the 19th, known as the Quinquatrus, i.e., the fifth day (counting inclusively) after the Ides, was again sacred to him: in the times when most of our authors wrote, two curious mistakes had altered the nature of this festival. It so happened that the temple of Minerva on the Aventine was dedicated on that day, and also the true meaning of the old-fashioned word had been forgotten, and it was imagined that it signified a festival lasting five days. Accordingly, for five days in the middle of Mars' month, the Romans from the second century B.C. onwards celebrated the intrusive goddess, her protégés, the craftsmen of all kinds, including those who practised the liberal arts, and not least the schoolmasters, keeping holiday, while the last-named expected a fee from their pupils."

The seven idols are the seven planets. For the festivals and other details the reader is asked to consult the classical dictionaries, to assist in which the Latin terms are here enumerated: *Minervalia, Saturnalia, Brumae, Carae Cognationis* (=Caristia), *strenuae, Septimontium, flaminicae*.

even the slave-boys must offer on the occasion of Saturn's feast. Your schoolmaster must put out his hand for new year presents and what he gets at the feast of the Seven Hills. He must exact the mid-winter dues and the offerings at the festival of Remembrance. The schools must be garlanded for Flora, the priests' wives and the newly appointed aediles bring their sacrifices, the school is bedecked for holy days. It is the same on an idol's birthday; the whole pomp of the devil is celebrated. Can you think this fitting for a Christian—unless you are prepared to think it just as fitting for a Christian who is not a schoolmaster?

I know it can be said: "If the servants of God are not allowed to teach letters, they will not be allowed to learn them either", and: "How could anyone be educated in everyday human wisdom or taught how to think and behave, since letters are a tool for every part of life. How can we reject the secular studies without which divine studies are impossible?"

Let us look into the necessity of a literary education. Let us recognize that it can be partly allowed and partly avoided. It is more allowable for Christians to learn letters than to teach them. The principles involved in learning and teaching are different. When a Christian *teaches* literature, he comes upon occasional praises of idols. In teaching them, he commends them; in handing them on, he confirms them; and in mentioning them, he bears testimony to them. He sets his seal to the gods under that very name, although, as I have said, the Law forbids us to call them gods and to take that name in vain.[36] Hence a child's belief is built up for the devil from the beginning of its education. [Question, whether one who catechizes about idols commits idolatry.][37]

But when a Christian *learns* these things, already understanding what idolatry is, he does not accept or admit them, all the more so if he has understood it for some time. Alternatively, when he is beginning to understand, he must first understand what he learned first, namely, about God and the faith. Thus he will reject and repudiate the idols, and will be as safe as one who wittingly takes poison from the unwitting and does not

---

36 Ex. 23:13. The following words arise out of Ex. 20:7, but Tertullian extends the sense to cover the application of the name of God to a "nothing," i.e., an idol, Isaiah's "vanity." So somewhat differently in *Prax*. 7. Cf. c. 20.

37 I should like to cut this sentence out as a gloss. Similarly the *Quaere* in c. 23. The latter strikes me as impossibly prosaic as Tertullian works up to his peroration; the present sentence would go out with the other.

drink it. He can plead necessity as an excuse because there is no other way he can learn. Just as it is easier not to teach letters than not to learn them, so it will be easier for the Christian pupil not to touch the other defilements of school life which arise out of public and scholastic festivals, than for the master not to frequent them.

11. If we consider the other sins according to their families, first avarice, the root of all evils, ensnared by which some have made shipwreck concerning the faith, (the same apostle twice calling avarice idolatry), and secondly lying, the servant of avarice—I say nothing of perjury, since it is not lawful even to take an oath—is business suitable for the servant of God?[38] Where there is no avarice, what motive remains for seeking gain, and where there is no motive for gain, there will be no necessity to engage in business. Granted, however, that there may be some just form of profit in which there is no need to keep watching against avarice and mendacity, I take it that the business which belongs to the very life and breath of the idols and fattens all the demons, will fall under the charge of idolatry. Is it not the primary idolatry? It is no defence that the same wares, the incense[39] and other foreign products imported for sacrifices to idols, are also used by men as medicines and by us Christians as aids to burial as well. When processions, priesthoods and idol-sacrifices are supplied at your risk, your loss, your damage, by your plans and flurries and business operations, you are plainly nothing but the idols' agent. It is no good maintaining that in this way every form of business becomes questionable. In proportion to the magnitude of the danger the more serious offences extend the sphere of vigilant care. We have to keep clear of the offenders no less than the offences. That an offence was committed by another does not lessen my guilt, if it was committed by my agency. At no point ought I to be an indispensable instrument to another man doing what I may not do myself. The mere fact that I am forbidden to do it should teach me to take care that it should not be done by my means. An example will establish the presumption that the guilt is no lighter. Since fornication is forbidden to me, I offer no assistance or connivance in it to others. By keeping my own body away from the brothels I acknowledge that I cannot

---

[38] I Tim. 6:10; 1:19; Col. 3:5; Eph. 5:5; Matt. 5:34–37; James 5:12.
[39] Cf. *Abodah Zara*, I, 5: "The following articles are forbidden to be sold to the heathen: fir-cones, white figs on their stems, frankincense and a white cock."

pander or make a profit of that sort on any one else's behalf. Again, the prohibition of murder shows me that a trainer [40] of gladiators must be kept out of the Church. He cannot escape responsibility for what he helps another to do. And here is a presumption more to the point. If a purveyor of victims [41] for public sacrifices comes over to the faith, will you permit him to continue in that occupation? Or if an already baptized Christian takes up such work, will you think it right to keep him in the Church? Surely not, unless you will wink at the incense-merchant also. I suppose the blood and the fragrance purveyed go to different beings! If idolatry, while still formless, [42] was carried on by means of these wares before there were any idols in the world, and if even today the service of idolatry is commonly performed by burning incense without any idol, does not the incense-merchant perform a greater service to the demons than the idol-maker? Idolatry can more easily dispense with an idol than with his wares. Let us question the Christian conscience. If a Christian incense-merchant walks through a temple, can he bring himself to spit and blow [43] on the smoking altars for which he has himself provided? Can he consistently exorcize his own foster-children, to whom he offers his own house for a pantry? Even if he has cast out a demon, he had better not be complacent about his faith. It was no enemy that he cast out. It should not have been difficult to get what he asked from one whom he is feeding every day. So no craft or profession or business that ministers to the making or equipping of idols can escape the charge of idolatry, unless by idolatry we mean something altogether different from the service of idol-worship.

12. It is wrong to cajole ourselves with the necessity of maintaining life by saying (after sealing our faith): "I have nothing to live on." I will give a complete answer at once to that rash suggestion. It comes too late. Thought should have been taken beforehand, like the highly provident builder in the parable who first counted the cost of the work, together with his means, lest he should blush at his failure after he had made a

---

[40] *Lanista.* One form of the *Egyptian Church Order* rejects gladiators and those who teach them.

[41] Cf. *Abodah Zara*, I, 6: "In no place whatsoever may one sell to them (heathen) large animals, calves and foals, perfect or maimed."

[42] *Informis*, cf. nn. 5, 6.

[43] *Despuet et exsufflabit*, not to blow the fire out, but to blow the spirit away, cf. *ad Uxor.*, II 5, *immundum flatu exspuis.*

start.[44] Now you have the Lord's words and examples, leaving you no excuse. Do you say: "I shall be poor?" The Lord calls the poor blessed. "I shall have no food." "Take no thought for food," he says. As for clothing, the lilies are our example. "I needed capital." But everything is to be sold and divided among the poor. "But I ought to provide for my sons and my descendants." "No one putting his hand to the plough and looking back is fit for the work." "But I was under contract." "No man can serve two masters." If you want to be the Lord's disciple, you must take up your cross and follow the Lord, that is, you must take up your straits and your tortures or at least your body, which is like a cross. Parents, wives, children are all to be left for God's sake. Are you hesitating about crafts and businesses and professions for the sake of children or parents? The proof that family as well as crafts and business are to be left for the Lord's sake was given us when James and John were called by the Lord and left both father and ship, when Matthew was roused from the seat of custom, when faith allowed no time even to bury a father. Not one of those whom the Lord chose said: "I have nothing to live on." Faith fears no hunger. It knows that hunger is to be despised, for God's sake, no less than any other form of death. Faith has learned not to be anxious for its life. How much more for a living?[45]

How many have fulfilled these conditions? What is difficult with men is easy with God. We must not comfort ourselves with the thought of God's kindness and clemency so far as to indulge our necessities to the verge of idolatry. We must keep our distance from every whiff of it like the plague. And this we must do not only in the cases already mentioned, but over the whole range of human superstition, whether it is appropriated to its gods or to dead men or to kings.[46] For it always belongs to the same unclean spirits, sometimes through sacrifices and priesthoods, sometimes through public shows and the like, sometimes through festivals.

13. Why speak of sacrifices and priesthoods? And I have already written a whole volume on shows and pleasures of that

---

[44] Luke 14:28–30.
[45] Luke 6:20; Matt. 6:25 ff.; Luke 9:62; Matt. 16:24; Luke 14:26; Matt. 4:21–22; 9:9; Luke 9:59–60 and parallels. This passage was drawn on by Jerome in his *Letter* 14 (p. 300).
[46] The Christian apologists jumped at every pagan concession to Euhemerism, the theory that the gods were deified heroes, cf. Tert., *Apol.*, 10, "You cannot deny that all your gods were once men." Cf. c. 15 below.

kind.[47] Here I must discuss the festivals and other extraordinary celebrations which we sometimes concede to our wantonness, and sometimes to our cowardice, joining with the heathen in idolatrous matters contrary to our faith and discipline. I shall first take up this issue. On such occasions, may the servant of God join with the heathen by way of clothing or food or any other kind of festive behaviour? When the Apostle said: "Rejoice with them that rejoice, and mourn with them that mourn", he was speaking about the brethren, exhorting them to be of the same mind. But in this instance there is no fellowship between light and darkness, between life and death—or we tear up what is written: "The world shall rejoice, but ye shall mourn."[48] If we rejoice with the world, it is to be feared that we shall also mourn with the world. Let us mourn while the world rejoices and afterwards rejoice when the world mourns. Thus Lazarus found refreshment in Hades in Abraham's bosom, while Dives was set in the torment of fire;[49] they balanced each other's vicissitudes of good and evil fortune by their contrasting reward and punishment.

There are certain days for gifts, which in some cases see the claims of rank discharged, in others the debt of wages.[50] Today, you say, I shall receive what is due to me, or pay back what I owe. This custom of consecrating days is rooted in superstition. If you are altogether free from the vanity of paganism, why do you participate in celebrations dedicated to idols, as if rules about days were binding upon you too, and you must discharge your debts or receive your dues only on the correct day? Tell me in what form you want to be dealt with. Why should you go into hiding, defiling your own conscience by another man's ignorance? If you are in fact known to be a Christian, you are on trial, and you go against another's conscience when you act as though you were not a Christian. But if you conceal your Christianity, you are tried and condemned. In one way or the other you are guilty of being ashamed of God. "Whosoever shall be ashamed of me before men, I also will be ashamed of him," he says, "before my Father which is in heaven."[51]

14. Many Christians today have come to think it pardonable

---

[47] *De Spectaculis.*   [48] Rom. 12:15, II Cor. 6:14; John 16:20.
[49] Luke 16:19ff. Hades translates *apud inferos.*
[50] *Mercedis debitum,* cf. *Mercedonios (dies) dixerunt a mercede solvenda,* in the Glossaries.
[51] Matt. 10:33; Luke 9:26.

to do as the world does "that the Name be not blasphemed."
There is indeed a blasphemy which we must avoid completely,
namely, that any of us should give a pagan good cause for
blasphemy by deceit or injury or insult or some other matter
justifying complaint in which the Name is deservedly blamed,
so that the Lord is deservedly angry. But if the words: "Because
of you my Name is blasphemed," [52] cover every blasphemy,
then we are all lost, since the whole [53] circus assails the Name,
for no fault of ours, with its wicked outcries. Let us stop being
Christians, and there will be no more blasphemy! No, let
blasphemy continue, so long as we are observing, not abandoning, our discipline, so long as we are being approved, not
reprobated. The blasphemy which attests my Christian faith
by detesting me because of it, is close to martyrdom. To curse
the keeping of our discipline is to bless our Name. "If I desired
to please men," he says, "I should not be the servant of Christ."

But, you may say, the Apostle elsewhere bids us take care to
please everybody: "Even as I please all men in all things."
Did he please men by celebrating the Saturnalia and the New
Year? Or was it by modesty and patience, by gravity, humanity,
and integrity? Again, when he says: "I am become all things to
all men, that I may gain all," did he become an idolater to the
idolaters? Did he become a heathen to the heathen, worldly
to the worldly? Even if he does not forbid us all converse with
idolaters and adulterers and other criminals, saying: "For then
must ye needs go out of the world," that does not imply such
a slackening of the reins of good behaviour that we can sin
with sinners merely because we have to live with them and mix
with them. It does not mean that where there is intercourse in
living (which the Apostle concedes), there can be sharing in
sin (which no one permits). We are allowed to live with the
heathen, but we are not allowed to die with them. Let us live
with all men, let us share their joys on the ground of a common
humanity, not a common superstition. We are like them in
possessing human souls, but not in the way we live. We share
the world with them, but not their error. [54]

But if we have no right to join with outsiders in such matters,
it is far more wicked to observe them among brethren. Who can
uphold or defend this? The Holy Spirit upbraids the Jews
for their feast-days: "Your sabbaths and new moons and

---

52 Isa. 52:5; Rom. 2:24; cf. I Peter 4:14–16. See also Tert., *Cult. Fem.*, II, 11.
53 *Totus*, perhaps "every."
54 Gal. 1:10; I Cor. 10:33; 9:22; 5:10.

ceremonies my soul hateth." [55] Do we who are strangers to the sabbaths and new moons and holy days once beloved by God, do we frequent the Saturnalia, the New Year and Midwinter festivals, the Feast of Matrons? [56] Do the presents and the New Year gifts come and go for us, the games resound and the banquets clatter for us? The heathen are more faithful to their own persuasion. They claim no Christian festival for themselves. They would not have shared the Lord's day or Pentecost with us even if they had known them. They would be afraid of being taken for Christians. We are not afraid of being proclaimed heathens. If the flesh is to be indulged at all, you have your own days, and more than they have. The heathen has a festival for each god on one day in the year only, you have one every week. Pick out all the heathen celebrations and put them in a row. They will not make up a Pentecost.

15. But "let your works shine," it says. [57] Now it is our shops and doors that shine. You can find more heathen doors without lamps and laurels than Christian. [58] What is your opinion of that kind of ceremony? If it is in honour of an idol, then honouring an idol is indubitably idolatry. If it is for a man, remember that all idolatry is for a man. Remember that all idolatry offers worship to men, since it is agreed even among the heathen that the gods themselves were once men. It makes no difference whether that superstitious worship is offered to men of the past or of today. Idolatry is not condemned on account of the persons set up to be worshipped, but of the attentions paid, which go to the demons. We must "render unto Caesar the things that are Caesar's"—happily he added: "And to God the things that are God's." [59] What then is Caesar's? Surely the subject of the original discussion, whether or not tribute should be paid to Caesar. That was why the Lord asked to see a coin and inquired whose image it bore. When he heard that it was Caesar's, he said: "Render to Caesar the things that are Caesar's, and unto God the things that are God's," that is, render to Caesar Caesar's image, which is on the coin, and to God God's image, which is on man. To Caesar, then, you should render money, to God yourself. If everything belongs to Caesar, what will be God's?

[55] Isa. 1:14.　　　　　[56] *Saturnalia, Ianuariae, Brumae, Matronales.*
[57] Matt. 5:16.
[58] Cf. *Abodah Zara*, I, 4: "A city in which idolatry is going on . . . the Wise decided that the shops with garlands are prohibited."
[59] Matt. 22:21.

Is it to honour a *god*, you ask, that the lamps are put before
doors and the laurels on posts? No indeed, they are not there
to honour a god, but a man, who is honoured as a god by such
attentions.[60] Or so it appears on the surface. What happens in
secret reaches the demons. For we ought to be well aware
(I give some details which may have escaped those not pro-
ficient in secular literature) that the Romans even have gods
of doorways.[61] There is Cardea, the goddess who gets her name
from hinges, there are Forculus, Limentinus, and Janus,
called after the doors, the threshold and the gate. Though
the names are idle fictions, we may be sure that they draw to
themselves demons and all manner of unclean spirits when they
are used superstitiously. Consecration creates a bond. Having
otherwise no individual names of their own, the demons find a
name where they find anything pledged to them. The same
with the Greeks. We read of Apollo Thyraeus and the Antelii,
the presiding demons of doorways. Foreseeing this from the
beginning, the Holy Spirit predicted through Enoch, oldest of
the prophets, that even doorways would come to a superstitious
use.[62] We see other doorways worshipped at the baths. So the
lanterns and laurels will belong to such as are worshipped in
the doorways. Whatever you do for a door, you do for an idol.
At this point I call a witness on the authority of God also, since
it is dangerous to suppress what has been shown[63] to one for
the sake of all. I know of a brother who was severely castigated
in a dream, the very same night, because, upon the unexpected
announcement of some public rejoicings, his slaves had garlanded his doors. He had not put the garlands out himself, or
ordered them. He had gone out before it happened and reproved it when he came back. This shows that in such matters
of discipline God judges us by our household.

So far as concerns the honours due to king or emperor, we

---

60 The Emperor.
61 The Apologists often ridicule Roman polytheism by going back to its
primitive stages when there was *numen* in everything. The material
mostly comes from Varro, and there is much of it in Tertullian and in
Augustine, *De Civitate Dei*. For the present passage cf. Rose, *op. cit.*,
30–32, e.g.: "To go through a door is to begin something, and beginnings
are heavily charged with magical significance. . . . So important was
the entrance-door that even its parts tended to assume a *numen* of their
own."
62 Cf. nn. 9–10.
63 *Ostensum . . . per visionem*, another possible touch of Montanism; but
Cyprian took dreams as supernatural warnings, and cf. Ambrose, *Letter*
51:14 (p. 257).

have a clear ruling to be subject in all obedience, according
to the Apostle's command, to magistrates and princes and those
in authority;[64] but within the limits of Christian discipline,
that is, so long as we keep ourselves free of idolatry. It was for
this reason that the familiar example of the three brethren
occurred before our time.[65] Obedient in other respects to
King Nebuchadnezzar, they quite firmly refused to honour his
image, and by this they proved that to extend the honour
proper to man beyond its due limits until it resembles the
sublimity of God is idolatry. Daniel, in the same way, subjected
himself to Darius in all points and performed his duty as long
as it did not imperil his religion.[66] To avoid that, he showed no
more fear of the king's lions than they had shown of the king's
fires.

So let those who have no light, light their lamps day by day.
Let those who have the threat of fire to face, fasten to their
door-posts laurels soon to burn. Fitting evidence of their darkness! Apt omen of their punishment! But you are the light of
the world, a tree ever green.[67] If you have renounced temples,
do not make your own gate a temple. I go further. If you have
renounced brothels, do not give your own house the appearance of a newly opened brothel.

16. So far as concerns the ceremonies[68] at private and family
festivals, such as putting on the white toga,[69] celebrating an
engagement or a marriage, or giving a name, I am disposed
to think that we are in no danger from the whiff of idolatry
which occurs at them. We must consider the causes of the ceremony. These, I think, are innocent in themselves, since neither
the man's clothing nor the ring nor the marriage bond originate
in honour paid to an idol. For instance, I do not find any kind
of clothing cursed by God except women's on a man. "Cursed
is every man," it says, "that putteth on a woman's garment."[70]
But the toga is expressly called "manly." Again, God no more

---

[64] Rom. 13:7; I Peter 2:13.   [65] Dan. 3.   [66] Dan. 6.
[67] Matt. 5:14; Ps. 1:3.
[68] *Officia*, which Tertullian uses with various shades of meaning in chs.
16–18. He does not speak of *pietas*, the duty of love and respect for the
gods and one's family, but of the more concrete "attentions" to both.
The sense "ceremonies" predominates in c. 16 with "in attendance on"
also important. Cf. "the office," "a service."
[69] *Toga pura*, and below, *vestitus virilis*, *toga virilis*, the white gown assumed
on reaching manhood in place of the *toga praetexta*, which had a purple
stripe, and was also worn by magistrates (cf. c. 18).
[70] Deut. 22:5.

prohibits the celebration of a marriage than the giving of a name.

It is objected that appropriate sacrifices take place. But if I am invited and the ceremony is not described as "assisting in the sacrifice," then I will give my assistance to their full satisfaction. Indeed I wish it were possible for us never to see what we must not do. But since the evil one has surrounded the world with idolatry, we may legitimately be present on some occasions when we are at the service of a man, not an idol. Of course, if I am invited to act as priest and perform a sacrifice, I shall not go, for that is strictly service to an idol. In such a case I shall not give my advice or my money or any assistance at all. If I attend when I have been invited because of the sacrifice, I shall be taking part in the idolatry. If there is something else that attaches me to the person offering the sacrifice, I shall only be an onlooker at it.[71]

17. Otherwise, what will Christian slaves and freedmen and magistrates' officers do when their masters or patrons or superiors are offering sacrifice and they are in attendance? If you hand wine to one who is sacrificing, indeed, if you help simply by pronouncing some word necessary to the sacrifice, you will be reckoned a minister of idolatry. Mindful of this rule, we can do our duty to magistrates and authorities like the patriarchs and other men of old, who attended upon idolatrous kings only so long as they could keep outside the confines of idolatry. A dispute arose recently on this point. Can a servant of God undertake an administrative office or function if, by favour or ingenuity, he can keep himself clear of every form of idolatry, as Joseph and Daniel, in royal purple, governed the whole of Egypt or Babylon, performing their administrative offices and functions without taint of idolatry? Grant that a man may succeed in holding his office, whatever it may be, quite nominally, never sacrifice, never authorize a sacrifice, never contract for sacrificial victims, never delegate the supervision of a temple, never handle their taxes, never give a show at his own expense or the State's, never preside over one, never announce or order a festival, never even take an oath; and on top of all that, in the exercise of his magisterial authority, never try anyone on a capital charge or one involving loss of civil status (you may tolerate inflicting a fine), never condemn

---

[71] It is unusual for Tertullian to make concessions. He does not allow a Christian to go to the circus *tantum spectator*, because he is under no kind of obligation to go. The concession is echoed in *Cult. Fem.*, II, 11.

to death by verdict or legislation, never put a man in irons or in prison, never put to torture—well, if you think that is possible, he may hold his office!

18. Now we have to consider the mere ornaments and trappings of office. Each has its proper dress for daily and for ceremonial use. In Egypt and Babylon the purple robe and gold necklace were marks of rank, just as our provincial priests have their golden wreaths and their robes of state, some with purple borders and some with palms embroidered on them.[72] But there was a difference in the obligation. They were conferred upon men who earned the king's friendship, simply as a mark of honour. Hence they were styled "Peers of the Royal Purple" after the purple robe, as we call candidates[73] after the white *toga candida*. The decoration was not attached to priesthoods or any idolatrous function. Had that been so, men of such holiness and constancy would at once have refused the garments as being defiled. It would have been seen at once (as it was seen a good deal later) that Daniel did not serve idols or worship Bel or the dragon.[74]

Purple as such, then, was not yet a mark of high office among the barbarians, but of free birth. As Joseph, who had been a slave, and Daniel, who had changed his status by captivity, attained the citizenship of Egypt or Babylon by means of the garments[75] which indicated free birth among the barbarians, so we Christians may, if necessary, allow the bordered *toga praetexta* to the boys and the stole to the girls as marks of birth, not authority, of family, not office, of class, not religion.

But the purple robe and other marks of rank and authority which were originally dedicated to the idolatry attaching to rank and authority,[76] these keep the stain of their profanation, since idols are still dressed up with robes of state, robes with

[72] *Praetextae vel trabeae vel palmatae.* For these and other details of dress see L. Wilson, *The Roman Toga* (1924), *id.*, *The Clothing of the Ancient Romans* (1938). On the religious associations and origins of the *corona* see Tert., *De Corona*, c. 12, and for the golden crowns of magistrates, c. 13.

[73] I.e., for magistracies at Rome.

[74] The Apocryphal book *Bel and the Dragon* is c. 14 of Daniel in the Vulgate. Tertullian presumably knew it as a continuation of Daniel, hence "later."

[75] Gen. 41:42; Dan. 5:16.

[76] "A magistrate was usually a priest as a part of his official functions, which is why, in Greek cities, they often wore wreaths, a very common mark of one engaged in religious duties, and in Rome all curule magistrates wore the *praetexta*." [*Oxford Classical Dict.*, s.v. *Priests*]. See also Rose, *op. cit.*, p. 42.

borders, robes with purple stripes, and still have rods and staves carried in front of them.[77] And rightly. After all, the demons are the magistrates of this world. They bear the rods and wear the purple to show they all belong to the one magisterial college. What will you gain by wearing the dress without performing its functions? No one can look clean in dirty clothes. If you put a dirty shirt on, you may not make it dirty, but you cannot be clean yourself while you are wearing it. As for your argument about Joseph and Daniel, you must recognize that one cannot always compare old and new, barbarous and civilized, beginnings and developments, servile and free. In status they were slaves. You are no man's slave, because you are Christ's alone, who has freed you from the captivity of this world. Therefore you must live after your Master's rule and pattern. He, the Lord and Master, walked humbly and meanly, uncertain of a home. For "the Son of Man," he says, "hath not where to lay his head." He went unkempt in clothing, or he would not have said: "Behold, they that wear soft raiment are in kings' houses."[78] In face and look he was without beauty, as Isaiah had prophesied.[79] If he did not exercise his rightful authority even over his own people, for whom he discharged his menial ministry, if, though conscious of his own kingdom, he refused to be made king, he gave his followers the fullest possible example to decline all parade and show, whether of rank or authority. Who could have employed them with better right than the Son of God? What rods of office would escort him, what purple flower from his shoulders, what gold gleam from his head, had he not counted worldly glory strange alike to himself and to his disciples? So he rejected the glory which he did not desire, and in rejecting it, condemned it, and in condemning it, set it down as the pomp of the devil. He would not have condemned it but for the fact that it was not his own; and what does not belong to God can belong to none but the devil. If you have forsworn the pomp of the devil, you should know that to touch it anywhere is idolatry. If you would be convinced that all authorities and ranks of this world are not merely strange to God, but also hostile to him, bear in mind

[77] *Praetextae, trabeae, laticlavi, fasces, virgae.*
[78] Luke 9:58; Matt. 11:8.
[79] *Inglorius*, cf. Isa. 53:2. Old Latin MSS. have *indecorus*. Tertullian takes this physically, some fathers negatively (not beautiful), some as referring to the lowliness of Christ.

that it is through them that punishments have been determined against God's servants, and through them that the penalties prepared for the impious remain unknown. You say that your birth and property make it difficult for you to avoid idolatry? [80] There can be no lack of remedies for that. And if all failed, there would remain that one remedy which would make you a happier magistrate, not on earth, but in heaven.

19. The last chapter may be thought to have decided the case of military service, [81] which is included in rank and authority. But at present it is being asked whether a baptized Christian can turn to military service and whether a soldier may be admitted to the faith, at least the rank and file who are not compelled to offer sacrifices or impose capital sentences.

There is no compatibility between the oath [82] to serve God and the oath to serve man, between the standard of Christ and the standard of the devil, the camp of light and the camp of darkness. One life cannot be owed to two masters, God and Caesar. Of course—if you like to make a jest of the subject— Moses carried a rod and Aaron wore a buckle, John had a leather belt, Joshua led an army and Peter made war. Yes, but tell me how he will make war, indeed how he will serve in peacetime, without a sword—which the Lord took away? Even if soldiers came to John and were given instructions to keep, even if the centurion believed, the Lord afterwards unbelted every soldier when he disarmed Peter. Among us no dress is lawful which is assigned to an unlawful activity.

20. Walking according to God's moral law is endangered by words as well as deeds. The Bible which says: "Behold the man and his deeds," says also: "Out of thy mouth thou shalt be justified." [83] Therefore we must remember to guard against the inroads of idolatry also in words let drop from fault of habit or cowardice. The Law does not actually forbid us to name the gods of the heathen. We may pronounce their names when daily life compels us to mention them. We often have to say: "You'll find him in the Temple of Aesculapius," or "in Isis Street," or "he's been made a priest of Jupiter," and much else of that sort, since names of this type are also bestowed upon

---

80 Because you are expected, or bound by inheritance, to hold magistracies. Many of no great position would be obliged to serve on town councils. *Codex Agobardinus* ends three words later.

81 For the subject of this chapter see the Introduction, and Tert., *De Corona Militis.*

82 *Sacramentum.*

83 John 19:5?; Matt. 12: 37.

men. If I address Saturnus by his own name, I am not honouring him, any more than I honour Marcus when I address him by the name of Marcus.

True, Scripture says: "Make no mention of the name of other gods, neither let it be heard out of thy mouth." What it lays down is that we should not call them gods. For in the first part of the Law it says: "Thou shalt not take the name of the Lord thy God in vain", that is, apply it to an idol. So anyone who honours an idol with the name of God falls into idolatry. If I am compelled to mention gods, I must add something to show that I do not call them gods. Scripture uses the name "gods," but adds "their" or "of the heathen," as when David, having used the name gods, says "but the gods of the heathen are demons." [84]

So much I have said rather to prepare for what follows. It is a bad habit to say, *Mehercule, Medius Fidius!* [85] Some even do not know that this is an oath by Hercules. An oath by those you have forsworn, what will that be but collusion between faith and idolatry? For surely we do honour to those by whom we swear.

21. It is cowardly to keep quiet in order to escape recognition as a Christian, when someone else binds you with an oath or some other attestation by his gods. In appearance you will be bound by them, and so you affirm their majesty just as much by keeping quiet as by speaking. What difference does it make whether you affirm the gods of the heathen by calling them gods or listening to them so called, whether you swear by an idol or acquiesce when you are sworn by someone else? Why cannot we recognize the tricks of Satan who, when he is unable to do it by his own lips, contrives by the lips of his servants to put idolatry into us through our ears? At all events, whoever it is that is binding you by this oath, you meet him on either friendly or unfriendly terms. If unfriendly, you are at once summoned to battle and know you have to fight. If friendly, will you not be much more secure if you transfer your pledge to the Lord, dissolving your obligation to a person through whom the evil one was trying to involve you in honouring an idol, that is, in idolatry?

All such sufferance is idolatry. You honour those to whom you showed respect when they were thrust upon you. Listen. In the course of some dispute, in public, a man said to an

---

[84] Ex. 23:13; 20:7, cf. n. 36; Ps. 96:5.
[85] An ancient oath by the Italian god Dius Fidius, connected with Jupiter.

acquaintance of mine: "Jupiter plague you." He (God forgive him!) replied: "No, you," just like a pagan who believed in Jupiter. Even if the curse he retorted had not been by Jupiter or anyone like Jupiter, he had affirmed Jupiter's deity. To return curse for curse proved that he was indignant at being cursed by Jupiter. Why be indignant about him, if you know he does not exist? If you fly into a rage, you at once affirm his existence. Your confession of fear will be idolatry. It is even worse when you curse back by Jupiter, for then you pay him the same honour as the person who provoked you. In an affair of that sort the Christian should smile, not fly into a rage. Indeed, according to the commandment, he should not even curse back by God, but of course should bless him by God. Thus you destroy idolatry, preach God and do your duty as a Christian.

22. Equally, we who are initiated into Christ will not tolerate being blessed by the gods of the heathen. We shall always repudiate an unclean blessing and cleanse it for ourselves by turning it to God. To be blessed by the gods of the heathen is to be cursed by God. If I give anyone alms or do him some kindness, and he prays his gods or the genius of the colony to be propitious to me, at once my offering or assistance becomes an honour done to the idols by whose means he returns me the favour of a blessing. But why should he not be made aware that I acted for God's sake, that God might be glorified, and not that the demons might be honoured by what I did for God? God may indeed see that I acted for his sake, but he sees no less that I was unwilling to show that I acted for his sake, and that, in a way, I turned his command into an offering to idols. Many say, no one is obliged to proclaim himself a Christian. Nor, I think, to deny that he is one. For you *are* denying it, if you dissemble your Christianity when for any reason you are taken for a pagan. And all denial is certainly idolatry, just as all idolatry is denial, whether by word or deed.

23. There is, however, a particular case, doubly sharp in word and deed and dangerous on both sides, though it cajoles you as if it were harmless on both. Nothing appears to have been done (the case runs) because no word was spoken.[86]

---

[86] Here is a very real difficulty for Christians engaged in business and on all sorts of occasions where legal instruments are required. Evidently they had tried to compromise, with the assistance of the pagans, making contracts without swearing oaths *viva voce*. The text is rather uncertain, without *Agobardinus*, and in places Tertullian is particularly tortuous.

Christians borrow money from pagans. They give pledge, security and bond under oath, and then deny it. Do they expect the day of prosecution and the place of judgment and the judge himself to be interested in their consciences? [87] Christ forbids us to take an oath, "I wrote it, he says, but I did not say anything." It is the tongue, not the letter, which kills! [88] Here I call nature and conscience to witness, nature because the hand can write nothing that the mind has not dictated, however still and motionless the tongue remains during the dictation; though the mind may have dictated to the tongue either something conceived by itself or something given to it by another. And now, in case it is pleaded that someone else dictated, I appeal here to conscience. Is it not the mind that accepts and transmits to the hand what that other dictated, whether the tongue acts in concert or keeps still? Fortunately the Lord spoke of sin in mind and conscience. "If (he said) concupiscence or malice rise up into the heart of man, thou art held guilty of the deed." [89] You gave your bond, then. Certainly it rose up into your heart. You cannot contend that you gave it in ignorance or against your will. When you gave your bond, you knew you were doing it, and in knowing it, you willed it; and it is done as much in deed as in thought. You cannot bar the weightier charge by a lighter one, admitting that you committed a fraud in that you did not perform the bond which you gave. "However, I did not deny God, because I took no oath." No, you will be said to have sworn if you consented to the act, even if you had done no such thing. If you take the pen, a silent voice is no valid plea; if you write, it is no defence that no sound was heard. On the contrary, when Zacharias was punished for a time with the loss of his voice, he conversed with his mind, over-riding the uselessness of his tongue. With the help of his hands he dictated from his heart, and without using his mouth he pronounced his son's name. [90] There speaks in his pen, there is heard in his tablet, a hand clearer than any sound, a letter more vocal

---

[87] I keep Reifferscheid-Wissowa's text—*se scire volunt scilicet tempus persecutionis et locus tribunalis et persona praesidis*—turn it into a question or exclamation, and make what I can of it. If they are brought into an earthly court, they will soon be found out if they reject their bonds on casuistical grounds and so it will be before the heavenly Judge. Kellner omits the passage, and there are many conjectures.

[88] This has usually been taken as part of what the offender says, but seems better as a sarcastic rejoinder. Is this how you treat II Cor. 3:6?

[89] Cf. Matt. 5:28.   [90] Luke 1.

than any mouth. [Question, whether he has spoken who is understood to have spoken.] [91]

Let us pray to the Lord that we may not fall into the necessity of any such contract, and that, if it so happens, he may give to the brethren the ability to assist us, or else to ourselves the constancy to break off every necessity. So may not those letters of denial, speaking instead of our mouths, be brought against us in the day of judgment, sealed no longer with the seals of lawyers, but of angels.

24. Among these rocks and inlets, these shoals and straits of idolatry, faith holds her course, her sails spread to the Breath of God, safe and sound if cautious and intent. But once overboard, no man swims back from those depths, once struck upon those rocks, no ship escapes its wreck, once sucked into that whirlpool of idolatry, no man breathes again. Every wave of it suffocates, every eddy of it swallows down into hell.

Let no one say: "Who can take precaution enough for safety? We shall have to depart from the world." [92] As if it were not a better bargain to depart than to stay in the world an idolater. Nothing is easier than to take precautions against idolatry, if the fear of it holds the first place. Any necessity is small in comparison with danger so great. When the apostles were in council, the Holy Spirit relaxed the bond and yoke for us precisely in order that we might devote ourselves to the avoidance of idolatry. [93] This will be our law, to be observed the more fully because it is not burdensome, our own Christian law, through which we are recognized and put to the test by the heathen. This law must be set before those who approach the faith and inculcated into those who enter upon the faith, that they may take thought as they approach, may persevere in its observance, and if they fail to observe it, may renounce themselves. We shall not be disturbed if, after the type of the Ark, the raven and the kite, the wolf, the dog and the serpent, are found in the Church. [94] If the Ark is the type, at any rate

91 See n. 37.
92 Cf. I Cor. 5:10.
93 Acts 15:28–9.
94 (1) Noah's ark is a regular type of the Church, e.g., Tert., *Bapt.*, 8, Cyprian, *Epp.*, 69:2; 74:11; 75:15; *De Unitate*, 6.

(2) The presence of clean and unclean animals in it is used as an argument against rigorists, e.g., by Callistus (ap. Hipp. *Phil.*, IX) and the unknown third cent. *Auctor ad Novatianum*, 2, and by Augustine against Donatists. Cyprian does not so use the ark, but applies the wheat and the tares in the same way (Ep. 54:3), as does Callistus.

no idolater is found in it. No animal is the figure of the idolater. What was not in the Ark can have no place in the Church.

(3) Tertullian says in *Apol.*, 41, that God will not hasten to make the separation, i.e., judgment, before the end of the world. In *Prax.*, 1, he hopes that the tares of Praxeas will be uprooted now, not simply at the end; but this is a special case. In *De Fuga*, 1, persecution is now separating the wheat of the martyrs from the chaff of apostates in the Church, the Lord's threshing-floor. But this is again a special case, not a principle of discipline to be applied by men.

(4) Here he is cautious. *Viderit* in Tertullian often dismisses a fact or a possibility, but can also mean, "I do not care if." Here *viderimus* seems to have the latter meaning. There may be unclean people in the Church, but at least no idolater. This would be quite consistent with catholic discipline as known to Tertullian, and is no proof of the Montanism of this treatise.

(5) Idolatry here means the real thing, I believe, not all the actions which he has dubbed idolatrous in the book. At least, he would not excommunicate all such offenders. No doubt they are all warned by this picture. But how does he know that no animal was a type of idolatry? Only because it has no place in the Church, a *petitio principii*.

(6) *Auct. ad Nov.* takes the raven to be a type of the unclean who depart from the Church and never return. That is, it could be a type of the apostate, though this author finds room for the return of the repentant lapsed under the figure of the dove which finds no resting-place outside and returns to the Church.

Cyprian

Cyprian

GENERAL INTRODUCTION

I

IT WAS CYPRIAN'S LOT TO BE BISHOP OF ONE OF THE greatest cities of the West at a critical period in the history of the Church, the years of persecution under Decius and Valerian. For his episcopate we have much evidence in his own writings, especially in the letters, of which eighty-one are extant, fifty-nine of them written by him, with six synodical letters issued on his authority, and sixteen written to him or included in his files. These are supplemented by the brief biography composed by the deacon, Pontius, who lived with him, and the *Acta Cypriani*, the official record of his martyrdom. Not much is known of his life before he became a bishop.

Like his compatriot Tertullian, Caecilius Cyprianus, "also known as Thascius" was brought up a pagan, well educated in rhetoric and perhaps in law. Until middle life he was teaching rhetoric professionally, and seems also to have practised occasionally as an advocate in the courts. He was a wealthy man at the time of his conversion to Christianity, which happened about 245–246. Cyprian regarded the Carthaginian presbyter Caecilianus as his spiritual father. Not long after his baptism he was ordained presbyter, and again it was not long before, on the death of Donatus, he was elected and consecrated Bishop of Carthage. This was in 249 (possibly 248); the new bishop was still near enough to his baptism to be called a neophyte and a *novellus*. He was to suffer for this from the jealousy and factious spirit of a group of senior presbyters.

The Church in Africa had enjoyed peace, so far as the State was concerned, since Tertullian's time, and was not well prepared to face the shock of renewed persecution when Decius ordered his subjects to attest their loyalty by sacrificing to the gods of the Empire. His edict took effect from the 1st January, 250. In Africa many Christians fell—"lapsed," as it was called —either by offering sacrifice or by purchasing certificates to say they had done so. Many of the faithful were imprisoned, pending sentence; some were put to death. The blow fell particularly upon the leaders, a deliberate policy. Pope Fabian, for example, was martyred on the 20th January, and it was not safe to fill the See until March, 251. Cyprian, impressed by the necessity of holding his flock together and guided, as he believed, by a dream, went into hiding and continued to direct his diocese by letters and, eventually, by a small commission of neighbouring bishops and presbyters. For the Bishop of Carthage was the most marked man in Latin Africa. It is unhappily easy to understand that the jealous presbyters made the most of their bishop's "desertion."

Cyprian's first major ecclesiastical controversy arose out of the problem of dealing with lapsed Christians who wished to be forgiven and taken back into communion. Former discipline was against this, and Cyprian was himself a disciplinarian, not quick to make concessions and with a strong sense that, if traditional discipline was to be altered on so important an issue, the change must have the approval of the Church. Accordingly he postponed a final decision until the slackening of persecution made it possible for an African council to meet after Easter, 251, when some concessions were made. Meanwhile he kept in touch with the widowed Church of Rome, where the most prominent personality was the presbyter, Novatianus. In Africa there was a demand for a much easier, "laxer," policy with the lapsed. Why not restore the penitent to communion at once? The five presbyters who opposed Cyprian on personal grounds, led by a certain Novatus, adopted this platform and secured the support of numerous confessors, who were persuaded that their spiritual authority as confessors enabled them to guarantee the forgiveness even of apostasy. They began by giving the penitents letters of recommendation to the bishop, and finished by demanding that the bishop should restore such pentitents to communion. Some presbyters disregarded the absentee bishop and acted in this sense on their own authority. Thus, besides the original problem of the proper disciplinary action to take, this first crisis involved questions about the authority of presbyters and of spiritual, but unordained, persons (we remember Tertullian's *spiritales*) *vis-à-vis* the bishop, and also of the relation of the individual bishop, in his disciplinary capacity, to the wider Church. All this led to the production of Cyprian's *De Unitate* early in A.D. 251. It is not surprising that his experience of faction led him to emphasize the authority of the bishop.

The second crisis arose out of the first. When Cornelius was made Bishop of Rome in March, 251, the presbyter Novatianus was, it seems, bitterly disappointed. Immediately he secured his own consecration as bishop, ostensibly of Rome, and headed the party which, so far from being lax in discipline, objected to any departure from the older rule that apostates must be excommunicated for life. For him, if he was sincere, this relaxation infringed the holiness of the Church to such an extent that it ceased to be the Church at all. Therefore Cornelius was not Bishop of Rome, and his party alone was the true "holy Church," and himself the lawful bishop. Cyprian, however, recognized Cornelius, after inquiry into the circumstances of both elections and consecrations. The Novatianist party soon spread into Africa, appointed another "bishop" of Carthage, and allied themselves, on the basis of common opposition to Cyprian, with the laxist group in Carthage, which before long appointed its own "bishop," Fortunatus. Cyprian had now to deal with formal, episcopal, schism in Africa.

The third crisis emerged from the second. After the excitement of the opening stages of controversy and schism, there were many Christians who wanted to return to, or enter into, communion with Cyprian. If they had been baptized before the schism, there was only a disciplinary issue, which caused no trouble except in the case of clergy. But some of them had been baptized in schism, by the Novatianists, and this raised a theological problem. Had they really been baptized at all? Could baptism be administered outside the Church? The Novatianists claimed to be the true Church, exclusively. So did those in communion with Cyprian at Carthage or Cornelius and his successors at Rome, whom, retrospectively, we can call the catholics. The first problem, then, was to decide which body was the true Church. Cyprian determines this—given orthodoxy on both sides—according to the principle of apostolic succession. Novatian had never become Bishop of Rome (or a bishop at all) since he did not succeed to a vacant See. It must be understood that neither Cyprian nor Stephen of Rome, bishop from 254, allowed that the Novatianists were *the* Church or *a* church or a part of the Church. They were outside.

But Stephen and Cyprian differed about what happened outside the Church. For Cyprian there was no spiritual life at all outside, no ministry, no sacraments, no salvation. Stephen also believed that there was no salvation and no gift of the Holy Ghost through baptism outside the Church. He thought, however, that baptism could be in some sense conferred outside, the *character* of a baptized Christian could be imparted, through the invocation of the Trinity and the use of water. This could become efficacious when the person so baptized entered the catholic Church, for which he need not be "re-baptized." Practically, this view made it easier for schismatics to return, since they need not repudiate their baptism. Theologically, it raises acute difficulties about the coherence of Church, Ministry, and Sacraments, and there is much to be said for Cyprian's attempt to hold these elements together, though we may be driven to a different conception of the Church if we are to do so. But Rome's point of view prevailed in time. Cyprian's arguments are fully enough expressed in his letters. Stephen's have to be taken at secondhand and from his opponents, unless the anonymous, but contemporary, tract, *De Rebaptismate*, fairly represents his position.

Cyprian would not budge. He was supported by practically the whole of the African episcopate, which refused, at its council in 256, to acknowledge heretical and schismatic baptism, and would not yield to the Bishop of Rome. Hence Cyprian's relations with Stephen are crucial in the controversy over the nature of the Roman primacy. That he respected Rome and recognized a considerable measure of authority in the apostolic see should not be questioned, but he stopped short of allowing it jurisdiction over other bishops, and he stood rather for a conciliar method of deciding controversies and a collegiate ideal of church government. How the immediate tension between Rome and Carthage would have ended we cannot say, for the situation was changed by the death of Stephen in August, 257 and a fresh outbreak of persecution at the same moment. The ranks were closed.

Valerian's first edict, issued in August, 257, ordered that bishops, presbyters, and deacons should sacrifice to the gods, on pain of exile, and forbade Christians to assemble for worship. Cyprian was arrested, brought before the Proconsul of Africa at Carthage on the 30th August, and banished to Curubis, not far from Carthage, where he had to remain for a year. The second edict ordered, among other things, that bishops should be put to death. Cyprian appeared before the new Proconsul on the 14th September, 258, refused to sacrifice, and was sentenced to death "under the emperors Valerian and Gallienus, but in the reign of our Lord Jesus Christ."

II

On his conversion Cyprian had renounced secular literature in favour of the Bible, a thing which he carried out with much more consistency than Jerome. Besides the letters, thirteen treatises are extant, if we count *Quod Idola Dii non sint*, the authorship of which is not certain. If it is Cyprian's, it may well be his earliest Christian work, the new convert's polemic against his former faith, nominal or real. The material is taken largely from Tertullian and, possibly, from Minucius Felix. Another early work, possibly the fruit of his studies under Caecilian, is the collection of biblical *Testimonia*, in three books, of which the first shows how the Jews have given place to the Church as the People of God, while the second is Christological and the third moral and disciplinary. The *Ad Donatum*, perhaps of 249, contrasts the blessings of baptism with the misery of the world; *De Habitu Virginum* imitates Tertullian in matter, though not in style. In 251 come the two most important treatises, the *De Unitate* (pp. 119–142) and the *De Lapsis*, the latter describing the consequences of the persecution and exhorting the lapsed to repentance. His disciplinary policy is defined more precisely in the relevant letters. Accepting the order in which Pontius mentions the treatises (*Vita*, c. 7, which seems to be chronological), the *De Dominica Oratione*, again modelled on Tertullian, may come in 252, followed by the two tracts evoked by the plague of 252, *De Mortalitate*, and *Ad Demetrianum*, replying to a pagan who blamed Christians for the occurrence of the calamity. *De Bono Patientiae*, much indebted to Tertullian's *De Patientia*, was certainly written in 256, and was followed by *De Zelo et Livore*, a slight tract on the evil of envy, with some reference to the faction and schism that beset him. *Ad Fortunatum* is an encouragement to face martyrdom, written in the autumn of 257 at Curubis. To these works may be added the *Sententiae* of the eighty-seven bishops at the Council of Carthage, 256, which begin and end with brief pronouncements from Cyprian as president. The majority of these treatises are of little importance. Nevertheless, though moral exhortations are not often thrilling reading to later generations, they can be of much practical importance in their own day, and in this respect Cyprian was a good bishop. His really important contributions to Christian thought and practice lie within the doctrine of the Church and the Ministry, and these are to be found in the *De Unitate* and the associated letters, samples of which are given in the present volume.

The Unity of the Catholic Church

INTRODUCTION

I

IN THE YEAR A.D. 251 EASTER SUNDAY FELL ON THE 23rd March. Not long afterwards, in April or just possibly in May, a Council was assembled at Carthage to decide the policy of the African Church towards the lapsed, and to this Council Cyprian, its president, read his two tracts (*libelli*), *On the Lapsed* and *On the Unity of the Catholic Church*, which he subsequently sent to Rome (*Ep.* 54:4). By that time he had perhaps revised them, at least the latter. Faction in Carthage, together with the desire to hold the African episcopate together in its disciplinary policy, would be sufficient cause for such a work as the *De Unitate*. In its present form, however, it shows knowledge of the troubled situation in Rome. After the long vacancy since the 20th January, 250, it had at last become possible to appoint a new bishop. This was Cornelius, the date of whose consecration is not precisely known, though it would seem overwhelmingly probable that it was in time for Easter. Soon afterwards (again, we do not know quite how soon) Novatian procured consecration in opposition to Cornelius.

These events appear to have been reported to the Council at Carthage in two stages. Having heard first of the election of Cornelius and of certain objections which were being raised, the Council sent two bishops to discover the facts. Before long they heard of Novatian's consecration, and sent two more. It would seem that the Council dispersed without having given formal recognition to Cornelius. Hence Cyprian's subsequent correspondence on the point. All this leaves us in some doubt whether Cyprian could have read the *De Unitate* to the Council in anything like its present form, with its plain rejection of Novatian. If he did, and it need not have been at the same time as the reading of the *De Lapsis*, it must have been at a late stage in the Council, which appears to have sat for a considerable time, and when he had made up his own mind about Novatian, even if no conciliar pronouncement had been made. At any rate, when he sent it to Rome, he had the situation there in mind as well as his own troubles in Carthage

II

Cyprian's conception of the catholic Church is akin to, and presumably in part derived from, that of Tertullian's *De Praescriptionibus Haereticorum*. The Church is a single, visible, body, using the apostolic Scriptures in addition to the Old Testament, maintaining the traditional apostolic faith, living under the institutions which have been handed down from apostolic times; and it is further linked with the apostles by the succession of bishops in each see. But circumstances have changed since Tertullian wrote, and the emphasis has changed with them. Cyprian has less need than Tertullian to worry about purity of doctrine. His principal concern is for unity, and with this in view he puts much more emphasis on the authority of bishops and their coherence as a college. To him the episcopate is still, of course, the guardian of the true faith, but in the immediate circumstances it is even more the guardian of unity. Hence the apostolic succession comes to the fore, partly as the means by which the true Church is distinguished from rivals and partly as the source of the bishop's right to obedience.

Theologically, Cyprian holds the unity of the Church to be axiomatic, or rather, biblically and divinely guaranteed. This does not mean simply that all Christians are inwardly and spiritually united (they may not be), but that there is only one concrete, visible body, only one communion, which is the Church, that true and only Church which the Lord established through the apostles. For Cyprian this unity is not ideal, but actual; it cannot be broken. And it is a unity with, or around, a structure, the episcopate in apostolic succession, the succession of the bishops in each local church. Outside the successions there is no church. No one can become a bishop unless he succeeds to a vacant see. Thus Novatian, for all his consecration by other bishops, was no bishop. It was not merely that he lacked jurisdiction. He lacked the character, the orders, of a bishop. Further, outside this one visible communion there is no spiritual vitality and no salvation, for the Holy Spirit and the gifts of the Spirit were and are bestowed by Christ upon the Church alone. The implications of this doctrine, apparent already in the *De Unitate*, were to be worked out more fully in the baptismal controversy. They are logical enough deductions from his premises.

Cyprian's teaching has the merit of clarity and coherence. It holds together Church, Ministry, and Sacraments in an intelligible and salutary fashion. But if it is true, the consequences are indeed terrible. Millions upon millions of *bona fide* Christians have found no salvation because they were outside the Church. If this conclusion is unacceptable, where did Cyprian go wrong? There are several possibilities. One may insist that the Holy Spirit works outside the Church, and that God is able to save whom he will outside the Church. Or one may dispute Cyprian's conception of the visibility of the Church and argue that the true Church, the Body of Christ, consists precisely of those who are saved by faith, and that the number of these elect is known to God alone, that the true Church is invisible to man. Again, Cyprian's concatenation of Church, Ministry, and Sacraments may be challenged. It may be allowed that baptism, at least, and perhaps a ministry and the eucharist, in some sense exist and "work" outside the Church as defined by Cyprian. This line of thought was explored in part by some who shared Cyprian's definition of the Church itself during the baptismal controversy of A.D. 255–256, when Rome held, against Africa and Asia, that heretical or schismatic baptism was so far valid outside the Church that it need not be repeated inside; but at that time it was far from clear what efficacy was attributed to such baptism. Augustine developed this theme and extended it to orders, leaving us with a strange structure of valid, but not efficacious, bishops and baptisms outside the Church, a pseudo-church which could perpetuate itself but bring no one to salvation inside itself. His teaching underlies much modern confusion. Another possibility is to question Cyprian's notion of the *visible* Church itself in terms of episcopal succession, and this may lead either to forms of congregationalism, local and visible groups of genuine Christians, each representing the catholic Church, or to an acknowledgment of schism within the Church catholic. In that case the disunity is recognized to be sinful, but it is held that Cyprian's criterion of apostolic succession is not adequate for the purpose for which he used it, and that there are other, and more important, means of continuity with the authentic Church of apostolic days, continuities of faith and life, and indeed of ministry and sacrament, which vouch for the catholicity, real if imperfect, of communions, denominations, within the one, holy, catholic and apostolic, but visibly divided, Church. Should this be sound, Cyprian's perception that Church, Ministry, and Sacrament are an indissoluble unity may be upheld as nearer to the truth than the superficially more charitable recognition of ministry and sacraments outside the Church. In any case the *De Unitate* is, historically and intrinsically, a major influence in the whole discussion.

III

It has been stated above that Cyprian probably revised his treatise after he had read it to the Council of Carthage in the spring of 251, in which case the version as originally read may not survive at all. There is the further complication that what has survived exists in two forms, with important differences in chapters 4 and 5, and some in chapter 19. Both extant versions have Novatian in mind. At first sight one version appears much more papalist than the other, the former being usually referred to now as the *Primacy Text*, and the latter, the episcopalian, as the *Textus Receptus*. In the present volume the latter is given in the body of the work, the Primacy Text as an appendix; conflated versions may be ignored. What are we to make of them? First, it is an intelligible position to hold that, since the *De Unitate* as evoked by the circumstances of 251 was not concerned with any questions about Roman primacy, but was concerned to hold bishops together, the episcopalian text, which indubitably has the better manuscript support, is the genuine one, and that the primacy phrases are later interpolations in the interest of Rome. But since Archbishop Benson argued this position at length, much labour has been devoted to the problem, and although the hypothesis of interpolation cannot be regarded as dead and may yet turn out to be correct, there is now a considerable measure of agreement that both texts are genuine and represent two editions. At least there is nothing in the wording of the primacy text which could not possibly be Cyprianic.

On the supposition that both are genuine there are two main theories of what happened. One is that Cyprian produced two somewhat different versions in 251, the first, the episcopalian, to meet the situation in Africa, the other for use in Rome. On this view the so-called primacy phrases would refer only to the schism in Rome, where to desert the chair of Peter and its occupant, Cornelius, in favour of Novatian, would be to put oneself outside the catholic Church, the Church of the lawful successions. This theory has received notable support, e.g., from Caspar. The alternative, it seems, and the theory at present most favoured, is to suppose that the primacy text was the original, and that Cyprian revised it in 256 since certain expressions could be used against him in his controversy with Stephen of Rome. This theory has been ably argued in recent years by Maurice Bévenot. The implications of Cyprian's changes and the precise meaning of his original words—on this hypothesis—are too big a subject to be argued out in this volume. It may be said, however, that some of the Roman Catholic scholars who have maintained the genuineness and priority of the primacy text do not consider that it is strictly papalist.

IV

The standard text of Cyprian's treatises is that of W. Hartel in the Vienna *Corpus*, Vol. III, 1 (1868), and the present translation has been made from it. For other English versions see the Bibliography at the end of this volume.

The Unity of the Catholic Church

THE TEXT

1. "Ye are the salt of the earth."[1] These words of the Lord convey a warning. Since he bids us be simple and innocent, yet prudent in our simplicity,[2] is it not proper, my dear brothers, that we should show foresight, uncovering the snares of our wily enemy and taking precautions against them by our anxious thought and watchful care? We who have put on Christ, the Wisdom of God the Father, must not lack the wisdom to safeguard our salvation. It is not only persecution that we have to fear, and the attack which advances openly to subvert and overthrow the servants of God. Caution is not difficult where the danger is obvious. When the adversary reveals himself, our minds are prepared for the encounter. There is more to fear, more care to be taken, with an enemy who creeps upon us secretly, tricks us with a show of peace, and hides his approach by serpentine deviations, true to his name of serpent. Cleverness of that kind, dark lurking deceit, has always been his way of circumventing us. That is how he has tricked us and deceived us from the very beginning of the world, his lies wheedling the inexperienced soul in its reckless confidence. That is how he tried to tempt the Lord himself, approaching him secretly as if to steal upon him again and trick him. But he was understood, turned back and laid low, because he was recognized and unmasked.

2. So we were taught by example to shun the way of the old man and tread in the footsteps of the victorious Christ, so that we may not be caught again in the snare of death through our heedlessness, but rather, being awake to our danger, take possession of the immortality we have received. And how can we possess immortality unless we keep the commandments of Christ by which death is conquered and defeated, as he warns us: "If thou wouldest enter into life, keep

[1] Matt. 5:13. [2] Matt. 10:16.

124

the commandments",[3] and again: "If ye do the things which I command you, henceforth I call you not servants, but friends"?[4] Mark what sort of men he calls strong and steadfast, founded securely upon a rock, established in unmovable and unshakable solidity against every storm and tempest of the world. He says: "He that heareth my words and doeth them, I will liken him unto a wise man, which built his house upon a rock; and the rain descended, and the floods came, and the winds blew and beat upon that house; and it fell not: for it was founded upon a rock."[5]

It is our duty to stand upon his words, to learn and do all that he taught and did. How can anyone profess faith in Christ without doing what Christ commanded? How can he come to the reward of faith without keeping faith with the commandments? He cannot but totter and wander, snatched up by the spirit of error and whirled about like dust scattered by the wind. One who leaves the true way of salvation will never find his own road to it.

3. We must guard against wily trickery and subtle deceit no less than open and obvious perils. And could anything more subtle and wily have been devised than this? The enemy had been exposed and laid low by the coming of Christ, light came to the nations, the sun of salvation shined to save mankind, so that the deaf received the hearing of spiritual grace, the blind opened their eyes to the Lord, the weak recovered strength in eternal health, the lame ran to church, the dumb prayed aloud. Yet, when he saw the idols abandoned and his seats and temples deserted through the host of believers, our enemy thought of a new trick, to deceive the unwary under cover of the name Christian. He invented heresies and schisms to undermine faith, pervert truth, and break unity. Unable to keep us in the dark ways of former error, he draws us into a new maze of deceit. He snatches men away from the Church itself and, just when they think they have drawn near to the light and escaped the night of the world, he plunges them unawares into a new darkness. Though they do not stand by the gospel and discipline and law of Christ, they call themselves Christians. Though they are walking in darkness, they think they are in the light, through the deceitful flattery of the adversary who, as the Apostle said, transforms himself into an angel of light and adorns his ministers as ministers of righteousness[6]

[3] Matt. 19:17.   [4] John 15:14–15.
[5] Matt. 7:24–25.   [6] II Cor. 11:14–15.

who call night day, death salvation, despair hope, perfidy faith, antichrist Christ, cunningly to frustrate truth by their lying show of truth. That is what happens, my brothers, when we do not return to the fount of truth, when we are not looking to the head and keeping the doctrine taught from heaven.

4. Due consideration of these points renders lengthy discussion and argument unnecessary. Faith finds ready proof when the truth is stated succinctly. The Lord says to Peter: "I say unto thee that thou art Peter, and upon this rock I will build my Church; and the gates of hell shall not prevail against it. I will give unto thee the keys of the kingdom of heaven: and whatsoever thou shalt bind on earth shall be bound in heaven; and whatsoever thou shalt loose on earth shall be loosed also in heaven." [7] He builds the Church upon one man. True, after the resurrection he assigned the like power to all the apostles, saying: "As the Father hath sent me, even so send I you. Receive ye the Holy Ghost: whose soever sins ye remit, they shall be remitted unto him; whose soever ye retain, they shall be retained." [8] Despite that, in order to make unity manifest, he arranged by his own authority that this unity should, from the start, take its beginning from one man. Certainly the rest of the apostles were exactly what Peter was; they were endowed with an equal share of office and power. [9] But there was unity at the beginning before any development, to demonstrate that the Church of Christ is one. This one Church is also intended in the *Song of Songs*, when the Holy Spirit says, in the person of the Lord: "My dove, my perfect one, is but one; she is the only one of her mother, the choice one of her that bare her." [10] Can one who does not keep this unity of the Church believe that he keeps the faith? Can one who resists and struggles against the Church be sure that he is in the Church? For the blessed apostle Paul gives the same teaching and declares the same mystery of unity when he says: "There is one body and one Spirit, one hope of your calling, one Lord, one faith, one baptism, one God." [11]

5. It is particularly incumbent upon those of us who preside over the Church as bishops to uphold this unity firmly and to be its champions, so that we may prove the episcopate also to be itself one and undivided. Let no one deceive the brotherhood

---

[7] Matt. 16:18–19.   [8] John 20:21–23.
[9] Equal, *parem*, equal with Peter's; office, *honoris*, possibly honour.
[10] S. of Sol. 6:9, cf. *Letter* 69:2 (p. 151).
[11] Eph. 4:4–6.

with lies or corrupt the true faith with faithless treachery. The episcopate is a single whole, in which each bishop's share gives him a right to, and a responsibility for, the whole.[12] So is the Church a single whole, though she spreads far and wide into a multitude of churches as her fertility increases. We may compare the sun, many rays but one light, or a tree, many branches but one firmly rooted trunk. When many streams flow from one spring, although the bountiful supply of water welling out has the appearance of plurality, unity is preserved in the source. Pluck a ray from the body of the sun, and its unity allows no division of the light. Break a branch from the tree, and when it is broken off it will not bud. Cut a stream off from its spring, and when it is cut off it dries up. In the same way the Church, bathed in the light of the Lord, spreads her rays throughout the world, yet the light everywhere diffused is one light and the unity of the body is not broken. In the abundance of her plenty she stretches her branches over the whole earth, far and wide she pours her generously flowing streams. Yet there is one head, one source, one mother boundlessly fruitful. Of her womb are we born, by her milk we are nourished, by her breath we are quickened.

6. The bride of Christ cannot be made an adulteress. She is undefiled and chaste. She knows but one home, she guards with virtuous chastity the sanctity of one bed-chamber. It is she who keeps us for God and seals for the kingdom the sons she has borne. If you abandon the Church and join yourself to an adulteress, you are cut off from the promises of the Church. If you leave the Church of Christ you will not come to Christ's rewards, you will be an alien, an outcast, an enemy. You

---

12 *Episcopatus unus est cuius a singulis in solidum pars tenetur.* This famous sentence is hard to translate. Cyprian uses a legal term *in solidum*, but not with precision. Its chief legal use is to express solidary obligation. Two men can each of them be responsible for the whole of a debt. This is one part of Cyprian's meaning here. Each bishop must exercise his own episcopal rights with a sense of responsibility to the whole college of bishops. Another sense is tenure upon a totality, the total being indivisible, but various people having rights to the whole. This sense is also present, for each bishop has full episcopal rights. Further, the word *episcopatus* has a double sense. Concretely, each bishop is a part of the whole college of bishops. Abstractly, he possesses the full power of episcopacy. And he is responsible to the whole, concrete, episcopate for his use of the full episcopacy. In 251 the sense of obligation, the primary legal sense, would predominate; in 256 he might well have in mind the complete rights of individual bishops, a point which comes out in the later letters and the *Sententiae*.

cannot have God for your father unless you have the Church for your mother. If you could escape outside Noah's ark, you could escape outside the Church.[13] The Lord warns us, saying: "He that is not with me is against me; and he that gathereth not with me, scattereth."[14] To break the peace and concord of Christ is to go against Christ. To gather somewhere outside the Church is to scatter Christ's Church. The Lord says: "I and the Father are one," and again, of Father, Son, and Holy Spirit it is written: "And the three are one."[15] Can you believe that this unity, which originates in the immutability of God and coheres in heavenly mysteries, can be broken in the Church and split by the divorce of clashing wills? He who does not keep this unity does not keep the law of God, nor the faith of the Father and the Son—nor life and salvation.[16]

7. In the Gospel there is a proof of this mystery of unity, this inseparable bond of harmony, when the coat of the Lord Jesus Christ is not cut or rent at all. The garment is received whole and the coat taken into possession unspoilt and undivided by those who casts lots for Christ's garment, asking who should put on Christ. Holy Scripture says of this: "But for the coat, because it was not sewn but woven from the top throughout, they said to each other, Let us not rend it, but cast lots for it, whose it shall be."[17] He showed a unity which came from the top, that is from heaven and the Father, a unity which could by no means be rent by one who received and possessed it. Its wholeness and unity remained solid and unbreakable for ever. He who rends and divides the Church cannot possess the garment of Christ. In contrast, when at Solomon's death his kingdom and people were being rent, the prophet Ahijah, meeting King Jeroboam in the field, rent his garment into twelve pieces, saying: "Take thee ten pieces: for thus saith the Lord, Behold, I rend the kingdom out of the hand of Solomon, and will give ten sceptres to thee; but he shall have two sceptres for my servant David's sake, and for Jerusalem's sake, the

---

13 For the Church as mother and virgin see A. J. Mason in Swete, *Essays on the Early History of the Church and the Ministry*, pp. 13–16, 36–38. For the ark, cf. Tert., *Idol.*, 24, and n. 94 (p. 109).

14 Matt. 12:30. *Colligit*, gathers, has a liturgical overtone, assemble for worship, form a schism.

15 John 10:30; I John 5:7a, the *comma Johanneum*. Tertullian likes to relate the Trinity to the Church, cf. *Bapt.*, 6; *Orat.*, 2; *Pudic.*, 21 (the last on p. 76)

16 An indirect form of the maxim, *extra ecclesiam nulla salus*, cf. *Letter* 73:21 (p.169).   17 John 19:23–24.

city which I have chosen, to put my name there." [18] When the twelve tribes of Israel were being rent, the prophet Ahijah rent his garment. But since Christ's people cannot be rent, his coat, woven throughout as a single whole, was not rent by its owners. Undivided, conjoined, coherent, it proves the unbroken harmony of our people who have put on Christ. By the type and symbol of his garment [19] he has manifested the unity of the Church.

8. Who then is so wicked and perfidious, so mad with the fury of discord as to believe that the unity of God, the garment of the Lord, the Church of Christ, can be rent—as to dare to rend it? He himself instructs us in his Gospel with words of warning: "And there shall be one flock and one shepherd." [20] A number of shepherds or of flocks in one place is unthinkable. Teaching us the same unity the apostle Paul exhorts us: "I beseech you, brethren, by the name of our Lord Jesus Christ, that ye all speak the same thing, and that there be no divisions among you; but that ye be perfected together in the same mind and in the same judgment." Again: "Sustaining one another in love, endeavouring to keep the unity of the Spirit in the bond of peace." [21] Do you think a man can abandon the Church, set up for himself another house and home, and yet stay alive, despite the words spoken to Rahab, the type of the Church: "Thou shalt gather unto thee into thy house thy father, and thy mother, and thy brethren, and all thy father's household. And it shall be that whosoever shall go out of the doors of thy house into the street, his blood shall be upon his head" [22] and despite the express requirement of the law of Exodus touching the Passover rite, that the lamb (whose killing prefigures Christ) should be eaten in one house? God says: "In one house shall it be eaten; ye shall not cast the flesh abroad out of the house." [23] The flesh of Christ and the holy thing of the Lord [24] cannot be cast out. The faithful have no home but the one Church. This home, this house [25] of unanimity, the Holy Spirit announces unmistakably in the Psalms: "God who maketh men to dwell together of one mind in an house." [26] In the house of God, in the

[18] I Kings 11:31–32, 36.   [19] *Sacramento vestis et signo.*
[20] John 10:16.   [21] I Cor. 1:10; Eph. 4:2.
[22] Josh. 2:18–19. For Rahab as a type of the Church cf. Jerome, *Letter* 52:3 (p. 318).
[23] Ex. 12:46.
[24] *Sanctum Domini*, the Eucharist, as in Jerome, *Letter* 15 (p. 308).
[25] *Hospitium*, perhaps hospice, but common as house.
[26] Ps. 68:6.

Church of Christ, they indeed live with one mind, they indeed persist in harmony and singleness of heart.

9. So also the Holy Spirit came as a dove, an innocent and happy creature, not bitter with gall, with no savage bite or lacerating claws. It loves human company and knows the fellowship of a single home. When they breed, they bring up their young together; when they go out, they fly close to each other. They pass their lives in mutual intercourse, marking their peace and concord with a kiss and fulfilling in every point the law of unanimity. The Church should exhibit their innocence and practise their affection. We should be like doves in brotherly love, like lambs and sheep in kindness and gentleness. What room is there in a Christian's breast for the fierceness of wolves, for the madness of dogs, the deadly poison of snakes, the bloody savagery of beasts? We may well congratulate ourselves when men like that are removed from the Church and Christ's doves and sheep are no longer the prey of their savage and poisonous contagion. There can be no fellowship between sweet and bitter, light and darkness, rain and sunshine, between war and peace, famine and plenty, drought and waters, calm and storm. Believe me, good men cannot leave the Church.[27] The wind does not carry off the grain, the storm does not bring down the tree with strong roots. It is the empty husks that are tossed away by the tempest, the feeble trees that are thrown down by the hurricane. And it is such men that John the Apostle upbraids and smites when he says: "They went out from us, but they were not of us; for if they had been of us, they would have continued with us." [28]

10. From such men have heresies often come, and still come. The twisted mind knows no peace and warring perfidy cannot keep unity. But the Lord allows such things out of respect for the freedom of the will, so that, when our hearts and minds are probed by the test of truth, the undamaged faith of such as are approved may shine out in manifest light. The Holy Spirit warns us through the Apostle: "There must be also heresies among you, that they which are approved may be made manifest among you." [29] In this way the faithful are approved and the faithless detected. Here and now, even before the Day of Judgment, the souls of the just and the unjust are parted and the chaff is separated from the wheat.[30]

From such men come those who, without divine appointment,

---

[27] Cf. Tert., *Praescr.*, 3 (p. 32).　　[28] I John 2:19.
[29] I Cor. 11:19.　　[30] See Tert., *Idol.*, n. 94 (p. 109).

set themselves over their rash associates, make themselves
prelates without any lawful ordination and call themselves
bishops though no one gives them a bishopric.[31] The Holy
Spirit portrays them in the Psalms "sitting in the seat of pestilence",[32] plagues and blights to faith, snake-mouthed traitors,
scheming to pervert truth, spewing deadly poisons from their
pestiferous tongues. Their words "spread like a canker",[33]
their teaching pours fatal venom into men's hearts and
breasts.

11. Against such men the Lord cries out, curbing and re-
calling his wandering people from them. "Hearken not unto
the words of the false prophets", he says, "for the visions of
their heart make them of no effect. They speak, but not out
of the mouth of the Lord. They say unto them that cast away
the word of God: Ye shall have peace, and every one that
walketh according to his own will; every one that walketh after
the error of his own heart, no evil shall come upon thee. I
spake not unto them, and they prophesied of themselves. If
they had stood in my substance and hearkened unto my
words and if they had taught my people, I should have turned
them from their evil thoughts." Again the Lord describes them:
"They have forsaken me the fountain of living water, and hewed
them out broken cisterns that can hold no water."[34] Although
there can be no other than the one baptism, they fancy they
baptize.[35] Forsaking the fountain of life, they promise the grace
of living and saving water. Men are not washed there, they
are dirtied; their sins are piled up, not purged. That birth makes
sons for the devil, not for God. Born of a lie, they cannot receive
the promises of truth; begotten of perfidy, they lose the grace
of faith. No one whose furious discord breaks the Lord's peace
can come to the reward of peace.

[31] It would seem that this must refer to Novatian. Cyprian's rival bishop
of Carthage, Fortunatus, was not consecrated until 252, and Maximus,
the Novatianist bishop of Carthage no earlier. Taken by themselves
Cyprian's words might suggest that no one consecrated Novatian, and
perhaps he did not yet know the circumstances. But Novatian was
consecrated—by bishops, however, who had no right to give him a see.
In *Letter* 69:3 (p. 152) Cyprian puts the real point. He succeeded to
nobody.

[32] Ps. 1:1. Seat is *cathedra*.

[33] II Tim. 2:17, so often quoted in this connexion.

[34] Jer. 23:16–17, 21–22; 2:13.

[35] A hint of controversy to come, cf. *Letters* 69, 73 (pp. 150–172). There
is no ground for supposing that this section was introduced for the first
time in an edition of 256.

12. Some deceive themselves with a vain interpretation of the words of the Lord: "Wheresoever two or three are gathered together in my name, I am with them." Corrupters and false interpreters of the Gospel, they set down the last words and omit what precedes them, remembering one part and craftily suppressing the other. Themselves cut off from the Church, they cut up the sense of a passage which must be taken as a whole. The Lord was urging peace and unanimity upon his disciples. "I say unto you, that if two of you shall agree on earth as touching anything that ye shall ask, it shall be done for you of my Father which is in heaven. For wheresoever two or three are gathered together in my name, I am with them."[36] These words prove that much is given not to the mere number but to the unanimity of those who pray. "If two of you shall *agree* on earth," he says, putting unanimity and peaceful concord first, teaching us to agree firmly and loyally. But how can one man agree with another when he disagrees with the body of the Church itself, with the whole brotherhood? How can two or three be gathered together in the name of Christ when they are known to be separated from Christ and his Gospel? For we did not go out from them, but they from us. Heresies and schisms were born after the Church, as men set up separate conventicles to suit themselves.[37] It is they who have abandoned the head and fount of truth.

The Lord's words were spoken about his own Church and addressed to members of the Church. If they are agreed, if, as he commanded, but two or three are gathered together and pray with one mind, then, although they are but two or three, they can obtain from the divine majesty what they ask. "Wheresoever two or three are gathered, I (he said) am with them." That means, of course, with the single-hearted and peaceable, with those who fear God and keep his commandments. With these, though but two or three, he declared his presence, as he was present also with the Three Children in the fiery furnace, and, because they continued single-hearted and of one mind, refreshed them with the breath of dew[38] as the flames surrounded them; or as he was present with the two apostles in prison, because they were single-hearted and of one mind, and himself opened the prison gates and set them again in the

---

[36] Matt. 18:19–20.
[37] Cf. Tert., *Praescr.*, *passim*, especially c. 31 (p. 52).
[38] LXX Dan. 3:50 (Song of the Three Children, verse 27). *Spiritu roris*, but "moist wind" in a modern version.

market-place to deliver to the crowds the word which they had been faithfully preaching.[39]

So when he lays down with authority: "Where two or three are gathered, I am with them," he is not separating men from the Church which he founded and created. Rebuking the faithless for their discord and with his own voice commending peace to the faithful, he shows that he is present with two or three praying with one mind rather than with a large number of dissidents, and that more can be obtained by the united prayer of a few than by the discordant petition of many.

13. So when he gave the rule of prayer[40] he added: "And when ye stand praying, forgive, if ye have aught against any one: that your Father also which is in heaven may forgive you your trespasses."[41] He calls back from the altar one going to the sacrifice with angry feelings and tells him first to be reconciled to his brother and then to come back and offer his gift to God.[42] For God had no respect to Cain's gifts, nor could he have God at peace with him when by his envious hate he had no peace with his brother. What peace can the enemies of their own brothers promise themselves? What sacrifices do the rivals of the priests[43] think they celebrate? Do those who gather themselves outside the Church fancy that Christ is with them when they are gathered together?

14. Suppose such men are put to death confessing the Name.[44] Their blood cannot wash away that stain, their suffering cannot purge the grievous and inexpiable guilt of discord. You cannot be a martyr if you are not in the Church. You cannot come into the kingdom if you desert her who is to reign there. Christ gave us peace, ordered us to be of one heart and mind, commanded us to keep the bonds of love and charity unharmed and inviolate. You cannot prove yourself a martyr if you have not kept brotherly charity. Witness the words of the apostle Paul: "Though I have faith, so that I could remove mountains, and have not charity, I am nothing. And though I bestow all my goods to feed the poor, and though I give my body to be burned, and have not charity, it profiteth me nothing. Charity suffereth long, and is kind; charity envieth not, is not puffed up, is not provoked, doth not behave itself unseemly,

[39] Acts 5:17ff., with two, Peter and John, assumed from Acts 3 and 4, despite 5:29.
[40] *Lex orandi.*   [41] Mark 11:25.   [42] Matt. 5:24.
[43] *Sacerdotum*, bishops, but here *qua* priests.
[44] Compare *Letter* 73:21 (p. 169).

thinketh no evil, loveth all things, believeth all things, hopeth all things, endureth all things. Charity will never fail." [45] Never, he says, will charity fail. There will always be charity in the kingdom, it will abide for ever in the unity of a harmonious brotherhood. Discord cannot enter the kingdom of heaven. One who has violated the love of Christ by faithless dissension cannot attain to the reward of a Christ who said: "This is my commandment, that ye love one another, even as I have loved you." [46] He who has not charity, has not God. It was the blessed apostle John who said: "God is love; and he that abideth in love abideth in God, and God abideth in him." [47] Those who have refused to be of one mind in the Church of God cannot abide with God. Though they give their bodies to be burned in flame and fire, though they expose themselves to wild beasts and lay down their lives, they shall have no crown of faith, but the penalty of perfidy, no glorious end of pious virtue, but the death of despair. Such a man may be killed; he cannot be crowned. He professes himself a Christian only as the devil not seldom feigns himself to be Christ. Of this the Lord himself warned us, saying: "Many shall come in my name, saying, I am Christ; and shall deceive many." [48] As the devil is not Christ, though he deceives in his name, so he who does not stand fast in Christ's Gospel and the true faith cannot be reckoned a Christian.

15. Grand and wonderful as it is to prophesy and cast out devils and do mighty works on earth, a man may do all this and yet not reach the heavenly kingdom unless he keeps strictly to the right and proper road. The Lord announces: "Many will say to me in that day, Lord, Lord, have we not prophesied in thy name? and in thy name have cast out devils? and in thy name done mighty works? And then will I say unto them, I never knew you: depart from me, ye that work iniquity." [49] We have need of right conduct to earn the favour of God when he judges us; we must obey his commands and instructions to obtain the reward of our merits. [50] In the Gospel, when he was giving us summary directions for the way of hope and faith, the Lord said: "The Lord thy God is one Lord: and thou shalt love the Lord thy God with all thy heart, and with all thy soul, and with all thy strength. This is the first commandment. And the second is like to it, Thou shalt love thy neighbour

---

[45] I Cor. 13:2–8.   [46] John 15:12.   [47] I John 4:16.
[48] Mark 13:6.   [49] Matt. 7:22–23.
[50] Note the teaching on merit, characteristic of Tertullian and Cyprian.

as thyself. On these two commandments hang all the law and the prophets." [51] His teaching required both unity and love, including all the prophets and the law in two commandments. But what sort of unity, what sort of love, is preserved or contemplated by the mad fury of discord that rends the Church, destroys faith, disturbs peace, scatters charity, profanes religion? [52]

16. This evil began long ago, my brothers in the faith. Now its cruel havoc has increased, now the poisonous plague of heretical perversity and schism is beginning to spring up and put out new shoots. So it must be at the end of the world, as the Holy Spirit foretells and forewarns through the Apostle: "In the last days perilous times shall come. Men shall be lovers of their own selves, proud, boasters, covetous, blasphemers, disobedient to parents, unthankful, unholy, without affection, truce-breakers, false accusers, incontinent, fierce, no lovers of good, traitors, wanton, puffed up with foolishness, lovers of pleasures more than lovers of God, having a form of godliness, but denying the power thereof. Of this sort are they which creep into houses, and take captive silly women laden with sins, led away by divers lusts, ever learning and never able to come to the knowledge of the truth. And like as Jannes and Mambres withstood Moses, so do these also withstand the truth. But they shall proceed little. For their folly shall be manifest unto all men, as theirs also was." [53]

Everything that was foretold is being fulfilled. Now it has come, testing men and time alike, as the end of the age draws near. More and more, by the adversary's rage, error deceives, folly exalts, envy inflames, greed blinds, impiety depraves, pride puffs up, discord embitters, anger throws headlong down.

17. We need not be troubled or disturbed by the extreme and sudden perfidy of so many. On the contrary, this verification of prophecy should confirm our faith. [54] It is in fulfil-ment of prophecy that some persons are appearing in this character, and the rest of the brethren would do well to take heed of such company, remembering another prophecy in which the Lord instructs us: "But take ye heed: behold, I have

[51] Mark 12:29–31; Matt. 22:40.
[52] *Sacramentum*, in the comprehensive sense, cf. Tert., *Praescr.*, cc. 20, 32 *ad fin*. Hardly "the sacrament" here.
[53] II Tim. 3:1–9.
[54] Compare the opening of Tert., *Praescr. Haer.*

foretold you all things." [55] Avoid such men, I beg you, and keep their pernicious conversation away from your hearts and your ears as the contagion of death, as it is written: "Hedge thine ears about with thorns and hearken not to an evil tongue." And again: "Evil communications corrupt good manners." The Lord warns us to depart from such men: "They be blind leaders of the blind. And if the blind lead the blind, both shall fall into the ditch." [56] One who separates himself from the Church is to be avoided and fled from. He is perverted, sinful, self-condemned. [57] Can any one believe he is with Christ when he works against Christ's priests and withdraws himself from the fellowship of his clergy and people? He is bearing arms against the Church, fighting against the providence of God. An enemy of the altar, a rebel against Christ's sacrifice, a traitor to his faith, a blasphemous renegade, a disobedient servant, an undutiful son, a hostile brother, he scorns the bishops, turns his back on God's priests, [58] and dares to set up another altar, to offer another prayer in unlawful words, to profane the true offering of the Lord with false sacrifices. Does he not know that the presumption which strives against the ordinance of God is punished by the chastisement of God?

18. Of this Korah, Dathan, and Abiram are an example. [59] When they tried to claim for themselves the right to sacrifice, in opposition to Moses and Aaron, they at once paid the penalty for their attempt. Bursting its bonds, the earth gaped deep asunder, and as the ground parted, the gulf swallowed them up alive where they stood. And it was not only the originators of this insane venture who were struck by the wrath of God's indignation. With speedy vengeance fire issuing from the Lord consumed the two hundred and fifty more who shared in it, their partners in audacity, clear proof that all wicked efforts to destroy the ordinance of God by human wills are rebellion against God himself. Similarly, when King Uzziah carried a censer and violently took upon himself to sacrifice, against the law of God, and refused to submit or give place, despite the opposition of Azariah the priest, he was confounded by God's indignation and defiled with the markings of leprosy on his

55 Mark 13:23.
56 Ecclus. 28:24; I Cor. 15:33; Matt. 15:14.
57 Cf. Tit. 3:11.
58 *Sacerdotibus*, not = presbyters, but a variant of *episcopis*, bishops, appropriate in the sacrificial context. The whole passage is attacking Novatian.
59 Num. 16. A stock passage for the condemnation of schism, cf. *Letter* 73:8 (p. 162).

forehead, branded by the Lord's anger upon that part of the body on which those who win the Lord's favour are sealed.[60] The sons of Aaron also, who set upon the altar a strange fire not commanded by the Lord, were at once blotted out in the sight of the avenging Lord.[61]

19. These examples, you will see, are being followed wherever the tradition which comes from God is despised by lovers of strange doctrine and replaced by teaching of merely human authority. The Lord rebukes and castigates them in his Gospel: "Ye reject the commandment of God that ye may establish your own tradition." [62] This is a worse offence than to fall before persecution, for the lapsed at least do penance for their offence and ask God's mercy with works of full satisfaction. The lapsed seek the Church and plead with it, the schismatic fights against the Church. In the one case there may have been constraint, in the other the will is guilty. The lapsed has harmed himself alone, the author of heresy or schism has deceived many, dragging them with him. With the former only one soul is lost, with the latter many are imperilled. The one knows his sin and laments it with tears, the other, puffed up by his sin and delighting in his offences, separates the sons from their mother, wheedles the sheep from their shepherd, and upsets the mysteries of God. While the lapsed sinned but once, he sins every day. Finally, it is possible for the lapsed, by undergoing martyrdom afterwards, to receive the promises of the kingdom, but if the schismatic is put to death outside the Church, he cannot attain to the rewards which belong to the Church.[63]

20. Do not be surprised, dear brothers, that even some of the confessors go to such lengths and sin, some of them, so wickedly and grievously. Confession does not guarantee immunity from the snares of the devil nor provide lasting security against the temptations, the perils, the attacks and assaults of the world, as long as you are in the world. Otherwise we should never see fraud and fornication and adultery in confessors after their confession, as we are now seeing in some of them, to our grief and pain. No matter who he is, the confessor is not greater or

60 II Chron. 26.   61 Lev. 10, cf. *Letter* 73:8.   62 Mark 7:9.
63 Throughout this chapter the lapsed and the schismatic are contrasted as *hic—ille* or *illic*, which I translate in various ways. In the MSS. which have the "interpolated" text of c. 4, *hic* and *illic* are inverted and there is a variant *hi qui sacrificaverunt* for *lapsi*. On the possible significance for the chronology of the editions see Bévenot in *J.T.S.*, April, 1954, pp. 68–72.

better or dearer to God than Solomon. And Solomon kept the grace which the Lord had given him as long as he walked in his ways, but lost the Lord's grace after he left the Lord's way. Therefore it is written: "Hold fast that which thou hast, that no other take thy crown." [64] Surely God would not threaten that the crown of righteousness might be taken away, if it were not necessary that when justice goes, the crown should go also.

21. Confession is the beginning of glory, it does not earn the crown at once. It does not perfect praise, but initiates honour. Scripture says: "He that endureth to the end shall be saved." [65] Therefore anything before the end can be no more than a step by which we climb to the summit of salvation, and not the goal where the mountain-top is already gained. He is a confessor —but after the confession the danger is greater, since the adversary is more provoked. He is a confessor—then, having obtained glory of the Lord through the Gospel, he is all the more bound to stand firmly by the Lord's Gospel. "To whom much is given, of him is much required: and to whom more honour is ascribed, of him more service is demanded." [66] Let no one perish through the example of a confessor, let no one learn unrighteousness or insolence or perfidy from a confessor's behaviour. He is a confessor—then let him be humble and peaceable, modest and disciplined in his conduct. One who is called a confessor of Christ should imitate the Christ whom he confesses. He says: "Every one that exalteth himself shall be humbled, and he that humbleth himself shall be exalted"; [67] and he was himself exalted by his Father because on earth he, the word and power and wisdom of God, humbled himself. How then can he love self-exaltation when his own law enjoins humility upon us and when he himself received from his Father the name above every name as the reward of humility? He is a confessor of Christ—but only if afterwards the majesty and dignity of Christ is not blasphemed through him. Let not the tongue which has confessed Christ be evil-speaking or turbulent, noisily abusive and quarrelsome, changing from words of praise to envenomed darts against the brethren and the priests of God. If a confessor afterwards becomes culpable and obnoxious, wasting his confession by evil living and staining his life with base filthiness, if, to conclude, he abandons the Church in which he became a confessor, rends the bond of unity and exchanges his first faith for faithlessness, he cannot flatter

[64] Rev. 3:11.   [65] Matt. 10:22.
[66] Luke 12:48.   [67] Luke 18:14.

himself, on the strength of his confession, that he is elect to the reward of glory, when for that very reason he deserves all the more punishment.

22. The Lord chose Judas among the apostles, and yet Judas afterwards betrayed the Lord. Even so, the defection of the traitor Judas from their company did not make the apostles fall from their own strong faith. Similarly, in the present case, the sanctity and worth of the confessors was not at once shattered because the faith of some few was broken. The blessed Apostle says in his epistle: "What if some of them fell from the faith? has their unfaithfulness made the faith of God of none effect? God forbid: for God is true, but every man a liar." [68] The larger and better part of the confessors stand firm in the strength of their faith and in the truth of the Lord's law and discipline. Mindful that, by the favour of God, they obtained grace in the Church, they do not secede from the peace of the Church. Their faith wins an ampler praise in that they have separated themselves from the perfidy of their fellow-confessors and escaped the infection of their crime. [69] Illumined by the true light of the Gospel and bathed in the pure, bright radiance of the Lord, they are as praiseworthy in keeping the peace of Christ as they were victorious in their encounter with the devil.

23. Dearest brothers, [70] my desire, my counsel, my exhortation to you is that, if it be possible, not one of the brethren perish, that our mother may joyfully gather into her bosom the one body of the People of God in full accord. But if some leaders of schism, some authors of faction, persist in their blind and stubborn madness, and cannot be recalled by wholesome counsel to the way of salvation, the rest of you, who were caught through your simplicity or led on by error or deceived by some clever trick, must set yourselves free from the snares of deceit. Free your wayward steps from wandering, mark the straight path to heaven. The Apostle bears witness: "We command you in the name of the Lord Jesus Christ, that ye withdraw yourselves from every brother that walketh disorderly, and not after the tradition which they received from us." And again:

[68] Rom. 3:3, 4.
[69] Here Cyprian is not thinking of the moral offences of some confessors, as in c. 20, but of their insubordination. See the introduction to *Letter* 33 (p. 143).
[70] Cyprian is always apt to address his words to the rhetorical object of them, not the literal audience. Cf. *Letter* 73:19. I think it rash to extract evidence as to chronology or editions from this, as some try to do.

"Let no man deceive you with vain words: for because of these
things cometh the wrath of God upon the sons of disobedience.
Be not ye therefore partakers with them." [71] You must withdraw,
you must fly from sinners. To join those who walk wickedly,
to journey with them on the roads of error and crime, straying
from the true path, involves you in the same crime. There is
one God and one Christ and one Church and one faith and one
people, fastened together into a solid corporate unity by the
glue [72] of concord. The unity cannot be rent, nor can the one
body be divided by breaking up its structure; it cannot be
broken into fragments by tearing and mangling the flesh.
Whatever leaves the womb cannot live and breathe apart.
It loses the substance of health. [73]

24. The Holy Spirit warns us: "What man is he that desireth
to live, and would fain see good days? Keep thy tongue from
evil and thy lips that they speak no guile. Depart from evil
and do good; seek peace and ensue it." The son of peace should
seek and ensue peace; he should keep his tongue from the evil
of faction if he knows and loves the bond of charity. On the
eve of his passion the Lord added this to his divine commands
and saving teaching: "Peace I leave with you; my peace I
give unto you." This is the inheritance which he gave to us.
Every gift and reward which he could promise he pledged to
the keeping of peace. If we are Christ's heirs, let us abide in
Christ's peace. If we are sons of God, we must be peace-
makers. "Blessed are the peace-makers", he said, "for they
shall be called sons of God." [74] The sons of God ought to be
peace-makers, gentle in heart, frank in speech, united in
affection, holding loyally to one another in the bonds of
unanimity.

25. This unanimity prevailed once, in the time of the
apostles. The new company of believers, keeping the Lord's
commandments, preserved its charity. There is scriptural proof
of this in the words: "And the multitude of them that believed

71 II Thess. 3:6; Eph. 5:6–7.
72 *Glutino*, cf. *Ep.* 68:3, a similar passage, and 66:8, of bishops, who are the
glue of the Church.
73 *Salutis*, translated "health" because of the physical metaphor, but
implying salvation. These sentences give a downright summary of
Cyprian's principles. He really does mean that the unity *cannot* be rent.
But where he says that whatever leaves the womb cannot live apart, he
is vulnerable. He expected schisms to wither away quickly. If they do not,
does that disprove his theology? Are they perhaps within the Church?
74 Ps. 34:12–14; John 14:27; Matt. 5:9.

were of one soul and of one mind." And again: "And they all continued of one mind in prayer, with the women and Mary, the mother of Jesus, and his brethren."[75] That is why their prayer was effectual, that is why they could be confident of obtaining whatever they asked of God's mercy.

26. In us, however, unanimity has diminished in proportion as liberality in good works has decayed. In those days they used to sell their houses and farms. Laying up for themselves treasure in heaven, they would offer the price to the apostles to be shared out among the poor. Now we do not even give a tithe of our patrimony, and though the Lord bids us sell, we prefer to buy and enlarge our estate. With us the vigour of faith has withered, the strength of belief has grown faint. And so, reviewing our times, the Lord says in his Gospel: "When the Son of man cometh, think you he shall find faith on the earth?"[76] We are seeing his prediction fulfilled. In the fear of God, in the law of righteousness, in love, in good works, our faith is nothing. No one meditates on the fear of things to come, no one takes to heart the day of the Lord and the wrath of God, the punishment in store for the unbeliever, the eternal torment appointed for the apostate. What our conscience would fear if it believed, it does not fear at all because it does not believe. If it believed, it would take care; if it took care, it would escape.

27. Dearest brothers, let us rouse ourselves to the full, let us break off the slumber of our former sloth and awake to observe and fulfil the Lord's commands. Behave as he taught us to behave when he said: "Let your loins be girded about and your lights burning; and ye yourselves like unto men that wait for their lord, when he will return from the wedding; that when he cometh and knocketh, they may open unto him. Blessed are those servants, whom the lord when he cometh shall find watching."[77]

We must gird ourselves, lest when the day of expedition comes, he find us impeded and encumbered. Let our light so shine and gleam in good works that it may lead us from the night of this world into the light of eternal day. Let us await the sudden advent of the Lord with ever-watchful care, that when he knocks our faith may be found awake to receive of him the reward of vigilance. If we keep these commandments, if we hold by these precepts and monitions, we cannot be

[75] Acts 4:32; 1:14.   [76] Luke 18:8.
[77] Luke 12:35-37.

overtaken in sleep by the wiles of the devil. As watchful servants, we shall reign with Christ in his kingdom.

Appendix: *The Primacy Text of* De Unitate *c. 4*

The text translated on p. 126 is the *Received Text* as printed, for example, by Hartel, pp. 212–213. The following is a translation of the Primacy Text as given by Bévenot:

[After Matt. 16:18–19] And after his resurrection he also says to him, Feed my sheep. On him he builds the Church, and to him he entrusts the sheep to be fed. And although he gives equal power to all the apostles, yet he established one chair (*cathedram*) and arranged by his own authority the origin and principle (*rationem*) of unity. Certainly the rest of the apostles were exactly what Peter was, but primacy is given to Peter (*primatus Petro datur*) and one Church and one chair is demonstrated. And they are all shepherds but the flock is shown to be one, which is to be fed by all the apostles in unanimous agreement. He who does not hold this unity of Peter, does he believe he holds the faith? He who deserts the chair of Peter on whom the Church was founded, does he trust that he is in the Church?

[Then straight to "the episcopate is a single whole," etc.]

Letter 33 : The Problem of the Lapsed

INTRODUCTION

THIS LETTER BELONGS TO A GROUP (25–40) written in the second half of A.D. 250. In the best manuscripts it has no address, but it was sent to a group of lapsed Christians. Though Cyprian was prepared to consider a change in the ancient discipline which sentenced apostates to permanent excommunication, he would not make one before a Council could meet to take a common decision. The humble lapsed of paragraph 2 know that they must wait. Others are demanding restoration in virtue of *libelli pacis* from confessors. Cyprian rejects their claim, asks who they are, and insists on precise detail. How indiscriminate the confessors could be may be seen in their formula *Communicet ille cum suis* (*Ep.* 15), where *suis*, "his people", might mean anything; and how naively insubordinate they sometimes became is illustrated in *Letter* 23, which is short enough to be quoted complete: "All the confessors to Pope Cyprian, greeting. Know that we have all granted peace to all who satisfy you as to their conduct since their offence. We wish you to make this ruling (*formam*) known to the other bishops. We hope that you have peace with the holy martyrs. Lucian wrote this in the presence of two of the clergy—an exorcist and a lector."

Cyprian did not admit any of the lapsed to communion till after the Council which met after Easter, 251. This decided that the penitent lapsed should at least be granted death-bed communion, and allowed individual circumstances to be taken into account and the period of penance shortened accordingly. With more persecution threatening in 252, another Council decided to receive back all truly penitent lapsed in order to fortify them with the communion of the Church against their new dangers.

As for the doctrine of the Church, it will be noticed that the lapsed are spiritually dead and outside the Church, that episcopacy is taken to be divinely ordained and necessary to the Church and that Peter is here the example and origin not of a Roman prerogative, but of episcopacy as such.

The manuscripts of Cyprian's letters are abundant and early, some of them dating from the seventh, and fragmentarily from the sixth, centuries. The edition now most often cited is that of W. Hartel in the Vienna *Corpus*, vol. iii, 2 (1871). Hartel has been much criticized, but his deficiencies affect the letters written by Cyprian himself less than the rest of the correspondence. There is a better edition by L. Bayard in the *Collection Budé*, 2 vols. Paris, 1925. It is this which has been used for the present volume.

Letter 33

THE TEXT

When our Lord, whose commands we ought to revere and keep, was settling the office of bishop and the constitution of his Church, he said to Peter in the Gospel: "I say unto thee, that thou art Peter, and upon this rock I will build my Church; and the gates of hell shall not prevail against it. And I will give unto thee the keys of the kingdom of heaven: and whatsoever thou shalt bind on earth shall be bound also in heaven: and whatsover thou shalt loose on earth shall be loosed also in heaven." [1] Thence, down the changes of years and successions, the appointment of bishops and the constitution of the Church runs on, so that the Church rests on the bishops and every act of the Church is governed by these same prelates.

This being established by divine law, I am astonished that certain persons have boldly and presumptuously taken on themselves to write to me in the name of the Church, though the Church is made up of the bishops and clergy and all who stand firm. May the Lord in his mercy and unconquered power never allow a collection of the lapsed to be called the Church, for it is written: "God is not the God of the dead, but of the living." [2] We want them all indeed to be brought to life, and with supplications and groanings we pray that they may be restored to their former state. But if some of them will have it that they are the Church, and if the Church is with them and in them, what remains but that we should request them to be so kind as to receive us into the Church? They ought to be submissive and quiet and modest. Remembering their offence, they should give satisfaction to God, and not write letters in the name of the Church when they know they should rather be writing to the Church.

2. Some of the lapsed, however, have written to me who are

[1] Matt. 16:18–19. [2] Matt. 22:32.

humble and meek, fearing and trembling before God, men who have always done great and noble works in their churches without ever demanding payment from the Lord for them, knowing that he said: "And when ye shall have done all these things, say, We are unprofitable servants: we have done that which it was our duty to do."[3] Keeping this in mind and taking no advantage of the certificate which they had received from the martyrs, they have written to me praying that their satisfaction may be acceptable to the Lord, telling me that they acknowledge their sin and are truly penitent, that they are not hurrying rashly or importunately to be reconciled, but are waiting for my presence. They say that the reconciliation which they receive in my presence will be all the sweeter to them. How warmly I have congratulated them, the Lord is witness, who deigned to show what such servants deserve of his goodness.

Having received their letter, and having now read your very different one, I must ask you to discriminate between your various desires, and whoever you are that have sent this letter, I must ask you to append your names to the certificate [4] and send it to me with all your names. I must first know whom I have to answer. Then I will answer each of your points as best fits my humble station and activity. I hope, brethren, that you are well and are living peacefully and quietly according to the discipline of the Lord. Farewell.

[3] Luke 17:10.
[4] *Libellus*, perhaps just "a paper."

Letters 69 and 73 : The Baptismal Controversy

INTRODUCTION

LETTER 69, WRITTEN TO AN UNKNOWN LAYMAN, Magnus, is the first document of the baptismal controversy between Carthage and Rome, and must date from A.D. 255. During that year thirty-one bishops of the proconsular province met at Carthage and informed eighteen Numidian bishops, who had consulted them, that they had confirmed the African practice of ignoring heretical or schismatic baptism and of baptizing, as for the first time, converts from heresy or schism to the Church. This decision was conveyed in *Letter* 70. About the same time, a Mauretanian bishop, Quintus, consulted the Bishop of Carthage direct, and Cyprian sent him *Letter* 71, enclosing a copy of *Letter* 70 with a few explanations of it, and referring also to the Council of bishops from Africa Proconsularis and Numidia held under Agrippinus of Carthage, which had come to the the same decision. This Council, mentioned also in *Letter* 73:3, cannot be exactly dated. Estimates range from *c.* 200 to *c.* 220.

The issue was being forced by the desire of Christians who had been baptized by Novatianists to enter what they had come to think, after all, the true Church. This was happening at Rome as well as in Africa. At Rome the new bishop, Stephen (254–257), held that, even outside the Church, baptism with water and the invocation of the Holy Trinity according to Christ's command ensured a "valid" baptism, that is, conferred the baptismal character, and need not and must not be repeated if the person concerned desired to enter the Church; it should be completed by the laying on of hands for the gift of the Holy Spirit. For Cyprian, as we have already seen, baptism outside the Church was meaningless and impossible. Each bishop claimed to have tradition behind him, and no doubt each was well supported by local custom. If Cyprian could not claim that African custom was universally on his side, he could eventually quote the support of Asia, assured him by the letter of Firmilian, Metropolitan of Cappadocia (*Letter* 75). While Stephen wanted to secure uniformity of practice, even threatening to excommunicate the Africans if they would not conform to Rome, Cyprian adhered to his own theology and to his ecclesiastical principles. The matter should be decided for Africa within Africa by a Council, and even then, though the bishops would be obliged to take account of the moral authority of the Council and the duty of acting in concert, each bishop was in the last resort responsible for his own flock to God, and must follow his conscience.

Accordingly, a Council of seventy-one bishops met at Carthage in the spring of 256. Its synodal letter (72) was sent to Stephen. Here, too, it is declared that every bishop has complete freedom in the administration of his church, subject to his ultimate responsibility to God. The Council, it would seem, tended to treat the issue as a disciplinary one, though for Cyprian it was undoubtedly doctrinal as well, and mainly. The letter contains a hint that Stephen is a stubborn man (§3) and hopes that peace will be maintained. Once again Cyprian was consulted by a fellow-bishop, Jubaianus, to whom he sent copies of *Letters* 71 and 72 with his own long *Letter* 73. This letter is important in many ways, not least because Augustine, in his *De Baptismo*, tries to refute it without contravening his great respect for the memory of Cyprian. But it is disappointing in so far as, in contrast to *Letter* 69, where Cyprian faces the more difficult problem of orthodox schism, in this one he jumps at a mention of Marcion in a letter which Jubaianus has sent for comment, and takes the easier line of denouncing heretical baptism.

Stephen answered the synodical *Letter* 72. His reply has not survived, but Cyprian comments on it in his letter (74) to a Tripolitanian bishop, Pompeius. Under threat of excommunication by Rome (and whether that means a breach of communion or exclusion from the catholic Church depends partly on what Stephen threatened and partly on the truth about the Roman primacy) Cyprian held another Council at Carthage on the 1st September, 256, when eighty-seven bishops unanimously declared that baptism outside the Church was entirely null and void. Their *Sententiae* are extant among Cyprian's works. Rome and Carthage were still at logger-heads when Stephen died and fresh persecution broke out in August, 257. What happened in the intervening year is obscure; Augustine says that no formal breach of communion took place.

The African tradition and theology was consonant with a certain severity in the genius of African Christianity, at least in these early centuries. Stephen was more politic and, in intention, more charitable (except to his opponents), whether or not he was theologically correct. In the fourth century the Donatist schism made the most of Cyprian, to the embarrassment of Augustine, while the catholic Church of the West, from the Council of Arles (314) onwards, if not before, adopted and developed the Roman practice.

Letter 69

THE TEXT

1. Cyprian to his son, Magnus, Greeting. In your concern for the duties of religion, dear son, you have asked me (a poor consultant!) whether those who come over from Novatian, after having received his profane washing, ought to be baptized and sanctified within the catholic Church, like all other heretics, with the only lawful and true baptism, that of the Church. On this point I will tell you what my own faith enables me to grasp and the holiness and truth of the divine Scriptures teach me, namely that no heretics or schismatics whatsoever have any power or right. Novatian therefore cannot properly be made an exception. He stays outside the Church, he works against the peace and love of Christ. Therefore he must be reckoned among the adversaries and the antichrists. When our Lord Jesus Christ testified in his Gospel that all who are not with him are his enemies, he did not point to any particular kind of heresy. In saying: "He that is not with me is against me; and he that gathereth not with me scattereth",[1] he showed that all who are not with him and scatter his flock by not gathering with him are his adversaries. Similarly, the blessed Apostle John made no distinction between one form of heresy or schism and another, nor did he single out any special class of separatists. He called all who had gone out of the Church and worked against it antichrists, saying: "Ye have heard that antichrist cometh, and even now are there many antichrists; whereby we know that it is the last hour. They went out from us, but they were not of us; for if they had been of us, they would have continued with us."[2] This makes it plain that all who are known to have withdrawn from the charity and unity of the catholic Church are adversaries of the Lord and antichrists. In addition, the Lord lays down in his Gospel: "But

[1] Luke 11:23.   [2] I John 2:18-19.

if he despise the Church, let him be unto thee as the heathen and the publican."[3] If those who despise the Church are counted heathen and publicans, it is even more necessary to reckon among them the rebellious enemies who invent false altars, illicit priesthoods,[4] sacrilegious sacrifices and spurious names,[5] when we see that less grave sinners, who merely despise the Church, are judged to be heathen and publicans by the Lord's own sentence.

2. That the Church is one is declared by the Holy Spirit, speaking in the person of Christ in the Song of Songs: "My dove, my perfect one, is but one; she is the only one of her mother, the choice one of her that bare her"; and again: "A garden inclosed is my sister, my spouse, a fountain sealed, a well of living water."[6] If then the spouse of Christ—which is the Church—is a garden enclosed, what is closed cannot be open to the stranger and the profane. If the Church is a sealed fountain, one who is outside, without access to the fountain, cannot drink from it or be sealed there. If there is but one well of living water—that which is within—then one who is without can have no life or grace from the water which only those within are allowed to use and drink. Peter established the same truth that the Church is one and that only those who are within the Church can be baptized: "In the ark of Noah few, that is, eight souls of men were saved by water; which thing also shall likewise save you, even baptism."[7] In saying this, he proves with his testimony that the one ark of Noah was a type of the one Church. At that time it was impossible for anyone not in the ark to be saved by water, in that baptism of a cleansed and purified world. Had it been possible, one who is not in the Church, the Church to which alone baptism has been vouchsafed, might perhaps be given life through baptism today! Paul makes the point even more clear and obvious in his epistle to the Ephesians: "Christ loved the Church, and gave himself up for it, that he might sanctify it, cleansing it with the washing of water."[8] If the Church which Christ loves is one Church and it alone is cleansed with his washing, how can he

---

[3] Matt. 18:17.

[4] *Inlicita sacerdotia*, claiming to be a bishop outside the succession.

[5] *Nomina adulterata*, in a double sense; Novatianists called themselves the *cathari*, "pure."

[6] S. of Sol. 6:9; 4:12.

[7] I Peter 3:20–21. For the Ark, cf. *De Unitate*, 6 and Tert., *Idol.*, 24, with notes.

[8] Eph. 5:25–26.

who is not in the Church be loved by Christ or washed and cleansed with his washing?

3. Therefore, since the Church alone possesses the water of life and the power to baptize and purify, no one can argue the efficacy of Novatianist baptism and sanctification without first proving that Novatian is in the Church, or presides over it. For the Church is one, and being one cannot be both inside and outside at once. If it is with Novatian, it was not with Cornelius. But if it was with Cornelius, who succeeded Bishop Fabian by a legitimate ordination and to whom, besides his episcopal rank, the Lord gave the honour of martyrdom, then Novatian is not in the Church and cannot be reckoned a bishop—a man who scorned the tradition of the Gospel and the apostles, succeeded no one and originated from himself! [9] For one who has not been ordained in the Church can by no means possess or govern the Church.

4. The Church is not outside. It cannot be rent or divided against itself, it maintains the unity of a single, indivisible house. So much is made clear with the authority of holy Scripture in the account of the Passover rite and the lamb which prefigured Christ: "In one house shall it be eaten; ye shall not cast the flesh abroad out of the house." [10] Rahab, who also was a type of the Church, expresses the same truth. The command given to her ran: "Thou shalt gather unto thee into thy house thy father, and thy mother, and thy brethren, and all thy father's household; and whosoever shall go out of the doors of thy house into the street, his blood shall be upon his head." [11] This figure [12] declares that all who are to live and escape the destruction of the world must be gathered into one house alone, the Church, while if any of the gathered goes outside, that is, if anyone who once obtained grace in the Church nevertheless abandons the Church, his blood will be upon his head, that is, he will have himself to blame for his damnation. The apostle Paul explains this, directing us to avoid a heretic as perverted, sinful and self-condemned. [13] For it is the heretic whose blood will be upon his head. He is not expelled by the bishop, but of his own accord runs away from the Church, condemning himself by his heretical presumption.

5. Therefore, to teach us that unity comes of divine authority,

[9] *Nemini succedens*, since Cornelius already occupied the *cathedra* of Rome, cf. *De Unit.*, 10, n. 31.
[10] Ex. 12:46, cf. *Unit.*, 8.   [11] Josh. 2:18–19, cf. *Unit.*, 8.
[12] *Sacramentum*.   [13] Titus 3:10–11, cf. Tert., *Praescr.*, 6.

the Lord affirms: "I and the Father are one"; and again, to bring his Church into that unity, he says: "And there shall be one flock and one shepherd." [14] If there is one flock, how can he be numbered with the flock who is not in the number of the flock? Or how can he be regarded as a shepherd who, while the true shepherd is alive and presides in the Church of God by virtue of an ordination in regular succession, succeeding nobody and beginning from himself, becomes a stranger and an alien, an enemy of the peace of the Lord and the unity of God, not dwelling in the house of God, namely the Church, in which dwell only men of one heart and mind. In the Psalms the Holy Spirit speaks of God "who maketh men to dwell together of one mind in an house." [15]

Again, the sacrifices of the Lord show how Christian unanimity is preserved by the strong and indissoluble bond of charity. When the Lord calls his body bread, bread which is made by the union of many grains of wheat, he is pointing to the union of our people, of which he was himself the figure. [16] When he calls his blood wine, wine which is pressed from many bunches and clusters and collected together, he is describing our flock similarly gathered together by the commingling of a multitude into unity. If Novatian is united to this bread of the Lord, if he is commingled with the cup of Christ, if, that is, it is established that he keeps the unity of the Church, then it will be possible to believe that he can possess the grace of the one and only baptism of the Church.

6. The sacred bond [17] of unity is indissoluble, and those who cause a schism, desert their bishop and set up a pseudo-bishop [18] for themselves outside the Church, are left without hope and bring utter ruin upon themselves from the wrath of God. Holy Scripture proves this in the Book of Kings where the ten tribes cut themselves off from the tribe of Judah and Benjamin, deserted their king and set up another for themselves outside: "And the Lord was very angry with all the seed of Israel, and removed them out of his sight, and delivered them into the hand of the spoilers, until he had cast them out of his sight. For Israel was scattered from the house of David; and

14 John 10:30, 16.   15 Ps. 68:6.
16 *Quem portabat.* Cyprian several times uses *portare* in this sense. For the many grains, cf. *Didache*, 9.
17 *Sacramentum,* perhaps mystery here.
18 *Pseudepiscopus.* Cyprian did not allow Novatian to be a bishop in any sense, despite his consecration by bishops. The word is used of Novatian's bishops in *Ep.* 55:24, and of Fortunatus in 59:9.

they made a king for themselves, Jeroboam the son of Nebat."[19] It says that the Lord was angry and gave them up to perdition because they had been scattered from unity and had set themselves up another king. So great was the wrath of the Lord against those who had caused the schism that the man of God sent to rebuke Jeroboam's sins and predict his coming punishment was even forbidden to eat bread and drink water among them. When he disobeyed and took food contrary to God's command, he was immediately smitten by the majesty of the divine judgment. On his journey home he was attacked and mauled to death by a lion. Does any of you dare to say that the saving water of baptism and heavenly grace can be shared with schismatics, when earthly, mundane drink cannot be shared with them? In his Gospel, the Lord satisfies us completely and makes it quite clear to our understanding that those who then cut themselves off from the tribe of Judah and Benjamin, deserted Jerusalem and seceded to Samaria, were to be reckoned among the profane and the heathen. For when he first sent his disciples to minister salvation, he instructed them: "Go not into the way of the Gentiles, and enter not into the city of the Samaritans."[20] Sending them first to the Jews, he orders them to pass by the Gentiles for the time being, and by adding that the schismatical city of the Samaritans was also to be left out, he shows that schismatics are on the same footing as Gentiles.

7. It may be objected that Novatian accepts the same law as the catholic Church, baptizes with the same creed,[21] acknowledges the same God the Father, the same Son Christ, the same Holy Spirit, and that he can exercise the power to baptize because, apparently, his baptismal interrogation is no different from ours. It must be recognized, however, in the first place that we and the schismatics do not in fact share a common credal law and a common baptismal interrogation.

---

[19] II Kings 17:20–21.   [20] Matt. 10:5.

[21] *Symbolum*, which I translate "creed," refers here rather to the interrogations than to a fixed declaratory creed. This is the first western use of the word in any such sense. Tertullian has it once in a technical, secular, sense in *Adv. Marc.*, V:1. See J. N. D. Kelly, *Early Christian Creeds*, pp. 46–47, 52–53, 56–57. Note remission through (*per*) the Church, also in *Ep.* 70:2, but nowhere else. But the normal eastern "baptism for the remission of sins" makes the same point. Cyprian's reasoning in c. 7 is not very convincing; c. 8 makes his real point, that, whether orthodox or not, they are outside the Church, and for that reason alone have no ministry or sacraments or Holy Spirit.

When they say, Do you believe in the remission of sins and eternal life through the holy Church? there is a lie implicit in their question, since they do not possess the Church. Further, their own lips confess that remission of sins cannot be given except through the holy Church, and since they do not possess the Church, they demonstrate that sins cannot be remitted among them.

8. The argument that they acknowledge the same God the Father, the same Son Christ and the same Holy Spirit, is no use to them either. Korah, Dathan and Abiram[22] acknowledged the same God as Aaron the priest and Moses. They lived by the same law and the same religious practices, invoking the one true God who should properly be worshipped and invoked. All the same, when they went beyond the limits of their own ministry and claimed for themselves authority to perform sacrifices in opposition to Aaron the priest, who had received the lawful priesthood by the favour of God and the ordination of the Lord, they were struck from on high and at once paid the penalty for their unlawful attempt. The sacrifices which they offered impiously and unlawfully against God's will and ordinance could be neither valid nor efficacious.[23] The very censers in which their illegal offering had been made were not to be used by the priests any longer. They were to keep alive the memory of God's avenging wrath for the correction of posterity. Melted down and purified by fire at the Lord's command, they were beaten into plates and fixed to the altar, as holy Scripture says: "A memorial unto the children of Israel, that no stranger, which is not of the seed of Aaron, come near to offer incense before the Lord; that he be not as Korah."[24] Yet they had not caused a schism. They had not gone out in shameless and hostile rebellion against the priests of God, like these men who are now rending the Church, rebelling against the peace and unity of Christ, and trying to set up a chair for themselves and assume a primacy[25] and claim authority to baptize and offer the sacrifice. How can those who strive unlawfully against God be successful in their attempts or secure anything by their unlawful endeavours? It is useless for the

[22] Num. 16, cf. *De Unitate*, 18.
[23] *Nec . . . rata esse et proficere.*　　　　　　　　[24] Num. 16:40.
[25] *Cathedram . . . primatum. Primatus* here is not primacy over the whole Church, but the bishop's position in his diocese. Korah, etc. are here spoken of as a faction, not a formal schism, but in general they are a type of schism.

champions of Novatian, or of any other schismatic like him, to contend that anyone can be baptized and sanctified with a saving baptism where it is agreed [26] that the minister of the baptism has not authority to baptize.

9. To help us understand God's verdict upon such audacity, we find that in a crime of this sort it is not only the leaders and authors of it who are marked out for punishment, but all who take part in it, unless they separate themselves from the communion of the wicked. The Lord commands through Moses: "Separate yourselves from the tents of these hardened men, and touch nothing of theirs, lest ye perish with them in their sins." [27] What the Lord had threatened through Moses he brought to pass. Everyone who did not separate himself from Korah, Dathan and Abiram paid the penalty at once for his impious communion with them. This example proves beyond all question that those who, with wicked temerity, join company with schismatics against the bishops who have been set over them, will all be held guilty and liable to punishment. As the Holy Spirit testifies by the prophet Hosea: "Their sacrifices shall be unto them as the bread of mourning; all that eat thereof shall be polluted." [28] Here he teaches plainly that the punishment inflicted upon the authors of schism is shared by all without exception who are polluted by their sin.

10. Where men are punished by God himself, what merit can they have in his sight? Or how can anyone justify and sanctify the baptized when he is an enemy of the bishops and tries to usurp functions forbidden to him, to which he has no right whatsoever? It is not surprising that they argue in favour of their wicked behaviour. Of course everyone defends his own actions. No one likes to give in easily when he is beaten, even if he knows that what he is doing is illegal. What is surprising, and calls more for indignation and grief than surprise, is the fact that Christians are standing by the antichrists, that inside the Church itself betrayers of the faith and traitors to the Church are opposing the Church. Still, obstinate and unteachable as they are in other ways, at least they admit that no heretic or schismatic anywhere possesses the Holy

---

[26] *Constet non habere*, which in Cyprian could easily be a periphrasis for *non habeant*. But in this case it was common ground between Cyprian and Stephen that the Novatianists had no authority to baptize and Cyprian uses this agreement as a premise. Similarly with the Holy Spirit in cc. 10–11 below.

[27] Num. 16:26.   [28] Hos. 9:4.

Spirit, and that, in consequence, while he can baptize, he cannot give the Holy Spirit. This admission makes it easy for us to prove to them that he who does not possess the Holy Spirit cannot baptize at all.

11. It is in baptism that we all of us receive the remission of sins. Now the Lord proves clearly in his Gospel that sins can be remitted only through those who possess the Holy Spirit. For when he sent his disciples out after the resurrection he said to them: "As the Father hath sent me, even so send I you. And when he had said this, he breathed on them, and saith unto them, Receive ye the Holy Ghost: whose soever sins ye remit, they shall be remitted unto him; whose soever sins ye retain, they shall be retained." [29] This passage shows that only he who possesses the Holy Spirit can baptize and give the remission of sins. To clinch the matter, John, who was to baptize Christ our Lord himself, received the Holy Spirit beforehand, while he was still in his mother's womb. This was done to make it quite certain and obvious that only those who possess the Holy Spirit can baptize. So will the champions of heretics and schismatics tell us whether they possess the Holy Spirit or not? If they do, why, when they come over to us, do those who were baptized in heresy or schism have hands laid on them so as to receive the Spirit? For surely he was already received where, if he was there, he could be given? But if outside the Church no heretic or schismatic gives the Holy Spirit, and if that is the reason why we lay hands on them, so that they may receive in the Church what neither exists nor can be given in schism, then it is obvious that those who admittedly do not possess the Holy Spirit cannot give the remission of sins either. Therefore, in order that according to God's ordinance and the truth of the Gospel they may receive the remission of sins and be sanctified and become temples of God, all without exception who come over to the Church of Christ from the adversaries and the antichrists are to be baptized with the baptism of the Church.

[The remainder of this letter (12–17) deals with an entirely different point. Magnus has asked whether baptism by affusion makes "legitimate" Christians. Cyprian replies that where the faith of the minister and the recipient is full and complete, the divine gifts are received, whether the method is washing (*lavacrum, loti*), affusion (*perfusi*), or sprinkling (*asparsio*).]

[29] John 20:21–23.

Letter 73

THE TEXT

Cyprian to his brother, Jubaianus, greeting.

1. You write to me, dearest brother, desiring me to tell you what I feel about the baptism of heretics who, though they are beyond the pale and outside the Church, claim for themselves something which is not within their right or power. I cannot hold this to be valid or legitimate, for we all know that they cannot lawfully possess it. As I have already expressed my views on this matter in my letters, to save time I am sending you a copy of them, showing you both what was decided at a Council which many of us attended, and also what I afterwards wrote to our colleague Quintus in reply to his questions on the subject. And now we have met again, seventy-one bishops of the province of Africa and of Numidia, and we have confirmed our previous decision, laying it down that there is *one* baptism, that of the catholic Church, and that in consequence we do not "rebaptize," but baptize, all those who, coming as they do from adulterous and unhallowed water, have to be washed and sanctified by the true water of salvation.

2. We are not disturbed, dearest brother, by the fact which you mentioned in your letter, that the Novatianists are rebaptizing those whom they entice from us. We are not in the least concerned with what the enemies of the Church do, provided we ourselves maintain a due regard for our position and hold firmly to reason and truth. Like a monkey imitating a man when he is not one, Novatian wants to claim for himself the authority and truth of the catholic Church, though he is not in the Church and indeed has set himself up as a rebel against the Church, and its enemy. Knowing that there is one baptism, he claims this for himself, so as to be able to say that the Church is with him, and make us heretics. We, however, who possess the source and root of the one Church, have

certain knowledge and full assurance that he has no rights outside the Church and that the one baptism is with us, among whom he was himself originally baptized when he still kept to the true principle of divine unity. If Novatian supposes that those who were baptized in the Church need to be rebaptized outside the Church, he should have begun with himself. The man who thinks they need baptism after the Church, indeed against the Church, should first get himself rebaptized with an extraneous and heretical baptism. Surely we are not bound to suppose that because Novatian dares to do this, we must not do it. Because Novatian usurps the honour of a bishop's throne, must I renounce my throne? Because Novatian ventures against all propriety to set up an altar and to offer sacrifice, must we abandon altar and sacrifices for fear of seeming to copy or resemble his rites? It would be altogether foolish and stupid of the Church to abandon the truth because Novatian arrogates to himself, outside the Church, an imitation of the truth.

3. To us it is no novelty and no sudden discovery that those who come to the Church from heresy must be baptized. Long years ago now, under Agrippinus of blessed memory, a great many bishops met together and decided this; and from that day to this many thousands of heretics[1] in our provinces have been converted to the Church and, far from disdaining it or holding back, have embraced with joy and with understanding the opportunity of obtaining a laver which gives life and a baptism which brings salvation. For it is not difficult for a teacher to explain what is true and lawful to one who has already condemned the depravity of the heretics and discovered the truth of the Church, and comes in order to learn and learns in order to live. If we can refrain from astounding the heretics by giving them our patronage and our consent, they will gladly and readily yield to the truth.

4. In the letter of which you sent me a copy[2] I find it said that we need not inquire who has performed[3] a baptism, since the

---

[1] An unexpected statement from Latin Africa. Were they mostly Marcionites or Gnostics of some sort, as Tertullian's writings may suggest?

[2] Not extant; its origin is unknown. Cyprian speaks guardedly of his immediate opponents. Some sections, especially at the end, suggest Rome, but he had some in Africa, cf. *Ep.* 71:1, *Quidam de collegis nostris.*

[3] The principle that the personal faith or morality of the minister does not destroy the efficacy of the sacrament is sound, but whether his lack of authority does is another question. According to Article 26 of the Church of England the unworthiness "hinders not" because they have Christ's commission and authority.

person baptized could receive remission of sins according to his belief. I cannot let this sentence pass, especially when I observe that the letter actually mentions Marcion and affirms that even converts from him ought not to be baptized because they have already been baptized in the name of Jesus Christ. We have therefore to consider the faith of believers outside, and ask whether they can obtain grace in some measure according to this faith of theirs. For if we and the heretics have one faith, it may be that we have one grace also. If the same Father, the same Son, the same Holy Spirit, the same Church are confessed with us by the Patripassians, the Anthropians, the disciples of Valentinus and Apelles, the Ophites, the Marcionites, and all the other pests and swords and poisons with which the heretics subvert truth, then perhaps they share one baptism with us, seeing that they share one faith.[4]

5. It would be tedious to run through the whole list of heresies and review the follies and ineptitudes of them all. There is no pleasure in saying what it is shocking or shameful to know. I shall therefore, for the time being, limit myself to Marcion, who is mentioned in the letter which you sent me, and I shall inquire whether his baptism is sound in principle. When the Lord sent his disciples out after the resurrection, he instructed them how to baptize, saying: "All power is given unto me in heaven and on earth. Go ye therefore, and teach all nations, baptizing them in the name of the Father, and of the Son, and of the Holy Ghost."[5] He taught them the Trinity, in whose name the nations were to be baptized. Does Marcion hold that Trinity?[6] Does he affirm the same God the Father, the Creator, as we do? Does he acknowledge the same Son, Christ, born of the Virgin Mary, the Word made flesh, who bore our sins, who by dying conquered death, who himself inaugurated the resurrection of the flesh and showed his disciples that he had risen in the same flesh? Very different is the faith of Marcion and the other heretics. No, with them there is nothing but unbelief and blasphemy and contention, things inimical to health and truth. How can we suppose that one who is baptized among

---

[4] Patripassians = Modalists, on the ground that their identification of the Father with the Son in Person crucifies the Father (so Tert., *Prax.*, 1); the rest Gnostic sects.

[5] Matt. 28:18–19.

[6] Marcion's God the Father was not the God of the Old Testament and Creator of the material universe, and his God the Son was not the Son and Messiah of the God of the Old Testament. Nor was the Son truly made flesh or risen in the flesh, i.e., his Christology was docetic.

them has obtained remission of sins and the grace of divine pardon by his faith when his faith is not the true one? For if, as some think, a man's faith enables him to receive something outside the Church, surely he receives what he believes. But if he believes what is false, he cannot receive what is true. He receives adulterous and unhallowed things, corresponding to his belief.

6. The prophet Jeremiah touched indirectly on this topic of unhallowed and adulterous baptism when he said: "Why do my tormentors prevail? My wound is stubborn, whence shall I be healed? When it was made, it became to me as lying water without faith." [7] Through the prophet the Holy Spirit makes mention of deceitful water without faith. What is this lying and faithless water? It must be that which simulates baptism and frustrates the grace of faith by its shadowy pretence. If any one could, according to his perverted faith, be baptized outside the Church and obtain remission of sins, then, by virtue of the same faith, he could also obtain the Holy Spirit, in which case it is not necessary to receive him into the Church with the laying on of hands so that he may obtain the Holy Spirit and be sealed. Either he could obtain both outside through his faith, or he received neither of them outside. [8]

7. Where, and through whom, can be given that remission of sins which is given in baptism is plain enough. The Lord founded the Church upon Peter, and taught and demonstrated that unity originated in him. [9] To Peter first he gave the power to loose on earth whatever he loosed. After the resurrection he said to the apostles as well: "As the Father hath sent me, even so send I you. And when he had said this, he breathed on them, and saith unto them, Receive ye the Holy Ghost: whose soever sins ye remit, they shall be remitted unto him: whose soever ye retain, they shall be retained." [10] From this we perceive that only

[7] Jer. 15:18.

[8] Cyprian in effect denies the distinction, or at least its relevance, between validity and efficacy. There is a weak point in his opponents' theology. They rest their case on the fact that Christ is the true minister of the sacraments, and will respond when the right form and matter is used, and, apparently, where the recipient has faith, whoever administers the sacrament (i.e., here, of baptism). Yet they deny full efficacy to what Christ himself does. For Cyprian's understanding of "sealing," and on the extent to which he associates the gift of the Spirit with the laying on of hands (Confirmation), see G. W. H. Lampe, *The Seal of the Spirit*, especially pp. 170–178.

[9] The point is unity, and the emphasis on "first," as in *De Unit.*, 4, not on headship of the Church. The inference drawn extends to all bishops.

[10] John 20:21–23.

those who preside in the Church and are established by the law of the Gospel and the ordinance of the Lord have the right to baptize and give the remission of sins, while nothing can be bound or loosed outside, where there is no one with power to bind or loose.

8. It is not without the authority of the divine Scriptures, dear brother, that I venture to say that God has disposed everything according to its definite law and particular ordinance, so that no one can arrogate to himself, in opposition to the bishops and priests, something which is not within his right and power. When Korah, Dathan and Abiram tried to arrogate to themselves the right to sacrifice, in opposition to Moses and Aaron the priest, they did not escape punishment for their unlawful endeavour.[11] So also the sons of Aaron, who set strange fire upon the altar, were at once blotted out in the sight of an angry Lord.[12] The same penalty awaits those who bring strange water to a false baptism. The censure and vengeance of God overtakes heretics who do, against the Church, what only the Church is allowed to do.

9. Some bring up the instance of those who had been baptized in Samaria.[13] "Only the laying on of hands was administered to them when the apostles Peter and John arrived, so that they might receive the Holy Spirit. They were not rebaptized." But this passage, my dear brother, strikes me as utterly irrelevant to the case before us. The Samaritan believers had come to the true faith and had been baptized by Philip the deacon, whom these very apostles had sent, within the one Church to which alone it has been granted to give the grace of baptism and to loose sins. Since they had already obtained the lawful baptism of the Church, it would have been wrong to baptize them any more. Peter and John supplied only what they lacked. By prayer and the laying on of hands the Holy Spirit was invoked and poured out upon them. We observe the same practice now. Those who are baptized in the Church are brought before the bishops of the Church, and, by our prayers and the imposition of our hands, they receive the Holy Spirit and are made perfect by the Lord's seal.[14]

---

11 Num. 16, cf. *Unit.*, 18; *Letter* 69:8.   12 Lev. 10.   13 Acts 8.

14 *Signaculo.* "It is possible that the *signaculum* is to be identified with the grace of the Holy Spirit by the laying on of hands, that is, that it denotes the 'seal of the Spirit'. If so, Cyprian is the first writer by whom the seal, in the full New Testament sense of the term, is directly associated with the ceremony of the imposition of hands; but it is more probable that it signifies the *consignatio*, the signing with the Cross which completes the convert's initiation, as in the *Apostolic Tradition*." (Lampe, *op. cit.*, 174).

10. It follows, dearest brother, that there is no need to suppose that we must yield to the heretics and hand over to them the baptism which was given to the one and only Church, and to no one else. It is the duty of a good soldier to defend his emperor's camp against rebels and enemies. It is the duty of a general of mark to keep the standards entrusted to him safe. It is written: "The Lord thy God is a jealous God." [15] We who have received the Spirit of God ought to be jealous for the faith of God, with that jealousy by which Phinehas [16] pleased God and earned his favour and allayed the wrath of his indignation when the people were perishing. Why should we credit anything spurious and foreign and hostile to divine unity, when we recognize only one Christ and his one Church? Like Paradise, the Church has enclosed fruit-trees within her walls, and if any of them does not bear good fruit, it is cut down and cast into the fire. These trees she waters with four rivers—the four Gospels [17]—by which, a saving and heavenly flood, she bestows the grace of baptism. Can one who is not in the Church water from the fountains of the Church? Can anyone receive the saving and health-giving draughts of Paradise from one who is perverted and self-condemned, banished from the fountains of Paradise, parched and faint with a thirst that will never be assuaged?

11. The Lord cries: "If anyone is athirst, let him come and drink" of the rivers of living water that flowed out of his belly. [18] If anyone is athirst, where shall he go? To the heretics, where there is no fountain and no river of life-giving water? Or to the Church, the one Church, established by the word of the Lord upon one man, who also received its keys? It is she alone who holds and possesses the whole power of her Spouse and Lord. In this Church we preside, for her honour and unity we fight, her grace and glory we defend alike with faithful devotion. It is we who, by divine permission, water the thirsty people of God, it is we who guard the boundaries of the fountains of life. If we maintain our right to their possession, if we recognize the sacrament of unity, why make ourselves into apostates from the truth, traitors to unity? The water of the Church, faithful and holy, the water of salvation, cannot be defiled and polluted, just as the Church herself is undefiled and chaste

[15] Deut. 4:24.   [16] Num. 25.
[17] Irenaeus has a long chapter (III. xi) to show by various natural and biblical analogies that there must be precisely four Gospels.
[18] John 7:37–38.

and pure. If heretics devote themselves to the Church, and become members of the Church, they can make use of her baptism and enjoy all her saving benefits. If they are not in the Church, but rather work against the Church, how can they baptize with the Church's baptism?

12. To credit their baptism is no small or light concession to the heretics, for baptism is the starting-point of our whole faith, the saving entrance into the hope of eternal life, the way by which God in his goodness purifies and gives life to his servants. If anyone could be baptized among the heretics, then he could obtain the remission of sins. If he obtained the remission of sins, he was sanctified, and if he was sanctified, he was made the temple of God. But of what God? I ask. The Creator?, Impossible; he did not believe in him. Christ? But he could not be made Christ's temple, for he denied the deity of Christ. The Holy Spirit? Since the Three are One, what pleasure could the Holy Spirit take in the enemy of the Father and the Son?

13. There are some who bring up custom as an objection against us when they are defeated by reason, as if custom were more important than truth, or as if, in spiritual matters, we were not bound to accept whatever improvement the Holy Spirit reveals to us.[19] This will not do. An error committed in good faith can be pardoned. The blessed apostle Paul says of himself: "I was before a blasphemer, and a persecutor, and injurious: but I obtained mercy, because I did it in ignorance." [20] But when inspiration and revelation have been vouchsafed, to persist knowingly and wittingly in one's error is to sin without the pardon granted to ignorance. For it means relying on prejudice and obstinacy when one is overcome by reason. And it is no good saying: "We observe what we received from the apostles." [21] The apostles handed down one Church only, and one baptism, which exists only in that same Church. We find no one admitted to communion by the apostles on the strength of a baptism received from heretics. There is no such evidence of the apostles having approved heretical baptism.

14. Some find support for the heretics in the words of the

---

19 This sounds almost Montanist. Cf. Tert. *Virg. Vel.*, 1: "Our Lord Christ called himself Truth, not Custom."
20 I Tim. 1:13.
21 Presumably addressed to Rome, cf. Firmilian to Cyprian (*Ep.* 75:6), "Those who at Rome do not observe what has been handed down from the beginning and vainly allege the authority of the apostles." Stephen "defames Peter and Paul."

apostle Paul: "Notwithstanding, every way, whether in pretence or in truth, Christ is preached." [22] I cannot see anything here, either, which the patrons and supporters of heresy can plead in its defence. Paul was not talking about heretics or their baptism in his letter, and he cannot be shown to have laid down anything relevant to this matter. Whether they were walking in a disorderly fashion and against the discipline of the Church, or were keeping the truth of the Gospel in the fear of God, he was talking about the *brethren*. He said that some of them spoke the word of the Lord steadfastly and without fear, while some acted in envy and strife, that some had preserved their good will and affection towards him, while others harboured ill will and faction. Nevertheless, he said, he endured everything patiently, provided that, whether in truth or in pretence, the name of Christ, which Paul preached, might come to the knowledge of many, and that the sowing of the word, still new and untaught, might spread through the preaching of those who spoke it. Again, it is one thing for those who are within the Church to speak about the name of Christ, and quite another for those who are outside and in opposition to the Church to baptize in the name of Christ. Therefore, if any one is protecting heretics, instead of producing what Paul said about the brethren, let him show where he thought fit to make any concession to a heretic or approved their faith or their baptism, or ruled that the faithless and the blasphemers could receive remission of sins outside the Church.

15. If, however, we try to discover what the apostles thought about heretics, we shall find that in all their letters they execrated and detested their blasphemous depravities. When they say: "Their word spreads as doth a canker," [23] how can the word which spreads like a canker into the ears of those who listen to it, give them the remission of their sins? When they say that there is no fellowship between righteousness and iniquity, and no communion between light and darkness, how can darkness illuminate or iniquity justify? When they say that they are not of God, but of the spirit of antichrist, how can the enemies of God, their hearts obsessed by the spirit of antichrist, minister spiritual and divine things? If we leave the errors of human contention behind and return with sincere and pious faith to the authority of the Gospel and the tradition of the apostles, we shall perceive that those who scatter and

22 Phil. 1:18. Cyprian treats the text very freely in what follows.
23 II Tim. 2:17, and for what follows cf. II Cor. 6:14; I John 4:3.

attack the Church of Christ have no rights over the saving grace of the Church. For Christ himself calls them his adversaries, and the apostles call them antichrists.

16. We must reject another attempt to circumvent Christian truth by bringing up the name of Christ. They say: "Wherever and however men have been baptized in the name of Jesus Christ, they received the grace of baptism." Yet Christ himself says: "Not everyone that saith unto me, Lord, Lord, shall enter into the kingdom of heaven." And again he warns and instructs us not to be lightly deceived by false prophets and false Christs using his name. "Many shall come in my name, saying, I am Christ; and shall deceive many." And afterwards he added: "But take ye heed: behold, I have foretold you all things." [24] From this it is clear that we are not at once to admit and accept every boast in the name of Christ, but only what is done in the truth of Christ.

17. It is true that in the Gospels and the letters of the apostles the name of Jesus Christ is used for the remission of sins. But this does not mean that the Son alone can profit any one, without the Father or in opposition to the Father. The Jews were always boasting that they had the Father, so this was done to show them that the Father would profit them nothing unless they believed in the Son whom he had sent. Those who knew God the Father, the Creator, ought also to know the Son, Christ. It was done to stop them flattering and applauding themselves about the Father alone without recognizing his Son, who in fact said: "No one cometh unto the Father, but by me." That it is the knowledge of both which saves, he himself makes manifest when he says: "This is life eternal, that they should know thee the only and true God, and Jesus Christ, whom thou hast sent." [25] Here we have Christ's own proclamation and witness that the Father who sent is to be known first, and then Christ who was sent, and that there can be no hope of salvation unless both are known together. How then can those who are alleged to have been baptized among the heretics in the name of Christ—heretics who do not know God the Father, indeed, who blaspheme him—how can they be reckoned to have obtained the remission of sins? In the time of the apostles the cases of the Jews and the Gentiles were altogether different. The Jews had already obtained that most ancient baptism of the Law and of Moses. [26] They needed to be baptized

24 Matt. 7:21–22; Mark 13:6, 23.
25 John 14:6; 17:3.   26 Cf. I Cor. 10:1–4.

in the name of Jesus Christ as well, as Peter puts to them in the Acts of the Apostles: "Repent, and be baptized every one of you in the name of Jesus Christ for the remission of sins, and ye shall receive the gift of the Holy Ghost. For to you is the promise, and to your children, and, after you, to all, as many as the Lord our God shall call unto him." [27] Peter makes mention of Jesus Christ with no intention of passing over the Father, but that the Son may be added to the Father.

18. Finally, when the Lord sent the apostles to the nations after the resurrection, he commanded them to baptize the Gentiles in the name of the Father and of the Son and of the Holy Ghost. How can it be said that "wherever and however" a Gentile is baptized, outside the Church, in opposition to the Church, "provided that it is in the name of Jesus Christ," he can obtain remission of sins, when Christ himself commands that the nations should be baptized in the full and united Trinity? Are we to believe that, while he who denies Christ is denied by Christ, he who denies his Father, whom Christ himself confessed, is not denied? that he who blasphemes against one whom Christ himself called Lord and God, is rewarded by Christ, and obtains remission of sins and sanctification in baptism? If a man denies that God is Christ's Creator,[28] by what power can he obtain remission of sins in baptism, when Christ received the very power by which we are baptized and sanctified from the same Father, whom he called greater than himself, by whom he prayed to be glorified, whose will he fulfilled even to the obedience of drinking the cup and submitting to death? To wish to maintain that one who gravely blasphemes and sins against the Father and Lord and God of Christ can receive remission of sins in the name of Christ, amounts to participation in the blasphemies of the heretics. And more, how can it be true both that one who denies the Son does not have the Father, and also that one who denies the Father has the Son? For the Son himself bears witness, saying: "No one can come unto me, except it be given unto him of the Father." [29] Thus it is evident that no one can receive remission of sins in baptism from the Son unless it is given to

[27] Acts 2:38–39.
[28] *Negans Deum Creatorem Christi*. Finding this phrase too unorthodox, some translators render "the Father of Christ." But (i) Cyprian is thinking of Christ in his humanity, and (ii) Marcion denied that the true God was the Creator of the Old Testament, to whom the Messiah "belonged."
[29] John 6:65.

him by the Father, especially as Christ says again: "Every plant which my heavenly Father hath not planted shall be rooted up."[30]

19. If the disciples of Christ will not learn from Christ how much veneration and honour is due to the name of Father, at least let them learn from examples of this world, and understand that it was not without grave reproof that Christ said: "The sons of this world are wiser than the sons of light."[31] In this world, if a father is insulted and his good name and honour are wounded by the wanton slanders of some malicious tongue, his son is indignant and angry, and tries with all his might to avenge the wrong done to his injured father. Do you think that Christ will let the impious blasphemers of his own Father go scot-free and remit their sins in baptism, when it is well known that even after baptism they go on heaping their curses upon the Father's person, sinning incessantly with their blasphemous tongues? Can a Christian, a servant of God, conceive or believe or utter any such thing? What will become of the divine precepts of the Law, "Honour thy father and thy mother?"[32] I suppose the word "father," which we are bidden to honour in man, may be violated with impunity in God! And what will become of Christ's own words in the Gospel: "He that curseth father or mother, let him die the death."?[33] I suppose the very person who orders that cursing one's parents after the flesh shall be punished with death, himself gives life to those who curse their heavenly and spiritual Father and hate the Church, their mother![34] "Whosoever shall blaspheme against the Holy Ghost shall be guilty of an eternal sin," he said.[35] Yet there are people ready to make the hateful and utterly detestable suggestion that, after such a threat, he sanctifies with saving baptism the blasphemers of God the Father. Do the people who believe that they ought to admit men like that to communion, when they come over to the Church, without first baptizing them, ever reflect that they are putting themselves in communion with other men's sins[36]—yes, and eternal sins? For that is what happens if you admit without baptism those who cannot put off the sins of their blasphemy except in baptism.

20. Again, how absurd and perverse it is if, when the heretics themselves repudiate and abandon their former error or crime

---

[30] Matt. 15:13.   [31] Luke 16:8.   [32] Ex. 20:12.
[33] Matt. 15:4.   [34] *Ecclesiae matris*, cf. §24.   [35] Mark 3:29.
[36] This principle of infection was seized on by the Donatists.

and acknowledge the truth of the Church, we ourselves mutilate the laws and sacraments of that very truth, telling those who come to us in penitence that they have already obtained the remission of sins—and that when they confess that they have sinned and come expressly to receive the pardon of the Church! Therefore, my dear brother, it is our duty to hold fast to the faith and truth of the catholic Church and teach it, and by means of every precept of the Gospels and the apostles, to demonstrate the character of the divine order and unity.

21. Can the power of baptism be greater and stronger than the confession which confesses Christ before men, and the suffering by which a man is baptized in his own blood? Yet not even this baptism can profit the heretic who, though he has confessed Christ, is put to death outside the Church.[37] Unless the patrons and protectors of the heretics proclaim them martyrs when they have been put to death for a false confession of Christ, unless, contrary to the testimony of the apostle (who said that, though they were burned and killed, it profited them nothing) they assign to them the martyr's crown and glory! But if not even the baptism of a public confession and of blood can profit a heretic for salvation, since there is no salvation outside the Church,[38] it can certainly not profit him to be baptized in a lair and den of robbers with the infection of polluted water, where, so far from putting off his old sins, he still loads himself with fresh and graver ones.

Baptism cannot be common to us and the heretics, for we do not have God the Father in common, nor Christ the Son, nor the Holy Ghost, nor the faith, nor the Church itself. Therefore those who come from heresy to the Church ought to be baptized, so that, being made ready for the kingdom of God by divine regeneration in the lawful and true and only baptism of the holy Church, they may be born of both sacraments, as it is written: "Except a man be born of water and the Spirit, he cannot enter into the kingdom of God."[39]

22. Referring to this passage and imagining that they can make void the truth of the Gospel teaching by human arguments, some bring up against us the case of catechumens. If a catechumen is arrested for the confession of the name and put to death before he is baptized in the Church, does he lose the

---

[37] Cf. *De Unit.*, 14.
[38] *Salus extra ecclesiam non est*, the original form of the Cyprianic maxim.
[39] John 3:5, *utroque sacramento*, water and the Spirit, the two parts of baptism, not baptism and eucharist.

hope of salvation and the reward of confession simply because
he was not first born again of water? Such champions and
supporters of heresy have to learn, first, that those catechumens
hold the faith and truth of the Church complete, and go out
from the camp of God to fight against the devil with a full and
sincere knowledge of God the Father and Christ and the Holy
Ghost, and, secondly, that they are not in fact deprived of the
sacrament of baptism, in that they are baptized with the most
glorious and most precious baptism of blood, of which the
Lord himself said: "I have another baptism to be baptized
with." [40] That those who are baptized in their own blood and
sanctified by suffering are made perfect and obtain the grace
which God promised is made plain by the Lord himself in the
Gospel, when he speaks to the thief who believed in him and
confessed him in the midst of his sufferings, and promises that
he will be with him in Paradise. Consequently, we who preside
over the faith and truth must not deceive and cheat those who
come to the faith and truth and do penance and ask for the
remission of their sins. We must correct them and reform them
and instruct them with heavenly teachings for the kingdom
of heaven.

23. It is objected: "What, then, will happen to those who
in times past came from heresy to the Church and were received
without baptism?" The Lord in his mercy is able to grant them
indulgence and not separate from the privileges of his Church
those who were received into the Church in good faith and have
fallen asleep in the Church. None the less, we are not to go on
making a mistake because it has been made once. It befits
wise and God-fearing men rather to obey the truth gladly and
instantly when it is laid open and made visible to them, than
to struggle persistently and obstinately against brethren and
bishops on behalf of heretics.

24. Let no one suppose that if heretics are faced with
baptism they stumble at it as though a second baptism is being
talked of, and so are held back from coming to the Church.
On the contrary, when the truth is pointed out and put con-
vincingly to them, they are the more impressed with the necessity of coming. If they see it decided and settled by our own
judgment that the baptism which they receive in heresy is to
be counted rightful and legitimate, they will think that they
rightfully and legitimately possess the Church as well, and all
the privileges of the Church. Then there will be no reason for

[40] Luke 12:50, *aliud*, another, is not in the normal Greek texts.

them to come to us, for, having baptism, they may be supposed to have all the rest. When, however, they come to see that there is no baptism outside, and that no remission of sins can be given outside the Church, they hurry to us all the more eagerly and promptly, and beg for the gifts and privileges of mother Church, being assured that they can by no means attain to the true grace of the divine promises unless they come first to the true Church. The heretics will not refuse to be baptized among us with the true and lawful baptism of the Church, when they learn from us how those who had already been baptized with John's baptism were baptized also by Paul, as we read in the Acts of the Apostles.[41]

25. Now some of our own people are upholding heretical baptism. They shrink from the odium of what seems like rebaptism. They count it a crime to baptize after the enemies of God. Yet we find that those whom John had baptized were baptized, and John was reckoned greater than all the prophets, John was filled with divine grace while he was yet in his mother's womb, John was upheld by the spirit and power of Elijah,[42] John was not the adversary of the Lord but his forerunner and herald, John did not merely announce the Lord in words before his coming, but pointed him out for men to see, John baptized the very Christ through whom all others are baptized.

If it is argued that a heretic can acquire the right to baptize by baptizing first, then baptism will belong not to those who are in lawful possession of it, but to those who seize it. Then, since baptism and Church are absolutely inseparable, the first to seize baptism will have seized the Church as well, and *you* begin to be the heretic to him, you who have been forestalled and find yourself left behind, you who, by yielding and throwing in your hand, have relinquished the right which you had received. How dangerous it is to give up one's right and power in the things of God is plain from holy Scripture. In Genesis, Esau lost his birthright and could not afterwards regain what he had once yielded.[43]

26. I have answered you briefly, my dear brother, and given you my poor best. I do not lay down the law to anyone. I do not condemn any bishop beforehand for doing what he thinks

[41] Acts 19:1–7. [42] Luke 1:15, 17.
[43] Gen. 27, cf. Heb. 12:16–17, which brings out the spiritual danger. Birthright is *primatus*, illustrating the element of temporal priority in this word, even as applied to Peter.

best. He has the right to use his own judgment freely.[44] So far as lies in me, I do not contend with my own colleagues and fellow-bishops for the sake of heretics.[45] I keep the harmony of God and the peace of the Lord with them, remembering the words of the Apostle: "If any man thinketh to be contentious, we have no such custom, neither the Church of God."[46] Charity of heart, the honour of our college, the bond of faith, the harmony of the episcopate, these I maintain in patience and gentleness. Accordingly, I have just written, as well as my modest talent allowed, with the permission and inspiration of the Lord, a small book on *The Benefit of Patience*,[47] which I am sending you in token of our mutual affection. Farewell, dearest brother.

[44] This passage is very important for Cyprian's idea of episcopal rights. Cf. *Sententiae*, Cyprian's opening words: "It remains that we should each of us express his opinion, not judging anyone or excommunicating anyone if he thinks differently. For none of us sets himself up as bishop of bishops (cf. Tert., *Pud.*, 1, on p. 74) or compels his colleagues to obey him by tyrannical terrorizing, since every bishop has freedom and power to use his own judgment, and cannot be judged by another."

[45] A hit at Stephen?

[46] I Cor. 11:16.

[47] *De Bono Patientiae*, extant, modelled on Tertullian's *De Patientia*.

Ambrose

Ambrose

GENERAL INTRODUCTION

IN OR ABOUT THE YEAR A.D. 339 AMBROSE WAS BORN at Augusta Treverorum (Trier), the son of Aurelius Ambrosius, Prefect of Gaul. After the death of his father he was educated at Rome, and about A.D. 365 he and his brother Satyrus obtained legal posts at Sirmium on the staff of the Prefect of Italy. A few years later (*c.* 370–372) Ambrose was appointed Governor (Consularis) of the province of Aemilia-Liguria in northern Italy. It was in this capacity that he was called upon to keep order at the election of a successor to the Arian bishop of Milan, Auxentius, an election which promised to be lively. Much to his consternation, he found himself chosen bishop by general acclamation, begun (it is said) by a child and taken up as an indication from heaven. Ambrose was the son of Christians and was brought up as a Christian, but, in the manner of his time, he had postponed baptism. When, despite his reluctance, the neighbouring bishops and the emperor Valentinian had approved his election, he was baptized (November 24th), ordained successively to the various grades of ministry and consecrated bishop on the 1st December, 373. He died in 397.

Notable as a writer and fairly entitled to rank as a doctor of the Church, Ambrose was nevertheless essentially a man of action. A faithful pastor and energetic administrator of his own diocese, he also, as bishop of a capital city, supervised the ecclesiastical affairs of the whole secular diocese of Italy, including Western Illyricum. We find him establishing new sees, consecrating bishops, presiding over great councils (Aquileia, 381, Capua, 391–392), and generally acting as primate of a large and autonomous region. For his respect for the See of Rome, which was real, did not extend to an acceptance of its jurisdiction over his own provinces; and in fact the bishops of

Gaul also were at this time tending to refer their problems to the Bishop of Milan and his Council.

As Bishop of Milan, Ambrose was in close touch with the emperors, who frequently resided there. During the greater part of his episcopate Milan, not Rome, was the administrative capital of the western empire and the seat of the Court. Some of the outstanding incidents in his relations with the Court are illustrated in this volume—the struggle over the Altar of Victory, the refusal to hand over a church to the Arians of Milan, the embassies to Maximus, the affair of Priscillian, the episodes at Callinicum and Thessalonica with the excommunication of Theodosius. It is probably not an exaggeration to say that Ambrose was in large part responsible for the change from toleration in religion, which was the policy of Valentinian I and, at first, of his son Gratian, to the establishment of orthodox Christianity as the religion of the State, the penalizing of heresy, and the suppression of the pagan cults; though it must not be supposed that so strong and able an emperor as Theodosius was merely a tool of the great ecclesiastic.

As a writer Ambrose was concerned above all with edification. He was neither an original thinker of the order of Augustine nor a scholar of the order of Jerome. Many of his writings are really sermons or catechetical instructions put together, perhaps quite hastily, from shorthand reports of what he had said. Of his attractiveness as a preacher and teacher we have the evidence of Augustine. His sermons are marked by an intimate knowledge of the Bible, which he interprets morally and allegorically after the example of Philo and Origen, whose work he knew. It was also upon Greek theologians—Athanasius, Didymus, Basil of Caesarea, Cyril of Jerusalem, Gregory of Nazianzus, Epiphanius—that he mainly relied for his dogmatic works. In this respect he was an important link between eastern and western Christianity.

The exegetical writings include the *Hexaemeron* (nine sermons on the six days of creation), works on the stories of Paradise, Cain and Abel, Noah, and the patriarchs from Abraham to Joseph, sermons on several psalms, especially Psalm 119 (118 to him), and a substantial collection of sermons on St. Luke. He did not write the important commentary on Paul's Epistles, now conventionally ascribed to "Ambrosiaster." Another big group contains his ascetic teaching—several books on virginity and widowhood, fasting, temperance, and almsgiving. The dogmatic works are partly controversial, directed for the most part against Arianism, like those *On the Faith*, *On the Holy Spirit*, and *On the Incarnation*, and partly instructions, like those *On the Mysteries* and *On the Sacraments*, the latter once more attributed with some confidence to Ambrose. He also wrote *On Penance* against the rigorist Novatianists. The ninety-one *Letters* are of great historical interest, and with these may be associated the funeral orations on Valentinian and Theodosius, together with the more personal lament over his brother Satyrus. There remains, among the major works, the *De Officiis Ministrorum*, worked up from sermons preached to his own clergy and nominally a treatise on the clerical life, but in fact the first substantial manual of Christian ethics. Its scheme is taken from Cicero's *De Officiis*, and its moral concepts are Stoic in pattern; but all is transformed by his Christian faith.

Ambrose taught a rounded "catholic" Christianity (one notices how often *fides* has to be translated "*the* faith"), his works as a whole contributing largely to the mediaeval catholicism of the West. The Bible is to him the fundamental authority for all life and thought, but, given the method of "spiritual" exegesis which reads meanings into the text, biblical authority tends to take second place to tradition and the accepted doctrines of the Church. "The Church to teach, the Bible to prove." Trinitarian and Christological orthodoxy has been established, no problems are raised about the nature and authority of the Church and its ministry, the sacraments of Baptism and the Holy Communion are inexplicable mysteries, miracles of grace. Ambrose's doctrine of the Fall and Original Sin is well on the way to Augustine's, his eucharistic teaching is not far from transubstantiation, though it is not based on a precise philosophy, and he teaches purgatorial fire, prayer for the dead and the invocation of saints. There is much legalism, much appeal to the concepts of merit and reward; and the double moral standard of precepts and counsels is accepted. Indeed, there is a serious danger of a religion of works. At the same time, however inconsistently in theory, he has a profound sense of divine grace, and a vein of mysticism which sees the essence of religion in the personal union of the faithful soul with its Saviour.

In the history of liturgy the name of Ambrose is attached to much more than can be safely attributed to him. He did, it seems, introduce into the West the eastern practice of antiphonal chanting by the congregation, and he did write some hymns, though perhaps only a dozen or so of the many subsequently believed to be his. The unquestioned hymns are *Aeterne*

12—E.L.T.

rerum conditor, Deus creator omnium, Jam surgit hora tertia, and *Veni redemptor gentium,* all mentioned by Augustine. The Ambrosian rite of later days is an amalgam of eastern, Roman and Gallican elements, and as such is not his work. Its eastern characteristics may have been brought to Milan by the Cappadocian bishop, Auxentius, Ambrose's Arian predecessor; and in that case Ambrose may have adapted them to western uses or may simply have removed any suggestion of Arianism. He did not compose the *Te Deum,* as one legend has it, but some modern scholars believe he wrote the Athanasian Creed. He undoubtedly influenced liturgical practice and the common life of the Church by the encouragement which he gave to the veneration of martyrs and the search for, and exchange of, relics.

He was a great prince of the Church in his own right. It was also given to him to help a greater man into the way of truth. Not that Augustine was ever intimate with him. But it was Ambrose whose preaching showed him how to understand the Old Testament and released him from some of his Manichaean difficulties, and it was Ambrose who baptized him, "the excellent steward of God whom I venerate as a father, for in Christ Jesus he begat me through the Gospel and by his ministry I received the washing of regeneration—the blessed Ambrose, whose grace, constancy, labours, perils for the catholic faith, whether in words or works, I have myself experienced, and the whole Roman world unhesitatingly proclaims with me."[1]

THE TEACHING OF AMBROSE ON THE RELATIONS BETWEEN CHURCH AND STATE

A treatise on Church and State from the pen of Ambrose would be an exciting thing to read, still more an intimate diary of his dealings with, and his thoughts about, his imperial masters. Failing any such thing, we have to put together the remarks drawn from him by political circumstances or made from time to time in the course of his exegesis of Scripture.

First, the State as such is good and within the purpose of God. In principle it precedes the Fall and is natural. The divinely appointed fellowship of Adam and Eve is the germ of the State, for fellowship implies mutual help and so justice and good-will, the twin principles of community and society. It is true that, but for sin, society would be more free and more

[1] Aug., *Contra Julianum Pelagianum,* I, 10.

equal than it is; some of its institutions, like slavery and private property, are the result of the Fall. So indeed is monarchy. While the State itself is natural, coercive power is the fruit of sin; not, however, as an invention of the devil, but as the divinely approved remedy for sin. Thus where there is a monarch, he must be accepted as the power ordained of God and given his due.

But what is his due? What is the sphere of his God-given authority? By the third century the totalitarianism of the Roman Empire assumed that nothing lay outside the control of the emperor. It seemed quite natural that he should be *Pontifex Maximus*, and the government had always felt free to control or suppress religious cults and associations in the interests of politics or morals. It was this tradition that Constantine inherited, and to it he added the conviction that he was raised up as God's servant, responsible to God for the welfare of both Church and State. It must have seemed to many Christians, confronted unexpectedly with the problem of the place of a Christian emperor in the life of the Church, that the best model was to be found in the Old Testament, where the anointed king is held responsible by God not only for what we might call secular policy, but also, and primarily, for what he does about his people's faith and worship and morals. Thus, although Constantine himself declared that the judgment of bishops is as the judgment of God, and deprecated any appeal from them to himself, the Church of his day expected him to be active in its affairs, and asked the State to enforce the decisions of Councils and to banish recalcitrant bishops.

The dangers inherent in this outlook became manifest as the century progressed and as emperor after emperor, often sincerely desiring peace and unity, used his authority to enforce his own views or the doctrine of whatever party he found it expedient to support. Hence came appeals for liberty in religion and theories of ecclesiastical independence. "What has the emperor to do with the Church?" said Donatus in A.D. 347, when Constans sent his officers to suppress Donatism in Africa. "Do not intrude yourself into ecclesiastical matters, do not give commands to us [bishops] concerning them," wrote Hosius of Cordova to Constantius after the Council of Milan of A.D. 355. "God has put the kingdom in your hands; he has entrusted the affairs of the Church to us. . . . Render to Caesar the things that are Caesar's, and to God the things that are God's."

Ambrose started from some such dualist theory of the separate spheres of Church and State, and never renounced it, though what he handed down to posterity was somewhat different. The emperor derives his power from God and within his proper sphere is to be obeyed. But he is not over the Church. "The palace belongs to the emperor, the churches to the bishop." In God's cause (*causa Dei, causa fidei, causa religionis*) the bishops are the judges and are directly responsible to God. The difficulty, of course, is to define the spheres of Church and State. When he came to work this out, which he did in practice more than in theory, Ambrose gave no support to the clear and radical dualism in which the State is entirely neutral and indifferent in matters of religion, while the Church lives its own life without any responsibility for the State. He is thinking of a Christian State. On the one hand, then, the State has far-reaching duties towards the Church. While the Christian emperor must not try to impose his own decisions in matters of faith and morals upon the Church, he should put the decisions of the Church (in practice, the bishops) into execution even by force, and he should protect the true religion and the true Church against its rivals, that is, he should prohibit heretical worship and the pagan cults. The Church, in its turn, as the guardian of the moral law, will speak its mind through the bishops to the emperor whenever political decisions or actions are held to be unchristian, and, if necessary, it will use its own kind of force, spiritual sanctions, excommunication, the threat of damnation. Thus Ambrose in effect excommunicated Theodosius, Maximus, and Eugenius. For the emperor, as a Christian, is within the Church, and, as a layman, is subordinate to the bishop. The bishop continues the function of the Old Testament prophet, of Nathan who rebuked David and Elijah who withstood Ahab. "Prophets and bishops must not rashly insult kings, if there are no grave sins for which they deserve reproach; but where there are grave sins, the bishop must not spare to correct them by his just remonstrances." [2] Again, "Although kings are above man's laws, they are subject to the punishment of God for their sins. [3]" *Ubi peccata graviora sunt, pro peccatis suis*—this is the mediaeval argument that kings and emperors are subject to the dictation of the Church *ratione peccati*, since the Church is ultimately responsible to God for the consciences and souls of her children. It is no longer a matter simply of protecting the exclusive right of the bishops

[2] *Enarr. in Ps.* 37, 43.   [3] *Enarr. in Ps.* 40, 14.

to define the faith or to exercise ecclesiastical discipline over
their flocks in matters plainly internal to the life of the Church.
This is no doctrine of mutually exclusive spheres, but an inter-
penetration of Church and State with ultimate authority in
the hands of the Church. Not that Ambrose himself worked it
out in detail, or pressed his claims to the full. For many pur-
poses a more obvious dualism was sufficient. But in principle
the inroads of the Church upon the authority of the State are
made at the most vital spot, and just where the New Testament
might seem to support the State—the working-out of political
justice, the preservation of public order, the exercise of that
coercive power for which, on Ambrose's own theory of the
State, government is ordained. For now the sovereign is not
responsible directly to God for his use of the sword, but to the
Church, and it may often rest with the Church to tell the faithful whether or not to obey the State.

The letters printed in this volume show Ambrose in action.
No one will doubt his courage and sincerity or deny the force
of his example in subsequent centuries. Later generations have
had to consider how far he was right and how what he rightly
desired can be secured without ecclesiastical tyranny.

Letter 10: *The Council of Aquileia, A.D. 381*

INTRODUCTION

IN A.D. 378 TWO ARIAN BISHOPS OF ILLYRICUM, threatened with the loss of their sees by the increasing movement back to Nicene orthodoxy, asked the emperor Gratian to summon a new General Council to discuss the disgreements in doctrine. He agreed, but the Gothic wars prevented the holding of such a council. One of the bishops, Palladius of Ratiaria, crossed swords with Ambrose by publishing a treatise *On the Faith* in reply to Ambrose's book of that name. In September, 380, he obtained an interview with Gratian, who consented to convene a General Council at Aquileia. This disturbed Ambrose, who suspected that many eastern bishops were still unorthodox and would support Palladius. He managed to persuade Gratian that a limited number of western bishops would suffice to settle the matter. So thirty-two bishops and two presbyter-deputies arrived, representing northern Italy, western Illyricum, Africa, and Gaul, in addition to Palladius and Secundianus, much aggrieved to find no eastern supporters present. After much wrangling about the validity of the Council as well as about doctrine, Palladius and Secundianus were condemned as Arians and excommunicated. At one stage Palladius had asked for a discussion before arbitrators, some of whom should be laymen of standing. Ambrose replied that bishops could not be judged by laymen, and that the very suggestion proved Palladius to be unworthy of his episcopal office.

According to the Acts of the Council, this took place on 3rd September, 381. Some scholars, disconcerted by the absence from the documents of the Council of any reference to the Council of Constantinople, which met from May to July, 381, have proposed to change this date. Palanque, followed by Dudden, at one time put the Council in May, but subsequently expressed his doubts. It may be that the silence of Aquileia about Constantinople was diplomatic, for the western bishops did not like some of its decisions.

The Council despatched several letters which are preserved among the correspondence of Ambrose. *Letter* 9 is a brief greeting to the churches of Gaul, thanking them for sending a delegation, and telling them of the condemnation of Palladius and Secundianus. The others are the work of Ambrose. *Letter* 10, addressed to all three emperors but really sent to Gratian, summarizes the work of the Council and asks the emperor to enforce its decisions. Ambrose has no scruples about invoking the secular arm, and it is clear that the Church thought it proper for the emperor to convene councils and to confirm such actions as the deposition of bishops. The Council even shows some anxiety in case Gratian should think it insufficiently authoritative, and emphasizes that his instructions have been followed. On the other hand, the emperor is urged to respect the name of bishop, to allow the bishops to appoint successors to Palladius and Secundianus, and, by enforcing the law against Photinian meetings, to secure respect *first* for the Church and secondly for the law; and he is promised divine favour if he does this. Together with the affirmation, in the course of the Council, that bishops cannot be judged by laymen, we have here an anticipation of Ambrose's later thoughts and actions.

Letter 11, also sent to Gratian, asks him somewhat anxiously to put an end to the schismatic (i.e., Ursinian) opposition to Pope Damasus. *Letter* 12, intended primarily for Theodosius, asks him to take steps to end the schism at Antioch by summoning a council at Alexandria. *Letters* 13 and 14, written perhaps a year later, continue this subject, which was decided against the wishes of the West.

Letter 10

THE TEXT

The Holy Council assembled at Aquileia to the most gracious and Christian emperors and most blessed princes, Gratian, Valentinian, and Theodosius.[1]

1. Blessed be God the Father of our Lord Jesus Christ, who has given to you the empire of Rome, and blessed be our Lord Jesus Christ, the only-begotten Son of God, who protects your reign with his goodness, before whom we offer our thanks to you, most gracious princes. We are grateful both for the proof of zealous faith shown in the trouble you have taken to convene a Council of bishops to end disputes, and for the honour done to the bishops by your considerate decision that no one who wished to be present should be absent, and no one be forced to attend against his will.[2]

---

[1] This letter, though addressed to all three emperors, was really intended for Gratian who is directly addressed in §2. As was usual at this time, Ambrose uses abstract nouns as imperial titles, like our "Your Highness" and "Your Grace." Sometimes they mean no more than "you", and often they might be translated "Your Majesty". But as the title chosen is sometimes relevant to the occasion—"Piety" in matters of religion, for example—I have decided to distinguish the words, though some, like "Your Tranquillity", will sound rather odd. I have translated *Clementia vestra* "Your Grace", since it is so close to a familiar title. It will be observed that Ambrose often chooses it when he wants to call on the emperor's graciousness or clemency; but frequently it is merely conventional. The vocative, *Imperator*, I usually translate "Sir", occasionally "Your Majesty."

[2] The Acts of the Council (*Gesta Concilii Aquileiensis*) are extant among Ambrose's letters, and something of Palladius's view of it may be gleaned from the *Dissertatio Maximini*. Gratian's rescript, cited in *Gesta* 3–4, shows that Ambrose had persuaded him to limit the scope of the Council. He has to emphasize that the Council met according to the terms of the rescript, since Palladius had previously been promised a General Council and now makes a grievance of the absence of eastern bishops and keeps saying that he will only answer in a full Council. Ambrose says that the

2. We assembled according to your gracious command, unhampered by excessive numbers and ready for discussion. No heretical bishops were found to be present except Palladius and Secundianus, men long notorious for their perfidy, on whose account people from the ends of the Roman world were asking that a Council should be convened. No one bent with the weight of his years, venerable if only for his grey hairs, has been compelled to come from the farthest shores of the ocean; yet the Council lacked nothing. No one, dragging along his feeble body, spent in the service of fasting, has been driven by the sufferings of his journey to weep over the hardships of his lost strength, and no one, above all, left without the means to come, has groaned over the poverty which is a bishop's glory. So it is, most gracious prince Gratian, that the praises of scripture have been fulfilled in you: "Blessed is he that considereth the poor and needy."[3]

3. It would indeed have been serious if, merely on account of two bishops rotten with perfidy, the churches throughout the world had been left without their bishops. Even if they could not come, owing to the length of the journey, they were all present, from almost all the provinces of the West, by sending representatives; and they made it known by express statements that they hold what we assert and that they agree with the formula of the Council of Nicaea, as the appended documents show. So now the peoples are everywhere praying in concert on behalf of your empire, and yet defenders of the faith have not been wanting as a result of your decision. For although the rulings of our predecessors were quite plain, we offered opportunities for discussion.

4. To begin with, we took up the question in its original form and thought it a good plan to read the letter of Arius,

eastern bishops had been informed that they could attend, but had themselves recognized that western Councils were for western bishops. Palladius and Secundianus were at this time western bishops by ecclesiastical and political allegiance. On this tricky point see my article in *Journal of Theological Studies*, XLVI (1945), p. 23. In a way, Ambrose was retorting upon the Arians the tactics employed by Valens and Ursacius in 359, when they persuaded Constantius to hold separate eastern and western Councils at Seleucia and Ariminum instead of the General Council originally planned. And Palladius and Secundianus were followers of Ursacius and Valens! Palladius was Bishop of Ratiaria (Artcher in Bulgaria), Secundianus of Singidunum (Belgrade), the See of Ursacius.

[3] Ps. 41:1.

the author of the Arian heresy, from whom it took its name.[4]
We intended that these men, who commonly deny that they
are Arians, should either attack and condemn the blasphemies
of Arius, or defend and uphold them or at least not repudiate
the name of the person whose impiety and perfidy they follow.
They had themselves challenged us to a discussion three
days before, had fixed the time and place, and had made their
appearance without waiting for a summons. However, as unwilling to approve their master as they were unable to condemn
him, despite their assertion that they would quickly prove
themselves to be Christians—a thing which we heard with
pleasure and hoped they would prove—on the spot they
suddenly began to shrink from the encounter and to refuse all
discussion.

5. Still, many words passed between us. The divine Scriptures were set out, we stretched our patience and gave them
the opportunity to discuss from daybreak to the seventh hour.
Would to God that they had not said much, or at least that we
could blot out what we heard! In blasphemous terms Arius
had described the Father as alone eternal, alone good, alone
very God, alone possessing immortality, alone wise, alone
almighty, impiously implying that the Son is without these
attributes. Palladius and Secundianus preferred to follow
Arius rather than confess the Son of God to be eternal God,
very God, good God, wise, almighty, possessing immortality.
Many hours we spent in vain. Their impiety grew, there was
no way of correcting it.

6. When at last they saw themselves hard pressed by the
blasphemies in Arius's letter (which we subjoin so that your
Grace also may abhor it), they interrupted half-way through
the reading of the letter and asked us to reply to their propositions. It was both out of order and unreasonable to interrupt
the procedure we had adopted, and we had already answered
that when they condemned the impieties of Arius, we would
reply to whatever objections they pleased to make, in due order
and place. However, we acquiesced in their wish to do things

[4] The letter of Arius to Alexander, Bishop of Alexandria, before the Council
of Nicaea. See Athanasius, *De Synodis*, 16. This calls Christ a creature.
Palladius does not go so far, and so claims not to be an Arian. He acknowledges that the Son is divine and only-begotten, but he subordinates the
Son to the Father in deity and will not call him very God. He belongs to
the homœan group, whose catchword was that the Son is "Like the
Father". It is made clear that he will not say that the Son is God in the
same absolute sense in which the Father is God.

the wrong way round. Then, misquoting the Gospel text, they put it to us that the Lord said: "He that sent me is greater than I", though the relevant biblical passages show that something quite different was written.[5]

7. Although they were convicted of misrepresentation and made to admit it, they were impervious to reason. When we said that the Son is described as less than the Father in respect of his taking of flesh, while, on the evidence of Scripture, he is proved to be like and equal to the Father in respect of deity, and that there can be no degrees of difference or greatness where there is unity of power, not only would they not correct their error, but they even began to press their insane notions further, saying that the Son is subordinate in deity,[6] as if there could be any subordination of God in his deity and majesty. In short, they refer his death not to the mystery of our salvation, but to some weakness in his deity.

8. We are horrified, most gracious princes, at sacrilege so terrible and teachers so depraved; and to prevent their peoples being any further deceived, we came to the conclusion that they ought to be deposed from their priesthood,[7] since they agreed with the impieties of the document appended. It is not fitting that they should lay claim to the priesthood of him whom they have denied. We beg you, out of regard for your own faith and honour, to show your respect for the Author of your empire, and, by letter of your Grace to the competent authorities, to decree that these champions of impiety and corrupters of truth be debarred from the threshold of the Church, and that holy bishops be put in the place of the condemned by the representatives of our humble selves.

9. The presbyter Attalus, who has not concealed his errors and adheres to the blasphemies of Palladius, is covered by a

5 This section is explained by *Gesta* 35–36. Instead of answering the Council, Palladius began to ask Ambrose questions. This is his "wrong way round" (*praepostera voluntas*). He plays his strong biblical card, "The Father is greater than I," but misquotes, conflating John 14:28 with the numerous references to the Father sending the Son.

6 *Subjectum secundum divinitatem.*

7 Latin *sacerdotio*. In earlier use, *sacerdos* almost always means bishop, and so usually still in Ambrose. Thus Ambrose applies Old Testament passages about priests to bishops, e.g., in *Letter* 63 (and cf. Cyprian, p. 162). Sometimes one must translate it priest, as here, because of the allusion to the priesthood of Christ; sometimes one must translate it bishop, or the point would be lost. Therefore, my *bishop* represents sometimes *sacerdos* and sometimes *episcopus*; and similarly with the adjectives.

similar decision. What are we to say of his master, Julianus Valens? [8] Though close at hand, he kept away from the episcopal Council for fear of being compelled to explain to the bishops why he had ruined his country and betrayed his fellow-citizens. Polluted by the impiety of the Goths, he dresses himself like the heathen, we are told, with collar and armlet, and dares to go about like that in the sight of a Roman army. That is unquestionably sacrilege not only in a bishop, but in any Christian; for [9] it is contrary to Roman custom. No doubt the idolatrous priests of the Goths are his model!

10. We trust your Piety will be moved by the name of bishop, which he dishonours with his sacrilege. He is convicted of a horrible crime even by the voice of his own people—if any of them can still be alive. At least let him go back home and not contaminate the cities of prosperous Italy. For at the moment he is associating like-minded persons with himself by unlawful ordinations and trying, by means of some abandoned wretches, to leave behind him a nursery for his own impiety and perfidy. And he has never even begun to be a bishop, for at Poetovio, to begin with, he supplanted the holy Marcus, a bishop whose memory is held in high esteem. Afterwards he was ignominiously turned out by the people, and, finding Poetovio impossible for him, is now prancing about at Milan, after the ruin—or, to speak bluntly, the betrayal—of his own country.

11. On all these points, Sirs, be pleased to take thought for us. We should not wish to give the impression of having assembled, in obedience to the instructions of your Tranquillity, to no purpose. Care must be taken that your decisions, even more than ours, should not be dishonoured. Therefore we ask your Grace to be pleased to give audience also to the legates of the Council, who are holy men, and to instruct them to return speedily with the information that you have given

---

[8] Julianus Valens, a presbyter from Noricum, had joined the Arians in Milan and given trouble to Ambrose some years before. He had then been intruded as Arian Bishop of Poetovio (Pettau) in place of Mark, but was not recognized by the catholics as a bishop. His treason took place in 379, after the Goths' victory of Adrianople, when he delivered his city into their hands. Afterwards he was expelled by the citizens, and went to Milan, where he intrigued with Ursinus (*Ep.* 11:3). The Council does not ask for his deposition, since they do not acknowledge him to be a bishop at all, but simply for his expulsion. Attalus was one of his followers.

[9] I wondered whether to translate *etenim* "and indeed", but Ambrose seems to give it the full sense of "for". If so his identification of Christianity and Roman civilization is revealing.

effect to our requests. You will be rewarded by Christ, the Lord God, whose churches you have cleansed from all stain of sacrilege.

12. There is also the matter of the Photinians.[10] By an earlier law you decreed that they should not assemble together, and by the law governing the episcopal Council, you forbade them to join us. We now learn that they are still attempting to meet inside the city of Sirmium, and ask your Grace once more to forbid their meetings and to order due respect to be shown first to the catholic Church and secondly to your own laws, so that, under God's protection, by your care for the peace and quiet of the Church, you may reign in triumph.

[10] Photeinus, Bishop of Sirmium, combined the modalism of Marcellus of Ancyra with an adoptianist doctrine of Christ, and was several times condemned by eastern and western Councils. Gratian had excluded the Photinians, with the Eunomians and Manichaeans, from his edict of toleration in 378; this law, the text of which is not extant, may well have forbidden these heretics to assemble within the cities. The other "law" referred to here is the rescript summoning the Council of Aquileia, which does not expressly forbid heretics, but only invites "the bishops."

Letter 17: The Altar of Victory

INTRODUCTION

AFTER THE BATTLE OF ACTIUM, OCTAVIAN, SOON TO be the Emperor Augustus, placed in the Roman Senate-House a Greek statue of the goddess Victoria, found at Tarentum. At her altar senators burned incense as they entered, and by it they took oaths of allegiance to each new emperor and pledged themselves annually with prayer for the welfare of the empire. So it continued until A.D. 357, when Constantius, visiting Rome, ordered the removal of the Altar of Victory. It was either restored as soon as his back was turned or else by Julian. Jovian and Valentinian I, though Christians, let it stay there. But in 382 Gratian, much under the influence of Ambrose, opened his campaign against paganism. He had perhaps renounced the title of Pontifex Maximus at his accession, though this too may have been done in 382. In that year he disendowed the official cults and priesthoods, including the Vestal virgins, and removed the Altar of Victory from the Senate. At this time the Roman Senate was still something of a stronghold of pagan conservatism under such leaders as Symmachus, Praetextatus, and Nicomachus Flavianus. Whether or not it had an absolute majority is a point on which Symmachus and Ambrose appear to contradict each other, but on this occasion at any rate the pagans mustered an effective majority and sent a deputation of protest to the emperor. Christian senators drew up a counter-petition which was sent through Pope Damasus to Ambrose, and by him presented to Gratian. He, as we learn from Symmachus, refused even to receive the official deputation. Defeated for the moment, the pagan party made capital out of the murder of Gratian in 383. Was this the reply of Heaven?

Early in the reign of the boy Valentinian II the pagan party secured some of the highest offices of State. Praetextatus became

Prefect of Italy, Symmachus Prefect of Rome; the powerful barbarian general, Count Bauto, was probably a pagan, and Count Rumoridus certainly one. Thus encouraged, the Senate again sent a deputation to the emperor, asking for the restoration of the religious subsidies and endowments and the return of the Altar of Victory. This was in the summer of 384. Symmachus drew up a *Memorial* pleading for religious liberty. The One whom all seek to worship cannot be found by all in the same way. Spoliation of any religion is sacrilege, and Valentinian is not being asked to make a gift, but to restore rights. The gods had already punished Rome with famine. There were Christians around Valentinian, as there had been in the Senate, who thought the request reasonable. Ambrose, therefore, hearing of what threatened, wrote quickly to Valentinian (*Letter* 17), claiming the right to intervene as bishop in a matter of religion and telling him that a Christian emperor or State cannot subsidize idolatry. When he had secured a copy of the *Memorial*, Ambrose wrote again, refuting its arguments in detail (*Letter* 18). His influence prevailed, and neither endowments nor Altar were restored. It was an acute conflict. Whatever the rights and wrongs of the immediate matters of dispute, the subsidies, the endowments, and the Altar (and even from a Christian standpoint there may be a case against him), Ambrose saw that this was intended to be a trial of strength between Christianity and paganism. He won it, and, as later events would show, Milan was to be for a time a more stable centre of Christianity than Rome. The pagan cause was further weakened by the death in 384 of Praetextatus. With his relative Symmachus, whom he admired as man and writer, Ambrose remained personally on good terms.

From time to time the pagan senators renewed their efforts, putting less emphasis on the Altar of Victory and more on the endowments and state support of the cults. Thus an approach was made to Theodosius in 389 or 390, at a time when he may have been thought to be fretting over his humiliation by Ambrose in the affair of Callinicum. The deputation arrived, Ambrose went to the palace to persuade the emperor against it, and, by his own account (*Letter* 57), got Theodosius to accept his advice. It looks, however, as if the emperor rather resented the bishop's officiousness. He refused the deputation's requests, but also gave orders to the members of his Consistory that they were not to communicate its secrets to Ambrose. Hence the awkward position in which Ambrose found himself at the time of the massacre at Thessalonica (*Letter* 51). Theodosius's own resolution to destroy paganism was soon demonstrated by the law *Nemo se hostiis* of February, 391, which forbade pagan sacrifices, the similar law addressed to Egypt in June, which resulted in the destruction of the *Serapeum* at Alexandria, and the law *Nullus omnino* of November, 392, which prohibited all forms of pagan worship.

Late in 391, when Valentinian II was in Gaul and Ambrose at Milan, another senatorial deputation arrived to ask for the return of the endowments. The Consistory favoured this, but Valentinian refused, this time without pressure from Ambrose. Soon afterwards he quarrelled with Count Arbogast and either committed suicide or was murdered on the 15th May, 392. In August the "usurper" Eugenius, nominally a Christian, was proclaimed emperor. Before long, two more petitions reached him from the Senate, appealing for the endowments. So long as he hoped to secure the recognition of Theodosius, it would have been highly inexpedient for Eugenius to consent; so he turned them away with kind words. But when Theodosius showed his hand in 393, Eugenius was compelled to woo the pagan party. He received another deputation, and this time he probably promised to restore the sacrifices and the Altar of Victory (though there is no direct proof of this) and he compromised ingeniously about the endowments. They were handed over to pagan senators as individuals, no doubt on the understanding that they would be applied to the cults. As a result of all this, Ambrose avoided Eugenius when he went to Milan, and in effect excommunicated him (*Letter* 57). But Eugenius had secured Italy. There was a brief pagan revival at Rome, until his victory at the River Frigidus made Theodosius's position secure, and with it his establishment of Christianity as the religion of the empire. The Altar of Victory was of course removed; the statue itself seems to have been replaced about 399, and, if so, was presumably banished for ever under the legislation of 408 against heathen statues.

Letter 17

THE TEXT

Bishop Ambrose to the most blessed prince and most Christian
emperor Valentinian.

1. As all who live under the sway of Rome serve you, the
emperors and princes of the world, so you serve Almighty God
and the holy faith. There can be no other assurance of prosperity than the universal and sincere worship of the true God,
the Christian God, by whom all things are governed. For he
alone is the true God, who is to be worshipped from the bottom
of the heart. "As for the Gods of the heathen, they are but
demons," as Scripture says.[1]

2. The servant of the true God, bound to worship him with
heartfelt affection, offers him not neglect or weakness of principle, but eager faith and devotion. Or if not that, at all events
he must not countenance any worship of idols or observance
of profane ceremonies. God is not mocked, unto whom all
the secrets of the heart are open.

3. Therefore, Sir, seeing that from a Christian emperor
God demands not faith alone, but zeal and care and devotion
in the exercise of faith, I wonder how some have come to hope
that you may feel it your duty to order the restoration of heathen
altars and to provide the funds necessary for profane sacrifices.
When the endowments have so long been appropriated to the
privy purse or the treasury,[2] it will be thought that you are
making a grant from your own resources rather than restoring
something of their own.

4. Who are they who are complaining about their losses?
The men who never spared our blood, the men who laid our
churches in ruins. They petition you for privileges when not
long ago, by Julian's law,[3] they denied us the common right

---

[1] Psalm 96 (95):3. [2] *Fisco vel arcae.*
[3] Julian's law *Magistros* of the 17th June, 362 (*C. Theod.*, XIII, iii, 5),

to speak and teach—privileges, too, by which even Christians were not seldom deceived. For by these privileges they frequently tried to trap Christians, sometimes through their inadvertence, sometimes because they were anxious to escape the burden of public duties.[4] And because all men are not firm, even under Christian emperors many fell.

5. Had these privileges not been removed already, I should recommend their abolition to you, Sir. As, however, they have been withdrawn and annulled for the greater part of the world by many former emperors,[5] while at Rome your Grace's brother Gratian, of august memory, in view of his loyalty to the true faith, removed and repealed them by rescripts, I beg you not to tear up decisions made out of regard for the faith, and not to rescind your brother's rescripts. No one thinks that his civil legislation should be treated lightly. Are his religious ordinances to be trampled under foot?

6. Let no one take advantage of your youth. If it is a pagan who makes this demand, he must not shackle your mind with the fetters of his own superstition. No, when you see him defending falsehood with all the passion of truth, his own zeal should teach and admonish you how zealous you should be for the true faith. That deference is due to the merits of distinguished men, I entirely agree.[6] But God, of course, is to be preferred to all men.

7. If counsel is required on military matters, one must look

enacted that all teachers must be patterns of morality, examined and appointed by the local magistrates and confirmed in office by the emperor himself. Julian's own *Letter* 61 and references by historians show that this was interpreted to exclude Christians from teaching grammar, rhetoric, or philosophy, on the ground that they could not honestly use the pagan classics.

[4] Some pagan priests were as such exempt from certain obligations to the State (*munera*), such as serving in the army or as town councillors. That Christians might square their consciences and undertake such priesthoods (which perhaps came to them by inheritance) is shown by the law of 386 (*C. Theod.* XII, i, 112) forbidding them to do so. Gratian's legislation of 382 included the removal of these privileges, so that their restoration was one of the objects of the senatorial deputation. There is a good deal of fourth century law on similar privileges for the Christian clergy. It is summarized in Fliche et Martin, *Histoire de l'Eglise*, III, 519–525.

[5] Constantine, Constans, and Constantius all passed laws against parts of the pagan cultus, though they were not strictly enforced. The official cults and priesthoods at Rome had been tolerated up to Gratian's time.

[6] An allusion to Symmachus.

for the opinion of a man versed in war and take his advice.[7]
When religion is under consideration, turn your mind to God.
No one is injured by having almighty God preferred to him.
The pagan has his own views. You do not compel him to worship anything against his will. You, Sir, should be allowed the
same freedom. No one should take it ill if he cannot extort
from the emperor what he would dislike the emperor wanting
to extort from him. Even for the heathen the apostate mind has
no attraction. A man should frankly defend his convictions
and adhere to his purpose.

8. If any nominal Christians think there should be some such
decree, I hope your mind will not be captured by mere words;
I trust empty names will not deceive you. To urge this—still
more to order it—is tantamount to offering sacrifice. Better,
no doubt, the sacrifice of one than the lapse of all. Every
Christian member of the Senate is endangered by this proposal.

9. Suppose today some pagan emperor (which God forbid!)
were to set up an altar to idols and compel Christians to meet
there, to be present while sacrifices are going on, to be choked
with ashes from the altar, with the cinders of sacrilege, with
smoke from the brazier, to vote in a Senate-House in which they
take the oath at the altar of an idol before they are asked for
their votes (for as they understand it, the altar is placed there
so that every meeting shall deliberate under oath to it), and all
this despite the present Christian majority in the Senate. Would
that not be regarded as persecution by a Christian who was
compelled to attend the Senate with such a choice before him?
And compulsion is often used. Improper means are adopted
to compel them to attend. With *you* emperor, then, are Christians to be forced to swear by an altar? An oath is an acknowledgment of divine power in him whom you invoke to guarantee
your good faith. With *you* emperor, are there petitions and
demands that you should order the erection of an altar and
provide funds for profane sacrifices?

10. No such decree can be made without sacrilege. Therefore
I ask you not to decree or order it, and not to put your signature
to any decrees of the kind. As a bishop of Christ, I appeal to
your faith. We should all have joined in appealing to you,
all the bishops, had not the news that something of the sort had
been put forward in your Consistory or been requested by the
Senate come so suddenly and been so hard to believe. But I
must not say that the Senate requested it. It was only a few

7 An allusion, probably, to Count Bauto.

pagans using the common name. When they tried to obtain this, some two years ago, the holy Damasus, by divine appointment Bishop of Rome, sent me a petition drawn up by Christian senators in large numbers, protesting that they had given no such authority, that they were not in agreement with pagan petitions like this, and did not consent to it. They complained both publicly and privately that they could not appear in the Senate-house if any such decree were made. Is it fitting that in your times, Christian times, Christian senators should be deprived of their rank,[8] in order that effect may be given to the godless wishes of pagan senators? I sent this petition to your Grace's brother, and it was established that the Senate had not charged any representatives with instructions about the expenses of superstition.

11. It may perhaps be asked why they were not present in the Senate on the occasion when the petition was drawn up. But their absence speaks clearly enough for their wishes, and it was sufficient for them to speak to the emperor. Can we be surprised that private citizens at Rome are robbed of their freedom of opposition by men who are unwilling that *you* should be free not to command what you disapprove, and free to observe what you think right.

12. Remembering therefore the mission lately entrusted to me,[9] I once more appeal to your faith, I appeal to your conscience, not to answer this heathen petition favourably and not to put a blasphemous signature to answers of that kind. At least refer the question to your Piety's kinsman,[10] Prince Theodosius, whom you have been accustomed to consult on almost all matters of importance. Nothing is more important than religion, nothing is higher than faith.

13. If this were a civil affair, the right to reply would be reserved for the opposing party. But it is an affair of religion. I appeal to you as a bishop. Let me be given a copy of the *Memorial* which was sent to you, so that I can reply to it in detail. Then let your Grace's kinsman be consulted on the

---

[8] Not literally, but effectively, since they would not be able to enter the Senate-house.

[9] I.e., by Damasus in 382, the "two years ago" of § 10.

[10] *Parens*, as again in § 13. Theodosius was not related by blood to Valentinian, but the usage is common within the imperial "family." Since Theodosius was *in loco parentis* to his young colleague, it could be translated "father" but for the reference to his real father (*pater*) below. It is true that Theodosius married Valentinian's sister, Galla, but this had not yet happened.

whole matter and vouchsafe to give us his answer. If anything different is decided, we bishops can certainly not accept it with equanimity and take no notice of it. You may come to church as you please, but you will find no bishop there, or else one who will resist you.

14. How will you answer a bishop who says to you: "The Church does not want your offerings, for you have adorned heathen temples with your offerings. The altar of Christ rejects your gifts, for you have made an altar to idols. It was your word, your hand, your signature, your doing. The Lord Jesus refuses and repudiates your service, for you have served idols. He told you: 'Ye cannot serve two masters'.[11] The virgins consecrated to God have no privileges from you. Do the Vestal virgins claim them? Why do you want God's priests, when you have preferred to them the godless petitions of the heathen? We cannot associate ourselves with another man's sin."?

15. How will you answer these words? That you are only a boy, and that is how you fell? But every age is made perfect in Christ, every age is fulfilled in God.[12] Childhood in faith is no excuse. Even children have confessed Christ fearlessly before their persecutors.

16. How will you answer your brother?[13] Will he not say to you: "I did not deem myself conquered, for I left you emperor. I did not grieve to die, for I left you my heir. I did not mourn my lost rule, for I believed that my rulings, especially concerning true religion, would endure for all ages. These were the record of my piety and virtue; these trophies of triumph over the world, these spoils of the devil, this booty won from our common adversary, were my offering, the offerings of an eternal victory. What more could my enemy have taken from me? You have repealed my decrees—a thing which he who took up arms against me has not done as yet. Now my body is struck by a deadlier weapon, for my ordinances are condemned by my brother. You are endangering a better part of me, for that was the death of my body, this is the death of my virtues. Only now is my rule ended, ended—to make the blow heavier—by your subjects, by my own subjects; and what is brought to an end is that which even my enemies praised in me. If you acquiesced willingly, you have condemned my faith; if you yielded against your will, you have betrayed your own. Therefore, I say (and this is the heavier blow), my danger lies in you."

11 Matt. 6: 24, slightly misquoted.   12 Perhaps *for* Christ, *for* God.
13 Gratian, his half-brother.

17. How will you answer your father,[14] who will address you with greater grief and say: "You have judged very ill of me, my son, if you thought I could ever have connived at idolatry. No one informed me that there was an altar in the Senate-House at Rome. I never imagined anything so wicked as that, in the common council of Christians and heathen, the heathen were offering sacrifice, that the heathen were triumphing over the Christians present, that Christians were being compelled against their wills to be present at sacrifices. Many different crimes were committed while I was emperor. I punished all that were detected. If any offender escaped my notice, shall he say that I approved what no one brought to my attention? You have judged very ill of me if you think that the superstition of others, and not my own faith, kept my empire safe."

18. You must see, Sir, that if you decree any such thing, you wrong first God, and then your father and brother. I beg that you will do that which you know will be profitable for your salvation in the sight of God.

[14] Valentinian I, who ruled the western empire mostly from Trier, and so can be represented as not understanding the effect upon Christians in Rome of his toleration of the Altar, etc. Symmachus more credibly refers to Valentinian's turning a blind eye (*dissimulatio proximorum*). It is noteworthy that Ambrose is here replying to the drift of Symmachus's *Relatio* even if he has not yet procured the full text of it.

Letters 20 and 21 : The Battle of the Basilicas

INTRODUCTION

AMBROSE'S TRIUMPH IN THE CASE OF THE ALTAR OF Victory in A.D. 384 was proof of his influence over Valentinian II, but no guarantee of continuously good relations with the imperial family. The empress-mother, Justina, was an Arian, and an aggressive one, with a grudge already against Ambrose because he had frustrated her attempt to secure the election of an Arian bishop for Sirmium when she was residing there. In Milan she became the natural centre of the Arian party, a party composed mainly of court officials and Gothic soldiers serving in the Roman army, the Goths having been converted to Christianity in an Arian form. If we can trust Ambrose on such a point, none of the citizens of Milan were Arians; though one would suppose that some few adherents of Auxentius survived. There were also refugees from Illyricum, a district in which Arianism flourished for a time. This party found a bishop in the person of a second Auxentius, usually identified with Auxentius, Bishop of Durostorum in Moesia, who was deposed from his see by Theodosius in A.D. 383.

Were the Arians of Milan to have their own place of worship? The easy solution of building one does not seem to have been tried; much better to score off the catholics by getting one of their churches. In 379 they secured one of the existing basilicas, but Gratian first sequestrated it and later restored it to Ambrose (*De Spiritu Sancto*, I, 1, 19–21). No further claim is heard of until 385. Whatever Ambrose might have thought about a church in his diocese built by Arians for Arians, he was not going to hand a catholic church over to heretics. The point of law might be arguable. On the one hand it was claimed that in the last resort all property belonged to the emperor. Thus Gratian had sequestrated a basilica, Theodosius, to the joy of the orthodox, had taken churches from Arian bishops, and Ambrose was to support the closing of pagan temples by law. On the other hand he could argue, as Symmachus had done, that by the ancient law and custom of Rome, temples and their belongings became the property of the god to whom they were dedicated, so that spoliation, even when done by the State under the forms of law, was always sacrilege. But Ambrose was not much concerned with the legal issues. This was to him a religious issue, a cause of God. Only the bishop could judge what was right, and he had a plain duty to God which he must perform at all costs. The battle of the basilicas very well illustrates Ambrose's attitude to the State, in theory and practice. Again he was victorious.

The highly dramatic course of events is related in three documents, *Letters* 20 and 21 and the *Sermon against Auxentius*. Unfortunately there are serious difficulties of chronology and topography, though these scarcely affect the value of the letters for the purpose of the present volume. One story, the more usual one, though minor variations are possible within it, runs as follows. First, during Lent 385, Ambrose was summoned before the Consistory and ordered to give the Portian basilica over to the Arians. He refused. A mob gathered outside the palace to support him, and this he dispelled at the request of the military commander. This incident is known from the *Sermon*, c. 29, where it is said to have happened "last year." Secondly, on the 4th April, 385, Ambrose was ordered to deliver up the *Basilica Nova*, and again refused. The government then tried once more to secure the *Portiana*, but gave up the attempt on Maundy Thursday. Ambrose tells the story of these days in a letter to his sister, *Letter* 20, written, on this view, in April, 385. Thirdly, after a pause of many months, Justina and Auxentius took their revenge, securing from Valentinian a law, promulgated on the 23rd January, 386, which allowed freedom of assembly for public worship to all who accepted the faith of the Council of Ariminum, 359, while those who opposed the law and tried to monopolize public worship were threatened with the death penalty for sedition. Ambrose was then ordered to surrender a basilica, but refused, exposing himself to this penalty. He was summoned before the Consistory, but refused to go, remonstrating with Valentinian in *Letter* 21 and preaching against Auxentius (perhaps on Palm Sunday); and so obviously had he the support of the citizens, and even of some of the Gothic soldiers, that the Court had again to give up its

demands. Auxentius disappears from history, and the prestige
of Ambrose was further enhanced by his discovery of the relics
of Gervasius and Protasius in June, 386.

The above chronology is retained by Dudden, though he
does not put the *Sermon* on Palm Sunday. Palanque, however,
working upon the hints of former scholars such as Seeck, places
Letter 20 in 386, after *Letter* 21 and the *Sermon*, partly because the
reasons adduced in favour of the other chronology are uncon-
vincing, and partly because the details of what, on the older
view, are two major incidents, are so similar as to point to only
one major crisis. In that case, the first episode, referred to in
the *Sermon*, c. 29, took place in 385 and was followed by Justina's plot and the law of January, 386, leading up to another
attack in Lent 386, to which *Letter* 21 refers, and coming to its
conclusion in Holy Week, as described in *Letter* 20.

There is much to be said for this reconstruction. It is certain
that *Letter* 21 and the *Sermon against Auxentius* belong together,
and that both are subsequent to the law promulgated in
January, 386. It is certain that *Letter* 20 covers a Palm Sunday.
It had been supposed by some that the *Sermon* was preached on
a Palm Sunday, since it refers to the reading of the Triumphal
Entry as a lesson; and as this could not be the Palm Sunday of
Letter 20, it appeared to follow that attacks occurred in two
Holy Weeks, 385 (*Letter* 20) and 386 (*Letter* 21 and *Sermon*).
But the lesson was read *casu*, by chance, and not in course, so
that the *Sermon* need not have been preached (one might say,
definitely was not preached) on a Palm Sunday. Dudden allows
this, and puts the incidents and the *Sermon* earlier in Lent, 386.
But this really takes away much of the case for supposing *Letter*
20 to refer to 385, and there are solid advantages in placing it
in 386. To take one example, *Letter* 20 tells how some Gothic
soldiers who were investing the basilica went over to the catholic side, while Augustine in his *Confessions* says that the introduction of antiphonal chanting and hymn-singing (he was
there) happened a year before his baptism, which took place
at Easter, 387. Now Paulinus, in his life of Ambrose, associates
the desertion of the Goths with the occasion of the changes in
singing, and it is unlikely that there were similar desertions in
successive years. Though the argument is not demonstrative,
since Paulinus is not very trustworthy on chronological details
and there were two investments of churches whichever chronology we adopt, the balance of probability seems to lie with
Palanque, and accordingly the letters are here printed in the

order 21, 20. That *Letter* 20 makes no reference to Auxentius
or the law of January, 386, need not disturb us, since Marcellina
plainly knew what had happened up to the point at which the
letter starts.

The topographical difficulty is twofold, to discover what
basilica Ambrose is speaking of at each stage, and to identify
them with later churches. The *Basilica Vetus* must be the ancient
cathedral of Milan, usually assumed to be outside the walls,
near one of the cemeteries. Savio identified it with SS. Nabore
e Felice, Cardinal Schuster with S. Lorenzo. The *Basilica Nova*,
within the walls, is certainly the later S. Tecla, on the site of
the present cathedral. In Ambrose's time it was beginning to
replace the *Vetus* as the effective cathedral. The *Portiana*, certainly outside the walls, is identified with S. Vittore ad Corpus
by Savio and many others, but with S. Eustorgio by Schuster.

If Letter 21 precedes *Letter* 20, it will have been occasioned
by the demand for the *Portiana*, and the *Sermon against Auxentius*
will have been preached in that church while it was surrounded
by troops. If 20 precedes 21, the basilica of the *Sermon* may have
been the *Nova*. Within *Letter* 20, it is fairly clear that Ambrose
is performing the Holy Week services in his cathedral proper,
the *Vetus*, up to Wednesday, but it seems likely that he was in
the *Portiana* on Maundy Thursday. Meanwhile, the *Nova* also
was invested. It is not clear whether all the references to the
hangings used to indicate confiscation to the State are to their
employment at the *Portiana* only, or, as seems likely, at the
Nova as well.

Letter 21

THE TEXT

Bishop Ambrose to the most gracious Emperor and most blessed Augustus Valentinian.

1. Dalmatius, tribune and secretary, cited me by order of your Grace, as he alleged, requiring me to choose judges, as Auxentius had done.[1] He did not mention the names of those who have been asked for, but added that the disputation would take place in the Consistory, with your Piety as the final arbiter.

2. To this I have, I believe, a sufficient answer. No one should regard me as contumacious when I assert what your father, of august memory, not only answered by word of mouth but also sanctioned by law, that in a matter of faith or ecclesiastical discipline the judge must not be inferior in office or different in standing. These are the words of the rescript, and they mean that he wished bishops to be judged by bishops. Again, if a bishop was to be prosecuted on other charges and a matter of conduct was to be examined, he wished that this also should come before a court of bishops.[2]

3. Who, then, has answered your Grace contumaciously? He who desires to see you like your father, or he who would have you different from him? Or are there perhaps some who set no store by that great emperor's opinion, despite the fact that his faith was proved by the constancy of his profession[3]

---

[1] *Judices*, here arbitrators almost, as if this were a personal dispute between Ambrose and Auxentius rather than a "cause of God."

[2] The law that bishops must be judged by their peers in matters of conduct as well as faith and ecclesiastical discipline is an omen of much to come, for example, the disputes between Becket and Henry II. It dates, apparently, from 367, but is known only from this passage and a reference to it by the Council of Rome, 378.

[3] According to Socrates, *H.E.*, III, 13, Jovian, Valentinian, and Valens all resigned their military offices under Julian rather than sacrifice. Sozomen, *H.E.* VI, 6, has a more elaborate story.

and his wisdom proclaimed by the improvement in the state of the country?

4. When did your gracious Majesty ever hear of laymen judging bishops in a matter of faith? Are we so prostrate with flattery as to forget the rights of a bishop? so that I should contemplate entrusting to others what God has given to me? What will happen next, if a bishop is to be instructed by a layman? The layman holding forth, the bishop listening, the bishop learning from the layman! In view of the holy Scriptures and the precedents of antiquity, it is impossible to deny that in a matter of faith—in a matter of faith, I repeat—it is the practice for bishops to judge Christian emperors, and not emperors bishops.

5. God willing, you will one day reach a riper age, and then you will know what to think of a bishop who allows laymen to trample on his episcopal rights. Your father, a man of mature years, by the favour of God, used to say: "It is not for me to judge between bishops." [4] Now your Grace is saying: "I must be the judge." He, baptized in Christ as he was, thought himself unequal to the responsibility of such a judgment. Do you, Sir, who have yet to earn the sacrament of baptism,[5] take upon yourself to pronounce judgment concerning the faith, when you do not yet know the sacraments of the faith?

6. What sort of judges he has chosen, when he is afraid to make their names known, can be left to the imagination. If he has found some, let them by all means come to church and listen with the people, not sitting as judges but deciding as individuals which side to choose when they have examined their own feelings. The matter before us concerns the Bishop of Milan. If the people listen to Auxentius and decide that he has the better case, let them follow his faith. I shall not be jealous.

7. I pass over the fact that the people themselves have already decided. I will not mention that they asked your Grace's father for their present bishop. I will not mention that your Piety's father guaranteed the chosen candidate freedom from

---

4 Valentinian I "considered that ecclesiastical matters were beyond the range of his jurisdiction" (Sozomen, *H.E.*, VI, 21). For a summary of his religious policy see Dudden, *St. Ambrose*, I, 84–86.

5 Valentinian II never was baptized, for he died while Ambrose was on his way to Gaul to baptize him (cf. p. 259). In his funeral oration Ambrose said that Valentinian had been washed by his piety and desire for baptism.

disturbance if he accepted the See. It was in reliance on those promises that I acted.[6]

8. But if he is priding himself on foreign supporters who think he should have the title of bishop, he had better be bishop of the place they come from. I neither accept him as bishop nor know where he comes from.

9. How can we decide a matter on which you have already made your own decision known, Sir; on which, indeed, you have already made it illegal to reach any other decision? In binding others by this rule, you bound yourself as well. The emperor should be the first to keep his own laws. Would you like me to make an experiment, to see whether the chosen judges will come contrary to your decree or whether they will excuse themselves on the ground that they cannot go against so stringent and peremptory an order from the emperor?

10. Only a bishop more contumacious than respectful would do such a thing. May I point out, Sir, that already you are partially rescinding your own law.[7] Would that it were wholly revoked! For I would not have your law above the law of God. God's law has taught us what to follow, a thing which man's laws cannot do. They often compel a change in the timid, but they cannot inspire faith.

11. The order was published simultaneously in many provinces: "Opposition to the emperor will be punished with death; all who fail to surrender the temple of God will be executed at once." Is it likely that anyone reading of that will have the courage to say to the emperor, by himself or as one of a small group: "I do not approve of your law"? If the bishops are not allowed to say this, are the laity? Shall judgment concerning the faith be given by one who is hoping for a favour or afraid to give offence?

12. Again, am I to sin by choosing as judges laymen who, if they are true to their faith, will be proscribed or put to death

---

[6] The people had decided when Ambrose was acclaimed as bishop. Valentinian had confirmed the election, "highly gratified to learn that the judges he had himself appointed were in demand as bishops" (Paulinus, *Vita Ambrosii*, 8).

[7] The law of the 23rd January, 386, threatened those who opposed it with death. Therefore (i) if any laymen agreed to act as arbitrators between Ambrose and Auxentius, they were in effect questioning the law and exposing themselves to its penalty (§§ 9, 12), and it would be wrong for a bishop to bring them into this danger; (ii) when Valentinian gives orders for this discussion between Ambrose and Auxentius, he is going back on his own law (cf. §16).

under the provisions of the law "Concerning the Faith"?
Am I to make them choose between apostasy and punishment?

13. Ambrose is not important enough to justify the degrada-
tion of the episcopal office on his account. One life is not as
precious as the dignity of the whole episcopate, on whose advice
I have written this letter.[8] Auxentius, they suggested, might well
choose a pagan or a Jew, and if we allowed them to pronounce
judgment concerning Christ, we should be giving them a
triumph over Christ. What more can they desire than to hear
Christ insulted? What could please them better than to have
Christ's divinity denied—which God forbid? Naturally they
are in entire agreement with the Arian who says that Christ is a
creature. No pagan or Jew will be slow to make that confession.

14. This word "creature" was accepted at the Synod of
Ariminum, a council I cannot but abhor, since I adhere to the
creed of the Council of Nicaea, from which neither death nor
the sword shall separate me.[9] This is the faith which your
Grace's father, the most blessed emperor Theodosius, approved
and follows.[10] This is the faith of Gaul and of Spain, upheld
by them together with pious confession of the Spirit of God.[11]

---

[8] Ambrose has gathered some neighbouring bishops to advise and support
him (cf. §17); but Palanque perhaps goes too far in wishing to rank this
as a Council of Milan.

[9] The Council of Ariminum of A.D. 359, composed of some four hundred
western bishops, began by reaffirming the Nicene faith (cf. §16), but the
legates whom it sent to Constantius at Constantinople were induced to
sign the homœan *Dated Creed* of the 22nd May, 359, which was then
accepted by the whole Council, as it was by the eastern churches, though
their Council of Seleucia had been a victory, if a short-lived one, of Basil
of Ancyra's homœousian party over the homœans. As Jerome said:
"the whole world groaned and was astonished to find itself Arian."
But even the *Dated Creed* did not use the word "creature." Ambrose,
who elsewhere makes the same charge against Ariminum, may have been
thinking of the equivocations of Valens and Ursacius, who said that they
had not, in their recantation at the beginning of the Council: "denied
that he was a creature, but that he was like other creatures" (Jerome,
Dial. adv. Luciferianos, 19). Justina's attempt to put the clock back to
359 was superficially clever, but entirely against the movement of thought
since that year.

[10] Theodosius was baptized by the "Nicene" Acholius, Bishop of Thessalonica, and had "established" orthodoxy and legislated against heresy in
380 and 382.

[11] The West reaffirmed its Nicene orthodoxy as soon as Constantius was
out of the way. The mention of Gaul and Spain reminds Valentinian
that Maximus proclaims himself a guardian of orthodoxy, and perhaps
even hints that catholic Christians may have to transfer their allegiance
to him if Valentinian betrays the faith.

15. If there must be discussion, I have learned to discuss in church, like my predecessors. If conference on the faith is necessary, it should be a conference of bishops, as under the emperor Constantine of august memory. He did not pass laws beforehand, but left the bishops free to decide. It was the same also under the emperor Constantius of august memory, a worthy heir to his father.[12] Though what began well, ended otherwise. For at first the bishops had subscribed to the pure faith, but some who wanted to let the palace decide concerning the faith, managed to get the bishops' first decisions altered by fraud.[13] But they at once revoked their perverted decision. There is no doubt that the majority at Ariminum approved the faith of the Council of Nicaea and condemned the Arian tenets.

16. Perhaps Auxentius will appeal to a synod to dispute about the faith. It is not necessary to weary so many bishops on account of a single person who, even if he were an angel from heaven, should not be preferred to the peace of the Church. However, when I hear of a synod assembling, I shall not be absent. So rescind the law, if you want us to hold a disputation.

17. I would have come to your Consistory, Sir, to put these considerations before you, had the bishops or the people allowed me to come. They said that discussion of the faith must take place in church in the presence of the people.

18. I could wish, Sir, that your message had not told me I might go into retirement wherever I pleased. I went out every day without any guards. You should have sent me wherever you pleased, for I was ready to submit to anything. But now the bishops are saying to me: "It makes little difference whether you leave the altar of Christ voluntarily or surrender it; if you leave it, you will be surrendering it."

19. If only it were clear to me that the church would not be handed over to the Arians, I would gladly submit to your Piety's will. But if I am the only trouble-maker, why has an order been given to invade all the other churches? If only it

12 *Paternae dignitatis herede.* It is odd to find Ambrose calling Constantius an heir to Constantine's *worth*, even with the qualification that follows; for he had all the time been attacking the Nicene party. But has the alternative translation, "heir to his father's throne (rank)" any point? Constantius had, of course, attacked paganism, which may be in Ambrose's mind. More particularly, Ariminum had *begun* without any imperial pressure on the bishops.

13 Primarily Valens and Ursacius, who were in regular attendance upon Constantius at Sirmium and even upon his travels, as at Arles, 353. They were responsible for the adoption of the *Dated Creed.*

were certain that no one would molest the churches, I would gladly accept any sentence passed upon me.

20. Be so good, Sir, as to accept my reasons for not coming to the Consistory. I have not learned how to stand up in the Consistory except on your behalf;[14] and I cannot dispute within the palace, for I neither know nor seek to know the secrets of the palace.

21. I, Bishop Ambrose, offer this remonstrance to the most gracious emperor and most blessed Augustus, Valentinian.

[14] A reference to his embassy to Maximus, *Letter* 24 § 3 (p. 221).

Letter 20

THE TEXT

(Ambrose to his sister, Marcellina)[1]

1. As nearly all your letters ask anxiously about the church, let me tell you what is happening. The day after I received the letter in which you told me how worried you were by your dreams, I began to feel the pressure of a heavy load of troubles. It was no longer the Portian Basilica, the one outside the walls, that was demanded, but the New Basilica, the one inside the walls, the larger one.

2. First some "mighty men of valour", Counts of the Consistory, called upon me to surrender the basilica and to ensure that the people made no disturbance. I answered that of course a bishop could not surrender God's temple.

3. Next day, this was applauded in church.[2] The Prefect himself came there and began to urge us to give up at least the Portian Basilica. The people shouted that down, so he went off, saying that he would report to the emperor.

4. The next day, Sunday, after the lessons and the sermon, when the catechumens had been dismissed, I was delivering the Creed to some candidates in the baptistery of the basilica. There I was informed that, having discovered that they had sent officials from the palace to the Portian Basilica and that they were putting up the hangings, some of the people were going

---

[1] Ambrose's sister, Marcellina, to whom this letter was sent, was older than himself. After the death of their father, she lived with her mother in Rome. In A.D. 353 she dedicated herself to virginity, living an ascetic life at home, as many of the great ladies of Rome did in the fourth century (see St. Jerome's letters, *passim*). She survived her brother. Other extant letters to her are 22, describing the finding of the bodies of Gervasius and Protasius, and 41 (p. 240).

[2] *Ecclesia* here, not *basilica*, and probably meaning the cathedral, the *Basilica Vetus*, cf. §10.

there. However, I went on with my duties and began to celebrate Mass.[3]

5. While I was offering, I was told that the people had
carried off a certain Castulus, a presbyter by Arian reckoning.
They had come upon him in the street as they went by. I
burst into tears, and during the oblation I prayed for God's
help to prevent any bloodshed over the church, or at least
that it should be my own blood that was shed, not only for the
sake of my people, but for the ungodly also. In short, I sent
presbyters and deacons and rescued the man from violence.

6. At once very heavy penalties were decreed, first upon the
whole body of merchants. So in Holy Week, when it is customary to release debtors from their bonds, we heard the grating of
chains put on innocent men's necks, and two hundred pounds'
weight of gold was demanded within three days. They replied
that they would give as much again, and double that, if they
were asked, provided they could keep their faith. The prisons
were full of business men.

7. All the functionaries of the palace—the secretaries, the
agents, the various magistrates' apparitors—were ordered to
stay indoors, on the pretext that they were being prevented from
getting involved in sedition. Men of rank were threatened
with severe trouble if they did not surrender the basilica.
Persecution was flaring up, and had the door been opened, it
seems likely that they would have broken out into violence without limit.

8. The counts and tribunes called on me to surrender the
basilica without delay. They said that the emperor was within
his rights, since everything came under his authority. I replied
that if he asked me for anything of my own, my estates, my
money, anything of mine like that, I should not refuse it, though
everything that belonged to me belonged to the poor. "But,"
I said, "the things of God are not subject to the authority of
the emperor. If he wants my patrimony, take it; if my body,
I will go at once. Do you mean to carry me off to prison, or to
death? I shall be delighted. I shall not shelter myself behind a
crowd of people. I shall not lay hold of the altar and beg for
my life. I will gladly sacrifice myself for the sake of the altar."

9. In fact, I was horrified to learn that armed men had been
sent to occupy the basilica of the church. I was afraid that in

---

[3] *Missam facere*, perhaps the earliest instance of this use. Some take it to
refer here to the dismissal of the catechumens, but "began" (*coepi*)
after the *dimissis catechumenis* above is against that interpretation.

defence of the basilica there might be some bloodshed, which would lead to the destruction of the whole city. I prayed that I might not survive the ruin of so great a city, or perhaps all Italy. I shrank with loathing from the odium of shedding blood; I offered my own throat. Some officers of the Goths were there, and I spoke to them, and said: "Did Rome give you a home so that you might show yourselves disturbers of public order? Where will you go next if these parts are destroyed?"

10. I was pressed to restrain the people. I said in return that while it lay in my power not to excite them, to pacify them was in God's hands. To conclude, if he thought that I was instigating them, I ought to be punished at once, or banished to whatever lonely part of the world he chose. At these words, they went off, and I stayed the whole day in the Old Basilica. Then I went back home to sleep, so that if anyone wanted to arrest me, he would find me ready.

11. Before daylight, when I set foot outside, the basilica was surrounded and occupied by soldiers. There was a rumour that the soldiers had sent word to the emperor that if he wished to go there, the way was clear. If they saw him joining the catholics, they would attend him. If not, they would go over to the congregation under Ambrose.

12. Not one of the Arians dared go there, for there were none among the citizens, just a few in the royal household, and some Goths. Being used to a waggon for a home, they were now making their waggon a church.[4] Everywhere that woman goes, she transports her sect with her.

13. I could tell from the laments of the people that the basilica was surrounded. But during the lessons I was informed that the New Basilica was also full of people, that the crowd seemed to be larger than when they were all free, and that they were calling for a Reader. In short, when the soldiers who had occupied the basilica learned that I had given orders for their excommunication, they began to come over to our congregation. Seeing them, the women were frightened, and one of them rushed out. However the soldiers explained that they had

---

[4] *Quibus ut olim plaustra sedes erat, ita nunc plaustrum ecclesia est.* This could mean that the Church becomes their waggon, that is, their means of transport, since that woman (Justina) takes her adherents round with her. But my translation tries to observe the order of words, *plaustrum ecclesia*, not *ecclesia plaustrum*, i.e., they are still peripatetic and have to worship *al fresco*, an unkind sneer in the circumstances. I hesitated between the two versions, but my translation receives some support from Jerome, *Letter* 107 §2, where see the note (p. 334).

come to pray, not to fight. The people shouted a little. With restraint, but persistently and faithfully, they asked that I should go to that basilica. It was said also that the people in that basilica were demanding my presence.

14. Then I began this sermon. "My sons, you have heard a lesson from the book of Job, the book appointed to be read through at this season. The devil also knew from our regular practice that we should read this book, in which the whole power of his temptations[5] is laid bare. So today he roused himself to greater energy. But thanks be to our God, who has thus strengthened you with faith and patience. I came up into the pulpit to praise one Job, and I find you all Jobs for me to praise. In each one of you Job has come to life again, in each one of you that holy man's patience and courage have shone out again. What more resolute words could have been spoken by Christian men than those which the Holy Spirit spoke in you today: "We petition, your Majesty, we do not fight; we are not afraid, we petition"? It becomes Christians to pray for peace and quiet, but not to abandon steadfast faith and truth even at the peril of death. For the Lord is our Leader, "who will save them that put their hope in him." [6]

15. But let us come to the lessons before us. You see that the devil is given leave to tempt us. This is to prove the good. The wicked one grudges progress in good and tempts in various ways. He tempted holy Job in his possessions, in his children, and in bodily pain. The stronger is tempted in his own body, the weaker in another's. From me too, he wanted to take my riches, the riches which I have in you. He was anxious to dissipate my possessions, which are your peace. You, my good children, he longed to snatch away from me, you for whom I daily renew the sacrifice. He tried to involve you in the ruins of public disorder. Already, then, I have undergone two kinds of temptation. And perhaps it was because the Lord God knew me to be too weak that he has not yet given him power over my body. Even if I desire it, even if I offer myself, perhaps he judges me still unequal to the conflict, and exercises me with divers labours. Job did not begin with that conflict. He ended with it.

---

[5] Throughout his comments on Job Ambrose is able to use the one word *tentare* and its cognates in senses which vary from "tempt" and "test" to "try" = "annoy". As the meaning "tempt" underlies his whole argument, I have kept it all through except that once, in §18, I translate *tentamina* "trials."

[6] Ps. 17 (16):7.

16. Job was tempted by one messenger of evil after another, and he was tempted also by his wife, who said: "Speak a word against God, and die." [7] You see what a multitude of things is suddenly set in motion against us—Goths, arms, heathen, the merchants' fine, the punishment of the saints. You observe what is commanded in the order. "Surrender the basilica"; in other words, "Speak a word against God, and die." But it is not only speak against God, but act against God. The order is, Surrender the altar of God.

17. So we are pressed by the emperor's commands, but strengthened by the words of Scripture, which answered: "Thou hast spoken as one of the foolish women." [8] This is no small temptation. We know how sharp are the temptations caused by women. Adam, for instance, was brought down by Eve, and so it came about that he departed from the commands of heaven. When he discovered his error, his guilty conscience accusing him, he was anxious to hide, but could not. So God said to him: "Adam, where art thou?" [9] That meant, what were you before? where have you gone now? where did I place you? where have you strayed to on your own? You know that you are naked because you have lost the clothing of good faith. Now you are trying to cover yourself with leaves. You threw away the fruit, you want to hide under the leaves of the Law, but you can be seen. For the sake of a woman you chose to leave the Lord your God, and so you are flying from him whom you used to look for. You have preferred to hide yourself away with a woman, leaving the mirror of the world, the abode of Paradise, the grace of Christ.

18. Need I mention how cruelly Jezebel persecuted Elijah? how Herodias had John the Baptist killed? All men suffer from some woman or other. As for me, the less my poor deserts, the heavier my trials. My strength is less, the danger greater. Woman follows woman, hatred succeeds to hatred, there is no end to their lies, the elders are sent for, all on the plea that the king is being injured. What reason is there for this grievous temptation of a worm like me, unless it is that they are persecuting not me, but the Church?

19. The order comes, Surrender the basilica. I reply: "It is not right for me to surrender it, nor good for your Majesty to receive it. When you have no right to violate the house of a private citizen, do you think that you can appropriate the house

[7] Job 2:9.   [8] Job 2:10.
[9] Gen. 3:9.

of God?" It is alleged that the emperor has the right to do anything, that everything belongs to him. I reply: "Do not burden
yourself, Sir, with the idea that you have any right as emperor
over the things of God. Do not exalt yourself; if you wish to
remain emperor, submit yourself to God. It is written, 'Unto
God the things that are God's, unto Caesar the things that are
Caesar's'.[10] Palaces belong to the emperor, churches to the
bishop. You have been entrusted with jurisdiction over public
buildings, but not over sacred ones." Again I am told that the
emperor's words were: "I also ought to have one basilica."
I answered: "It is not lawful for thee to have her.[11] What have
you to do with an adulteress? For she who is not joined to
Christ in lawful wedlock is an adulteress."

20. While I was preaching, I was told that the imperial
hangings had been taken down, and that the basilica was
packed with people demanding my presence. At once I turned
my sermon in that direction, and said: "How deep and profound are the oracles of the Holy Spirit! You remember,
brethren, the psalm that was read at Matins, how we responded
with heavy hearts: 'O God, the heathen are come into thine
inheritance.'[12] And truly the heathen came, and worse than
heathen. Goths came, and the men of divers nations. They
came in arms, they surrounded and occupied the basilica.
Ignorant of the depth of thy ways, we were grieved at this.
But we were foolish and mistaken.

21. The heathen came. Yes, truly they came into thine
inheritance. Those who came as heathen, became Christians;
those who came to invade thine inheritance, were made co-
heirs of God. I have defenders whom I thought enemies, allies
whom I accounted adversaries. That is fulfilled which the
prophet David sang concerning the Lord Jesus, 'His dwelling
is in peace', and, 'There brake he the horns of the bow, the
shield, the sword, and the battle'.[13] For whose is this gift, this
work, but thine, Lord Jesus? Thou sawest armed men coming
to thy temple; on the one hand, the people groaning and
thronging God's basilica, that they might not be thought to
be surrendering it, on the other hand, the soldiers ordered to
use force. Death was before my eyes, I feared that madness
might have free play. But thou, O Lord, didst set thyself
between and make the twain one. Thou didst restrain the

10 Matt. 22:21.
11 Matt. 14:4. If handed over to Arians, the basilica would be adulterous.
12 Ps. 79 (78):1.   13 Ps. 76 (75):2, 3.

armed men, saying: 'Assuredly, if ye have recourse to arms, if those shut up in my temple are troubled, what profit is there in my blood?' Thanks be to thee, O Christ. No ambassador, no messenger, but thou, O Lord, hast delivered thy people. 'Thou hast put off my sackcloth and girded me with gladness'."[14]

22. So I spoke, wondering that the emperor's mind could be softened by the zeal of the soldiers, the entreaties of the counts, and the people's prayers.[15] Meanwhile I was informed that a secretary had been sent to me with a message. I retired for a while and he gave me the message. "What is in your mind in acting against my pleasure?", it read. I replied: "I do not know the emperor's pleasure, and when it says that I am acting imprudently, I do not understand what is meant." It said: "Why did you send presbyters to the basilica? If you are a usurper, please tell me, so that I may know how to prepare myself against you." I replied that I had done nothing to put the Church in the wrong, but that when I had heard that the basilica was occupied by soldiers, I had only given freer course to my laments; and that when many exhorted me to go there, I had said: "I cannot surrender the basilica, but I must not fight." After I had heard that the imperial hangings had been taken away from it, when the people were demanding that I should go there, I had sent presbyters there, but had refused to go myself, saying: "I believe in Christ that the emperor himself will be with us."

23. If this looks like usurpation, indeed I have arms, but only in the name of Christ. I have the power to offer my own body. Why does he delay to strike, if he thinks me a usurper. By ancient right priests have conferred sovereignty, not usurped it. It is a common saying that sovereigns have coveted priesthood more than priests have coveted sovereignty. Christ fled, that he might not be made king.[16] We have our own power. The priest's power is his weakness. "When I am weak, then am I strong."[17] God has raised up no adversary against him. Let him beware of making a usurper for himself. Maximus does not say that I am usurping Valentinian's authority, though he complains that my embassy prevented him from crossing into Italy.[18] I added that priests had never been usurpers, though they had often suffered from them.

[14] Ps. 30 (29): 11.
[15] The removal of the hangings showed that the emperor had yielded, at least about one of the basilicas.
[16] John 6:15.   [17] II Cor. 12:10.   [18] Cf. *Letter* 24 (p. 222).

24. That whole day was one of distress to me, though the children were amusing themselves by tearing up the imperial hangings. I could not go home, for the soldiers guarding the basilica were all around. We said the psalms with the brethren in the smaller basilica of the church.

25. Next day, the book of Jonah was duly read, and when that was done, I began to preach. "My brothers, the book has been read in which the prophet speaks of sinners turning to repentance. They are accepted in the hope that their present state is an earnest of the future. That righteous man (I added) was ready to incur God's wrath, rather than see or announce the destruction of the city. And because the word of the Lord was gloomy, he was also sad that the gourd withered. And God said to the prophet: 'Art thou sad for the gourd?' Jonah answered, 'Yes, I am sad.'[19] The Lord said, if Jonah was grieved because the gourd withered, how much more ought He to care for the salvation of so many people? and therefore He had put away the destruction prepared for the whole city."

26. Just as I said this, I was told that the emperor had ordered that the troops should be withdrawn from the basilica, and that the money which the merchants had been condemned to pay should be given back. How all the people shouted with joy and gratitude! It was the day on which the Lord gave himself up for us, the day on which the Church brings penance to an end.[20] The soldiers vied with one another in spreading the news, running to the altar and giving the kiss of peace. Then I understood that God had smitten "the worm when the morning rose," [21] that the whole city might be saved.

27. That is the story so far, and I wish it were the end of the matter. But the emperor is talking in an excited way that bodes worse trouble. He calls me a usurper and worse than a usurper. When the counts asked him to go to church, and told him that they were asking this at the request of the soldiers, he replied: "If Ambrose ordered it, you would hand me over to him in chains." After such words, you can judge for yourself what is coming next. Everyone was horrified to hear them; but he has people about him who exasperate him.

[19] Jonah 4:9.
[20] Maundy Thursday, cf. Ambrose, *Hexaemeron*, V, 90, on the fifth day, and preached on a Thursday: "It is the time when the forgiveness of sins (*indulgentia*) is celebrated ... now let the passion of the Lord Jesus hasten on."
[21] Jonah 4:7.

28. To give you an example, the Grand Chamberlain Calligonus [22] dared to address me in particularly violent terms. "Do you flout Valentinian while I am alive? I will have your head off." I answered: "God grant you carry out your threat. I shall suffer as bishops suffer, you will act as eunuchs act." May God keep them from the Church, may they turn all their weapons upon me, and satisfy their thirst in my blood.

[22] Calligonus was himself executed *gladio*, i.e., decapitated, some two years later, cf. Ambrose, *De Joseph*, 33; Augustine, *Contra Julianum Pelagianum*, vi, 41.

Letter 24: Ambrose and Maximus

INTRODUCTION

IN A.D. 383 THE ARMY IN BRITAIN REVOLTED AGAINST Gratian, under the leadership of Magnus Maximus. Gratian was murdered on the 25th August, and Maximus secured control of Britain and Gaul, which he ruled from Trier. He aspired to be acknowledged as a legitimate Augustus, and invited the boy Valentinian II to place himself under his parental care at Trier, which would have made him master of the whole of the West. Milan, now the residence of Valentinian and his mother Justina, feared an invasion of Italy; and so, while Count Bauto occupied the Alpine passes, Ambrose was asked to negotiate peace with Maximus—so far as is known, the first employment of a bishop on a secular diplomatic mission. Its story is told retrospectively in *Letter* 24. Up to a point it was satisfactory to both parties, for peace was secured and Maximus was acknowledged as Augustus, even—after a time—by Theodosius. But Maximus afterwards claimed that he had been deceived by ambiguous words about a promised visit of Valentinian and so cajoled out of his contemplated invasion of Italy.

In A.D. 386[1] Milan once more expected invasion from Gaul, and once more Ambrose was sent to Trier to make peace. This time his mission, reported in *Letter* 24, was a complete failure. Indeed, so undiplomatic was his behaviour that one can only conclude that he had never seen any possibility of conciliation. It has even been suggested that Justina had planned that, if she could not have peace, she should at least be able to discredit her unsuccessful ambassador. Ambrose, for his part, took care not to compromise himself by association with Maximus, and the last words of his letter warn Valentinian to expect

[1] The old date was 387 (e.g., Tillemont). Rauschen put this second embassy in 384, and was followed by Seeck and von Campenhausen. Palanque argues the case for 386 in his *Saint Ambroise*, pp. 516–518. Dudden follows Palanque.

war. When it came in the autumn of 387, Valentinian fled with
Justina to Thessalonica, and Maximus easily secured Italy.
Stirred to action at last, Theodosius marched against Maximus,
who was defeated and executed near Aquileia in August, 388.
Valentinian went to administer Gaul, and Theodosius took
charge of Italy as well as the East, thus being brought into
closer touch with Ambrose at Milan.

One passage in the letter needs further explanation. In the
370's the Spanish church was troubled, for good or ill, by an
ascetic movement inspired by a certain Priscillian. Some
bishops approved it, others suspected it of dualistic (Gnostic or
Manichaean) errors. Though some of its irregularities were
condemned by the small Council of Saragossa in A.D. 380, the
movement was not expressly denounced as heretical, and soon
afterwards Priscillian became Bishop of Avila. At this point
Ydacius, Bishop of Merida, himself accused of misconduct by
Priscillian, brought the State into the business and, as Metropolitan of Lusitania, obtained from Gratian a rescript expelling
"pseudo-bishops and Manichaeans" from their sees. Though
Priscillian and his friends could get no sympathy from Damasus
of Rome or Ambrose, bribery enabled them to have the rescript quashed. But on the death of Gratian, Ithacius, Bishop of
Ossonoba, got the ear of Maximus, who gave orders that the
Priscillianists should be tried by an ecclesiastical Council at
Bordeaux (A.D. 384). From this court Priscillian appealed back
to the Emperor. To be brief, Martin of Tours failed to deter
Maximus from taking cognizance of the case, Priscillian found
himself charged by Ithacius with sorcery, a crime and a capital
offence, was found guilty and executed. Subsequently, Martin
refused to communicate with the "Ithacians," the bishops who
had promoted the secular trial and approved the death penalty,
and extended his refusal even to Felix, the new Bishop of Trier,
good man though he was, because he had been consecrated by,
and remained in communion with, the Ithacians. Like Martin,
Ambrose was horrified at this abuse of the secular arm,[2] though
he did not question Priscillian's heresy, and it is these Ithacian
bishops who are referred to in §12. The case of Felix was considered by a Council of Milan in 390 (*Letter* 51, §6), but Ambrose and his suffragans were unable to extend their communion to him. Throughout this affair, Ambrose is standing
upon his fundamental dualism of Church and State.

[2] On the question of whether Priscillian had yet been executed, see the
note on §12 (p. 224).

Letter 24

THE TEXT
(Ambrose to the Emperor Valentinian)

1. You showed your confidence in my former mission by not calling me to account for it. Indeed, the fact that I was detained some days in Gaul made it sufficiently clear that I had not accepted anything to please Maximus or agreed to any proposals tending to suit him rather than to secure peace. Nor would you have entrusted me with a second mission if you had not approved the first. However, as on my second visit I was unable to avoid a clash with Maximus, I have thought it best to tell you in this letter how I have fared with my mission. By this means I hope to forestall the circulation of reports containing more invention than fact before my return enables me to publish the full and plain story with every mark of truth.

2. The day after I reached Trier, I made my way to the palace. The Grand Chamberlain Gallicanus, one of the emperor's eunuchs, came out to meet me. I requested an audience, he asked whether I brought any reply from your Grace.[1] I said yes. He replied that the interview could only take place in the Consistory. I said this was not usual for a bishop, and that in any case there were matters of importance which I ought to talk over with his master. To be brief, he went off to consult him, but came back with the same answer. It was plain that his first statement had been prompted by Maximus himself. I said that although this was inconsistent with my office, I would not abandon the duty I had undertaken, and that I was glad to humble myself in your service in particular, and, of course, in the service of brotherly piety.

3. When he had taken his seat in the Consistory, I went in.

[1] That is, to Maximus's invitation to Valentinian to come and live with him, cf. § 7.

He rose to kiss me. I stood still among the councillors. Some
urged me to go up to the throne, and he called to me. I replied:
"Why kiss one whom you do not recognize. If you had recognized me, you would not be receiving me in this place." "You
are upset, bishop," he said. "It is not that I am angry at the
insult," I said, "but I am ashamed to find myself standing in
a strange place." [2] "On your first mission you came into the
Consistory," he said. "That was not my fault," I said. "The
blame lay with the one who summoned me, not with me for
coming." "Why did you come?" he said. "Because at that
time," I said, "I was asking for peace on behalf of one who was
in an inferior position, whereas now I am asking for it on behalf
of an equal." "Equal!" he said. "Who made him that?"
"Almighty God," I said, "who has upheld Valentinian in the
kingdom which he had given him."

4. When I said that, he burst out: "You tricked me, you and
that Bauto who wanted to claim the kingdom for himself,
though he pretended it was for the boy. Yes, and he let barbarians loose against me. As if I had none of my own to bring!
There are thousands of barbarians in my service and my pay.
If I had not been held back at the time you came, no one could
have resisted me and my power."

5. I said mildly: "You need not get so angry, there is no
reason for that. Please listen patiently while I answer your
charges. I have come here precisely because of your allegation
that on my first mission you trusted me and I deceived you. I
am proud to have done even that for the sake of an orphan
emperor. Whom should we bishops protect more than orphans?
For Scripture says: "Give judgment for the fatherless, do right
for the widow, and relieve the oppressed," and in another place:
"A judge of widows and a father of the fatherless."[3]

6. But I shall not reproach Valentinian with my services. [4]

----

2 *Verecundia quod alieno consisto loco.* If *verecundia* means "shyness" here,
Ambrose is being ironical. More probably he means that, though he will
refrain from anger, it remains true that he is being humiliated *qua*
bishop. *Alieno* means "the wrong place for a bishop," rather than "strange
to me personally." But there is some play on words all through this
section. *Consisto* (stand) is chosen to go with *consistorium*, but adds to the
note of humiliation—the bishop is kept standing in a public audience.

3 Isa. 1:17, Ps. 68 (67):5.

4 Reading *exprobrabo.* "I do not want to suggest that the charges you bring
against me are true and that my troubles arise out of my services to
Valentinian, for your charges are false." The *Library of the Fathers* translates "make a boast of," either reducing the sense or, possibly, reading
(*ex*)*probabo.*

To speak the truth, when did I oppose your legions and prevent
you from entering Italy? What rocks did I use, what forces,
what units? Did I close the Alps to you with my body? If only
I could! I should not be afraid of your reproaches and accusa-
tions then. By what promises did I trick you into consenting
to peace? When Count Victor met me in Gaul, near the city
of Mainz, had you not sent him to ask for peace? [5] How then
did Valentinian deceive you, seeing that you asked him for
peace before he asked you? How did Bauto's devotion to his own
emperor deceive you? Because he did not betray his master?

7. And how did I circumvent you? Was it that, when I first
arrived and you said that Valentinian should come to you as a
son to a father, I replied that it was not reasonable for the boy
and his widowed mother to cross the Alps in the depths of
winter, or to commit himself, in delicate circumstances, to so long
a journey without his mother, that I had been entrusted with a
mission about peace, not with a promise that he would come?
It is clear that I had no power to pledge myself to anything
beyond my instructions, and that in fact I gave no such pledge.
For you said yourself: "Let us wait to see what answer Victor
brings back." It is well known that, while I was detained, he
reached Milan and was refused what he asked. Our agreement
went no further than peace; we were not agreed about the
emperor coming, which should never have been suggested.
I was present when Victor arrived back. How then could I
have dissuaded Valentinian from coming? The envoys sent to
Gaul subsequently, to say that he would not come, found me
still in Gaul, at Valence. On my way back I came across soldiers
of both sides, set to guard the mountain passes. What armies of
yours did I send back? What eagles did I turn back from Italy?
What barbarians did Bauto let loose?

8. It would not have been surprising if Bauto had done so,
Frank as he is by birth, when you threaten the Roman empire
with barbarian auxiliaries and troops from across the frontier,
whose maintenance was paid for by the taxes of the provincials.
Mark the difference between your menaces and the conciliatory
behaviour of the young Emperor Valentinian. You were demanding entrance to Italy with hordes of barbarians round you,

---

[5] Victor was the son of Maximus, and was sent to Milan to invite Valentinian to Trier, offering peace—Maximus would say, on that condition.
His mission crossed with Ambrose's near Mainz. Ambrose adduces
this as proof that he had not himself inveigled Maximus into offering
peace.

Valentinian turned back the Huns and Alans who were approaching Gaul through German territory. Why be annoyed with Bauto for pitting barbarian against barbarian? For while you were holding down a Roman army and he confronted you on two sides, in the very heart of the Roman empire the Juthungi[6] were laying Rhaetia waste. It was against the Juthungi that the Huns were called in. Yet when they were overrunning Germany on your frontier and already threatening Gaul with imminent disaster, they were obliged to relinquish their triumphs to save you from alarm. Compare his actions with yours. You were responsible for the invasion of Rhaetia, Valentinian bought peace for you with his own gold.

9. Now look at the man who is standing on your right.[7] When Valentinian could have avenged his own grief, he sent him back to you with honour. He had him in his own territory, and even when the news of his brother's murder came, he curbed his anger. They were the same relation, if not the same rank, yet he did not retaliate on you. Compare his actions with yours, and judge for yourself. He sent you back your brother alive. At least restore his brother dead. He did not refuse you assistance against himself. Why do you refuse him his brother's mortal remains?[8]

10. You are afraid—or so you say—that the return of the body may revive the grief of the troops. If they deserted him in life, will they defend him in death? You could have saved him, but you killed him. Why are you afraid of him now that he is dead? "I destroyed my enemy," you say. No, he was not your enemy; you were his. Well, no defence affects him now. Consider the case yourself. If someone thought to usurp your rule in these parts today, tell me, would you call yourself his enemy, or him yours? If I am not mistaken, a usurper makes war, an emperor defends his own rights. It was wrong of you to kill him. Must you refuse his body? Let the Emperor Valentinian have at least the remains of his brother as your hostage

---

[6] An Alemannic tribe, which invaded Rhaetia. Bauto (or Theodosius) then invited the Huns and Alans, already approaching Gaul, to attack the territory of the Alemanni, hoping thus to induce the Juthungi to return home. Maximus protested when the Huns were thus brought to his own borders, and Valentinian, to keep peace with Maximus, had to buy them off. There is no other evidence that the raid into Rhaetia was instigated by Maximus.

[7] Marcellinus, the younger brother of Maximus.

[8] The request for Gratian's body was a secondary object of the mission, and probably, after so long, no more than a pretext for it.

for peace. How could you assert that you did not order his death when you deny him burial? If you grudge him even burial, will it be believed that you did not grudge him his life?

11. But I will return to myself. You complain, I hear, that the Emperor Valentinian's adherents turned rather to the Emperor Theodosius than to you. What did you expect to happen when you threatened to punish the fugitives and put those you captured to death, while Theodosius lavished gifts on them and loaded them with honours?" [9] "Who did I kill?" he said. "Vallio," I answered. "And what a man, what a soldier! Did his fidelity to his emperor justify his fate?" "I did not order his death," he said. "I heard that an order was given for him to be put to death," I answered. "No," he said, "if he had not laid hands on himself, I had ordered that he should be taken to Chalons [10] and burnt alive there." I replied: "That was why it was believed that you had put him to death. And could anyone suppose that his own life would be spared when so valiant a warrior, so faithful a soldier, so good a counsellor, had been put to death?"

Then I went away, on the understanding that he would think it over.

12. Afterwards, when he saw that I held aloof from the bishops who were in communion with him or who were demanding the infliction of the death penalty upon certain heretics, he grew angry at this and ordered me to depart without delay. Though many thought that I should walk into a trap, I was glad to begin my journey. My only regret was the discovery that the aged bishop Hyginus, now almost at his last gasp, was being taken off into exile. When I appealed to his guards not to let him be hustled off without covering or feather-bed, I was hustled off myself. [11]

[9] Gratian was captured near Lyons and put to death by Maximus's general, Andragathius, 25th August, 383. Accounts are given in Socrates, H.E., V, 11, and Sozomen, H.E., VII, 13, and by Ambrose himself in In ps. 61 enarr., 23-25. There was no wholesale proscription of Gratian's adherents, but a few of the outstanding men lost their lives—Vallio, hanged in his own house, and Merobaudes, Gratian's generals, and Macedonius, Master of the Offices.

[10] Cabillonum, Chalon-sur-Saône. Reading exuri, burned, the answer is extraordinary. Should we read exhiberi (exhri), kept alive?

[11] Hyginus was Bishop of Cordova. He had denounced Priscillianism to Ydacius of Merida, but had afterwards communicated with Priscillian. On the circumstances of this section, see the introduction to this letter. But there is a particular problem not discussed there. Was Ambrose in Trier before or after the execution of Priscillian? Dating the mission in

13. That is the story of my mission. Farewell, Sir. Be on your guard against a man who conceals war under a cloak of peace.

387, the older scholars said that Priscillian was already dead. Rauschen emphasized *ad necem petebant*—Ambrose refused to communicate with the Ithacian group who were then pressing for the execution of Priscillian. So, dating the execution in 385, he put the mission in 384 (for this reason among others). Palanque accepts this reasoning, but, putting the mission in 386, places the execution late in the same year. Dudden puts the mission in 386, but the execution in 385, without arguing the point. D'Alès, *Priscillien*, 1936, accepts Palanque's conclusions. If they are not accepted, *petebant* must be used for the pluperfect to keep step with *communicabant*, or to mean "the sort of bishops who demanded."

Letters 40 and 41: The Synagogue at Callinicum

INTRODUCTION

IN THE SUMMER OF A.D. 388 THE CHRISTIANS OF Callinicum, a town and military station on the Euphrates, were stimulated by their bishop to set fire to a Jewish synagogue, and some monks destroyed the neighbouring chapel of the Valentinians, a Gnostic sect. The Count of the East reported the incidents to the Emperor Theodosius who, having defeated the usurper Maximus, reached Milan in October. Theodosius sent orders to the Count that the bishop should rebuild the synagogue and punish the monks. The Gnostics were a sect outside the law, and could have no lawful place of meeting inside a city; but this chapel seems to have been out in the country. The Jews, at any rate, were legally permitted to assemble for worship, and had every right to the protection which, in the previous decades, had too often been denied them. Five years after this incident, which may well have worsened their position for a time, a fresh law was enacted to penalize those who attacked synagogues.

Ambrose was at Aquileia when he heard what the emperor had decided. At once, apparently, he sent *Letter* 40 to Theodosius, arguing in it that a Christian bishop could not possibly build a synagogue, and even that it should not be rebuilt with any Christian money, including that of the Christian State. He requests an interview with the emperor, and ends his letter with a scarcely veiled threat of excommunication. In *Letter* 41 Ambrose tells his sister what happened. Theodosius, it seems, had not granted the interview. So when he went to church, Ambrose preached him a sermon which, based on the Lessons, worked round skilfully from the bishop's duty to speak out, through a commendation of the forgiving spirit and a comparison of the Church and the synagogue, which suggested that the Jews had no claims on the emperor's good offices, to a direct accusation of ingratitude for the favour shown by God to Theodosius. At the end of the sermon, Ambrose refused to continue with the celebration of the eucharist until the emperor had solemnly promised not only to rescind the first order (which in fact he had already done—so that he had taken some notice of Ambrose), but even to drop the whole affair. Ambrose had applied spiritual sanctions, though short of excommunication, in an affair of State.

Both letters are of outstanding interest. Ambrose was plainly wrong. It is strange that one who had been a provincial governor should show so little regard for justice and public order. Concentration on one aspect of the matter warped his judgment to the point of bigotry. For we need not suspect him of deliberately snatching at an opportunity to try his strength against Theodosius, the authority of the Church against the power of the State. He convinced himself that it was wrong in principle for any Christian, bishop or emperor, to construct a building for non-Christian worship. Therefore this case was for him a "cause of God," not one of secular administration. The basis of *Letter* 40 is a dualism of the spheres of Church and State. In God's cause the bishop must decide, and cannot be constrained by the emperor. This was Ambrose's normal view; but something more is creeping in when he says that the demands of public order must yield to those of religion.

Some may find the sermon tedious. It will serve incidentally, however, as an example of his spiritual exegesis of Scripture, and what he says of the Church suits the general purpose of this volume. But if we envisage the scene, the sermon is charged with drama. Theodosius perhaps saw what was coming, as Ambrose spoke of forgiveness and disparaged the Jews, even before he repeated the parallel between David and the emperor which he had used in his letter. The congregation could only then have perceived what it all meant, and one can imagine the shock when the preacher addressed the emperor by name. Think of it happening today—a bishop confronting the head of the State in church and refusing to celebrate until the demands of the Church had been met! At least we can commend Ambrose's courage, and the self-restraint of Theodosius. Fortunately Ambrose was to use his authority in a better cause two years later.

Note on the Date of Letter 40

The chronology is not quite certain. The Valentinian chapel

was attacked on the Feast of the Maccabaean Martyrs, 1st August, 388. Theodosius reached Milan, after the defeat of Maximus, early in October. Ambrose was probably at Aquileia in December for the funeral of Bishop Valerian (d. 26th November) and the consecration of his successor, Chromatius; but there is no proof that it was on this occasion that he sent *Letter* 40. In any case, this letter was not his first action in the affair, as 40:9 (I have asked, etc.) and 41:1 (I took etc.) demonstrate. By the time of the incident described in *Letter* 41, Theodosius had altered the original decision, attacked in 40, that the bishop should rebuild the synagogue. It is probable enough, however, that it was during his December visit to Aquileia that Ambrose heard that Theodosius had actually sent off the original rescript. What he does not know, or diplomatically pretends not to know, is whether any counter-order has been sent.

Letter 40

THE TEXT

Bishop Ambrose to the most gracious prince and most blessed emperor, Theodosius Augustus.

1. My Lord Emperor, although I am constantly harassed by well-nigh unceasing cares, I have never been in such a fret of anxiety as now, when I see how careful I must be not to expose myself to a charge of high treason. I beg you to listen patiently to what I have to say. If I am not fit to have your ear, then I am not fit to make the offering for you or to have your prayers and petitions entrusted to me. You want me to be heard when I pray for you. Will you not hear me yourself? You have heard me pleading for others. Will you not hear me pleading for myself? Are you not alarmed at your own decision? If you judge me unfit to hear you, you make me unfit to be heard for you.

2. An emperor ought not to deny freedom of speech, and a bishop ought not to conceal his opinions. Nothing so much commends an emperor to the love of his people as the encouragement of liberty in those who are subject to him by the obligations of public service. Indeed the love of liberty or of slavery is what distinguishes good emperors from bad, while in a bishop there is nothing so perilous before God or so disgraceful before men as not to speak his thoughts freely. For it is written: "I spake of thy testimonies before kings, and was not ashamed,"[1] and in another place: "Son of man, I have made thee a watchman unto the house of Israel, to the intent (it says) that if a righteous man doth turn from his righteousness, and commit iniquity, because thou hast not given him warning (that is, not told him what to guard against), his righteousness shall not be remembered, and his blood will I require at thine

[1] Ps. 119 (118):46.

229

hand. Nevertheless if thou warn the righteous man, that he sin not, and he doth not sin, the righteous shall surely live, because thou hast warned him; and thou shalt deliver thy soul." [2]

3. I would rather share good than evil with you, Sir; so your Grace should disapprove the bishop's silence and approve his freedom. You are imperilled by my silence, you are benefited by my freedom. I am not an officious meddler in matters outside my province, intruding myself into the affairs of others. I am doing my duty, I am obeying our God's commands. I am acting in the first place out of love for you, out of regard for your interest, out of zeal for your welfare. But if you do not believe this or forbid me to act on these motives, then I speak in fear of the wrath of God. If my peril would set you free, I would patiently offer myself for you—patiently, but not gladly. Better that you should be acceptable to God and glorious without peril to me. But if I am to be burdened with the guilt of my silence and dissimulation without delivering you, I would rather have you think me importunate than useless or base. For the holy apostle Paul, whose teaching you cannot reject, said: "Be instant in season, out of season; reprove, exhort, rebuke, with all long-suffering and teaching." [3]

4. We bishops have one whom we offend at our peril. Emperors are not displeased that everyone should discharge his own function, and you listen patiently to anyone who makes suggestions within his own department. Indeed, you reprove persons who do not carry out the appointed duties of their service. If you welcome this in your own officials, can you take it ill in the case of bishops? For we speak not as we will, but as we are bidden. You know the passage: "When ye shall stand before kings and governors, take no thought what ye shall speak: for it shall be given you in that hour what ye shall speak. For it is not ye that speak, but the Spirit of your Father that speaketh in you." [4] If I had to speak on political affairs, I should feel less apprehension at being refused a hearing, though in them also justice must be maintained. But in God's cause who will you listen to, if not the bishop, whose peril is increased if sin is committed? Who will dare to tell you the truth if the bishop will not?

5. I know that you are pious, merciful, kind and peaceable, having at heart the faith and fear of the Lord. But things often escape our notice. Some men "have a zeal for God, but not

[2] Ezek. 3:17, 20, 21.　　　[3] II Tim. 4:2.　　　[4] Matt. 10:19, 20.

according to knowledge." [5] I think we have to take care that
this does not steal even into faithful souls. I know your piety
towards God, your leniency towards men. I am myself obliged
to you for kind favours. That is why I am the more afraid,
the more anxious, lest afterwards you should yourself condemn
me on the ground that, owing to my dissimulation or flattery,
you had not escaped a fall. If I were to see you sinning against
myself, I ought not to keep silence. For it is written: "If thy
brother sin against thee, first tell him his fault, then rebuke
him before two or three witnesses. If he refuse to hear thee,
tell it unto the church." [6] Shall I keep silence when the cause
is God's? Let us then consider what it is that I fear.

6. The Count of the Eastern forces [7] reported the burning of a
synagogue at the instigation of the bishop. You ordered that
the others should be punished and the synagogue be rebuilt
by the bishop himself. I do not press the point that you should
have waited for the bishop's own statement. Bishops check
mobs and work for peace, except when they are themselves
stirred by wrong done to God or insult offered to the Church.
Suppose, however, that the bishop was too zealous in setting
fire to the synagogue and suppose he is too timid when called
to account. Do you feel no alarm at his acquiescence in your
verdict, no apprehension at his fall?

7. Again, are you not afraid—as will happen—that he may
meet your count with a refusal? Then it will be necessary to
make him either an apostate or a martyr. Both are foreign to
your times, both savour of persecution, whether he is driven to
apostasy or martyrdom. You see how the case is likely to turn
out. If you think the bishop firm, take care not to drive a firm
man to martyrdom. If you think him irresolute, refrain from
causing a frail man to fall. A heavy responsibility lies on one
who compels the weak to fall.

8. When the terms are put to him, I fancy the bishop will
say that he himself spread the flames, gathered the crowds and
led the people to the spot. He will not lose the opportunity of
martyrdom, and he will put the stronger to the test instead of
the weak. Blessed falsehood, that wins for him the pardon of
others, and for himself grace. Sir, this is my own request, that

---

[5] Rom. 10:2.   [6] Matt. 18:15–17.
[7] *Comes Orientis militarium partium*, not the natural way to refer to the
Count of the East, head of the Diocese *Oriens* (Syria, Mesopotamia,
etc.). Nevertheless, it is usually supposed that Ambrose intends him.
Some suggest a purely military official, e.g., the *Dux* of Osrhoene.

you turn your vengeance upon me, and, if you think this a crime, that you ascribe it to me. Why do you enforce judgment against the absent? You have the offender before you, confessing his guilt. I declare that I set fire to the synagogue, at least that I instructed them to do it, that there might be no place in which Christ is denied. If I am asked why I have not burned the synagogue here,[8] the answer is that the flames have already begun to attack it by God's own judgment; there was nothing for me to do. To tell the truth, I was slack just because I thought it would not be punished. Why do something which, being unpunished, would be unrewarded? If what I say offends modesty, it also calls for gratitude, by preventing an offence against God most high.

9. However, suppose no one cites the bishop to perform this obligation. For I have asked this boon of your Grace, and though I have not yet read that the order has been revoked, still, let us suppose that it has been. What if other more timid folk, afraid of death, offer to repair the synagogue at their own expense? What if the count, knowing the previous decision, himself orders it to be rebuilt from the funds of the Christians? Then, Sir, you will have an apostate count. Will you entrust to him the standards of victory, the Labarum[9] consecrated with the name of Christ—to him who is restoring a synagogue that does not know Christ? Tell him to carry the Labarum into the synagogue, and see whether they do not resist.

10. So the unbelieving Jews are to have a place erected out of the spoils of the Church? The patrimony acquired by the favour of Christ for Christians is to be made over to the treasury of unbelief? We read that of old temples were built for idols from the plunder of the Cimbri and the spoils of other enemies. The Jews will put this inscription on the facade of their synagogue: "The Temple of Impiety erected out of the spoils of the Christians"!

11. But, Sir, you are concerned for the preservation of

---

[8] *Hic*, i.e., Milan. This has caused some to argue that the letter was written from Milan, not Aquileia. But the word could easily be used by a writer who has Milan in mind all the time. Nothing else is known of the act of God, possibly lightning, which had burned the synagogue at Milan.

[9] The sacred standard. It was a pole with a cross-bar, plated with gold; at the top a gold wreath contained the *Chi Rho* monogram, standing for Christ, while from the cross-bar hung the banner with the imperial portraits. Constantine used it after his conversion in the campaigns against Maxentius (312) and Licinius (324).

discipline. Which is more important, a parade of discipline or the cause of religion? Punishment must give place to piety.

12. Have you not heard, Sir, that when Julian ordered the repair of the temple at Jerusalem, the men who were clearing the site were consumed by fire from above? Take care that the same does not happen again. That Julian ordered it is good enough reason for you not to order it.[10]

13. What is your real concern? Is it that a public building of any kind has been set on fire, or specifically a synagogue? If you are concerned at the burning of a building of the cheapest sort (and what else could there be in so obscure a town?), do you not recall, Sir, how many Prefects' houses have been set on fire in Rome without any punishment?[11] Indeed, if ever any emperor decided to punish the deed at all severely, he only aggravated the case of those who had suffered such a loss. If we are to talk of the *duty* of punishment, which will you count more deserving of it—to burn down a few buildings in the town of Callinicum[12] or to set fire to the city of Rome? At Constantinople recently the bishop's house was burnt, and your Grace's son interceded with his father, asking that you would not punish the wrong done to himself, the emperor's son, and the burning of the episcopal house.[13] Have you considered, Sir, whether, if you order the punishment of the present offence, he may not again intervene against it? It was good that the son obtained that boon from his father, for it was proper that he should first pardon the wrong done to himself. That the son should be petitioned for his own injury and the father for the son's was a good distribution of favours. Thus there is nothing you keep from your son; see that you withhold nothing from God.

14. The burning of a single building, I submit, does not warrant so great a disturbance as the severe punishment of the whole people, and the less so when it was a synagogue that was

10 Julian intended to rebuild the Temple of the Jews, not the Temple of Zeus on its site. Ammianus Marcellinus tells the story to which Ambrose alludes (XXIII, i, 2–3), as well as the ecclesiastical historians, e.g., Socrates, *H.E.*, III, 20.

11 The house of the elder Symmachus, Prefect of Rome, was attacked in A.D. 365, and there had just been an attack on the estates of the younger Symmachus, also Prefect of Rome, at Ostia.

12 Callinicum was more prosperous than Ambrose allows. Ammianus calls it a strongly fortified place with plenty of trade (*munimentum robustum et commercandi opimitate gratissimum*, XXIII, iii, 7).

13 In summer, 388, the house of Nectarius was burnt during an Arian riot (Socrates, *H.E.*, V, 13).

burnt, a place of unbelief, a home of impiety, a refuge of insanity, damned by God himself. For so we read the words of the Lord God by the mouth of Jeremiah: "And I will do unto the house, which is called by my name, wherein ye trust, and unto the place which I gave to you and to your fathers, as I have done to Shiloh. And I will cast you out of my sight, as I have cast out your brethren, the whole seed of Ephraim. And pray not thou for this people, neither ask mercy for them, nor make intercession to me for them: for I will not hear thee. Seest thou not what they do in the cities of Judah?" [14] God forbids him to intercede for the very people whom you think it right to avenge.

15. If I were pleading according to the law of the nations, I should undoubtedly relate how many church buildings the Jews burned in Julian's reign—two at Damascus, one of which has scarcely now been repaired, and that at the expense of the Church, not the synagogue, while the other church is a forbidding tangle of shapeless ruins. Churches were burnt also at Gaza, Ascalon, Berytus, and at most places thereabouts, and no one asked for punishment. At Alexandria the finest church of all was burnt by the heathen and the Jews. The Church has not been avenged. Is the synagogue to be?

16. And is the burning of the Valentinian "temple" to be punished? For what is it but a temple, seeing that the heathen congregate there? Though the heathen call on twelve gods only the Valentinians worship thirty-two aeons, whom they call gods. [15] I find that a report was made about them also and an order obtained for the punishment of certain monks. The Valentinians blocked the road to them when they were on their way to celebrate the feast of the Maccabaean Martyrs, singing psalms, as is their normal custom. Roused by such insolence, the monks set fire to a temple of theirs which had been hastily put up in some country village.

17. How many see themselves confronted with the same choice, when they remember how in Julian's time a man who overthrew an altar and disturbed the sacrifice was condemned by the judge and suffered martyrdom! The judge who heard the

14 Jer. 7:14–17.
15 Valentinus was one of the chief Gnostic teachers; he went from Alexandria to Rome in the middle of the second century. He developed the theory of Deity as a Pleroma of aeons, ogdoad+decad+dodecad. To him, of course, the individual aeons were not separate gods. There is for him an underlying monism. See further Tertullian, *Praescr. Haer.*, 30 (p. 50).

case was always regarded as a persecutor. No one was prepared to meet him or salute him. If he were not already dead, Sir, I should be afraid that you would be punishing him; though he has not escaped the punishment of heaven, having lived to see his son and heir die before him.[16]

18. It is reported that the judge has been instructed to hold an enquiry and informed that he should not have referred the case, but should have inflicted punishment; and that the offerings taken away are to be recovered. Other points I will pass over, but churches have been burnt by Jews and nothing returned, nothing asked back, no enquiry made. What could the synagogue have possessed in that frontier township? Everything in the town put together would amount to very little; there could be nothing of any value, no wealth, there. What could a fire take from those scheming Jews? These are tricks of the Jews, trying to bring a false charge. They hope that, as a result of their complaints, an extraordinary military tribunal may be set up, and an officer sent who will perhaps say what was once said here, before your accession, Sir: "How can Christ help us when we fight for the Jews against Christ, when we are sent to avenge Jews? They have lost their own armies, and now they want to destroy ours."

19. One can imagine how far they will go with their false charges, when they accused even Christ on false evidence. If they can lie with regard to God, there will be no limit to their calumnies. They will accuse anyone they please of causing sedition, they will aim even at people they do not know. What they want is to see row upon row of Christians in chains, the faithful with their necks under the yoke, the servants of God confined in dark prisons, beheaded with the axe, given to the flames, or sent to the mines to prolong their pains.

20. Will you give the Jews this triumph over the Church of God, this victory over the people of Christ? Will you give this joy to the unbeliever, Sir, this festival to the synagogue, these sorrows to the Church? The Jews will set this celebration among their feast-days and number it with the days of their triumph over the Amorites and the Canaanites, or the days of their

16 Dudden says that this section alludes to the martyrdom of Mark of Arethusa, but the details in Sozomen and Theodoret are very different. *Judex* was commonly used for provincial governors and other high officials, e.g., the Count in §18, and should perhaps be translated "magistrate." In the last sentence "avenging" would make better sense than "punishing," but *vindicare in eum* should mean punish. In the absence of a critical text, I cannot say whether there is any case for omitting the *in*.

deliverance from Pharaoh, King of Egypt, or from the hand of Nebuchadnezzar, King of Babylon. Now they will add this festival to commemorate their triumph over the people of Christ.

21. They say that they are not bound by the laws of Rome, even regarding the laws as criminal. Yet now they claim to be avenged by Roman law! Where were these laws when they burned the roofs of consecrated churches? If Julian did not avenge the Church because he was an apostate, will you, Sir, avenge the synagogue's wrongs because you are a Christian?

22. And what will Christ have to say to you hereafter? Do you not recall what he said to holy David through Nathan the prophet? [17] "It is I that chose thee, the youngest of thy brethren, and from a private person made thee emperor. Of the fruit of thy loins have I set upon the imperial throne. I made barbarian nations subject to thee, I gave thee peace, I delivered thine enemy captive into thy power. Thou hadst no corn to feed thine army. By the hand of the enemy himself, I threw open the gates to thee, I opened the barns. Thine enemy gave thee his stores, which he had made ready for himself. I confounded thine enemy's counsels, that he laid himself bare. The usurper of empire I so bound and so fettered in mind that, though he still had the means to fly, he shut himself up with all his force, as if afraid that any should escape thee. His commander and his army on the other element, whom I had previously dispersed that they should not join in the battle, I gathered together to complete thy victory. Thine own army, assembled from many untamed tribes, I bade keep faith and peace and concord as though they had been one nation. When the supreme danger threatened, that the treacherous plots of the barbarians might penetrate the Alps, I gave thee victory within the very wall of the Alps, that thou mightest win the day without loss. I made thee to triumph over thine enemy— and thou art giving mine enemies a triumph over my people."

23. Why was Maximus abandoned? Was it not because, a few days before he set out on his campaign, when he heard that a synagogue had been burnt at Rome, he had sent an edict to Rome, posing as the guardian of public order? As a result,

---

[17] Here and in the sermon retold in *Letter* 41 Ambrose works out a parallel between David and Theodosius. Like David, he was not a member of the royal family. Arcadius, made Augustus before the death of Theodosius, is Solomon, proclaimed before David's death, Goths = Philistines; the enemy, Athanaric, surrendered to Theodosius, reminiscent perhaps of Saul being delivered into David's hands, and the usurper, Maximus, resembles Absalom. Andragathius was the commander of the fleet.

Christian people said: "There is nothing good in store for him. This king has turned Jew. We heard of him as the defender of order, but Christ, who died for sinners, soon put him to the test." If this was said of words alone, what will be said of punishment? So Maximus was at once defeated, by the Franks, by the Saxon people, in Sicily, at Siscia, at Poetovio, in short, everywhere.[18] What has a pious man in common with the impious? The evidences of impiety must be done away with at the same time as the impious himself. That which caused his downfall, that by which the conquered gave offence, the conqueror must not imitate, but condemn.

24. I have not reviewed these facts for you as if you were ungrateful. I have recounted them as rightly given to you, so that, mindful of them, you may love the more, as one to whom more has been given. When Simon gave this answer, the Lord Jesus said: "Thou hast rightly judged." And turning at once to the woman who anointed his feet with ointment (she was a type of the Church), he said to Simon: "Wherefore I say unto thee, her sins, which are many, are forgiven; for she loved much; but to whom little is forgiven, the same loveth little." [19] This is the woman who entered into the Pharisee's house and cast out the Jew, but gained Christ. For the Church has shut out the synagogue. Why this new attempt to let the synagogue shut out the Church in the servant of Christ, from the faithful heart, I mean, from the abode of Christ?

25. The words which I have put together spring from my affection and regard for you, Sir. At my request you have freed many from exile, from prison, from the extreme penalty of death. I owe it to these kindnesses to prefer the risk of offending you, for the sake of your own salvation, to the loss, in a single moment, of that episcopal privilege which I have so long enjoyed.[20] I can say this because sincere love gives complete

18 There is no other allusion to Maximus and the Roman synagogue. The curious sentence "we heard . . . test" is absent from at least one MS., and the Benedictine editors suggest omitting it. Maximus took the initiative against Theodosius, marching through Italy into Illyricum. Theodosius left Thessalonica in June, 388. The invasion of Gaul by the Franks and Saxons held back Maximus's reinforcements, his fleet was defeated off Sicily, and his armies at Siscia and Poetovio. He was finally defeated and executed near Aquileia, 28th August, 388.

19 Luke 7:43 ff., and more fully in *Letter* 41.

20 The privilege is that of interceding for the condemned, which had by this time become almost a right to obtain pardons. Hence bishops are to use it with discretion. For Ambrose as intercessor, see Dudden, pp. 120–121. Cf. *Letter* 57 §12 (p. 264).

confidence. At least no one should injure the man who is con-
sulting his interest. However, it is not the loss of privilege that
I deprecate, but the danger to salvation.

26. It is of great importance, Sir, that you should not think
of investigating or punishing what to this day no one has investi-
gated or ever punished. It is a serious thing to hazard your
faith for the sake of the Jews. When Gideon killed the consecrated calf, the heathen said: "Let the gods themselves avenge
their own wrong." [21] Who is to avenge the synagogue? Christ,
whom they slew, whom they denied? Will God the Father
avenge those who do not even accept the Father, in that they
did not accept the Son? Who is to avenge the heresy of the
Valentinians? How can your Piety avenge them when you have
ordered their exclusion and denied them leave to meet together?
If I put Josiah to you as a king approved by God, will you
condemn in their case action which was approved in him? [22]

27. If you distrust me, summon what bishops you please,
and discuss what ought to be done, Sir, without injury to the
faith. If you consult your ministers on matters of finance, it is
surely even more fitting that you should consult the bishops of
the Lord on matters of religion.

28. I beg your Grace to consider how many are plotting
against the Church and spying upon her. Wherever they detect
a crack, they will plant a dart. I speak after the manner of men;
but God is feared more than men, and God is rightly preferred
even to emperors. If it is sometimes thought proper to defer to
friend or parent or relative, am I not right in deciding to defer
to God and to prefer him above all else? Consult your own
interest, Sir, or allow me to consult mine.

29. What shall I answer hereafter, if it becomes known that,
on authority sent from here, Christians have been put to death
by sword or club or leaded scourge? How shall I explain that
away? How shall I excuse it before the bishops who are
already giving vent to their indignation that men who have
been presbyters for thirty years and a good deal more, or
deacons of the Church, are being withdrawn from their
sacred function and assigned to municipal office? [23] Your

21 Cf. Judg. 6:31.
22 Because he destroyed the idols and high places (II Kings 23).
23 Under a law of Constantius, men who belonged to families liable to
hold municipal office (*curiales*) might escape their responsibilities in order
to become bishops. Other clergy must renounce their property in favour of
the municipality or give it to another member of their family who would
assume the obligations. If that member died, clergy could be called upon

servants are retained in your service for a stated period. How much more should you consider the servants of God! How, I repeat, shall I excuse this to the bishops who complain about their clergy and write that their churches are being laid waste by a burdensome oppression?

30. I wanted this to come to the notice of your Grace. You will vouchsafe to take counsel and to regulate it as you please, following your own judgment. But as to that which troubles me, and rightly troubles me, banish it, cast it out. You yourself do whatever you order to be done. Or if the count is not going to do it, I would rather have you merciful than see him not doing what he has been ordered to do.

31. You have those for whom you must still invoke and merit the mercy of the Lord towards the Roman empire.[24] You have those for whom you hope more than for yourself. Let their interest, their welfare, appeal to you as I speak. I fear you may commit your case to the judgment of others. All is still in your own hands. On this point I pledge myself to our God for you, and you need not be afraid for your oath. Can God be displeased with an amendment made for his honour? You need change nothing in the first letter, whether it has been sent yet or not. Have another letter written, full of faith and piety. It is open to you to amend; it is not open to me to hide the truth.

32. You forgave the people of Antioch the wrong which they did to you. You sent for your enemy's daughters and gave them to a relative to bring up, you sent money from your own treasury to your adversary's mother.[25] Such piety as this, such faith towards God, will be obscured by the present action. You spared armed foes and preserved your enemies. Do not, I beg you, insist so eagerly upon the punishment of Christians.

33. Now, Sir, I beseech you not to spurn my fears for you and for myself. It was a holy man who said: "Wherefore was I born to see the destruction of my people", incurring the wrath of God?[26] I at least have acted with all possible respect. It is better for you to hear me in the palace than—if the necessity should arise—in church.

to resume the obligations. Cf. Ambrose, *Ep.* 18:14. Some translators make the sentence in *Letter* 40 refer to the bishops themselves, which seems to me unnecessary and most unlikely.

[24] His sons, Honorius and Arcadius.

[25] Antioch—the riots of 387; enemy and adversary—Maximus.

[26] I Macc. 2:7.

Letter 41

THE TEXT

From Brother to Sister

1. My dear and holy sister, it was good of you to write and tell me that you are still anxious because I told you of my own anxiety. It surprises me that you have not received my letter telling you that my composure has been restored. It had been reported that a Jewish synagogue had been set on fire by Christians, at the instigation of the bishop, and also a Valentinian chapel. While I was at Aquileia, orders had been sent that the bishop should rebuild the synagogue, and the monks, who burned down the Valentinian building, be punished. I took the matter up energetically, but achieved nothing. So I composed a letter to the emperor and sent it off at once. When he went to church, I preached this sermon:—

2. In the book of the prophet it is written: "Take to thyself the rod of an almond tree."[1] We have to consider why the Lord said this to the prophet. It was not written without purpose, since in the Pentateuch also we read that the almond rod of Aaron the priest blossomed after it had been long laid up.[2] The rod appears to signify that prophecy or priestly authority ought to be forthright, commending not what is pleasant, but what is advantageous.

3. The prophet is bidden to take an almond rod because the fruit of this tree has a bitter rind and a hard shell, but is sweet inside. Like it, the prophet also offers hard and bitter things and does not shrink from declaring what is painful. It is the same with the priest,[3] whose injunctions may seem bitter to some for a time, and, like Aaron's rod, long laid up in the ears of dissemblers, may yet blossom one day when men think they have withered.

[1] Jer. 1:11. [2] Num. 17:8.
[3] *Sacerdos*, with the double meaning of Old Testament priest and Christian bishop.

4. Accordingly, the Apostle says: "What will ye? shall I come unto you with a rod, or in love and a spirit of meekness?" [4] He mentioned a rod first, striking those who were astray as with an almond rod, that he might afterwards comfort them with the spirit of meekness. So the man whom the rod deprived of the heavenly sacraments was restored by meekness. [5] He gave similar instructions to his disciple also, saying: "Reprove, exhort, rebuke," [6] two stern words and one gentle, but stern only so that he might soften them. Just as to bodies sick with excess of gall bitter food and drink taste sweet and, on the other hand, sweet dishes taste bitter, so, when the mind is wounded, it sickens under the attentions of an unctuous flattery and is again tempered by the bitterness of correction.

5. So much for what we learn from the reading of prophets. Let us also consider what the Gospel lesson has to say to us. "And one of the Pharisees desired the Lord Jesus that he would eat with him. And he entered into the Pharisee's house, and sat down to meat. And behold, a woman which was in the city, a sinner, when she knew that Jesus sat at meat in the Pharisee's house, brought an alabaster cruse of ointment, and standing behind at his feet, began to wet his feet with tears." [7] And he recited the rest as far as the place: "Thy faith hath saved thee; go in peace." How simple in language, I went on, but how profound in counsel is the Gospel lesson! Therefore, since it is the word of the "great counsellor", [8] let us consider its deepest meaning.

6. Our Lord Jesus Christ judged that men can be more effectively constrained and challenged to do what is right by kindnesses than by fear. He knew that for correction love is of more use than terror. So when he came, born of a Virgin, he sent grace first, forgiving our sins in baptism to make us more grateful to him. [9] Then he declared in this woman that if we

---

[4] I Cor. 4:21.   [5] II Cor. 2:10.   [6] II Tim. 4:2.

[7] Luke 7:36–38. Note the liturgical alteration of the text to "the Lord Jesus."

[8] Isa. 9:6.

[9] In this section Ambrose makes much of the varying senses of *gratia*, *gratus*. In the incarnation and in baptism God's grace is prevenient. Receiving it makes us (i) more acceptable to God, and (ii) grateful (cf. §9). If we express our gratitude in actions, it in turn earns a reward, the reward of further grace. It is not always easy to be sure how Ambrose is using the words, especially when the extra complications of attractiveness, beauty, favour, privilege, are brought in (cf. §28 and *Letter* 63, §56 on p. 272).

repay him with the services fitting to grateful men, we shall all have a reward for that gratitude. If he had simply forgiven us our original debts, he would have seemed more cautious than merciful, more careful for correction than munificent in reward. Merely to entice is the cunning of a narrow mind. It befits God to advance those whom he has invited by grace with increases of that grace. Therefore he first forgives us through baptism and afterwards bestows ampler gifts on those who serve him well. Thus the kindnesses of Christ are both the incentive to virtue and also its reward.

7. No one need shudder at the word money-lender. Formerly we were in the clutches of a harsh lender, who could only be paid off and satisfied by the death of the debtor. The Lord Jesus came, and saw us tied by a heavy loan. No one could discharge the loan from the patrimony of his own innocence. I could have nothing of my own with which to free myself. He offered me a new form of acquittance, to change my creditor, since I had no means to pay the loan. It was guilt, not nature, that had made us debtors. By our own sins we contracted heavy debts, so that, whereas we were free, we came to be bound. A debtor is one who has taken some of a lender's money. Now sin comes from the devil, as though this were the wealth which the evil one has for his patrimony. As Christ's riches are virtues, so the devil's wealth is crime. He had brought the human race into the everlasting captivity of an inherited liability by that heavy loan which our debt-laden ancestor had transmitted to his posterity in an encumbered succession.[10] Jesus Christ came, offered his death for the death of all, and poured out his blood for the blood of all.

8. So we have changed our creditor, but we have not escaped. Or rather we have escaped, for though a debt remains, the loan is cancelled. The Lord Jesus says "to them that are in chains, Come out; to them that are in prison, Go forth."[11] Therefore your sins are forgiven, and there is no one whom he has not released from his bonds. For it is written that he forgave "all trespasses, blotting out the bond written in ordinances that

10 Ambrose taught a full-blooded doctrine of the Fall, Original Sin, and Original Guilt. Like Tertullian, he describes the effect of Adam's sin on his posterity sometimes in legal, sometimes in physical or medical terms. With the present passage compare *In ps.* 48 *enarr.* 8: *Adam . . . obnoxiam haereditatem successionis humanae suo vulnere dereliquit*, where the mixture of terms appears. On his doctrine of the Fall in general see Dudden, pp. 612–624.
11 Isa. 49:9.

was against us."[12] Why then do we hold other men's bonds, why do we want to demand what others owe us, when we are enjoying the remission granted to ourselves? He who pardoned all, demands of all that they forgive others what each remembers to have been forgiven to himself.

9. Take care that you do not find yourself in a worse case as lender than debtor, like the man in the Gospel[13] to whom his lord forgave all his debt and who afterwards began to demand from his fellow-servant what he himself had not paid; which so angered his lord that he demanded of him, with bitter reproach, what he had previously forgiven. So we must take care lest, by not forgiving the debts owed to us, we should find ourselves having to pay what had previously been forgiven. For so is it written, in the words of the Lord Jesus: "So shall my heavenly Father do also unto you, if ye forgive not every one his brother from your hearts." Let us, then, to whom much has been pardoned, forgive a little, and let us understand that the more we pardon, the more acceptable we shall be to God; for the more we have been forgiven, the more grateful we are to God.

10. When the Lord asked him: "Which loves him the more?", the Pharisee answered: "He, I suppose, to whom he forgave the more." And the Lord said to him: "Thou hast rightly judged".[14] The Pharisee's judgment is praised, but his feelings are blamed. About others he judges well, but what he thinks about others, he does not believe to be true in his own case. You hear a Jew praising the discipline of the Church, proclaiming its real grace, honouring the bishops of the Church. You urge him to believe; he refuses. What he praises in us, he does not himself pursue. So Simon's praise was not complete just because he heard Christ say: "Thou hast rightly judged." Cain also offered rightly, but did not divide rightly. So God said to him: "If thou offerest rightly, but dost not divide rightly, thou hast sinned; be silent."[15] Simon also offered rightly, in that he judged that Christ will be the more loved by Christians because he forgave us many sins. But he did not divide rightly, in that he thought that he who forgave men their sins could possibly be ignorant of them.

11. So he says to Simon: "Seest thou this woman? I entered into thine house, thou gavest me no water for my feet: but she hath wetted my feet with her tears."[16] We are all one Body of

---

[12] Col. 2:13, 14.
[14] Luke 7: 42, 43.   [15] Gen. 4:7 (LXX).
[13] Matt. 18: 23–35.
[16] Luke 7:44.

Christ, God being the head and we the members. Some, maybe, are the eyes, like the prophets; some are teeth, like the apostles who admitted to our breasts the preaching of the Gospel. Scripture well says: "His eyes shall be bright with wine, and his teeth whiter than milk." [17] His hands are those who carry out good works. Those who bestow upon the poor the means of nourishment are his belly. Some, then, are his feet; and would that I were counted fit to be his heel! So he who forgives the lowest their sins, pours water upon Christ's feet; and in setting the lowly free, he washes the sole of Christ's feet.

12. Again, he who cleanses his conscience from the filth of sin, pours water upon Christ's feet; for Christ walks in all our hearts. Take care then not to have an unclean conscience and make the feet of Christ dirty. Take care lest he strike against the thorn of wickedness in you, so that his heel is wounded as he walks in you. It was because he had not a mind clean from the filth of unbelief that the Pharisee did not give Christ water for his feet. How could he cleanse his conscience when he had not received the water of Christ? But the Church has both water and tears, the water of baptism and the tears of penitence. For faith, which weeps over the sins of old, has learned to guard against new ones. So Simon the Pharisee, having no water, had no tears either. How could he have tears, when he showed no penitence?[18] Since he did not believe in Christ, he had no tears. If he had had them, he would have washed his eyes to see Christ, whom he did not yet see, though he sat at meat with him. Had he seen him, he would not have doubted his power.

13. The Pharisee had no hair, for he could not recognize the Nazarite. The Church, which was looking for the Nazarite, had hair. Hair is reckoned among the inessential parts of the body. Yet, if it is anointed, it gives out a good odour and is an ornament to the head; though if it is not anointed with oil, it is an encumbrance. Just so riches are a burden if you do not know how to use them, if you do not sprinkle them with the odour of Christ. But if you feed the poor, wash their wounds, and wipe off their filth, you have wiped the feet of Christ.

14. "Thou gavest me no kiss: but she, since the time I came

---

[17] Gen. 49:12.

[18] *Paenitentiam non gerebat.* In many cases in Ambrose's writings the context does not make it quite clear whether he is thinking of repentance or penance. Here there is at least an allusion to " doing penance" as a sacrament which "the Church has", cf. *Letter* 51 §11 (p. 256).

in, hath not ceased to kiss my feet." [19] A kiss is the sign of love. What kiss could the Jew have, seeing that he has not known peace, has not received peace from Christ, who said: "My peace I give unto you, my peace I leave with you?" [20] The synagogue has no kiss. The Church has the kiss, the Church which waited for Christ, which loved him, which said: "Let him kiss me with the kisses of his mouth." [21] Her long and ardent desire had grown with waiting for the Lord's coming. She sought to quench it, drop by drop, with his kiss, to satisfy her thirst with the boon. Therefore the holy prophet says: "Thou shalt open my mouth, and it shall show forth thy praise." [22] He who praises the Lord Jesus, kisses him; and he that kisses him, surely believes in him. David himself says: "I believed, and therefore have I spoken," [23] and earlier: "Let my mouth be filled with thy praise, and let me sing of thy glory." [24]

15. Concerning the pouring of special [25] grace upon us, the same Scripture teaches you that he who receives the Spirit kisses Christ, when the prophet says: "I opened my mouth and drew in the Spirit." [26] He who confesses Christ kisses him, "For with the heart man believeth unto righteousness; but with the mouth confession is made unto salvation." [27] He kisses Christ's feet who, as he reads the Gospel, comes to know the deeds of the Lord Jesus and wonders at them with pious affection, and so, with the kiss of religion, caresses, as it were, the prints of the Lord as he walks. So we kiss Christ with the kiss of communion—"let him that readeth understand." [28]

16. How can the Jew have this kiss? Not believing in his coming, he did not believe in his passion. How could he believe that he had suffered, when he did not believe that he had come? So the Pharisee had no kiss, except perhaps the kiss of the traitor Judas. But Judas had no kiss either; and that was why, when he wanted to show the Jews the kiss he had promised them as the sign of betrayal, the Lord said to him: "Judas, betrayest thou the Son of man with a kiss?" [29] He meant, do you offer a kiss when you have not the love which goes with a

---

[19] Luke 7:45.   [20] John 14:27.   [21] S. of Sol. 1:2.
[22] Ps. 51:15 (50:17).   [23] Ps. 116 (115):10.   [24] Ps. 71 (70):8.
[25] Reading *specialem* with the Benedictine text. But *spiritualem?*
[26] Ps. 119 (118):131. Spirit, *spiritum* also = breath.
[27] Rom. 10:10.
[28] Matt. 24:15. This is an instance of the *Disciplina Arcani*, reserve in speaking of the sacraments, which, curiously enough, was stronger about this date than earlier.
[29] Luke 22:48.

kiss, do you offer a kiss when you do not know the mystery[30] of the kiss? It is not the kiss of the lips which is required, but the kiss of heart and mind.

17. But you say: "He kissed the Lord." Yes, but only with his lips. The Jewish people has that kiss, and therefore it was said: "This people honoureth me with their lips, but their heart is far from me."[31] He who has no faith and charity has no kiss. A kiss conveys the force of love, and where there is no love, no faith, no affection, what sweetness can there be in kisses?

18. But the Church does not cease to kiss Christ's feet. So, in the *Song of Songs*, she asks not one, but many kisses.[32] Like holy Mary, she is intent upon his every utterance, takes in all his words when the Gospel is read, or the prophet, and keeps all his sayings in her heart.[33] The Church alone has kisses as a bride, for the kiss is, as it were, the pledge of marriage and the privilege of wedlock. How can the Jew have kisses, when he does not believe in the Bridegroom? How can the Jew have kisses when he does not know that the Bridegroom has already come?

19. Not only has he no kisses; he has no oil either, with which to anoint the feet of Christ. If he had had any oil, he would surely by now have softened his own neck. Moses says: "This people is stiff-necked",[34] and the Lord told how the Levite and the priest passed by, and neither of them poured oil or wine upon the wounds of the man who had been beaten by robbers.[35] They had nothing to pour. If they had had any oil, they would have poured it upon their own wounds. Isaiah cries: "They cannot apply ointment or oil or bandage."[36]

20. But the Church has oil, with which she tends the wounds of her children, that the wound may not harden and spread deep. She has oil which she has received secretly. With this oil Asher washed his feet, as it is written: "A blessed son is Asher, and he shall be accepted by his brethren, and he shall dip his foot in oil."[37] With this oil, then, the Church anoints the necks of her children that they may take the yoke of Christ. With this oil she anointed the martyrs, that she might wipe off from them the dust of this world. With this oil she anointed the confessors, that they might not give in to their labours or succumb

---

[30] *Sacramentum*, the increased significance; but with reference also to the original sense of an oath of loyalty.
[31] Isa. 29:13; Matt. 15:8.
[32] S. of Sol. 1:2. [33] Luke 2:51. [34] Ex. 34:9.
[35] Luke 10:31, 32. [36] Isa. 1:6. [37] Deut. 33:24.

to fatigue, that they might not be overcome by the heat of this world. She anointed them to refresh them with the oil of the Spirit.

21. This oil is not for the synagogue, since it does not possess the olive and did not understand the dove which brought back the olive branch after the Flood.[38] For that dove descended afterwards, when Christ was being baptized, and abode upon him, as John bare witness in the Gospel saying: "I saw the Spirit descending from heaven as a dove, and it abode upon him."[39] How could he see the dove who did not see him upon whom the Spirit descended as a dove?

22. The Church, then, washes Christ's feet and wipes them with her hair and anoints them with oil and pours ointment upon them, in that she not only cares for the wounded and tends the weary, but also sprinkles them with the sweet odour of grace. She pours the same grace not only upon the rich and mighty, but also upon men of low estate, she weighs them all in an equal balance, gathers them all into the same bosom, cherishes them in the same lap.

23. Christ died once and was buried once, but he would have his feet anointed every day. What feet of Christ do we anoint? Those feet of which he said: "Inasmuch as ye have done it unto one of these least, ye have done it unto me".[40] These are the feet which the woman in the Gospel refreshes, these that she wets with her tears, when sin is remitted to the lowest, guilt washed away and pardon granted. These feet he kisses who loves the lowest of the holy people. These feet he anoints who confers the favours of his gentleness even upon the poor. In these, the Lord Jesus tells us, the martyrs, the apostles, the Lord himself, are honoured.

24. You see how the Lord is teaching you a lesson, challenging you to goodness by his own example, teaching you even when he reproves. When accusing the Jews, for instance, he says: "O my people, what have I done unto thee? or wherein have I grieved thee? or wherein have I offended thee? Answer me. Is it because I brought thee out of the land of Egypt, and delivered thee out of the house of bondage?" adding: "And I sent before thy face Moses and Aaron and Miriam."[41] Remember what Balak[42] consulted against thee (that is, seeking assistance from the art of magic); yet I did not let him hurt thee. Thou wast indeed oppressed, an exile in foreign lands, laden

[38] Gen. 8:11.   [39] John 1:32.   [40] Matt. 25:40.
[41] Micah 6:3, 4.   [42] Micah 6:5 with Num. 23.

with heavy burdens. I sent before thy face Moses and Aaron and Miriam, and he who spoiled the exile was first spoiled himself. Thou who hadst lost thine own didst gain another's. Thou wast freed from the foes that encompassed thee; safe in the midst of the waters, thou sawest the destruction of thine enemies, when the same wave which had surrounded thee and borne thee on, poured back and drowned the foe.[43] When food was lacking as thou wentest through the wilderness, did I not bring thee nourishing rain, and supply thee on all sides, whithersoever thou didst go?[44] Did I not subdue all thine enemies, and bring thee into the place of the cluster of grapes?[45] Did I not deliver to thee Sihon, King of the Amorites, the "proud one", the prince of "them that provoked thee"?[46] Did I not deliver alive to thee the King of Ai, whom thou didst condemn with the ancient curse, nailing him to a tree and hanging him on a cross?[47] Shall I speak of the hosts of the five kings, slaughtered because they strove to deny thee the lands due to thee?[48] And now, in return for all these things, what else is required of thee, O man, but to do justice and righteousness, to love mercy, and to be ready to walk with the Lord thy God?[49]

25. How did he expostulate, through Nathan the prophet, with King David, that pious and gentle man?[50] "I chose thee, the youngest of thy brethren, I filled thee with the spirit of gentleness. By the hand of Samuel, in whom I dwelt, and my Name dwelt, I anointed thee king. I removed the former king, who was driven by an evil spirit to persecute the priests of the Lord, and from an exile I made thee a conqueror. Of thy seed have I set one upon thy throne to be thy consort before he is thy heir. I made even strangers subject to thee, that they who warred upon thee might be thy servants. And thou, wilt thou deliver my servants into the power of my enemies? Wilt thou take away that which belonged to a servant of mine, at once branding thyself with sin and giving my adversaries occasion to triumph over me?"

[43] Ex. 14:29.   [44] Ex. 16:4.   [45] Num. 13:24, Eshcol.
[46] Num. 21:21 ff. Sihon could mean "bold," but Ambrose's interpretation of Amorites will not do.
[47] Josh. 8:23, 29; cf. Deut. 21:23; Gal. 3:13.
[48] Josh. 10:26.   [49] Micah 6:8.
[50] In § 24 Ambrose has been working round to Theodosius, and this becomes obvious in § 25, parallel to *Letter* 40:22, where see the notes. Here Ambrose adds a reference to the former king Valens, an Arian who persecuted the orthodox and whose death at the battle of Adrianople, 378, left room for Theodosius.

26. Therefore, Sir—to speak no longer about you, but to you—since you see how severely the Lord is wont to censure, be sure that, the more glorious you become, the more completely must you submit yourself to your Maker. For it is written: "When the Lord thy God shall bring thee into the land of others, and thou shalt eat the fruit of others, say not: 'My strength and my righteousness have given me this'," [51] but: "The Lord God gave it, Christ in his mercy bestowed it." Love, therefore, the Body of Christ, which is the Church. Give water for his feet, kiss his feet, not only forgiving those who are taken in sin, but also restoring them to concord by your pardon, releasing them in peace. Anoint his feet, that the whole house where Christ sits may be filled with your ointment, and all that sit at meat with him delight in its odours. I mean, Sir, so honour the least that the angels may rejoice at their pardon, the apostles exult, the prophets be glad, as over one sinner that repenteth. [52] "For the eyes cannot say to the hand, We have no need of thee: or the head to the feet, I have no need of you." [53] Therefore, because all are necessary, do you protect the whole Body of the Lord Jesus, that he also may guard your kingdom with his heavenly favour.

27. When I came down, he said to me: "You have been preaching about me." I replied: "The sermon was meant for your own good." Then he said: "It is true that it was somewhat harsh of me to order the bishop to repair the synagogue, but that has been corrected. The monks do many wrong things." [54] At this the general Timasius [55] began to abuse the monks violently, and I answered him: "I am dealing with the emperor as is proper, for I know that he fears God. I shall have to deal differently with you if you are so rude."

28. Then, standing still for a time, I said to the emperor: "Let me offer for you with a clear conscience; set my mind at rest." He sat there and nodded, but did not promise openly; and as I continued to stand, he said he would alter the rescript. At once I asked him to stop the whole investigation, [56] in case the count should take advantage of it to do some injury to the

[51] Deut. 8:17; 9:4.   [52] Luke 15:10.   [53] I Cor. 12:21.

[54] Theodosius's position at this point is that the synagogue must be rebuilt, but not at the expense of the bishop; that is, the State will pay. The monks are those who destroyed the Valentinian chapel. His remark is only too true, as was shown even more in the Christological controversies of the next centuries.

[55] Timasius was *Magister Militum*, and was Consul in 389.

[56] That is, nothing will be done and no one punished.

Christians. He promised he would do so. I said to him: "I act [57] on your honour," and I repeated: "I act on your honour." "Act on my honour", he said. Only then did I go to the altar, and I would not have gone unless he had distinctly promised. And truly the offering was so full of grace that I felt myself that the favour he had granted was acceptable to God, and that the divine presence had not been withheld. So all was done as I wished.

[57] *Ago*, which has here the technical meaning of "celebrate," though, in view of the repetition, it would be clumsy to translate it so.

Letter 51: The Massacre at Thessalonica

INTRODUCTION

IN A.D. 387 THE PEOPLE OF ANTIOCH HAD DEMON-
strated against the burden of taxation and had torn down
the imperial statues. Theodosius had at first ordered stern
punishment, but eventually pardoned the city, though its
conduct was legally treason. It was possibly with this clemency
in mind that he determined to teach the citizens of Thessalonica a sharper lesson when, in the summer of A.D. 390, they
rioted against the barbarian garrison and murdered its
commander.

His plan became known to Ambrose, who told him that it
was utterly atrocious and came to think that Theodosius
had given it up. But other interests inflamed his quick temper,
so that he sent the order, only to countermand it—too late.
The Thessalonians were invited to an exhibition in the Circus
and were there massacred to the number of seven thousand.
This happened in August. Ambrose heard of it while he was
presiding over a council of bishops from Italy and Gaul.
Shocked though they all were, they left any definite action to
Ambrose, who deliberately withdrew from Milan before
Theodosius returned to it from a visit to Verona. A few days
later, in the middle of September, he wrote privately to the
emperor, saying that he could not "offer the Sacrifice" if
Theodosius came to church before he had done penance.
After an unsuccessful attempt to secure a compromise through
Rufinus, the Master of the Offices, the emperor, to his great
credit, accepted the humiliation of public penance, went to
church for some weeks as an excommunicate penitent, and
was readmitted to communion at Christmas.

The story has found its way into art and literature in a
somewhat legendary form. Sozomen, writing at Constantinople in the middle of the fifth century, believed that the

251

emperor did go to church, only to be met at the door by Ambrose and turned away. Theodoret, writing slightly later than Sozomen, has a different and more elaborate account of Theodosius's submission to terms dictated by Ambrose in the sacristy. Neither story is supported by any words of Ambrose or by his biographer, Paulinus. Indeed, the bare truth needed no elaboration. Ambrose's private letter was kind, in the circumstances, but firm enough, and the emperor's submission to public penance was sufficient. No doubt the dramatic elements in the later versions have reinforced the Church's victory in the mind of subsequent generations.

But what kind of victory was it? The action ordered by Theodosius was indefensible, as he admitted. There is no good reason to suppose that Ambrose was happily seizing an opportunity to display the authority of the Church. As bishop, he had to demand penitence and, by the discipline of the Church, public penance, for so grievous a sin. At the same time, however, this sin was an act of State, an exercise of the coercive jurisdiction entrusted by God to the civil power, for which, on a strictly dualist view of the two spheres of Church and State, the ruler might be considered responsible directly to God, and to God only. Ambrose is not simply protesting against a wicked deed. He is, in principle, subjecting the emperor's political and administrative actions to a measure of ecclesiastical control through his private status as a layman of the Church. *Imperator intra ecclesiam est.* Taking the incident by itself, one cannot but admire and approve what Ambrose did. But as a precedent, the application of spiritual sanctions (as distinct from moral protest) to acts of State has its own spiritual dangers, manifest in history. For bishops, as well as princes, may be mistaken or greedy or ambitious. Yet, by some means or other, as Ambrose so often says, God must be set above all men and the Church must vindicate the cause of God.

Letter 51

THE TEXT

Bishop Ambrose to the most august Emperor Theodosius.

1. It is pleasant to me to recall our long-standing friendship, and I remember with gratitude the many favours which you have most graciously bestowed upon others at my intercession. From this you can be sure that it is no feeling of ingratitude which has induced me to avoid meeting you on your arrival,[1] which I had once so eagerly awaited. Why I did this, I will briefly explain.

2. I saw that in all your Court I alone was denied the natural right of hearing, and so was deprived of the power of speech as well. For you were frequently annoyed that decisions taken in your Consistory had come to my knowledge.[2] And so I am allowed no part in the common ways of mankind! For the Lord Jesus says: "Nothing is hid, that shall not be made manifest."[3] With all respect, then, I complied with your imperial will as best I could. For you I have provided that you shall have no cause for annoyance, by arranging that no word of imperial decisions reaches me; and for myself, that I shall not be compelled, by being present, either not to listen, for fear of everyone, and so let myself be spoken of as conniving at what is decided, or else to listen with my ears open, but my voice stopped, unable to tell what I have heard, for fear of hurting and bringing into danger those who come under suspicion of betraying secrets.

[1] Theodosius was at Verona from the 18th August to the 8th September. Ambrose left Milan for the country before he returned.
[2] After the Callinicum incident Ambrose was not on the best of terms with Theodosius, who showed some irritation on the occasion of the senatorial deputation, 389–390 (cf. *Letter* 57:4, p. 262). He ordered his Consistory not to divulge secrets of State to Ambrose, who for some time kept away from the Court. Some of the legislation of A.D. 390 is distinctly anti-clerical.
[3] Luke 8:17.

3. What was I to do? Not listen? I could not stop my ears with wax, as in the old stories.[4] Was I to tell what I heard? But I had to take care that what I apprehended from your commands should not result from my own words—bloodshed. Say nothing? That would be the most wretched thing of all, one's conscience bound and one's lips closed. In that case, what of the passage of Scripture: "If the priest speaketh not to the wayward, the wayward shall die in his iniquity, and the priest shall incur punishment, because he warned not the wayward."[5]

4. Please listen, your Majesty. That you have a zealous faith, I cannot deny. I am sure that you fear God. But you have a naturally hot temper. If it is soothed, you quickly change to mercy, but if it is encouraged, you are so excited that you can scarcely control it. Would to God that, if no one is moderating it, no one inflames it![6] I am willing enough to leave it to yourself, for you do recover yourself and you do overcome your natural temper by your religious zeal.

5. I preferred to leave this temper of yours privately to your own consideration. That was better than perhaps arousing it in public by my actions. I would rather fall somewhat short in my duty than in humility, and I would rather that others should miss episcopal authority in me than that you should feel any lack of respect in your devoted friend. I wanted you, with your temper under control, to have an unimpaired power to choose what course to adopt. I excused myself on the ground of illness, which was indeed severe, and scarcely to be alleviated except by gentler company.[7] Yet I would rather have died than not wait two or three days for your arrival. But I could not do so.

6. Something unparalleled in history has happened at Thessalonica, something which I tried in vain to prevent. Indeed, before it happened, when I was plying you with petitions against it, I said that it would be utterly atrocious; and when it happened, what you yourself condemned by trying—too late—to revoke, I could not extenuate. When news of it first came, a council was in session to meet the bishops from

4 Ulysses stopped the ears of his crew with wax against the attractions of the Sirens' song (Homer, *Odyssey*, XII, 173 ff.).

5 Ezek. 3:18. Again *sacerdos* links priest and bishop.

6 Perhaps especially Rufinus, Master of the Offices. Paulinus says that the courtiers worked on the emperor secretly (*Vita Amb.*, 24).

7 The MSS. have *viris*, but something to do with climate or country air seems to be required. *Auris*, breezes, has been conjectured.

Gaul.[8] Everyone deplored it, no one made light of it. The mere fact of being in communion with Ambrose would not have procured your pardon. The odium of your deed would only have been heaped higher on my head, if no one had said that you must be reconciled with our God.

7. Are you ashamed, Sir, to do as David did—David, the king and the prophet, the ancestor of Christ according to the flesh? He was told of the rich man who had exceeding many flocks and yet, when a guest arrived, took the poor man's one ewe lamb and killed it; and when he recognized that he was himself condemned by the story, he said: "I have sinned against the Lord."[9] Therefore do not take it ill, Sir, if what was said to King David is said to you: "Thou art the man."[10] For if you listen with attention and say: "I have sinned against the Lord," if you say, in the words of the royal prophet: "O come, let us worship and fall down, and weep before the Lord our Maker,"[11] then it will be said to you also: "Because thou repentest, the Lord putteth away thy sin; thou shalt not die."[12]

8. Another time, when David had commanded that the people should be numbered, his heart smote him and he said to the Lord: "I have sinned greatly in that I have done this deed: and now, O Lord, take away the iniquity of thy servant, for I have offended greatly."[13] And again Nathan the prophet was sent to him, offering him the choice of three things, to choose which he would: famine in the land for three years, or to flee from before the face of his enemies for three months, or death in the land for three days. And David answered: "Between these three things I am in a great strait. But let me fall into the hand of the Lord; for his mercies are exceeding many: and let me not fall into the hand of man."[14] His fault was that he wanted to know the number of the whole people with him, which he ought to have left to God alone to know.

9. And, we are told, when death came upon the people, on the very first day at the hour of dinner, David saw the angel smiting the people and said: "I have sinned, and I, the shepherd, have done wickedly: but these sheep, what have they done? Let thine hand be against me, and against my father's

---

[8] The Council of Milan which considered the problem of communion with Felix of Trier. See the introduction to *Letter* 24 and the notes on §12 of it (pp. 218, 224).

[9] II Sam. 12:13.   [10] II Sam. 12:7.   [11] Ps. 95 (94):6.

[12] II Sam. 12:13.   [13] II Sam. 24:10.

[14] II Sam. 24:14. For *death* A.V. has *pestilence*, Vulgate *pestilentia*. Ambrose's *mors* follows LXX *thanatos*. Cf. *Letter* 63:51 and note.

house." [15] So the Lord repented him, and he commanded the angel to spare the people, and David to offer sacrifice. For in those days there were sacrifices for sins, whereas now there are the sacrifices of penitence. And so he became more acceptable to God by his humility. That man sins is no cause for surprise. What is blameworthy is his failure to acknowledge his error and humble himself before God.

10. Job, a holy man and powerful in this world also, said: "I hid not my sin, but declared it before all the people." [16] To the fierce King Saul himself, his son Jonathan said: "Sin not against thy servant David", and: "Wherefore dost thou sin against innocent blood, to slay David without a cause?" [17] Though a king, he would have been sinning if he had put the innocent to death. When, for instance, David had come into possession of his kingdom and had heard that the innocent Abner had been slain by Joab, the captain of his host, he said: "I and my kingdom are guiltless henceforth and for ever from the blood of Abner, the son of Ner;" [18] and he fasted for sorrow.

11. I have not written this to put you to shame, but to induce you, by royal examples, to put this sin away from your kingdom. That you will do by humbling your soul before God. You are a man, and temptation has come to you. Conquer it. Sin is only put away by tears and penitence. No angel can do it, no archangel. If we sin, the Lord himself, who alone can say: "I am with you", [19] gives remission only to those who offer penitence. [20]

12. I advise, I entreat, I exhort, I admonish. I am grieved that you, who were an example of unheard-of piety, who exercised consummate clemency, who would not suffer individual offenders to be placed in jeopardy, that you, I say, should feel no pain at the destruction of so many innocent persons. You have been most successful in war, and in other ways you have deserved praise; yet piety has ever been the crown of your achievements. The devil grudged you your chief excellence. Conquer him, while you still have the means to conquer. Do not add sin to sin by following a course which has injured many.

13. For my part, though in all other respects I am a debtor to your goodness, for which I can never be ungrateful—a goodness in which I am sure you surpass many emperors and are

---

[15] II Sam. 24:17.   [16] Job 31:33, 34.   [17] I Sam. 19:4, 5.
[18] II Sam. 3:28.   [19] Matt. 28:20.
[20] *Paenitentiam deferentibus.* Repentance in the first place, but Ambrose intends to put Theodosius under penance. Cf. *Letter* 41:12, note.

equalled by one [21] only—for my part, I say, I have no reason to be contumacious towards you, but I have some cause for fear, and I dare not offer the Sacrifice if you intend to be present. Can what was not allowed when the blood of one innocent man only was shed, be allowed when the blood of many has been shed? I think not.

14. Finally, I am writing with my own hand for you alone to read. [22] As I trust in the Lord to deliver me from all tribulations, it was not by man or through man that I was forbidden to do this, but directly. In my anxiety I was preparing to go away. That very night I dreamed that you came to church, but I was not allowed to offer the Sacrifice. I pass over other things which I could have avoided, but bore for love of you, I think. The Lord grant that everything ends peaceably. Our God warns us in many different ways, by signs from heaven, [23] by the injunctions of the prophets. By visions granted even to sinners he would have us learn to ask him to end disturbances and preserve peace for you, our emperors, and to maintain the Church, whose good it is that emperors should be Christian and pious, in faith and tranquillity.

15. Doubtless you wish to be approved by God. "To every thing there is a time," [24] as it is written. "It is time to act, Lord," [25] it says, and "It is an acceptable time, O God." [26] You shall make your oblation when you are given permission to sacrifice, when your offering is acceptable to God. Should I not be delighted to have the emperor's favour and do as you wish, if the case allowed it? Prayer by itself, however, is a sacrifice. It wins pardon, while to offer would cause offence. It shows humility; the other would suggest contempt. God himself has said that he would rather have his commandments obeyed than sacrifice offered to him. God proclaims this, Moses declares it to the people of Israel, Paul preaches it to the nations. Do that which you see is better for the time. "I desire mercy more than sacrifice", [27] it says. Are not those who condemn their sin truer Christians than those who think to defend it? "The just accuses himself in the beginning of his words." [28] He who accuses himself when he sins is just, not he who praises himself.

---

[21] Gratian.

[22] The letter was indeed secret, and was not known to Paulinus and the early ecclesiastical historians.

[23] A comet was visible 22nd August–17th September, 390.

[24] Eccl. 3:1.   [25] Ps. 119 (118):126.   [26] Ps. 69 (68):13.

[27] Hos. 6:6; Matt. 9:13.   [28] Prov. 18:17.

16. I wish, Sir, that I had before this trusted myself rather than your habit of mind, thinking how you quickly pardon and quickly revoke your orders, as you have often done. You have been anticipated and I have not shrunk from what it was my duty not to shun. But thanks be to the Lord who willeth to chastise his servants, that he may not destroy them. I share this now with the prophets; you will share it one day with the saints.

17. Shall I not value the father of Gratian [29] more than my own eyes? Your other sacred offspring must pardon me. I have put a name sweet to me before those whom I love equally. I love you, I hold you in affection, I attend you with my prayers. If you believe me, do as I say. If you believe me, acknowledge the truth of my words. If you do not believe me, forgive me for putting God first. May your Majesty be blessed with all happiness and prosperity, and, together with your sacred offspring, enjoy perpetual peace.

[29] If Gratian here is still the emperor, as Palanque and Dudden suppose, with the Benedictine editors, "father" is applied to the older emperor. But we should have far better sense if we could accept the theory of Rauschen that Theodosius had had a son by his second wife, Galla, and named him Gratian. Then Ambrose gracefully apologizes to the elder brothers Arcadius and Honorius, sons of Flaccilla, for mentioning the baby first (antetuli).

Letter 57: Ambrose and Eugenius

INTRODUCTION

VALENTINIAN'S POSITION IN THE WEST DEPENDED on the support and loyalty of the Frankish Count Arbogast, commander of the Roman army in Gaul. They quarrelled, and the young emperor, having vainly attempted to dismiss the Count, turned to Theodosius for help, which was not given in time. Ambrose was on his way to Gaul to baptize Valentinian when he heard that the emperor had been found dead in his palace on the 15th May, A.D. 392. Whether it was murder or suicide we do not now know. As Theodosius did not at once reveal his policy, Ambrose did nothing about Arbogast, and when in August the general, who as a pagan could have no hope of the imperial throne, raised Eugenius to the purple, it was again uncertain whether Theodosius would acknowledge him as his legitimate colleague. So Ambrose did not answer the two letters in which Eugenius sought recognition by the bishop of the western capital.

Early in 393 it became clear that Theodosius intended to break with Eugenius, who therefore turned to the pagan party for assistance, and, with Arbogast, entered Italy, where he was not opposed. Ambrose avoided him by leaving Milan. *Letter 57*, which treats him as at least *de facto* emperor, upbraids him for his concessions to paganism and, without using the word, excommunicates him, once again using spiritual sanctions for actions which Ambrose looked at from the standpoint of religion and took to be under a bishop's disciplinary authority, but which were also acts of State for which a case might be made.

The introduction to *Letter 17* (p. 190) will help to explain many details in the present letter. While Eugenius was at Milan, the ecclesiastical situation there must have been very difficult, for the clergy would not admit him to communion.

259

Ambrose absented himself, mostly at Florence. The decisive clash between Theodosius and Eugenius took place in the Julian Alps on 5th and 6th September, A.D. 394, when the victory of Theodosius at the River Frigidus put an end to the pagan revival. Ambrose afterwards found it necessary to assure Theodosius that he had not withdrawn from Milan because he despaired of the Christian emperor's success, but in order to avoid the sacrilegious Eugenius. He had returned on the 1st August, as soon as Eugenius left the city.

Letter 57

THE TEXT

Bishop Ambrose to the most gracious Emperor Eugenius.

1. The reason for my departure was the fear of the Lord, by whom I endeavour to direct all my actions. It has never been my way to turn my mind away from him, or to count any man's favour of more value than the favour of Christ. I wrong no one when I prefer God to all, and, trusting in him, I am not afraid to say to you emperors what, to the best of my ability, I think right. So I shall not refrain from saying to you, most gracious Emperor, what I have not refrained from saying to emperors before you. To keep the order of events, I will review concisely the relevant facts.

2. When the most honourable Symmachus was Prefect of Rome, he sent a *Memorial* to the Emperor Valentinian II of august memory, asking him to order the restoration of their confiscated revenues to the temples. He did his duty in accordance with his own feeling and his own religion. It was no less incumbent upon me to take account of my duty as bishop. I presented two petitions to the emperors in which I pointed out that a Christian could not restore funds for sacrifices. I said that I had not been responsible for their confiscation, though I did now propose that they should not be decreed. I added that he would be thought to be granting them to the idols himself, not restoring them. He could not really restore what he had not personally taken away. Rather, he was of his own motion making a gift to meet the expenses of superstition. Finally, if he did it, either he should not come to church, or else, if he came, he would not find a bishop there or he would find one prepared to resist him in church. I told him that he could not excuse himself on the ground that he was only a catechumen, since even catechumens are not allowed to provide funds for idols.

261

3. My petitions were read in the Consistory. The most honourable Count Bauto, holding the office of Magister Militum, was present, and so was Rumoridus, a man of the same rank and an adherent of heathen worship from his early childhood. At that time Valentinian listened to my advice and did nothing contrary to the necessary demands of our faith. The counts also agreed with their master.[1]

4. Later, I gave my views verbally to the most gracious Emperor Theodosius, not hesitating to speak to him face to face. When he was informed of the delegation from the Senate (though the request did not come from the whole Senate), he at last accepted my version of the affair, and then for a few days I did not go to see him. He did not take this ill, because I was not seeking my own advantage, but, to his benefit and my own soul's, "I was not ashamed to speak in the sight of the king".[2]

5. A second delegation from the Senate to prince Valentinian of august memory, when he was in Gaul, failed to extort anything from him. I was not there, and had not written to him on that occasion.

6. Sometime after your Grace had taken up the reins of government, we learned that the revenues had been granted subsequently to persons eminent indeed in public life, but pagans by religion. And it may perhaps be said, your Majesty, that you did not restore them to the temples but granted them to men who had deserved well of you. But you know that the fear of God requires us to act with constancy, as is often done in the cause of liberty, not only by bishops, but also by those in your service and by the ordinary inhabitant of the provinces. When you became emperor, the delegates asked you to restore the funds to the temples. You did not. A second time others made the same request. You refused. And subsequently you thought fit to give them to the very men who made the petition!

7. The power of the emperor is indeed great; but consider, Sir, how great God is. He sees the hearts of all, he questions the innermost conscience, he "knows all things before they are done",[3] he knows the secrets of your breast. You do not allow anyone to deceive you, and do you expect to hide anything from

---

1 The Benedictine text has *adquieverunt etiam comiti suo*, which is nonsense. Palanque accepted Seeck's conjecture *comites duo*. Wytzes, feeling that *duo* here would be unusual Latin, suggested *dno*, i.e., *domino*; and Palanque, reviewing his book, accepted this.

2 Ps. 119 (118):46.   3 Ecclus. 23:20.

God? That cannot have entered your mind. For however stubbornly they pressed their suit, was it not your duty, Sir, out of reverence for the most high and true and living God, to resist them with even greater stubbornness and refuse what was derogatory to the Law of God?

8. Who grudges your giving others what you please? We do not pry into your generosity, we do not grudge others their advantages. But we are the interpreters of the faith. How will you offer your gifts to Christ? Few will judge of your actions, everyone will judge of your intentions. Whatever they do will be ascribed to you, whatever they do not do, to themselves. Indeed you are emperor; all the more must you submit yourself to God. How will Christ's bishops be able to dispense your benefactions?

9. There was a question of this kind in the days of old, but even persecution yielded to the faith of our fathers, and heathendom gave way.[4] For "when certain games that came every fifth year were kept at Tyre", and the villainous King of Antioch had come to see them, Jason ordered the temple stewards, as Antiochians of Jerusalem, to take three hundred silver didrachmas and give them to the sacrifice of Hercules. But our fathers did not give the money to the heathen. They sent faithful men to protest that it was not paid for sacrifices to the gods, which was not fitting, but given for other expenses. And it was declared that, as he had said that the money was sent for the sacrifice of Hercules, it should be used for the purpose for which it had been sent. But when those who brought it replied in accordance with their own feelings and their own religion that it was not available for the sacrifice, but for other necessities, the money was handed over to build ships. Although they sent the money under compulsion it was not used for the sacrifice, but for other State expenses.

10. Of course those who brought it could have said nothing; but that would have done violence to their faith, for they knew for what purpose it was given. So they sent men who feared God to secure that what was sent should not be assigned to the temple but to pay for ships. They entrusted the money to them to plead the cause of the holy Law. The result was judge, and

---

[4] II Macc. 4:18–20. To judge from the rhythm, *rex sceleratissimus*, Ambrose transfers "villainous" from Jason to Antiochus. But I have not followed Wytzes, who also transfers *Antiochenses* to the didrachmas, but have assumed that the clumsy Latin preserves the original sense. Verse 9 explains why they were Antiochians of Jerusalem.

this declared them innocent. If men who were in the power of another took such precautions, there can be no doubt, Sir, what your duty was. You were under no compulsion, in no one's power, and you should have taken the advice of a bishop.

11. For my part, although I was the only one to resist, I was not the only one to desire and counsel resistance. Therefore I am bound by my own words before God and before all men, and I have come to see that I have no other choice and no other duty than to consult my own interests. For I could not honestly give in to you. I have for a long time repressed my grief and long concealed it, thinking it right to say nothing to anyone. But now I must not dissemble, I am not at liberty to be silent. When you wrote to me at the beginning of your reign, I did not reply, because I foresaw that this would happen. When I did not answer and you demanded a reply, I said: "The reason for this is that I think it will be extorted from him."

12. But when occasion arose for the exercise of my office on behalf of persons anxious about their fate, I wrote and interceded for them,[5] showing that, while in the cause of God I feel a proper fear and do not set flattery above the good of my soul, in cases where petition should properly be made to you, I too show the deference due to your authority. For it is written: "Honour to whom honour, tribute to whom tribute." When I cordially deferred to the private citizen, how could I not defer to the emperor? But since you desire deference to yourself, allow me to defer to him whom you wish to be considered the author of your empire.

5 For Ambrose's use of episcopal *intercessio* see the note to *Letter* 40:25.

Letter 63: The Episcopal Election at Vercellae

INTRODUCTION

AMBROSE'S LONGEST EXTANT LETTER, AND ONE OF his last, was written in A.D. 396 to the Christians of Vercellae, some forty-five miles west of Milan, during the vacancy of the See. Until *c.* 345–350 Vercellae had been within the diocese of Milan, which probably had no precise boundaries then, at any rate to the north and west. Its first bishop was Eusebius, a Sardinian, who was a Reader at Rome, when he was chosen for the new See. He came to be one of the outstanding bishops of his time. Faithful to the creed of Nicaea, he withstood Constantius at the Council of Milan, A.D. 355, and was banished to Scythopolis in Palestine, whose bishop was an Arian. Under Julian's edict of toleration he was able to return from exile, took part with Athanasius in the Council of Alexandria of A.D. 362, and was sent from it to Antioch to negotiate an end of the schism there, only to be forestalled and frustrated by Lucifer of Cagliari (his fellow-confessor at Milan), who consecrated Paulinus as Bishop of Antioch. At Vercellae he introduced the practice of having his clergy live together under a monastic rule.

A letter written by Eusebius from exile gives us some idea of the great extent of his diocese, and *a fortiori* of the diocese of Milan before Vercellae had been subtracted from it. It is addressed to his congregations (*plebes*) in four cities, Vercellae, Novara, Hippo Regia (Eporedia, Ivrea) and Dertona (Tortona). The diocesanization of North Italy quickened its pace in the second half of the fourth century, and by the time Ambrose wrote *Letter* 63, Dertona certainly and Eporedia possibly had become separate dioceses. Ambrose intended to give Novara a bishop, but this was in fact done by his successor.

Eusebius died about A.D. 370, and was succeeded by Limenius, who was present at the Council of Aquileia, 381. By the sixth century he was being venerated as a saint, but it is note-worthy that in the present letter, with its lavish praise of Euse-bius, nothing is said of his successor.

The death of Limenius was followed by a long vacancy, the people being unable to decide upon a candidate. Ambrose, as metropolitan, intervened with the present letter. It may be that the division of the diocese had caused some difficulty, though of this there is no evidence. It may be that Limenius was some-how responsible for the existence of party strife, since he is not commended by Ambrose. The principal cause of controversy, however, is plain enough, and calls for a word about Jovinian.

Once a monk in Ambrose's own monastery outside the walls of Milan, Jovinian reacted against asceticism, went to Rome, and began to attack not simply the practice of celibacy and abstin-ence, but the prevalent notion that these states and virtues of themselves earned a higher reward in heaven. He made his position more precarious by denying the perpetual virginity of Mary. He was excommunicated by Pope Siricius in 392 and went to Milan, pursued by a letter from Siricius to the northern bishops, warning them against him. He was accordingly con-demned by a Milanese council, oddly enough as a Manichaean (Ambrose, *Letter* 42, gives the details), and was attacked about the same time in Jerome's *Adversus Jovinianum*, a work which shows Jerome at his worst. Jovinian was expelled from Milan, and is heard of no more; but two of his disciples, Sarmatio and Barbatianus, also ex-monks, are found at work in Vercellae, where they seem to have secured a considerable backing. It might be conjectured that Limenius had given them some encourage-ment, though again there is no proof of this. It might also be conjectured that one of the divisive issues was whether or not the clergy should live under a monastic rule. Of course, it may be only that the more easy-going and wealthier laymen of Ver-cellae did not want a bishop who would be always exhorting them to fasting, poverty and celibacy, while others favoured this ideal.

Ambrose, who had founded a monastery and written numer-ous ascetic works, was naturally eager to stamp out any traces of Jovinianism and to see that the clergy of Vercellae should still—or again—live under a monastic rule. His praise of Euse-bius must be understood in the light of this intention. Ambrose is not merely saying to them: "You had a good bishop once, make sure of finding another." Again, although much of the letter consists at first sight of ordinary moral teaching such as any bishop might give to any congregation, it is probable that most of it bears directly on the matters which were dividing the people. The letter is also interesting as showing how great a part the laity might play at this period in the choice of their bishop, and how much store was set by unanimity or substantial agreement as a token of divine approbation. After the election by the clergy and people, the candidate had to be approved by the metropolitan and consecrated by the bishops of the province. Thus local knowledge was balanced with a wider outlook and experience.

The letter was not successful in ending the strife, and Ambrose found it necessary to go to Vercellae. Eventually Honoratus was appointed, a presbyter who had been with Eusebius in exile and presumably shared his views. To him fell the sad duty of administering the last rites to Ambrose on the 4th April, A.D. 397.

Letter 63

THE TEXT

Ambrose, the servant of Christ, called to be a bishop, to the church at Vercellae and to those who call upon the name of our Lord Jesus Christ: Grace be multiplied unto you from God the Father and his only-begotten Son in the Holy Ghost.

1. I am very greatly distressed that the church of the Lord which is among you has still no bishop, and now alone in all the provinces of Liguria, Aemilia, Venetia, and the adjacent parts of Italy is without that office which other churches have so often sought from it for themselves. And I am ashamed to learn that the contention among you, which has been the obstacle, is put down to me. While you are divided, what can I decide? How can you elect anybody? How can anyone accept, taking upon himself, with his people divided, a burden which it is not easy to carry even when there is unity?

2. Has the teaching of a confessor come to this? Are these the sons of the righteous fathers who approved the holy Eusebius at first sight, though he was an utter stranger to them, setting their own countrymen aside and approving him the moment they saw him? The choice of the whole church, no wonder he turned out so great a man! Asked for unanimously, no wonder it was believed that he had been chosen by divine providence! You should follow the example of your fathers. Indeed, you ought to excel them in proportion to the excellence of the teacher who instructed you. For you have been taught by a holy confessor. You ought to give proof of your moderation and unity by your agreement in the choice of a bishop.

3. The Lord has told us that if two are agreed on earth as touching anything that they shall ask: "It shall be done for them of my Father which is in heaven. For where two or three are gathered together in my name, there am I in the midst of

268

them."[1] When, therefore, a whole congregation is gathered together in the name of the Lord and all ask for the same man, it would surely be wrong of us to doubt that the Lord Jesus is present with them to prompt their wills and decide what they ask, to preside over the ordination and bestow grace.

4. Therefore make yourselves worthy to have Christ in your midst. . . .

[Ambrose now turns to the causes of the dissension at Vercellae, chief among which were two followers of Jovinian, a vigorous critic of the monastic and ascetic ideals. Ambrose therefore praises fasting, temperance, and, at some length, virginity. This last theme leads him back to the Church, "a virgin without spot or wrinkle", and so to the episcopal election.]

46. While all our actions should be free from hidden malevolence, this is particularly the case in the selection of a bishop, whose life is the pattern for all his flock. Calm and pacific judgment is called for if you are to prefer to all his fellows a man who will be elected by all and who will heal all dissension. "The gentle man is the physician of the heart".[2] In the Gospel the Lord declared himself the physician of the heart when he said: "They that are whole have no need of a physician, but they that are sick."[3]

47. He is the good physician, who has taken our infirmities upon him and healed our sicknesses. Yet he, as it is written: "glorified not himself to be made an high priest, but the Father that spake unto him said, 'Thou art my Son, this day have I begotten thee': as he saith also in another place, 'Thou art a priest for ever after the order of Melchizedek'."[4] He (because he was to be the type of all priests) took flesh, "that in the days of his flesh he might offer up prayers and supplications with strong crying and tears to God the Father; and, though he was the Son of God, might be seen to learn obedience from the things which he suffered, which he might teach us, that he might become unto us the author of salvation."[5] Then, having accomplished his sufferings, as being himself made perfect, he gave health to all and bore the sin of all.

48. He himself chose Aaron to be high priest[6] in order that in the election of a priest the grace of God might have more weight than human ambition. No one should put himself forward, no one should take it upon himself. It must be a call

1 Matt. 18:19, 20. 2 Prov. 14:30. 3 Matt. 9:12.
4 Heb. 5:5,6. 5 Heb. 5:7-9. 6 Cf. Num. 17:8.

from above, "that he may offer gifts for sins who can have compassion on the erring, for that (it says) he himself also is compassed with infirmity." [7] No man should "take the honour unto himself, but when he is called of God, as was Aaron". [8] So also Christ did not demand priesthood, but received it.

49. When the hereditary succession from Aaron contained more heirs by birth than in righteousness, there came, after the type of that Melchizedek of whom we read in the Old Testament, the true Melchizedek, the true king of peace, the true king of righteousness (for that is what the name means), "without father, without mother, without genealogy, havir ; neither beginning of days, nor end of life." [9] This refers to the Son of God, who in his divine generation knew no mother and in his birth of the Virgin Mary knew no father; who, born of the Father alone before the worlds and sprung from the Virgin alone in this world, could have no beginning of days, for he was in the beginning. [10] And how could he who is the author of life to all have an end of life? He is "the beginning and the ending" of all. [11] But the passage also shows by way of example that the bishop [12] ought to be without father and without mother in the sense that he is not chosen for his noble birth, but for his moral reputation and pre-eminence in virtue.

50. He must have faith and a settled character, not one without the other, but both in one, together with good works and deeds. The apostle Paul wants us to be imitators of them who, as he says, "through faith and patience inherit the promises of Abraham", [13] who by patience was counted worthy to receive and inherit the grace of the blessing promised to him. The prophet David admonishes us to imitate holy Aaron, setting him before us among the saints of the Lord as an example, "Moses and Aaron among his priests, and Samuel among such as call upon his name." [14]

51. Aaron was indeed a man fit to be set before all as an example to follow. When, in consequence of the rebellion, dread death was spreading among the people, he threw himself between the living and the dying to stay death, that no more should perish. [15] Truly a man of episcopal [16] heart and mind,

---

[7] Heb. 5: 1, 2.   [8] Heb. 5:4.   [9] Gen. 14:18–20; Heb. 7:1–3.
[10] John 1:1.   [11] Rev. 1:8.   [12] *Sacerdos.*
[13] Heb. 6:12–15.   [14] Ps. 99 (98):6.
[15] Num. 16:48. For "death" (*mors*), the Vulgate has *plaga*, the A.V. "plague." The LXX has *thrausis*, breaking or shattering, which Ambrose does not follow this time. Cf. *Letter* 51:8 and note.
[16] *Sacerdotalis.*

offering himself in loyal affection for the Lord's flock, as a good shepherd. Thus he broke the sting of death, stayed its onset, denied it passage. His loyalty increased his merit, for he offered himself for those who were resisting him.

52. Therefore let the dissident learn to fear the displeasure of the Lord and to be at peace with his priests. Were not Dathan, Abiram and Korah swallowed up by an earthquake because of their dissidence?[17] When Korah, Dathan and Abiram had provoked two hundred and fifty men to separate themselves from Moses and Aaron, they rose up against them and said: "Enough for you that all the congregation are holy, every one of them, and the Lord is among them".[18]

53. At this the Lord was angry, and spoke to the whole congregation. The Lord considered and knew who were his, and brought his holy ones near unto him. Those whom he did not choose, he did not bring near unto him. And the Lord commanded Korah and all those who had risen up with him against Moses and Aaron, the priests of the Lord, to take them censers and put incense upon them, that he whom the Lord had chosen might be established as holy among the Levites of the Lord.

54. And Moses said to Korah: "Hear me, ye sons of Levi, is it a small thing unto you, that God hath separated you from the congregation of Israel, and brought you near to himself, to minister the service of the tabernacle of the Lord?" And below, "Seek ye the priesthood? Thus art thou and all thy company gathered together against God. And Aaron, what is he that ye murmur concerning him?"[19]

55. When therefore they considered the causes of the offence, namely that men unworthy of it wanted to hold the office of priest and were therefore causing dissension, murmuring against God and censuring his judgment in the choice of his priest, the whole people was seized with a great fear, and dread of punishment overwhelmed them. But when they all besought God that all might not perish for the insolence of a few, the guilty were marked off, the two hundred and fifty men and their leaders were separated from the body of the people, there was a sound of roaring and the earth clave asunder in the midst of the people, a deep gulf opened, the offenders were snatched

---

[17] The story of Korah in Numbers 16 is naturally used by the Fathers as a stock warning against schism, faction, and disobedience to authority. Cyprian often quotes it, e.g., in *Letter* 73:8 (p. 162).

[18] Num. 16:3. [19] Num. 16:8-11.

away and removed from all contact with the elements of this world. Not for them to pollute the air by breathing it or heaven by looking at it, to contaminate the sea with their touch or the earth with their tombs!

56. Their punishment came to an end, but not their wickedness. At this there arose a murmuring among them that the people had perished by means of the priests. Then the Lord was moved to indignation and would have destroyed them all, had he not first bowed to the prayers of Moses and Aaron, and afterwards, at the intervention of Aaron his priest, chosen to increase the humiliation of their pardon by giving them, ungrateful as they were, to the very men whose favour [20] they were repudiating.

57. Even the prophetess Miriam, who had crossed the sea with her brothers on foot, not yet understanding the mystery of the Ethiopian woman, murmured against her brother Moses, and was covered with leprous spots; and she would scarcely have been freed from the terrible infection without the prayers of Moses. [21] This murmuring of hers, however, is to be taken as a type of the synagogue. Not understanding the mystery [22] of the Ethiopian woman, that is, the Church of the Gentiles, she daily abuses and envies and murmurs against the people by whose faith she will herself be freed from the leprosy of her unbelief. For we read that "blindness in part hath befallen Israel until the fulness of the Gentiles be come in, and so all Israel shall be saved." [23]

58. Another example will show us that it is divine rather than human grace which works in priests. Of all the rods which Moses had taken from the tribes and laid up, only Aaron's blossomed. [24] In this way the people learned to see in a priest an office conferred by divine appointment, and they stopped claiming to possess an equal grace by human appointment, although previously they believed themselves to have an equal prerogative. [25] The rod was simply intended to show that priestly grace never withers and, with the utmost humility,

---

[20] *Gratia*, translated "privilege" in the *Library of the Fathers* and by Romestin. It is true that they were rebelling against priestly privilege; but here they are *ingratos*, ungrateful, to those who interceded for them and saved them. If this is correct, it could be translated "kindness" or "benefits." "Favour" can include, if necessary, the priests' favour with God.

[21] Num. 12:1 and 10. A. V.: Ethiopian, R. V.: Cushite woman whom Moses married.

[22] *Sacramentum.*   [23] Rom. 11: 25.   [24] Num. 17:8.

[25] *Parem gratiam . . . parem praerogativam.*

bears in the exercise of its office the blossom of the authority committed to it. This too must be taken mystically.[26] It is not without significance, I think, that this happened towards the end of Aaron's life. It seems to indicate that the ancient people, decaying through the age-long infidelity of its priests, will in the last days be transformed to zealous faith and devotion by the example of the Church, and will again put forth, with renewed grace, its long-dead blossom.

59. Again, after the death of Aaron, God did not command the whole people, but only Moses, who was among the priests of the Lord, to strip Aaron the priest of his garments and put them upon his son, Eleazar.[27] The whole point of this is to make us see that it must be a bishop who consecrates a bishop, clothes him with the vestments—that is, the virtues—of a bishop and, when he is sure that no vestment is lacking and that all is in order, conducts him to the holy altar. For if he is to offer prayer for the people, he must be chosen by God and approved by the bishops. There must be no grave cause of offence in one whose office it is to intercede for the offences of others. To be a bishop calls for no small virtue. He must keep himself from the tiniest sins, not merely from the graver ones. He must be quick to show pity, he must keep his promise, he must raise the fallen, sympathize with pain, be always kind, love piety, dispel or repress anger. He must be a trumpet to rouse his people to devotion or soothe them into tranquillity.

60. There is an old saying: "Learn to be one",[28] so that your life may be like a portrait, always presenting the same likeness. But you cannot "be one" if you are inflamed with anger at one moment, boiling with extreme indignation at another, your face now flushed, now pale, changing colour every moment. Admittedly, it is natural to be angry, or there is generally cause for anger. Still, it is our duty as human beings to moderate our anger, and not be carried away by a brutal fury knowing no restraint. It is our duty not to sow strife, not to exacerbate family

---

[26] *Mysterium.*

[27] Num. 20:26, where Moses consecrates Eleazar. Ambrose is on slightly delicate ground here, since Moses was not spoken of as a priest in the same way as Aaron. So he quotes Psalm 99:6 in § 50, and inserts the words "the priests of the Lord" into the passage from Numbers 16 which he is using in § 53. What if Moses were taken as a type of the godly prince? However, he was a Levite.

[28] I.e., single-minded, consistent. I presume that the old saying was a crisp one, not extending beyond the three words *adsuesce unus esse*, which I translate literally.

quarrels. "A wrathful man diggeth up sin." [29] You cannot "be one" if you are double-minded, if you cannot control yourself when you are angry, of which David well says: "Be ye angry, and sin not." [30] He is not commanding us to be angry, but making allowances for human nature. The anger which we cannot help feeling we can at least moderate. So, even if we are angry, our emotions may be stirred in accordance with nature, but we must not sin, contrary to nature. If a man cannot govern himself, it is intolerable that he should undertake to govern others.

61. So the Apostle has given us a pattern, since "the bishop must be without reproach." Elsewhere he says: "For the bishop must be blameless, as God's steward; not proud, not soon angry, not given to wine, no striker, not greedy of filthy lucre." [31] What agreement can there be between the compassion of the generous and the avarice of the greedy?

62. I have put down the faults which I have been taught to avoid. But it is the Apostle who is the teacher of virtues. He teaches a bishop "to convince the gainsayers" patiently, and bids him be "the husband of one wife", [32] not excluding him from marriage altogether (for that would go beyond the precepts [33] of the law), but encouraging him by chastity in marriage to preserve the grace of his baptism. And he gives him no inducement by apostolic authority to beget sons again once he has become a bishop, for he speaks of him as "having children", not begetting them or marrying a second time.

63. I could not pass over this matter because there are many who argue that "husband of one wife" is said of marriage after baptism, on the ground that the fault which would constitute an impediment has been washed away in baptism. It is of course true that all faults and sins are washed away, so that a man who has defiled his body with many women, none of them bound to him in lawful matrimony, is forgiven everything. But where there has been a second marriage, it is not dissolved. Sin is washed away in baptism, law is not. For though there is

---

[29] Prov. 15:18.   [30] Ps. 4:4.
[31] I Tim. 3:2; Titus 1:7.   [32] Titus 1:9 and 6.
[33] Celibacy is a counsel, not a precept, where this distinction is used. It looks rather as if "digamy" was an issue in the episcopal election at Vercellae, Ambrose implicitly excluding a digamous candidate. Unable to find biblical authority forbidding married clergy to beget children, Ambrose has to content himself with pointing out that Paul does not positively authorize them to do so. By this time (but probably not much earlier) it was customary in the West for the clergy to abstain from physical intercourse with their wives, if they were not celibate.

no sin in marriage, there is law in it, and therefore what is lawful is not remitted as sin, but retained as law.[34] Now the Apostle has laid down a law, namely: "If any man is blameless, the husband of one wife". Consequently, anyone who is blameless and the husband of one wife comes within the law governing the qualifications of a bishop, while a man who has married again, though he commits no sin and is not polluted thereby, is disqualified for the prerogative of episcopacy.[35]

64. I have been speaking of the demands of law. I shall go on to say what reason prescribes. But first take note that in addition to the Apostle's ruling on bishops and presbyters, the Fathers at the Council of Nicaea decreed that no one who contracts a second marriage shall be ordained at all.[36] For how can he comfort and honour a widow, how can he exhort her to remain a widow and keep faith with her husband, when he has not kept faith with his own first wife? Again, what difference would there be between bishop and people if both were bound by the same laws? As the bishop is pre-eminent in grace, so must he be pre-eminent in virtue. He who binds others by his own precepts must observe in his own life the precepts of the law.

65. How I struggled against being ordained![37] And when at last I was forced to it, how hard I tried at least to get my ordination postponed! But the pressure was too strong for the rules. However, the bishops of the West decided to approve my ordination, and the eastern bishops showed their approval by following its example[38]—though it is forbidden to ordain "a

---

34 There is a closely parallel passage in *De Officiis*, I, 247.

35 The eastern churches allowed the ordination of a man who had not been married twice after baptism (e.g., *Apostolic Canons*, 17), and Jerome defends this (*Letter* 69). Ambrose's view soon became normal in the West (e.g., Augustine and Innocent I accept it), if it was not already so. For his teaching on clerical celibacy see Dudden, pp. 124–125, and on marriage and virginity in general, pp. 144–159.

36 Nicaea did not legislate against digamy at all, in the sense of successive marriages. On the contrary, it required Novatianist clergy returning to the catholic Church to abjure their rigorist rule of excommunicating those who married twice.

37 For Ambrose's devices to avoid or delay consecration see Paulinus, *Vita Amb.*, 7–8.

38 He does not mean that the western bishops subsequently decided (in a Council or otherwise) to approve his consecration, but that the consecrating bishops decided to overlook the fact that he was not baptized, taking general acclamation to be a proof of divine choice. In the East, the unbaptized Nectarius, like Ambrose a civil servant, was made Bishop of Constantinople in 381. Against this there really was a Nicene canon (no. 2).

novice, lest he be lifted up with pride".[39] If my ordination was not postponed, it was under constraint; and where the humility proper to a bishop is not wanting, he will not be blamed when he was not responsible.

66. If so much consideration is needed in ordaining a bishop for other churches, how much care is called for in the church of Vercellae, where two things are equally demanded of the bishop, monastic asceticism and ecclesiastical discipline. For Eusebius of holy memory was the first in western parts to bring these different systems together. Though living in a city, he observed monastic rules, and while governing his church he practised fasting and self-discipline. A bishop's services are greatly enhanced if he obliges the younger clergy to practise abstinence and accept the rule of chastity, if, while they live in the city, he keeps them away from its mode of life.[40]

67. Hence the illustrious line of Elijah, Elisha, and John, the son of Elizabeth, who, clothed in sheepskins and goatskins, needy and destitute, afflicted with pains and torments, wandered in deserts, among mountain heights and thickets, among pathless rocks and gloomy caves, in marshy bogs, of whose life the world was not worthy.[41] Hence Daniel, Ananias, Azarias, and Misael, although they were nourished in the king's palace, eat only coarse food, with water to drink, fasting as if they were in the desert.[42] Rightly did the king's servants prevail over kingdoms, throw off the yoke and scorn captivity, subdue powers, conquer the elements, quench the power of fire, dull the flames, blunt the edge of the sword, stop the mouths of lions. Where they had been counted weak, they were found strong.[43] They did not shrink from the mockery of men, for they hoped for a heavenly reward. They did not dread the darkness of prison, for the grace of eternal light was shining upon them.

68. Following their example, the holy Eusebius went out from his own country and kindred, choosing to live in a strange land rather than take his ease at home.[44] For the sake of his faith he preferred the hardships of exile, in company with Dionysius of holy memory, who set a voluntary exile above the emperor's friendship.[45] So when these never-to-be-forgotten

[39] I Tim. 3:6.
[40] Can monasticism be practised in a city? See Jerome, *Letter* 14:6, 7 (p. 296).
[41] Heb. 11:37, 38 elaborated.   [42] Dan. 1:16.
[43] Heb. 11: 33, 34 elaborated.   [44] Like Abraham, Gen. 12:1; Heb. 11:8.
[45] Dionysius of Milan and Eusebius were banished after the Council of Milan, A.D. 355, where they defied Constantius. The details are given

heroes were carried off from the cathedral, surrounded and jostled by men in arms, they triumphed over the might of empire. Purchasing to themselves by earthly shame a resolution of spirit and a royal power, no troops of soldiers, no clash of arms, could take their faith away from them, and they subdued the bestial ferocity of mind which had no power to hurt the saints. For, as you read in Proverbs: "The king's wrath is as the wrath of a lion." [46]

69. He confessed himself beaten when he asked them to change their minds. They thought their pens of reed stronger than swords of iron. Then was unbelief wounded and brought low, not the faith of the saints. They did not need a grave in their own country; a heavenly mansion was prepared for them. They wandered over the world as having nothing, and possessing all things. [47] Wherever they were sent, it was to them a paradise. Abounding in the riches of faith, they could lack nothing. Poor in money, but rich in grace, they made others rich. [48] They were tempted, but not slain; in fastings, in labours, in imprisonments, in watchings. [49] Out of weakness they were made strong. [50] They looked for no tempting delicacies; hunger filled them to the full. The summer heat did not parch them; they were refreshed with the hope of eternal grace. The frosts of icy regions did not crush them; their own devotion brought them the warm breath of spring. They feared no human chains; Jesus had set them free. They did not ask to be rescued from death; they took for granted that Christ would raise them from the dead.

70. In answer to his prayers, the holy Dionysius laid down his life in exile. Not for him to return and find his devoted clergy and people brought to confusion by the habits and practices of unbelievers. He obtained this favour, with tranquil mind to carry the peace of the Lord with him to the grave. And so, as holy Eusebius was the first to raise the confessor's standard, blessed Dionysius, expiring in his place of exile, was the first to win the martyr's name. [51]

in Hilary's *Collectio Anti-Ariana* (C.S.E.L., 65). It is Constantius who is referred to here and in § 69. [46] Prov. 19:12.
[47] II Cor. 6:10. [48] II Cor. 6:10. [49] II Cor. 6:5. [50] Heb. 11:34.
[51] *Priori martyribus titulo* in the Benedictine text, which the editors explain as *potiori*, better than, martyrdom, in that his long sufferings in exile surpassed the brief pains of martyrdom. They are followed by the English translators. But is not the point simply that, although Eusebius was the first to be a confessor (Hilary tells how and why), Dionysius was the first to die a martyr (Eusebius did not)? *Martyrii* would be simpler.

71. In holy Eusebius endurance grew with monastic discipline, and, becoming accustomed to a harder rule, he drew from
it the power to carry his burdens. It will not be questioned that
there are two outstanding forms of unreserved[52] Christian
devotion, the clerical office and the monastic rule. The former
schools us in forbearance and courtesy, the latter inures us to
abstinence and endurance. The one lives as on a stage, the
other in secret, the one is watched, the other hidden. It was a
good athlete who said: "We are made a spectacle unto this
world, and to angels."[53] And truly he was worthy to be watched
by the angels as he strove to win the prize of Christ, as he
struggled to establish the life of angels on earth and confound
the wickedness of angels in heaven. For he wrestled with
spiritual wickedness. Rightly did the world watch him, in
order to follow his example.

[Ambrose then illustrates the ascetic life from the stories of
Elijah, warns Vercellae that if it wants clergy who will give
themselves to reading and hard work, fast and keep themselves
from women, they will need a good teacher; and that the people
will be unable to choose such a bishop until they have settled
their own disputes. Thus he is able to conclude with general
moral instruction.]

52 *Adtentiore*, more advanced, more whole-hearted. Ambrose thinks of the
   monastic and clerical states as intrinsically higher states of life than lay
   Christianity.
53 I Cor. 4:9.

Jerome

Jerome

GENERAL INTRODUCTION

I

EUSEBIUS HIERONYMUS WAS BORN ABOUT A.D. 347 at Stridon near Aquileia, of a prosperous middle-class family. "I was born a Christian, of Christian parents," Jerome said, and "From my cradle I have been nourished with catholic milk." When he was about twelve years old he was sent to Rome, together with his friend Bonosus, to continue his education. For four years he studied "grammar" (that is, literature), having as his master the famous Aelius Donatus, the commentator on Terence and Virgil, whose elementary grammars were standard works in the Middle Ages. After this Jerome went on to another four years' study of "rhetoric" and philosophy. He was an ardent student of literature and a lover of books, always eager to build up his library. His moral life was far from blameless—of course the later ascetic may exaggerate his youthful sins—but he never strayed far from his Christianity and was baptized in Rome near the end of his studies, very probably at Easter, A.D. 366.

Soon afterwards Jerome and Bonosus paid a visit to the court of Valentinian at Augusta Treverorum (Trier), probably in the hope of obtaining employment in the imperial service. The outcome was something very different, for in this distant western city they came upon evidences of the anchoretic life. Athanasius had been there and made known the practices of the Egyptian desert. His life of St. Antony was read in Trier, and some had tried to follow the hermit's example, as we know from Augustine's *Confessions*. The young men vowed to do the same one day. Bonosus found himself able to do this quite soon, and without going far from home, but Jerome was more restless. For a time he associated with the brilliant group of

282   JEROME

clergy at Aquileia—the choir of the blessed, as he called them—
which included Chromatius, later bishop, and Rufinus, and
through which he became known to Evagrius, the Antiochene
presbyter and friend of Eusebius of Vercellae. Eventually,
however, he decided to break away and go to the East, the true
home of the ascetic life. In 373 or 374[1] he arrived at Antioch,
where he was entertained and assisted by Evagrius. There he
was visited by his friend Heliodorus of Altinum, who had
left the army with the intention of adopting the monastic life in
some form and was on a pilgrimage to the Holy Places. Jerome
tried vainly to persuade him to share with him the life of a
hermit in the desert. Heliodorus went back to Italy, and in
374 or 375 Jerome set out for the desert of Chalcis.

It was either at Antioch or in the desert that he had his
famous dream, related in one of his letters (22:30). "Suddenly
I was caught up in the spirit and brought before the Judgment-
seat. I was asked my condition, and said that I was a Christian.
'Thou liest', said the Judge. 'Thou art a Ciceronian, not a
Christian. For where thy treasure is, there will thy heart be
also.' ... I took an oath, calling upon his name, and said,
'Lord, if ever I possess worldly books or read them, I have
denied thee' ... Henceforth I read God's books with greater
zeal than I had ever read men's books." If he did not keep his
promise literally, he kept it in spirit, and the first fruit of his
new biblical studies was a commentary on Obadiah, a work
which caused him some rueful amusement in later days. He
had tried to expound an allegorical interpretation of the
prophet before he had understood the literal sense. He had
read that to faith all things are possible, and had not understood that there are diversities of gifts, and that his knowledge
of profane letters would not unlock the secrets of a sealed book.
He hoped his youthful essay might lie hidden in some corner of
a library. If it does, no one has yet found it. About this time,
too, he wrote the first of his romances of the desert, the *Life of
Paul the Hermit*. By 377 at latest he had returned to Antioch,
still under thirty and altogether unaware of the venerable
figure he would cut in the art of many centuries to come.

In Antioch Jerome was ordained presbyter by Paulinus,
whom the West recognized as bishop of the city, and soon
afterwards he went to Constantinople, where he studied
theology and the Bible under Gregory of Nazianzus, who (it
may fairly be presumed) made him conscious of the riches of

[1] On the date see the introduction to *Letter* 15 (p. 302).

Origen's biblical commentaries. He was in Constantinople for the Council of A.D. 381 and came to know Gregory of Nyssa. In the next year, owing partly to the continued disputes about the episcopal succession at Antioch, Jerome accompanied Paulinus to Rome, where he stayed for three years, eminent both as a scholar and as a spiritual director dedicated to the promotion of the ascetic life. As a scholar, he was secretary to Pope Damasus, who commissioned him to revise the current Latin versions of the Bible and produce a standard text. While at Rome he revised the Gospels and some of the remainder of the New Testament, at any rate the Pauline Epistles. This he did, of course, from the Greek original. He also revised the Psalms, but only from the Greek text of the Septuagint, without recourse to the Hebrew. This is the *Psalterium Romanum*. As an ascetic teacher and spiritual director, Jerome had a great following among Roman ladies of high birth and ample fortune, many of whom figure largely in his correspondence. Some of them lived lives of abstinence and charity at home, others went in time to the monasteries of Jerusalem and Bethlehem. The impulse to this domestic asceticism had been given by Athanasius when he was in Rome in A.D. 340, attended by two Egyptian monks. Entertained by the rich widow Albina in her house on the Aventine, Athanasius had so much impressed her daughter Marcella that, becoming a widow within a few months of marriage, she devoted herself to a life of piety and renunciation in her mother's home, which became a centre for others of like mind. Marcellina, Ambrose's sister, joined them after her own mother's death. Marcella was one of Jerome's most frequent correspondents. Another of the circle was Paula, who became head of Jerome's convent at Bethlehem and was succeeded in this office by her daughter Eustochium. Another great lady, Melania the Elder, founded a convent on the Mount of Olives, working there with Rufinus.

In Rome Jerome could not escape controversy. He wrote against the Luciferians, followers of Lucifer of Cagliari who would not communicate with the bishops who had "lapsed" in the Arian controversy, particularly at Ariminum in 359, even when they were reconciled with the Church in general. This book is moderate in tone, for Jerome, and may have been written earlier. Certainly of this period is his attack on Helvidius, an opponent of asceticism, whose teaching was taken up a little later by Jovinian.

When Damasus died in December, 384, there were rumours

that Jerome might succeed him. "In the opinion of most people," said Jerome himself, "I was fit for the *summum sacerdotium.*" And although in other circumstances, *summum sacerdotium* might mean no more than a bishopric, it is pretty clear that in its context it means the bishopric of Rome. We must conclude that he was a disappointed man. There was opposition to his unfamiliar text of the Bible, and even greater opposition to his extreme ascetic teaching, and probably to his biting tongue and pen. If it is true that he had hoped for the Chair of Peter, he might not be altogether welcome to the new Pope, Siricius. Be that as it may, he left Rome for the East in August, 385, and made Palestine his home for the rest of his life.

II

Jerome sailed with his brother Paulinian and the Roman presbyter Vincent to Cyprus, where he was entertained by Epiphanius, Bishop of Salamis, and so to Antioch, where he again consorted with Paulinus and Evagrius. Meanwhile Paula and Eustochium had also left Rome. They joined Jerome's party at Salamis and Antioch, from which they all started on a long pilgrimage to the biblical sites of Palestine, reaching Jerusalem in mid-winter and continuing to Bethlehem and then back into Galilee. After that they all went to Egypt, the classic home of monasticism. At Alexandria Jerome met the theologian Didymus the Blind, whom he counted among his revered masters. When they returned to Bethlehem in the summer of 386, Jerome and Paula set about establishing monasteries there. The story of this pilgrimage is told in his *Letter* 108. The buildings, constructed by means of Paula's money and credit, were not ready until 389. There were separate monasteries for men and women and a hospice for pilgrims. These monasteries were organized as distinct communities, the men under Jerome, the women under Paula, but both groups met for worship on Sundays in the Church of the Nativity. A similar pair of monasteries had been established some years previously by Rufinus of Aquileia and Melania on the Mount of Olives, and at this time John, Bishop of Jerusalem, was on friendly terms with the whole Latin community in his diocese.

Established once and for all in his monastery, Jerome devoted himself to study and writing. Lives of Malchus and Hilarion continued the romantic descriptions of famous hermits. He translated Didymus's *On the Holy Spirit*, wrote many biblical commentaries, and, now equipped with a knowledge of Hebrew, tackled the translation of the Old Testament, which he did not complete until A.D. 405. Unfortunately the peace which he needed for the work which called out his best qualities was broken by a dispute which stimulated his worst. The Origenistic controversy is much too involved to be related here. Up to A.D. 392 Jerome, proud to call himself the pupil of Gregory of Nazianzus and Didymus of Alexandria, and familiar with the library at Caesarea, was a devoted student of Origen, translated his works, accepted his principles of exegesis, and introduced the substance of his commentaries into his own. At Bethlehem he had translated Origen's *Homilies on St. Luke*, and the notice of him in the *De Viris Illustribus* (written *c.* 392) is still full of praise. But in 393 a certain Atarbius, otherwise unknown, arrived in Palestine and began to go round the monasteries, calling on the monks to denounce Origen as a heretic. Jerome was disturbed, but Rufinus shut the door on the intruder. This herald was soon followed by his principal, Epiphanius of Salamis, a man of holy life but a narrow-minded and pedantic heresy-hunter. Rufinus held out for Origen, and John of Jerusalem was not disposed to denounce his teaching, especially when urged to do so by a bishop who showed no regard for his colleague's jurisdiction. But Jerome was not only anxious to be strictly orthodox, but also had the deepest respect for Epiphanius as a man of ascetic life. So he took his side. Soon Epiphanius ordained Jerome's brother, Paulinian, against his will and against all canonical propriety, in another bishop's diocese. Consequently relations between Jerusalem and Bethlehem were strained almost to breaking-point. In 395, when threat of invasion by the Huns caused a panic in Palestine, Jerome thought of returning to the West. Some of his company did go, but Jerome stayed. It was not long before John of Jerusalem tried to make sure of his departure by getting an imperial order for his expulsion, but it was not put into effect; possibly it lapsed through the fall and death of the great minister, Rufinus, in November, 395. In autumn 396 Jerome wrote a virulent pamphlet against John, but in 397, by the mediation of Theophilus of Alexandria (who had not yet come out against Origen), a reconciliation was effected between Jerome and his old friend Rufinus, which pacified John as well.

The reconciliation with Rufinus was brief, for he returned to the West as a champion of Origen against all adversaries.

His translation of the *Apology for Origen* composed by the martyr
Pamphilus with the help of the scholar Eusebius of Caesarea,
was a clever move. When he followed it with a version—with
improvements!—of Origen's *De Principiis*, the fat was in the
fire. Jerome pursued him relentlessly, even for some years
after Rufinus had refused to enter into any further controversy
with him. When Theophilus turned against Origen, Jerome
supported him in his campaign against John Chrysostom,
Bishop of Constantinople. To a large extent, John of Jerusalem
stood aloof from the conflict after the reconciliation of 397,
though he wrote to Pope Anastasius in favour of Rufinus.

The unhappy controversy did not occupy Jerome's whole
attention. He continued with his Old Testament translation
until its completion in 405, and wrote more commentaries.
His controversy with the opponents of asceticism went on. To
the work against Helvidius he had added a bitter refutation of
Jovinian in 393, which was followed in 406 by the *Contra
Vigilantium*. From 394 or 395 he was corresponding with
Augustine (mostly in 404), discussing among other things the
advisability of making biblical versions from the Hebrew, which
might upset people used to translations made from the Septuagint, and the possibility that Peter and Paul, in the story told
in Galatians, might have exercised a little expedient dissimulation, a notion of Jerome's which horrified Augustine. The
correspondence was sometimes friendly, sometimes distinctly
cool. But when Jerome was drawn into the Pelagian controversy he was entirely on Augustine's side, and wrote against
the heretic. No doubt he could do this *ex animo*, but we may
suspect that his zeal was not diminished by the fact that John
of Jerusalem had received Pelagius kindly.

As Jerome grew old, he had to suffer from the loss of his
friends. Paula died in 404, Marcella in 411, soon after the sack
of Rome by the Goths, Eustochium, who had succeeded her
mother at Bethlehem, at the turn of 418–19. Jerome himself
died in September 419 or 420.[2]

III

Jerome's writings are numerous and bulky. First, he translated the whole of the Old Testament from the Hebrew into

---

[2] The date usually accepted is 420. Cavallera argues for 419, but it is an
argument from silence (the absence of letters definitely assignable to
420), and not conclusive.

Latin, besides making two versions of the Psalms and one of Job from Greek; and he translated the New Testament books from the Greek. Secondly, he wrote commentaries, some of them substantial, on each of the prophets, the Psalms, Ecclesiastes, Matthew, Galatians, Ephesians, Philemon, and Titus. These vary considerably in nature and value, the later ones tending to be more literal and historical than the earlier, showing a revulsion from the influence of Origen. Some of them are composed mainly of extracts from Greek commentators. With these we may group the translations of Origen's *Homilies* on Isaiah, Jeremiah, Ezekiel, Canticles, and Luke. There are also a book on difficult passages in Genesis, the handbooks on Hebrew names and place-names, largely taken from Eusebius, and some notes and sermons on the Psalms and on Mark.

The controversial works include the group against the opponents of asceticism, viz. Helvidius, Jovinian, and Vigilantius, the treatises against the Luciferians and the Pelagians, and the anti-Origenist works, viz. the three books against Rufinus and the pamphlet against John of Jerusalem.

Purporting to be historical, but perhaps without intent to deceive, are the lives of the hermits, Paul, Malchus, and Hilarion. The truly historical works are the translation of Eusebius's *Chronicon* and its continuation to A.D. 378, and the very valuable collection of Christian bio-bibliographies called *De Viris Illustribus*. Unfortunately Jerome did not carry out his project of writing a history of his own time. The 154 letters are, of course, full of the most important historical materials; some of them are really treatises, like the famous *Letter* 22 to Eustochium on *Virginity* or *Letter* 52 to Nepotian on the *Duties of the Clergy*. Jerome also translated the *De Spiritu Sancto* of Didymus and the *Rule* of Pachomius. Some of his translations have not survived, including that of the *De Principiis* of Origen, which he made to show up how Rufinus had doctored his own version in the interest of Origen's orthodoxy.

IV

Jerome's faults of character are obvious enough. He lacked breadth of mind, and would rarely try to understand the other point of view. He nursed his animosities and grievances, and only too often let his clever and satirical pen run away with him. With this want of restraint and judgment he would, humanly speaking, have made a poor bishop and an impossible pope. It is not difficult to gather a highly unfavourable impression of his personality from his letters and certain other works. Yet he had high qualities, even apart from his scholarship. He was capable of the warmest human affections, he schooled himself to endure hardship, and he worked with almost incredible assiduity.

No doubt judgment on his ascetic teaching will vary with the judge, for here the whole course of Christian history is involved, and any attempt to strike a balance can only be very tentative. There are imponderables which elude us. On the one hand, he tramples on natural affections and social duties in a way which no Christian society can accept as normative, even if it is ever proper in particular cases; and he proclaims a double standard of morality, with a tariff of rewards, which is insidiously demoralizing and false to the Gospel. Not that he invented all this, and he shared this outlook, alas, with such great men as Athanasius and Ambrose; but it has to be remembered that his writings ranked high among the clerical studies of the Middle Ages. On the other hand, the strong challenge to self-sacrifice and simplicity of life was of enormous value as the Church emerged from the shadows of unpopularity and persecution to a place in the sun, tempted every moment to compromise with the world. Jerome's teaching and example led many to dedicate themselves to a life of charity and piety and prayer.

Though he was no philosopher and not really a constructive, certainly not an original, theologian, he was the outstanding scholar of his time—and it is seldom that one can thus single a man out with such confidence. If in many respects his scholarship was superficial and unreliable, and if this was sometimes the result of a more or less culpable haste and impatience, it was more often due to the absence of those tools of systematic learning which have slowly accumulated in subsequent centuries and to which he himself contributed not a little. He had the instincts of a scholar. Without him our picture of his age would be much poorer and much less vivid. As an exegete he had much more concern than was usual in his day for textual and historical matters, and he shared with Ambrose and Hilary of Poitiers the merit of revealing the riches of Greek biblical scholarship to the churches of the Latin West.

Then there is the Vulgate, his chief claim upon the gratitude of the Church. In the first place, he provided a standard text for all those who wanted to read the Bible in Latin, and that in itself was no small benefit at a time when a welter of widely different translations—as many versions as manuscripts—was confusing the Christian reader. Secondly, he established, against much opposition, the principles that, where possible, Scripture should be studied in the original tongues, and that translations, above all when they are intended for common use in the Church, should be made from the original. Finally, the version which he produced was, with all its faults, a very good one, far more reliable than anything available up to his own time, and not to be superseded in the West for many centuries. It is still of cardinal importance to the student of the text of the Scriptures, and still the official Bible of a great multitude of Christians.

Letter 14 : To Heliodorus

INTRODUCTION

HELIODORUS WAS A NATIVE OF ALTINUM IN Venetia, near Aquileia, and was probably educated with Jerome in Rome. He became an officer in the army, but abandoned this profession with the intention of devoting himself to some form of the ascetic life. On a pilgrimage to the Holy Land he stayed at Antioch with Jerome, who was eager that the two friends should go out into the desert of Chalcis, some fifty miles away, to live there as hermits. But Heliodorus went back to Italy. From the desert Jerome sent this further appeal, written probably in A.D. 375 or 376. His pleading was again unsuccessful. The comparison of the monastic life, held almost to guarantee salvation, with the difficult duties and manifold temptations of the clergy, suggests that Jerome knew of his friend's inclination to be ordained and work "in the world".[1] In the event, Heliodorus became Bishop of Altinum, the first recorded and probably the first in fact, and was present in this capacity at the Council of Aquileia, A.D. 381. Despite his decision, Jerome remained on excellent terms with him. With Chromatius of Aquileia Heliodorus encouraged and assisted Jerome's biblical work, sending him money to pay for parchment and copyists, and they received his thanks in the dedications and prefaces of the translations of "Solomon" (Proverbs, Canticles, Ecclesiastes), Judith and Tobit. Heliodorus was the uncle of Nepotian (*Letter* 52) and in 396 received from Jerome the touching elegy on his nephew (*Letter* 60). He was still alive in A.D. 405.

Jerome's attitude towards the lives and prospects of monks and secular clergy respectively is illuminating, and certain passages in the *Letter* (e.g. the end of §2) are extreme examples

[1] I think Fremantle is wrong in concluding that Heliodorus was already a presbyter.

of his repudiation of family affection and duty, about which a psychologist might find a good deal to say. What Jerome himself came to say about his early production may be read in *Letter* 52:1 (p. 315), but though he there regrets his flowery language, he never reached a full appreciation of the ties of family life as *duties*. The letter failed to convince Heliodorus, but was highly esteemed by the ascetics. Fabiola knew it by heart (*Letter* 77). It cannot therefore be regarded simply as a private and personal document.

Letter 14 : To Heliodorus

THE TEXT

1. So conscious are you of the affection which exists between us that you cannot but recognize the love and passion with which I strove to prolong our common sojourn in the desert. This very letter—blotted, as you see, with tears—gives evidence of the lamentation and weeping with which I accompanied your departure. With the pretty ways of a child you then softened your refusal by soothing words, and I, being off my guard, knew not what to do. Was I to hold my peace? I could not conceal my eagerness by a show of indifference. Or was I to entreat you yet more earnestly? You would have refused to listen, for your love was not like mine. Despised affection has taken the one course open to it. Unable to keep you when present, it goes in search of you when absent. You asked me yourself, when you were going away, to invite you to the desert when I took up my quarters there, and I for my part promised to do so. Accordingly I invite you now; come, and quickly. Do not call to mind old ties; the desert is for those who have left all.[1] Nor let the hardships of your former travels deter you. You believe in Christ, believe also in his words: "Seek ye first the kingdom of God and all these things shall be added unto you."[2] Take neither scrip nor staff.[3] He is rich enough who is poor—with Christ.

2. But what is this, and why do I foolishly importune you again? Away with entreaties, an end to coaxing words. Offended love does well to be angry. You have spurned my petition; perhaps you will listen to my remonstrance. What keeps you, pampered soldier,[4] in your father's house? Where are

---

[1] Literally, "the desert loves the naked." But *necessitates* (ties) may mean privations.   [2] Matt. 6:33.   [3] Cf. Matt. 10:10.

[4] The military passage is imitated closely from Tertullian, *Ad Martyras* 3. That Heliodorus had been a soldier gives it special point.

your ramparts and trenches? When have you spent a winter in the field? Lo, the trumpet sounds from heaven! Lo, the Leader comes with clouds! He is armed to subdue the world; and out of the King's mouth proceeds a two-edged sword to mow down all that encounters it.[5] But as for you, what will you do? Pass straight from your chamber to the battlefield, and from the cool shade into the burning sun? Nay, a body used to a tunic cannot endure a buckler; a head that has worn a cap refuses a helmet; a hand made tender by idleness is galled by a sword-hilt. Hear the proclamation of your King: "He that is not with me is against me, and he that gathereth not with me scattereth."[6] Remember the day on which you enlisted, when, buried with Christ in baptism, you swore fealty[7] to him, declaring that for his sake you would spare neither father nor mother. Lo, the enemy is striving to slay Christ in your breast. Lo, the ranks of the foe sigh for that bounty which you received when you entered his service. Should your little nephew[8] hang on your neck, pay no regard to him; should your mother with ashes on her hair and garments rent show you the breasts at which she nursed you, heed her not; should your father prostrate himself on the threshold, trample him under foot[9] and go your way. With dry eyes fly to the standard of the cross. In such cases cruelty is the only true affection.

3. Hereafter there shall come a day when you will return a victor to your true country, and will walk through the heavenly Jerusalem crowned with the crown of valour. Then will you receive the citizenship thereof with Paul.[10] Then will you seek the like privilege for your parents. Then will you intercede for me who have urged you forward on the path of victory.

I am not ignorant of the fetters which you may plead as hindrances. My breast is not of iron nor my heart of stone. I was not born of flint or suckled by a Hyrcanian tigress.[11] I have passed through troubles like yours myself. Now it is a widowed sister who throws her caressing arms around you. Now it is the slaves, your foster-brothers, who cry: "To what master are you leaving us?"[12] Now it is a nurse bowed with age, and a body-

[5] Rev. 1:7, 16.   [6] Matt. 12:30.

[7] *In sacramenti verba, sacramentum* combining the senses of military oath and sacrament.

[8] Nepotian.

[9] A literary reminiscence of Seneca (*Controv.*, I, 8, 15) "*patrem calca,*" the same words, and so not so fierce as it seems.

[10] Cf. Acts. 22:25–29; Phil. 3:20.

[11] Vergil, *Aeneid*, IV, 366–367.   [12] *Ibid.*, II, 677–678.

servant loved only less than a father, who exclaim: "Only wait till we die and follow us to our graves." Perhaps, too, your foster-mother, with sunken bosom and furrowed brow, will recall your lullaby of old and sing it again.[13] The learned may call you, if they please,

> "The sole support and pillar of your house."[14]

The love of God and the fear of hell will easily break such bonds.

Scripture, you will argue, bids us obey our parents. Yes, but whoso loves them more than Christ loses his own soul. The enemy takes sword in hand to slay me, and shall I think of a mother's tears? Or shall I desert the service of Christ for the sake of a father to whom, if I am Christ's servant, I owe no rites of burial, albeit if I am Christ's true servant I owe these to all?[15] Peter with his cowardly advice was an offence to the Lord on the way to his passion; and to the brethren who strove to restrain him from going up to Jerusalem, Paul's one answer was: "What mean ye to weep and to break my heart? For I am ready not to be bound only, but also to die at Jerusalem for the name of our Lord Jesus Christ."[16] The battering-ram of natural affection which so often shatters faith must recoil powerless from the wall of the Gospel. "My mother and my brethren are these, whosoever do the will of my Father which is in heaven."[17] If they believe in Christ let them bid me Godspeed, for I go to fight in his name. And if they do not believe, "let the dead bury their dead."[18]

4. But all this, you argue, only touches the case of martyrs. Ah! my brother, you are mistaken, you are mistaken, if you suppose that there is ever a time when the Christian does not suffer persecution. Then are you most hardly beset when you know not that you are beset at all. "Our adversary as a roaring lion walketh about seeking whom he may devour,"[19] and do you think of peace? "He sitteth in ambush with the rich: in the secret places that he may murder the innocent; his eyes are set against the poor. He lieth in wait secretly as a lion in his den; he lieth in wait to catch the poor;"[20] and do you slumber softly under a shady tree,[21] so as to fall an easy prey? On one

13 Persius, III, 18.   14 Verg., *Aen.*, XII, 59.
15 Luke 9:59, 60.   16 Acts 21:13.
17 Matt. 12:50; Luke 8:21.   18 Luke 9:60.
19 I Peter 5:8.   20 Ps. 10:8, 9 (as LXX 9:29, 30).
21 Cf. Verg., *Georgics*, II, 470.

side self-indulgence presses me hard; on another covetousness
strives to make an inroad; my belly wishes to be a god to me,[22]
in place of Christ, and lust presses me to drive away the Holy
Spirit that dwells in me and defile his temple.[23] I am pursued,
I say, by an enemy,

"Whose name is Legion and his wiles untold";[24]

and, hapless wretch that I am, how shall I hold myself a victor
when I am being led away a captive?

5. My dear brother, weigh well the various forms of transgression, and think not that the sins which I have mentioned
are less flagrant than that of idolatry. Nay, hear the Apostle's
view of the matter. "For this ye know," he writes, "that no
whoremonger or unclean person, nor defrauder, which is
idolatry, hath any inheritance in the kingdom of Christ and of
God."[25] In a general way all that is of the devil savours of
enmity to God, and what is of the devil is idolatry, since all
idols are subject to him.[26] Yet Paul elsewhere lays down the
law in express and unmistakable terms, saying: "Mortify
your members, which are upon the earth, laying aside fornication, uncleanness, evil concupiscence and covetousness, which
are the service of idols, for which things' sake the wrath of God
cometh."[27]

Idolatry is not confined to casting incense upon an altar
with finger and thumb, or to pouring libations of wine out of a
cup into a bowl. Covetousness is idolatry, or else the selling of
the Lord for thirty pieces of silver was a righteous act. Lust
involves sacrilege, or else men may defile with common harlots
those members of Christ which should be "a living sacrifice
acceptable to God."[28] Fraud is idolatry, or else they are worthy
of imitation who, in the Acts of the Apostles, sold their inheritance, and because they kept back part of the price, perished
by an instant doom.[29] Consider well, my brother; nothing is
yours to keep. "Every man," the Lord says, "that forsaketh
not all that he hath, he cannot be my disciple."[30]

22 Phil. 3:19.   23 I Cor. 3:16–17.   24 Verg., *Aen.*, VII, 337, *mille nomina.*
25 Eph. 5:5. Jerome has *fraudator* here instead of "covetous."
26 With this and the remainder of the chapter compare Tertullian, *On
Idolatry, passim,* and especially chapters 1 and 2 (pp. 83–84). Section 6
comes largely from *On Idolatry,* 12.
27 Col. 3:5. *Cupidatem* here for covetousness.   28 Rom. 12:1.
29 Ananias and Sapphira, Acts 5. I have retained Fremantle's translation
here, since it makes some sense of a difficult passage. But his underlying
text differs from Hilberg's.   30 Luke 14:33.

6. Why are you such a half-hearted Christian? See how they left their father and their net; see how the publican rose from the receipt of custom.[31] In a moment he became an apostle. "The Son of man hath not where to lay his head,"[32] and do you plan wide porticos and spacious halls? Do you look to inherit the world, you, a joint-heir with Christ?[33] Translate the word "monk",[34] the name you bear. What brings you, a solitary, into the crowd? I am no experienced mariner who has never lost either ship or cargo, advising those who have never known a gale. Lately shipwrecked as I have been myself, my warnings to other voyagers spring from my own fears. On one side, like Charybdis, self-indulgence sucks into its vortex the soul's salvation. On the other, like Scylla, lust, with a smile on her girlish face, lures it on to wreck its chastity. Here a savage coast, there the devil, a pirate with his crew, carrying irons to fetter his captives. Be not credulous, be not over-confident. The sea may be as smooth and smiling as a pond, its quiet surface may be scarcely ruffled by a breath of air, yet the great plain has its mountains. There is danger in its depths, the foe is lurking there. Stow your tackle, reef your sails, fasten the cross of the yard-arm on your prow. Your calm means a storm.

"Why so?" you will perhaps argue; "are not those who live in a city Christians?"[35] Your case, I reply, is not that of others. Listen to the words of the Lord: "If thou wilt be perfect, go, sell all that thou hast, and give to the poor, and come, follow me."[36] You have already promised to be perfect. For when you forsook the army and made yourself an eunuch for the kingdom of heaven's sake,[37] you did so that you might follow the perfect life. Now the perfect servant of Christ has nothing beside Christ. Or if he have anything beside Christ he is not perfect. And if he be not perfect when he has promised God to be so, his profession is a lie. But "the mouth that lieth slayeth the soul."[38] To conclude, then, if you are perfect you will not set your heart on your father's goods; and if you are not perfect you have deceived the Lord. The Gospel thunders forth its divine warning: "Ye cannot serve two masters,"[39] and does any one dare to make Christ a liar by serving at once both God

---

[31] Matt. 4:22; 9:9.   [32] Matt. 8:20.   [33] Rom. 8:17.
[34] *Monachus*, from Greek *monos*, alone; so solitary.
[35] Cf. Ambrose, *Letter* 63:66 (p. 276).
[36] Matt. 19:21.
[37] Matt. 19:12, here meaning "vowed to celibacy."
[38] Wisdom 1:11.   [39] Matt. 6:24.

and Mammon? Repeatedly does he proclaim: "If any one will come after me let him deny himself and take up his cross and follow me." [40] If I load myself with gold can I think that I am following Christ? Surely not. "He that saith he abideth in Christ ought himself also so to walk even as he walked." [41]

7. I know you will rejoin that you possess nothing. Why, then, if you are so well prepared for battle, do you not take the field? Perhaps you think that *you* can wage war in your own country, although the Lord could do no signs in his? Why not? you ask. Take the reason which comes to you with his authority: "No prophet is honoured in his own country." [42] But, you will say, I do not seek honour; the approval of my conscience is enough for me. Neither did the Lord seek it; for when the multitudes would have made him a king he fled from them. [43] But where there is no honour there is contempt; and where there is contempt there is frequent rudeness; and where there is rudeness there is vexation; and where there is vexation there is no rest; and where there is no rest the mind is apt to be diverted from its purpose. Again, where, through restlessness, earnestness loses any of its force, it is lessened by what it loses, and that which is lessened cannot be called perfect. The upshot of all which is that a monk cannot be perfect in his own country. Now, not to aim at perfection is itself a sin.

8. Driven from this line of defence you will appeal to the example of the clergy. These, you will say, remain in their cities, and yet they are surely above criticism. Far be it from me to censure the successors of the apostles, who with holy words make the body of Christ, [44] and through whom we are made Christians. [45] Having the keys of the kingdom of heaven they judge men to some extent before the day of judgment, and, in sober chastity, guard the bride of Christ. But, as I have before hinted, the case of monks is different from that of the clergy. The clergy feed the sheep; I am fed by them. They live of the altar; I, if I bring no gift to it, have the axe laid to my root as to that of a barren tree. Nor can I plead poverty as an excuse, for in the Gospel I see an aged widow casting into the treasury the last two coins that she had. [46] I may not sit in the presence of a presbyter; [47] he, if I sin, may deliver me to Satan, "for the destruction of the flesh

---

[40] Matt. 16:24.   [41] I John 2:6.   [42] Matt. 13:57–58; John 4:44.
[43] John 6:15.   [44] *Christi corpus conficiunt.*   [45] In baptism.
[46] I Cor. 9:13–14; Matt. 3:10; Luke 21:1–4.
[47] Jerome had not yet been ordained. For "sitting" cf. *Letter* 146:2 (p. 388).

that the spirit may be saved." [48] Under the old law he who
disobeyed the priests was put outside the camp and stoned
by the people, or else he was beheaded and expiated his contempt with his blood. [49] But now the disobedient person is cut
down with the spiritual sword, or he is expelled from the Church
and torn to pieces by ravening demons. Should the entreaties
of your brethren induce you to take orders, I shall rejoice that
you are lifted up, and fear lest you may be cast down. You will
say: "If a man desire the office of a bishop, he desireth a good
work." I know that; but you should add what follows: such an
one "must be blameless, the husband of one wife, sober, chaste,
prudent, well-prepared, given to hospitality, apt to teach, not
given to wine, no striker but patient." [50] After fully explaining
the qualifications of a bishop the Apostle speaks of ministers
of the third degree with equal care. "Likewise must the
deacons be chaste," he writes, "not double-tongued, not given
to much wine, not greedy of filthy lucre, holding the mystery
of the faith in a pure conscience. And let these also first be
proved; and then let them minister, being found blameless." [51]
Woe to the man who goes in to the supper without a wedding
garment. Nothing remains for him but the stern question:
"Friend, how camest thou in hither?" And when he is speech-
less the order will be given to the servants: "Bind him hand and
foot, and take him away, and cast him into outer darkness;
there shall be weeping and gnashing of teeth." [52] Woe to him
who, when he has received a talent, has bound it in a napkin;
and, whilst others make profits, only preserves what he has
received. His angry lord shall rebuke him in a moment. "Thou
wicked servant," he will say, "wherefore gavest thou not my
money into the bank that at my coming I might have required
mine own with usury? [53] That is to say, you should have laid
before the altar what you were not able to bear. For whilst you,
a slothful trader, keep a penny in your hands, you occupy

[48] I Cor. 5:5.   [49] Deut. 17:5, 12.
[50] I Tim. 3:1–3. Here Jerome has *ornatum* for the Greek *kosmion* (otherwise,
"orderly") and so still in the Vulgate, translated "of good behaviour"
in the Douai Bible, and "well-behaved" by Knox. These seem to go back
to the Greek. Labourt renders *ornatum* here "cultivé"; it can mean, "well-
furnished." For *didaktikon*, "apt to teach," Jerome has *docibilem* here,
perhaps still understood as "teachable." The Vulgate has *doctorem*.
[51] I Tim. 3:8–10. Here Jerome has *pudicos*, "chaste," for the Greek, *semnous*,
"grave"; and so also in the Vulgate.
[52] Matt. 22:11–13. The Latin here means literally, "Remove him by his
hands and feet." "Bind" is not represented.
[53] Luke 19:22.

the place of another who might double the money. Wherefore, as he who ministers well purchases to himself a good degree, so he who approaches the cup of the Lord unworthily shall be guilty of the body and blood of the Lord.[54]

9. Not all bishops are bishops indeed. You notice Peter; mark Judas as well. You look up to Stephen; look also on Nicholas, whom in the Apocalypse the Lord abominates, whose wicked and shameful imaginations gave rise to the heresy of the Ophites.[55] "Let a man examine himself and so let him come."[56] For it is not ecclesiastical rank that makes a man a Christian. The centurion Cornelius was still a heathen when the gift of the Holy Spirit was poured out upon him. Daniel was but a child when he judged the elders.[57] Amos was stripping mulberry bushes when, in a moment, he was made a prophet. David was only a shepherd when he was chosen to be king. And the least of his disciples was the one whom Jesus loved the most. My brother, sit down in the lower room, that when one less honourable comes you may be bidden to go up higher. Upon whom does the Lord rest but upon him that is lowly and of a contrite spirit, and that trembleth at his word? To whom God has committed much, of him he will ask the more. "Mighty men shall be mightily tormented."[58] No man need pride himself in the day of judgment on merely physical chastity, for then shall men give account for every idle word, and the reviling of a brother shall be counted as the sin of murder. It is not easy to stand in the place of Paul, or to hold the rank of those who already reign with Christ. There may come an angel to rend the veil of your temple, and to remove your candlestick out of its place. If you intend to build the tower, first count the cost. Salt that has lost its savour is good for nothing but to be cast out and to be trodden under foot of swine. If a monk fall, a priest[59] shall intercede for him; but who shall intercede for a fallen priest?

10. At last my discourse is clear of the reefs; at last this frail bark has passed from the breakers into deep water. I may now spread my sails to the breeze; and, as I leave the rocks of

---

[54] I Tim. 3:13; 1 Cor. 11:27.
[55] Rev. 2:6. Nicholas is more usually given as the founder of the Nicolaitans, a Gnostic sect of easy morals. The supposedly similar Ophites were said to worship the serpent.
[56] I Cor. 11:28.   [57] Susanna (Daniel 13).   [58] Wisdom 6:6.
[59] *Sacerdos*, probably bishop, as Jerome has come round again to think of the successors of the apostles. Vallarsi's text, followed by Fremantle (but corrected above), mentions Peter as well as Paul.

controversy astern, my epilogue will be like the joyful shout of mariners. O desert, bright with the flowers of Christ! O solitude whence come the stones of which, in the Apocalypse, the city of the great king is built! [60] O wilderness, gladdened with God's especial presence! What keeps you in the world, my brother, you who are above the world? [61] How long shall gloomy roofs oppress you? How long shall smoky cities immure you? Believe me, I have more light than you. Sweet it is to lay aside the weight of the body and to soar into the pure bright ether. Do you dread poverty? Christ calls the poor blessed. Does toil frighten you? No athlete is crowned but in the sweat of his brow. Are you anxious as regards food? Faith fears no famine. [62] Do you dread the bare ground for limbs wasted with fasting? The Lord lies there beside you. Do you recoil from an unwashed head and uncombed hair? Christ is your head. Does the boundless solitude of the desert terrify you? In the spirit you may walk always in paradise. Do but turn your thoughts thither and you will be no more in the desert. Is your skin rough and scaly because you no longer bathe? He that is once washed in Christ needeth not to wash again. [63] To all your objections the Apostle gives this one brief answer: "The sufferings of this present time are not worthy to be compared with the glory" which shall come after them, "which shall be revealed in us." [64] You are pampered indeed, dearest brother, if you wish to rejoice with the world here, and to reign with Christ hereafter.

11. It shall come, it shall come, that day when this corruptible shall put on incorruption, and this mortal shall put on immortality. [65] Then shall that servant be blessed whom the Lord shall find watching. [66] Then at the sound of the trumpet the earth and its peoples shall tremble, but you shall rejoice. The world shall lament and groan when the Lord comes to judge it, and the tribes of the earth shall smite the breast. Once mighty kings shall shiver in their nakedness. Then shall Jupiter, with all his progeny, indeed be shown in flames; and Plato, with his disciples, will be but a fool. Aristotle's arguments shall be of no avail. You may be a poor man and country bred, but then you shall exult and laugh, and say:

[60] Rev. 21:19, 20. [61] Cf. Cyprian, *Ad Donatum*, 14, fin.

[62] Tert., *Idol.*, 12 (p. 96). The rest of the section is based on Cyprian, *Ep.* 76:2.

[63] John 13:10. [64] Rom. 8:18.

[65] I Cor. 15:53. [66] Matt. 24:46.

Behold the crucified, my God, behold my judge. This is he who was once an infant wrapped in swaddling clothes and crying in a manger. This is he whose parents were a working man and a woman who worked for wages. This is he, who, carried in his mother's bosom, though he was God, fled into Egypt before the face of man. This is he who was clothed in a scarlet robe and crowned with thorns. This is he who was called a sorcerer and a man with a devil and a Samaritan. Jew, behold the hands which you nailed to the cross. Roman, behold the side which you pierced with the spear. See both of you whether it was this body that the disciples stole secretly and by night, as you said. [67]

O my brother, if you are to say these words, if you are to see that triumph, what labour can be hard now?

[67] Jerome's peroration is based on the peroration to Tertullian's *De Spectaculis* (§30).

Letter 15 : To Pope Damasus

INTRODUCTION

I

THIS LETTER WAS NECESSITATED, OR AT LEAST, elicited, by the Antiochene or Meletian schism. Soon after the Council of Nicaea (325) Eustathius, Bishop of Antioch, a staunch champion of the Nicene faith, had been deposed from his see and banished. The next few bishops were somewhat shaky in their faith, from the strictly Nicene point of view, but they were not condemned and most Antiochene Christians accepted them as their lawful bishops. A small group, faithful to Eustathius, held aloof from them and worshipped apart. Their leader was a presbyter, Paulinus, and in theology and terminology they remained consistently Nicene. Although the western Council of Sardica excommunicated Stephen of Antioch in 342, so that Athanasius, when he visited Antioch in 346, communicated with Paulinus, the official bishops were generally accepted in the East until Eudoxius came out openly on the Arian side, and in an extreme form, and was deposed by the Council of Seleucia in 359. He was succeeded by Meletius, nominally Bishop of Sebaste at the time, though he had never taken possession of his see.

Meletius had an Arian past. He had belonged to the" homœan" group which was content to say that the Son is like the Father, under which formula they could be as orthodox as they liked, or as Arian. Many of them wanted peace. Meletius was presumably expected to maintain the more or less Arian, but not too sharply defined, tradition of the See of Antioch before Eudoxius. However, he at once proclaimed his orthodoxy, preaching before Constantius on Proverbs 8:22 in a way which moved the Emperor to send him off quickly into exile.

Euzoius, a real Arian, was appointed in his place. So at this point there were three allegiances in Antioch—to Euzoius, to Meletius in exile, and to the Eustathian group under the presbyter Paulinus. Constantius died in 361, and when Meletius returned from his sufferings for the faith and, before long, professed full Nicene, "homoousian", orthodoxy, he might well have expected the support of the Eustathians.

Meanwhile, however, Athanasius had taken advantage of his own return from exile to hold a council at Alexandria (362), which, it was hoped, might plan how to unite with the Nicene party those in the East who, though long suspicious of the *homoousion* ("being of one substance") as modalist or Sabellian, were substantially orthodox as regards the Deity of Christ. The eastern terminology was now sympathetically reviewed, instead of being dismissed out of hand, and it was seen that the term *hypostasis* could be, and was being, used in two senses, one in which it was equivalent to *ousia*, substance, so that there could be only one *hypostasis* of God (the Nicene and western use), the other in which it was distinguished from *ousia* and employed to designate the three Persons of the Trinity (the eastern use). It was now recognized that the eastern terminology was not inherently tritheistic or Arian, and it was agreed that the Nicene West and Alexandria need no longer insist on the East abandoning its three *hypostaseis* as a condition of communion where the Nicene *homoousion* was accepted. It was hoped, further, that the "homœousians" who, for fear of Sabellianism, would so far only say that the Son is like the Father in substance, would accept the assurance that the Creed of Nicaea and the churches of the West were not modalist, and, with the use of the three *hypostaseis* admitted, would now accept the *homoousion*. And in particular it was expected that the troubled situation in Antioch could be cleared up, since Meletius, who accepted *homoousion* but spoke of three *hypostaseis*, could now be recognized as the Bishop of Antioch and brought into communion with the West. Accordingly, a deputation was sent to Antioch under Eusebius of Vercellae.

These conciliatory plans were upset by the fanatical Lucifer of Cagliari, who reached Antioch and consecrated Paulinus as bishop before Eusebius arrived. This placed Eusebius and Athanasius in an awkward position, for Athanasius, at least, had formerly communicated with Paulinus. Eusebius reserved his judgment, but Athanasius went in person to Antioch, apparently intending to communicate with Meletius. But something went wrong, and he recognized Paulinus after all. The West followed him, though not all at once. Damasus of Rome did not declare his position for ten or a dozen years.

The trouble at Antioch was not merely local in its effect. It was straining the relations between the great sees of Christendom and holding up the defeat of Arianism in the East. A brave effort was therefore made by Basil, Bishop of Caesarea in Cappadocia from 370 to 379, to heal the schism. While always on Meletius' side, he saw that the latter had erred in his conduct towards Athanasius and that the whole matter needed the mediation of the West, provided the West would look at it afresh and on the basis of adequate information. The missions which he sent to Athanasius, and through him to Rome and other western cities, can be studied in part in his correspondence. But Athanasius died in 373 and Basil's efforts were fruitless, for the West continued to acknowledge Paulinus, and at last, in 375 on the accepted chronology, Damasus recognized him. This was not acceptable either to Basil or to the bulk of the eastern bishops, with whose continued support Meletius presided over the early stages of the Council of Constantinople, A.D. 381, and enthroned the new bishop of that city, Gregory of Nazianzus. Jerome was there. When Meletius died during the Council, Gregory thought the proper course would be to accept Paulinus, whom the West already recognized, as the lawful Bishop of Antioch, thus securing peace. However, the eastern bishops in general would not offer this slight to the memory of Meletius (no doubt they were by this time thoroughly antagonistic to Paulinus), so they chose Flavian, one of his presbyters, to succeed him. Gregory thereupon resigned the See of Constantinople.

In 382 a Council met at Rome, largely to determine the attitude of the West to certain aspects and activities of the Council of Constantinople. Paulinus was there, attended by Jerome (*Letter* 108:6, p. 351, cf. 127:7). Paulinus was once more recognized as Bishop of Antioch, and he continued in communion with Rome and Alexandria until his death in 388, when he was succeeded by Jerome's friend, Evagrius. Indeed Paulinus had done his best to secure this succession by consecrating Evagrius before his own death. This was a mistake, as it turned out, for the uncanonical procedure shocked the West, and, after a good deal of trouble and negotiation which is here irrelevant, Flavian was universally accepted. The East had prevailed over the West.

II

When Jerome wrote to Damasus from the desert of Chalcis, what was his position? Was his letter sincere? Much depends on the chronology. It used to be the custom to put the letter in 374, before the recognition of Paulinus by Damasus in his letter *Per filium meum* or, it may be, in the previous letter (not extant) which it implies. Then Jerome's *Letter* 15 can perhaps be taken as a straightforward request for guidance, though one which makes his own preference perfectly clear. To put it in 376-7, as Cavallera does, raised a host of problems, for by that time, unless we redate *Per filium* and several of Basil's letters, Jerome must have known of Paulinus's changed position. His own early letters show that Evagrius visited him frequently in the desert, and brought him news and letters. We might then have to conjecture that *Per filium* was not regarded as decisive enough, or that Damasus, beset by Basil's emissaries, was thought likely to waver. In that case there would be a good deal of pretence in Jerome's letter; we should suspect a plot between him and Evagrius, who had already been employed by Damasus as his messenger to Basil. But perhaps there is a way to save Jerome's good faith. Cavallera's chronology for these years rests to a very considerable extent on taking the consecration of Ambrose as Bishop of Milan for his starting-point; and this he puts in December, 374. But with Palanque's dating of this event to 373, which has been widely accepted, it does not seem difficult to put Jerome's journey to Antioch in 373 and his flight to the desert in 374. Then he could have written this letter before, or without knowledge of, Damasus's decision. Not that this chronology is without difficulty, for (i) there has still to be time for *Letter* 16, and, more seriously, (ii) *Letter* 15 puts Vitalis on a par with Paulinus and Meletius, as if he were already claiming to be Bishop of Antioch, and this is very difficult to reconcile with *Per Filium*, if that dates to 375. Perhaps Jerome is only thinking of him as a party-leader and potential schismatic. The other difficulty is not serious, for we do not know how long an interval Jerome would leave before he wrote again to Damasus.

III

Even if we put this *Letter* 15 in 374 or 375, it is hard to think of it as quite sincere. He asks Damasus with whom he—a

western Christian on a visit to the East—is to communicate
at Antioch; he professes his willingness to do what Damasus
tells him. Yet he was in reality deeply committed to Paulinus,
through his friend Evagrius, and even apart from that, it is
clear that he will be horrified if he is told to communicate
with the Meletians and accept the three hypostases. He treats
the Meletians as Arians in disguise. He lectures the Pope,
although he can hardly have had time yet to grasp the subtle-
ties of Greek trinitarian theology and terminology, if he ever
did.

Jerome received no reply from Damasus, from which fact
one might argue in favour of the 374–5 date of the letter, on
the supposition that Damasus would not yet declare himself, or
might suppose that Damasus knew his decision would reach
Jerome before long, perhaps crossing his letter. Jerome did
write again, still from the desert, in similar terms. When he
returned to Antioch he was ordained presbyter by Paulinus
and later accompanied him to Rome, as we have seen. By the
time of his ordination, on any dating of *Letters* 15 and 16,
Damasus's acceptance of Paulinus will have become known to
him.

Jerome's loyalty to the Bishop of Rome is expressed in this
letter in strong terms. Later in life his relations with Rome were
less cordial, as *Letter* 146 may seem to show. But just as that
letter does not really prove that he had abandoned the position
of *Letter* 15, so the implications of *Letter* 15 must not be exag-
gerated in favour of the claims of Rome. Jerome writes as a
westerner, indeed as a Roman, as he says, to the church of his
baptism. He had not accepted any ecclesiastical allegiance in
the East, and did not want to put himself out of communion
with the western bishops. This was an attitude which he tried
to retain, for he only accepted ordination on the condition that
it did not make him one of Paulinus's own presbyters canonic-
ally, and during the long years at Bethlehem he wanted to
think of his monasteries as a Latin enclave in the diocese of
Jerusalem.

Letter 15 : To Pope Damasus

THE TEXT

1. Since the East, shattered as it is by the long-standing feuds subsisting between its peoples, is bit by bit tearing into shreds the seamless vest of the Lord, "woven from the top throughout," since the foxes are destroying the vineyard of Christ, and since among the broken cisterns that hold no water it is hard to discover "the sealed fountain" and "the garden inclosed," [1] I think it my duty to consult the chair of Peter, and to turn to a church whose faith has been praised by Paul.[2] I appeal for spiritual food to the church from which I once received the garb of Christ.[3] The wide space of sea and land that lies between us cannot deter me from searching for the pearl of great price. "Wheresoever the body is, thither will the eagles also be gathered together." [4] Evil children have squandered their patrimony; you alone keep your heritage intact. Your fruitful soil, when it receives the pure seed of the Lord, bears fruit an hundredfold; but here the seed corn is choked in the furrows and nothing grows but darnel and oats. In the West the sun of righteousness is even now rising; in the East, Lucifer, who fell from heaven, has once more set his throne above the stars.[5] "Ye are the light of the world," "ye are the salt of the earth," ye are "vessels of gold and of silver." Here are vessels of wood or of earth, which wait for the rod of iron and eternal fire.[6]

2. Yet, though your greatness terrifies me, your kindness

---

1 John 19:23; S. of Sol. 2:15; Jer. 2:13; S. of Sol. 4:12. These were standard texts to indicate the unity of the Church, together with the lamb and ark and citation of Luke 11:23 in §2. Most of them occur in Cyprian, *De Unitate.*
2 Rom. 1:8.
3 He was baptized in Rome; hence §3, "a Roman."
4 Luke 17:37. 5 Isa. 14:12.
6 Matt. 5:13–14; II Tim. 2:20; Rev. 2:27; 18:9.

307

attracts me. From the priest I demand the safe-keeping of the victim, from the shepherd the protection due to the sheep.[7] Away with the envied glory; let the pride of Roman majesty withdraw. My words are spoken to the successor of the fisherman, to the disciple of the cross. As I follow no leader save Christ, so I communicate with none but your blessedness, that is with the chair of Peter. For this, I know, is the rock on which the Church is built.[8] This is the house where alone the paschal lamb can be rightly eaten. This is the ark of Noah, and he who is not found in it shall perish when the flood prevails.[9] But since by reason of my sins I have betaken myself to this desert which lies between Syria and the uncivilized waste, I cannot, owing to the great distance between us, always ask of your sanctity the holy thing of the Lord.[10] Consequently I here follow the Egyptian confessors who share your faith, and hide my frail craft in the wake of their great argosies.[11] I know nothing of Vitalis; I reject Meletius; I have nothing to do with Paulinus.[12] He that gathers not with you scatters; he that is not of Christ is of Antichrist.[13]

3. Just now, I am sorry to say, those offspring of Arians, the Campenses,[14] are trying to extort from me, a Roman, their

---

[7] *Sacerdos, pastor,* both as bishop.

[8] Matt. 16:18. In *Ep.* 16, to Damasus, Jerome says: "He who is joined to the chair of Peter is my man."

[9] Ex. 12:22; Gen. 7:23, cf. Cyprian, *De Unitate,* 8 and 6.

[10] *Sanctum Domini,* the eucharist.

[11] In A.D. 373 the eastern emperor Valens, an Arian, banished some orthodox Egyptians to Syria. Some were at Heliopolis (Baalbek). Jerome mentions a group of them, visited by an Alexandrian presbyter, in *Ep.* 3. Damasus was in communion with Alexandria, so Jerome was safe in communicating with them.

[12] In *Ep.* 16, these three claim to be adhering to Damasus. For Meletius and Paulinus see the *Introduction.* Vitalis had been a presbyter of Meletius, but became a disciple of Apollinarius, whose lectures Jerome attended in Antioch. As such, Vitalis was orthodox as to the *homoousion,* but unorthodox as to the Incarnation. He went to Rome, and was sent back to Antioch with a letter which charged Paulinus to look into his orthodoxy. This implied that Damasus recognized Paulinus, not Meletius. The date is usually given as 375. About this time Apollinarius consecrated Vitalis as bishop, and so he too claimed to be Bishop of Antioch. Had this happened when Jerome wrote? The chronology is not clear. Epiphanius does not mention Vitalis in his *Ancoratus,* written in 374.

[13] Luke 11:23.

[14] The origin of the nickname *Campenses* is uncertain. Some think it goes back to the time when the Meletian party had lost possession of the city churches to the Arian bishop Euzoius, and were compelled to worship in the fields; others connect it with the plain (*campus*) of Cilicia

unheard-of formula of three hypostases. And this, too, after the definition of Nicaea and the decree of Alexandria, in which the West has joined.[15] Where, I should like to know, are the apostles of these doctrines? Where is their Paul, their new doctor of the Gentiles? I ask them what three hypostases are supposed to mean. They reply three Persons subsisting. I rejoin that this is my belief. They are not satisfied with the meaning, they demand the term. Surely some secret venom lurks in the words. "If any man refuse," I cry, "to acknowledge three hypostases in the sense of three things hypostatized, that is three Persons subsisting, let him be anathema." Yet, because I do not enounce their words, I am counted a heretic. "But, if any one, understanding by hypostasis *ousia*, deny that in the three persons there is one hypostasis, he has no part in Christ." Because this is my confession I, like you, am branded with the stigma of Sabellianism.[16]

4. Give a decision, I beg you. If you so decide, I shall not hesitate to speak of three hypostases. Order a new creed to supersede the Nicene; and then, whether we are Arians or orthodox, one confession will do for us all. In the whole range of secular learning hypostasis never means anything but *ousia*.[17] And can any one, I ask, be so profane as to speak of three substances in the Godhead? There is one nature of God and one only; and this, and this alone, truly *is*. For it derives its being from no other source but is all its own. All other things, that is all things created, although they appear to be, are not. For there was a time when they were not, and that which once was not, may again cease to be. God alone who is eternal, that is to say, who has no beginning, really deserves to be called an essence. Therefore also he says to Moses from the bush: "I AM THAT I AM," and Moses says of him: "I AM hath sent

and the alliance between the Meletians and the theologians of Tarsus, for which see §5 and note.

15 Jerome will not face the fact that the "decree" of the Council of Alexandria, 362, was entirely against the line he was taking. But he has right on his side to the extent that, according to this decree, he could not be compelled to accept the three hypostases as a mark of his own orthodoxy. Presumably there were supporters of Meletius among the monks of Chalcis, as well as in Antioch.

16 *Cauterio unionis*, that is, the doctrine that God is one Person in three aspects or modes. This was taught by Sabellius early in the third century, and the East suspected that the West used the *homoousion* in a Sabellian or modalist sense.

17 This is not true. For *hypostasis* see Prestige, *God in Patristic Thought*, pp. 162–190.

me." [18] As the angels, the sky, the earth, the seas, all existed at the time, how could God claim for himself that name of essence which was common to all? But because his nature alone is uncreated, and because in the three Persons there subsists but one Godhead, there is only one nature which truly *is*; whosoever in the name of religion declares that there are in the Godhead three elements, that is three hypostases, is trying to predicate three natures of God. And if this is true, why are we severed by walls from Arius, when in unbelief we are one with him? Let Ursinus be made the colleague of your blessedness; let Auxentius be associated with Ambrose. [19] But may the faith of Rome never come to such a pass! May the devout hearts of your people never be infected with such sacrilege! Let us be satisfied to speak of one substance and of three subsisting Persons—perfect, equal, coeternal. Let us keep to one hypostasis, if such be your pleasure, and say nothing of three. It is a bad sign when those who mean the same thing use different words. Let us be satisfied with the form of creed which I have mentioned. Or, if you think it correct, write and explain how we should speak of three hypostases. I am ready to submit. But, believe me, there is poison hidden under their honey; the angel of Satan has transformed himself into an angel of light. [20] They give a plausible explanation of the term hypostasis; yet when I profess to hold the doctrine which they expound, they count me a heretic. Why are they so tenacious of a word? Why do they shelter themselves under ambiguous language? If their belief corresponds to their explanation of it, I do not condemn them for keeping it. On the other hand, if my belief corresponds to their alleged opinions, they should allow me to set forth their meaning in my own words.

6. I implore your blessedness, therefore, by the crucified, the salvation of the world, and by the consubstantial Trinity, to authorize me by letter either to use or to refuse this formula of three hypostases. And lest the obscurity of my present abode may baffle the bearers of your letter, I pray you to address it

[18] Ex. 3:14.

[19] Ursinus was the rival of Pope Damasus ever since their disputed election of A.D. 366. Auxentius is either Ambrose's Arian predecessor or, less probably, Auxentius of Durostorum, for whom see Ambrose, *Letters*, 20, 21 (pp. 199–217). If the latter, Jerome had unexpectedly good information about Milan, perhaps through Evagrius; though his own home was in the orbit of Milan.

[20] II Cor. 11:14.

to Evagrius,[21] the presbyter, with whom you are well acquainted. I beg you also to signify with whom I am to communicate at Antioch. For the Campenses, with their allies the heretics of Tarsus,[22] desire nothing more than, with the support and authority of communion with you, to preach the three hypostases in the old sense of the word.[23]

[21] Evagrius was a presbyter of Antioch, an adherent of Paulinus. He went to Italy with Eusebius of Vercellae when the latter returned from exile, was respected in the West as a man of letters and an ardent "Nicene", and used his influence on behalf of Paulinus, whom he succeeded in 388. There is a valuable appendix on Evagrius, the "Little Church" at Antioch and Jerome, in Labourt's edition of the *Letters*, vol. III, 248–259.

[22] Silvanus, Bishop of Tarsus, and Theophilus, Bishop of Castabala, came to orthodoxy through the "homœousian" party, in which they were prominent. They were in communion with Meletius, and Jerome, who does not accept their orthodoxy, regards Meletius as tarred with the same Arian brush. But they were in communion with Pope Liberius according to Socrates, *H.E.*, IV, 12.

[23] The old sense was, at least to Jerome, three different hypostases of different quality. The Council of Constantinople of A.D. 381 accepted the three hypostases, and so has the West, despite Jerome.

Letter 52 : To Nepotianus

INTRODUCTION

NEPOTIAN WAS THE NEPHEW OF HELIODORUS OF Altinum, to whom *Letter* 14 had been sent in or about A.D. 376. One of Heliodorus' reasons for returning to Italy had been the claims of his widowed sister and her small (*parvulus*) son. Nepotian was brought up by his uncle, joined the army, as he had done, and like him left it with a desire for the ascetic life. Like him again, he decided to enter the ministry of the Church. Most of what we know about Nepotian comes from the letter which Jerome wrote to Heliodorus in A.D. 396 when the young man died, not long after his ordination as presbyter. The present letter gives an indication of its own date in the last section. It was written ten years—not, perhaps, an exact figure—after the famous letter to Eustochium on Virginity (22), which can be dated fairly closely to the end of 383 or the beginning of 384.

Nepotian, we are told in *Letter* 60 (§§ 9–13 give the biographical details), had served in the army in order to have means for charity, a kindly way of putting it. When he left the service, he gave all his savings to the poor, desiring to be perfect. He burned to visit the monasteries of Egypt or Mesopotamia, or at least the hermits of the Dalmatian islands, but he could not bring himself to leave his uncle, who had brought him up and educated him in holiness. So passing through the usual grades of ministry, he was ordained presbyter,[1] making the expected protestations of unwillingness and unworthiness. It was for him not an honour, but a burden, *non honor sed onus*.

---

[1] He was still young, and there was some grumbling about his youth (*Ep.* 60:10). The question of canonical age at this date is obscure. The early Council of Neocaesarea had given thirty as the minimum age for a presbyter, Pope Siricius thirty-five. Presumably Nepotian was younger than this.

As a presbyter he showed himself humble, chaste, charitable and industrious. So much might be common form in the obituary of a respectable and regretted clergyman. There are other details which seem more individual. While he did his duty as a priest in the world, at home he lived with monastic severity; fasting in particular is mentioned. He studied the Bible assiduously, and became acquainted with the Fathers. If Jerome's pen has not run away with him, Nepotian could quote from Tertullian and Cyprian, from Lactantius, Hilary, Minucius Felix, Victorinus and Arnobius; all of them Latin, it should be noticed, which indicates either that Jerome is close to the facts or that, aware that Nepotian did not read Greek, he was respecting historical verisimilitude. We are told also that he took great care of the church buildings and furniture, adorned the church and the chapels of the martyrs with flowers and trees, was careful about his ceremonial, and could usually be found in church.[2] When he died, still young, all Altinum, all Italy, lamented him. Jerome was sure that he would have been a bishop had he lived.

The letter on the duties of the clergy was written in answer to Nepotian's own request. It was, of course, intended to be something more than a letter. Jerome tells fondly and proudly how Nepotian valued it, how he took it to bed with him, learned it by heart, read it to his friends. Though Jerome begins it with a little criticism of the youthful extravagances of his letter to Heliodorus, there are plenty of literary graces to come, and he indulges himself in the new kind of extravagance more congenial to his middle age, the mystical interpretation of Scripture. Nepotian must have wondered when he was coming to the point. When he did, there was still a stern note of

[2] I take it that this all refers to the Cathedral of Altinum, of which he would be one of the presbyters under his uncle. Wright's translation "his church" and "its presbyter" suggests a parochial system, which is, I suppose, not impossible, but unlikely at this date in the north of Italy, even if Altinum, which was quite an important place before the raids of the Huns, had more than one church. The phrase *basilicas ecclesiae et martyrum conciliabula* in 60:12 is interesting. With the singular *ecclesiae*, the plural *basilicas* may mean parts of one church, like the double cathedrals at Milan, Trier, and elsewhere; and the "little meeting-places" of the martyrs bear witness to the popularity of the cult of martyrs which was spreading so fast about this time. In North Italy it had the strong encouragement of Ambrose. Altinum may have had martyrs of its own, though there is no good evidence of this (there are very late and very unreliable stories of the *cult* of Theonestus there); it would seem more likely that this is a case of the translation of relics.

asceticism, but, compared with *Letter* 14, a much more genuine understanding of the pastoral work of the clergy. There is nothing very profound, nothing very unusual; but Jerome had seen the temptations to which the clergy might be exposed, and his advice is usually sensible. It is not difficult to translate it into terms of some kinds of clerical life today.

Letter 52 : To Nepotianus

THE TEXT

1. Again and again you ask me, my dear Nepotian, in your letters from over the sea, to draw for you a few rules of life, showing how one who has renounced the service of the world to become a monk or a clergyman may keep the straight path of Christ, and not be drawn aside into the haunts of vice. As a young man, or rather as a boy, and while I was curbing by the hard life of the desert the first onslaughts of youthful passion, I sent a letter of remonstrance to your reverend uncle, Heliodorus, which, by the tears and complainings with which it was filled, showed him the feelings of the friend whom he had deserted. In that work I indulged my youthful fancy, and as I was still aglow with the methods and maxims of the rhetoricians, I decked it out a good deal with the flourishes of the schools. Now, however, my head is grey, my brow is furrowed, a dewlap like that of an ox hangs from my chin, and, as the poet says:

"The chilly blood stands still around my heart."

Elsewhere he sings:

"Old age bears all, even the mind, away."

And a little further on:

"So many of my songs are gone from me,
And even my very voice has left me now."[1]

2. But that I may not seem to quote only profane literature, listen to the mystical teaching of the sacred writings. Once David had been a man of war, but at seventy age had chilled

[1] For the Vergilian reminiscences in this passage cf. *Aen.*, VII, 417; *Geor.*, III, 53; II, 484; *Buc.*, IX, 51–54.

him so that nothing would make him warm. A girl is accordingly sought from all the coasts of Israel—Abishag the Shunamite—to sleep with the king and warm his aged frame.[2] Does it not seem to you—if you keep to the letter that killeth—like some farcical story or some broad jest from an Atellan play? A chilly old man is wrapped up in blankets, and only grows warm in a girl's embrace. Bathsheba was still living. Abigail was still left, and the remainder of those wives and concubines whose names the Scripture mentions. Yet they are all rejected as cold, and only in the one young girl's embrace does the old man become warm. Abraham was far older than David; still, so long as Sarah lived he sought no other wife. Isaac counted twice the years of David, yet never felt cold with Rebecca, old though she was. I say nothing of the antediluvians, who, although after nine hundred years their limbs must have been not old merely but decayed with age, had no recourse to girls' embraces. Moses, the leader of the Israelites, counted one hundred and twenty years, yet sought no change from Zipporah.

3. Who, then, is this Shunamite, this wife and maid, so glowing as to warm the cold, yet so holy as not to arouse passion in him whom she warmed? Let Solomon, wisest of men, tell us of his father's favourite; let the man of peace recount to us the embraces of the man of war. "Get wisdom, get understanding: forget it not; neither decline from the words of my mouth. Forsake her not and she shall hold to thee: love her and she shall keep thee. The beginning of wisdom is: get wisdom, and with all thy getting get understanding. Embrace her and she shall promote thee. Honour her, and she shall embrace thee, that she may give to thine head a crown of grace, that she may protect thee with a crown of delight."[3]

Almost all bodily excellences alter with age, and while wisdom alone increases all things else decay. Fasting, sleeping on the ground, moving from place to place, hospitality to travellers, pleading for the poor, perseverance in standing at prayer, the visitation of the sick, manual labour to supply money for almsgiving—all acts, in short, of which the body is the medium decrease with its decay.

Now there are young men and men of riper age who, by toil and ardent study, as well as by holiness of life and constant prayer to God, have obtained knowledge. I do not speak of these, or say that in them the love of wisdom is cold, for this withers in many of the old by reason of age. What I mean is that youth, as such, has to cope with the assaults of passion, and amid the allurements of vice and the tinglings of the flesh is stifled like a fire fed with wood too green, and cannot develop its proper brightness. But when men have employed their youth in commendable pursuits and have meditated on the law of the Lord day and night, they learn with the lapse of time, fresh experience and wisdom come as the years go by, and so from the pursuits of the past their old age—their old age, I repeat—reaps a harvest of delight. Hence that wise man of Greece,[4] perceiving, after the expiration of one hundred and seven years, that he was on the verge of the grave, is reported to have said that he regretted extremely having to leave life just when he was beginning to grow wise. Plato died in his eight-first year, his pen still in his hand. Isocrates completed ninety and nine years in the midst of literary and scholastic work. I say nothing of other philosophers, such as Pythagoras, Democritus, Xenocrates, Zeno, and Cleanthes, who in extreme old age displayed the vigour of youth in the pursuit of wisdom. I pass on to the poets, Homer, Hesiod, Simonides, Stesichorus, who all lived to a great age, yet at the approach of death sang each of them a swan song sweeter than their wont. Sophocles, when charged by his sons with dotage on account of his advanced years and his neglect of his property, read out to the judges his recently composed play of *Oedipus*, and made so great a display of wisdom—in spite of the inroads of time—that he changed the severity of the law court into the applause of the theatre. Nor should we wonder that Cato, that most eloquent of Romans, after he had been censor and in his old age, neither blushed at the thought of learning Greek nor despaired of succeeding. Homer, for his part, relates that from the tongue of Nestor, even when quite aged and almost decrepit, there flowed speech sweeter than honey.[5]

Even the very name Abishag in its mystic meaning points to the greater wisdom of old men. For the translation of it is: "My father is over and above," or "my father's roaring."[6] The term "over and above" is obscure, but in this passage is indicative of excellence, and implies that the old have a larger stock of wisdom, and that it even overflows by reason of its abundance.

[4] Theophrastus. In the following passage Jerome draws on Cicero, *Tusc. Disp.*, III, 69, and *De Senectate*.
[5] *Iliad* I, 248–249.
[6] The meaning is uncertain, and may be "father has wandered."

In another passage "over and above" forms an antithesis to
"necessary." Moreover, "*shag*", that is "roaring", is properly
used of the sound which the waves make, and of the murmur
which we hear coming from the sea.[7] From which it is plain
that the thunder of the divine voice dwells in old men's ears
with a volume of sound beyond the voices of men. Again, in
our tongue Shunamite means "scarlet",[8] a hint that the love
of wisdom becomes warm and glowing through the study of
Scripture. For though the colour may point to the mystery of
the Lord's blood, it also sets forth the warm glow of wisdom.
Hence it is a scarlet thread that the midwife in Genesis binds
upon the hand of Pharez—Pharez "the divider", so called because he divided the wall of partition which had before separated two peoples.[9] So, too, with a mystic reference to the shedding of blood, it was a scarlet cord which the harlot Rahab
(a type of the Church) hung in her window that she might be
saved at the destruction of Jericho.[10] Hence, in another place
Scripture says of holy men: "These are the Kenites which came
from the warmth of the house of Rechab."[11] And in the gospel
the Lord says: "I am come to cast fire upon the earth, and fain
am I to see it kindled."[12] This was the fire which, when it was
kindled in the disciples' hearts, constrained them to say: "Did
not our heart burn within us while he talked with us by the
way, and while he opened to us the Scriptures?"[13]

4. To what end, you ask, these far-fetched references? To
show that you need not expect from me boyish declamation,
flowery sentiments, a meretricious style, and at the close of
every paragraph terse and pointed aphorisms to call forth
approving shouts from those who hear them. Let Wisdom alone
embrace me; let her nestle in my bosom, my Abishag who
grows not old. Undefiled truly is she, and ever virgin; for
although she daily conceives and unceasingly brings to
birth, like Mary she remains inviolate. Hence, I suppose,
the apostle says "be fervent in spirit."[14] And when the Lord
in the Gospel declares that in the end of the world—when the

---

[7] Heb. *shaag*, mostly of lions. A different word is used for waves (*hamah*).
But cf. Job 3:24 (*sheagh*).

[8] The place-name, Shunem, has the same consonants as *shani*, *shanim*,
scarlet.

[9] Gen. 38:28–30.

[10] Josh. 2:18, 21. Rahab was a stock type of the Church. See Cyprian,
De Unitate, 8 (p. 129), *Letter* 69, 4.

[11] I Chron. 2:55, Vulg. *de Calore*.

[12] Luke 12:49.   [13] Luke 24:32.   [14] Rom: 12:11.

shepherd shall grow foolish, according to tne prophecy of Zechariah[15]—"the love of many shall wax cold,"[16] he means that wisdom shall decay. Hear, therefore—to quote the blessed Cyprian—"words forcible rather than elegant."[17] Hear one who, though he is your brother in orders, is in years your father; who can conduct you from the cradle of faith to perfect manhood; and who, while he builds up stage by stage the rules of holy living, can instruct others in instructing you. I know, of course, that from your reverend uncle, Heliodorus, now a bishop of Christ, you have learned and are daily learning all that is holy; and that in him you have before you a rule of life and a pattern of virtue. Take, then, my suggestions for what they are worth, and add this little book to the one I sent to him. One will teach you to be a perfect monk, and this will show you the whole duty of a clergyman.

5. A clergyman, then, as he serves Christ's Church, must first understand what his name means; and then, when he has defined it, must endeavour to be that which he is called. For since the Greek word κλῆρος means "lot," the clergy are so called either because they are the lot of the Lord, or else because the Lord himself is their lot and portion.[18] Now, he who in his own person is the Lord's portion, or has the Lord for his portion, must so bear himself as to possess the Lord and to be possessed by him. He who possesses the Lord, and who says with the prophet: "The Lord is my portion,"[19] can hold to nothing beside the Lord. For if he hold to something beside the Lord, the Lord will not be his portion. Suppose, for instance, that he holds to gold or silver, or estates or inlaid furniture; with such portions as these the Lord will not deign to be his portion. I, if I am the portion of the Lord, and the line of his heritage,[20] receive no portion among the remaining tribes; but, like the priest and the Levite, I live on the tithe, and serving the altar, am supported by its offerings. Having food and raiment, I shall be content with these, and naked I shall follow the naked Cross.[21] I beseech you, therefore and

"Again and yet again admonish you,"[22]

do not look to your military experience for a standard of clerical

[15] Zech. 11:15.   [16] Matt. 24:12.
[17] *Ad Donatum*, 2.   [18] *Sors, id est pars.*
[19] Ps. 16 (15):5; 73 (72):26.   [20] Ps. 16 (15):5, 6; cf. Deut. 32:9.
[21] Deut. 18:1–2; Num. 18:24; I Cor. 9:13; I Tim. 6:8.
[22] Verg., *Aen.*, III, 436.

obligation. Under Christ's banner seek for no worldly gain, lest
having more than when you first became a clergyman, you
hear men say, to your shame: "Their portions shall not profit
them." [23] Welcome poor men and strangers to your homely
board, that with them Christ may be your guest. A clergyman
who engages in business, and who rises from poverty to wealth
and from obscurity to a high position, avoid as you would the
plague. "Evil communications corrupt good manners." [24] You
despise gold; he loves it. You spurn wealth; he eagerly pursues
it. You love silence, meekness, privacy; he takes delight in
talking and effrontery, in squares, and streets, and apothe-
caries' shops. What unity of feeling can there be where there
is so wide a divergency of manners?

A woman's foot should seldom, if ever, cross the threshold of
your humble home. To all maidens and all Christ's virgins
show the same disregard or the same affection. Do not remain
under the same roof with them, and do not rely on your past
continence. You cannot be holier than David or wiser than
Solomon. Always bear in mind that it was a woman who
expelled the tiller of paradise from his heritage. In case you
are sick, one of the brethren may attend you; your sister also
or your mother or some woman whose faith is approved by all.
But if you have no persons so connected with you or so marked
out by chaste behaviour, the Church maintains many elderly
women who by their ministrations may oblige you and benefit
themselves so that even your sickness may bear fruit in the
shape of almsgiving. I know of cases where the recovery of the
body has but preluded the sickness of the soul. There is danger
for you in the service of one whose face you are always
watching. If in the course of your clerical duty you have to
visit a widow or a virgin, never enter the house alone. Let
your companions be persons association with whom will not
disgrace you. If you take a reader with you or an acolyte or a
psalm-singer, let their character, not their garb, be their adorn-
ment; let them use no tongs to curl their hair; rather let their
mien be an index of their chastity. You must not sit alone with
a woman secretly and without witnesses. If she has anything
confidential to disclose, she is sure to have some nurse or house-
keeper, some virgin, some widow, some married woman. She
cannot be so friendless as to have none save you to whom she
can venture to confide her secret. Beware of all that gives

[23] Jer. 12:13, LXX, with pun on *cleri* (κλῆροι) as (i) portions, (ii) clergy.
[24] I Cor. 15:33.

occasion for suspicion; and, to avoid scandal, shun every act that may give colour to it. Frequent gifts of handkerchiefs and scarves, of favours pressed to the lips and choice dishes—to say nothing of tender *billets-doux*—of such things as these a holy love knows nothing. Such endearing and alluring expressions as "my honey, my light, my darling", the ridiculous courtesies of lovers and their foolish doings, we blush for on the stage and abhor in men of the world. How much more do we loathe them in clergymen, and above all in clergy who are monks, who adorn the priesthood by their vows while their vows are adorned by the priesthood. I speak thus not because I dread such evils for you or for men of saintly life, but because in all ranks and callings and among both men and women there are found both good and bad, and in condemning the bad I commend the good.

6. Shameful to say, idol-priests, play-actors, jockeys and prostitutes can inherit property: clergyman and monks alone lie under a legal disability, a disability enacted not by persecutors but by Christian emperors.[25] I do not complain of the law, but I grieve that we have deserved a statute so harsh. Cauterizing is a good thing, no doubt; but how is it that I have a wound which makes me need it? The law is strict and farseeing, yet even so rapacity goes on unchecked. By a fiction of trusteeship we set the statute at defiance; and, as if imperial decrees outweigh the mandates of Christ, we fear the laws and despise the Gospels. If heir there must be, the mother has first claim upon her children, the Church upon her flock—the members of which she has borne and reared and nourished. Why do we thrust ourselves in between mother and children?

It is the glory of a bishop to make provision for the wants of the poor; but it is the shame of all priests to amass private fortunes. I who was born (suppose) in a poor man's house, in a country cottage, and who could scarcely get enough millet and coarse bread to fill an empty stomach, am now come to disdain the finest wheat flour and honey. I know the several kinds of fish by name. I can tell unerringly on what coast an oyster has been picked.[26] I can distinguish by the flavour the province from which a bird comes. Dainty dishes delight me because their ingredients are scarce and I end by finding pleasure in their ruinous cost.[27]

[25] Valentinian I in A.D. 368 forbade the clergy to receive legacies from widows and unmarried women (*Cod. Theod.*, XVI, ii, 20). Ambrose refers to this in *Ep.* 18:14.
[26] Cf. Juvenal, IV, 140.   [27] Cf. Petronius, 119, v, 36.

I hear also of servile attention shewn by some towards old men and women when these are childless. They fetch the basin, beset the bed and perform with their own hands the most revolting offices. They anxiously await the advent of the doctor and with trembling lips ask whether the patient is better. If for a little while the old fellow shews signs of returning vigour, they are in agonies. They pretend to be delighted, but their covetous hearts undergo secret torture. For they are afraid that their labours may go for nothing and compare an old man with a clinging to life to the patriarch Methuselah. How great a reward might they have with God if their hearts were not set on a temporal prize! With what great exertions do they pursue an empty heritage! Less labour might have purchased for them the pearl of Christ.

7. Read the divine scriptures constantly; never, indeed, let the sacred volume be out of your hand. Learn what you have to teach. "Hold fast the faithful word which is according to the teaching, that you may be able to exhort in the sound doctrine and to convict the gainsayers. Continue thou in the things that thou hast learned and that have been entrusted to thee, knowing of whom thou hast learned them;" and "be ready always to give satisfaction to every man that asketh you a reason of the hope that is in you." [28] Do not let your deeds belie your words; lest when you speak in church someone may mentally reply, "Why do you not practise what you preach?" He is a fine and dainty master who, with his stomach full, reads us a homily on fasting. Let the robber accuse others of covetousness if he will. In a priest of Christ mind and mouth should be at one.

Be obedient to your bishop and welcome him as your spiritual father. Sons love and slaves fear. "If I be a father," he says, "where is mine honour? And if I be a master, where is my fear?" [29] In your case one man combines in himself many titles to your respect. He is at once monk, bishop, and uncle. But the bishops also should know themselves to be priests, not lords. Let them render to the clergy the honour which is their due, that the clergy may offer to them the respect which belongs to bishops. There is a saying of the orator Domitius which is here to the point: "Why am I to recognize you as leader of the Senate when you will not recognize my rights as a private member?" [30] We should realize that a bishop and his presbyters

28 Titus 1:9; II Tim. 3:14; I Peter 3:15.   29 Mal. 1:6.
30 Cicero, *De Oratore*, III, 4; Quintilian, *Inst. Or.*, VIII, 3, 89; XI, 1, 37.

are like Aaron and his sons. As there is but one Lord and one
temple, so also should there be but one ministry. Let us ever
bear in mind the charge which the apostle Peter gives to priests:
"Feed the flock of God which is among you, taking the over-
sight thereof not by constraint but willingly, as God would have
you; not for filthy lucre but of a ready mind; neither as being
lords over the heritage but being ensamples to the flock,"
and that gladly; that, "when the chief shepherd shall appear,
ye may receive a crown of glory which fadeth not away." [31] It
is a bad custom which prevails in certain churches for presbyters to be silent when bishops are present, on the ground
that they would be jealous or impatient hearers. [32] "If anything," writes the apostle Paul, "be revealed to another that
sitteth by, let the first hold his peace. For ye may all prophesy
one by one, that all may learn and all may be comforted;
and the spirits of the prophets are subject to the prophets.
For God is not the author of confusion but of peace." [33] "A
wise son is the glory of his father;" [34] and a bishop should rejoice
in the discrimination which has led him to choose such for the
priests of Christ.

8. When teaching in church seek to call forth not plaudits
but groans. Let the tears of your hearers be your glory. A presbyter's words ought to be seasoned by his reading of Scripture.
Be not a declaimer or a ranter, one who gabbles without rhyme
or reason; but shew yourself skilled in the deep things and
versed in the mysteries of God. To roll your words out and by
your quickness of utterance astonish the unlettered crowd is
a mark of ignorance. Assurance often explains that of which
it knows nothing; and when it has convinced others imposes
on itself. My teacher, Gregory of Nazianzus, [35] when I once
asked him to explain Luke's phrase δευτερόπρωτον, [36] that
is "the second-first Sabbath," wittily evaded my request saying: "I will tell you about it in church, and there, when all

---

[31] I Peter 5:2–4. For heritage the Latin has *in cleris*, with a double meaning.
[32] In the West it was rare for presbyters to preach in the presence of bishops,
until the end of the fourth century. Augustine was an exception, cf.
Possidius, *Vit. Aug.*, 6 and Aug., *Ep.* 41. For Jerome's views on bishops
and presbyters see *Letter* 146 (p. 383).
[33] I Cor. 14:30–33.   [34] Prov. 10:1.
[35] Jerome was in Constantinople A.D. 379–382, and for part of the time
studied with Gregory, one of the chief theologians of the early centuries
of Christianity, and for a short time Bishop of Constantinople.
[36] Luke 6:1. For the problem itself the commentaries on St. Luke must be
consulted.

the people applaud me, you will be forced against your will to know what you do not know at all. For, if you alone remain silent, every one will put you down for a fool." There is nothing so easy as by sheer volubility to deceive a common crowd or an uneducated congregation: such most admire what they fail to understand. Hear Marcus Tullius, the subject of that noble eulogy: "You would have been the first of orators but for Demosthenes: he would have been the only one but for you."[37] Hear what in his speech for Quintus Gallius[38] he has to say about unskilled speakers and popular applause. "What I am telling you," said he, "is a recent experience of my own. At these games a certain poet and literary man has been carrying off all the prizes. He has written a book entitled *Conversations*[39] *of Poets and Philosophers*. In this he represents Euripides as conversing with Menander and Socrates with Epicurus—men whose lives we know to be separated not by years but by generations. Nevertheless he calls forth limitless applause and endless acclamations. For the theatre contains many who went to the same school as he: and like him they learned nothing."

9. In dress avoid sombre colours as much as bright ones. Showiness and slovenliness are alike to be shunned; for the one savours of vanity and the other of ostentation. To go about without a linen scarf on is nothing: what is praiseworthy is to be without money to buy one. It is disgraceful and absurd to boast of having neither napkin nor handkerchief and yet to carry a well-filled purse.

Some bestow a trifle on the poor to receive a larger sum themselves and under the cloak of almsgiving do but seek for riches. Such are almshunters rather than almsgivers. Their methods are those by which birds, beasts, and fishes are taken. A morsel of bait is put on the hook—to land a fine lady's purse! The Church is committed to the bishop; he knows whom he should appoint to be his almoner. It is better for me to have no money to give away than to beg shamelessly. It is a form of arrogance, too, to wish to seem more liberal than he who is Christ's bishop. "All things are not open to us all."[40] In the Church one is the eye, another is the tongue, another the hand, another the foot, others ears, belly, and so on. Read Paul's epistle to the Corinthians and learn how the one body is made up of different members. The rude and simple brother must not suppose himself a saint just because he knows nothing; and he who is educated

[37] Source unknown.   [38] Not extant.
[39] *Convivia, symposia.*   [40] Verg., *Buc.,* VIII, 63.

and eloquent must not measure his saintliness merely by his
fluency. Of two imperfect things holy rusticity is better than
sinful eloquence.

10. Many build the walls of churches nowadays, but undermine the pillars of the Church.[41] Their marbles gleam, their
ceilings glitter with gold, their altars are studded with jewels;
yet to the choice of Christ's ministers no heed is paid. And let no
one allege against me the wealth of the temple in Judaea, its
altar, its lamps, its censers, its dishes, its cups, its spoons, and the
rest of its golden vessels. If these were approved by the Lord it
was at a time when the priests had to offer victims and when the
blood of sheep was the redemption of sins. They were figures
typifying things still future and were "written for our admoni-
tion upon whom the ends of the world are come." [42] But now
our Lord by his poverty has consecrated the poverty of his
house. Let us, therefore, think of his cross and count riches to
be but dirt. Why do we admire what Christ calls "the mammon
of unrighteousness"? Why do we cherish and love what it is
Peter's boast not to possess? [43] Or if we insist on keeping to the
letter and, in the case of gold and wealth, find our pleasure in
a purely historical exegesis, let us keep to everything else as
well as the gold. Let the bishops of Christ be bound to marry
wives, who must be virgins. Let the best-intentioned priest be
deprived of his office if he bear a scar and be disfigured. Let
bodily leprosy be counted worse than spots upon the soul. Let
us be fruitful and multiply and replenish the earth, but let us
slay no lamb and celebrate no mystic passover, for where there
is no temple, the law forbids these acts. Let us pitch tents in
the seventh month and noise abroad a solemn fast with the
sound of a horn.[44] But if we compare all these things as spiritual
with things which are spiritual; and if we allow with Paul
that "the Law is spiritual" and call to mind David's words:
"open thou mine eyes and I shall behold wondrous things
out of thy law;" and if on these grounds we interpret it as our
Lord also interprets it (he has explained the Sabbath in this
way) [45]; then, rejecting the superstitions of the Jews, we must
also reject the gold; or else, approving the gold, we must

41 I read *subtrahunt* with Hilberg. Wright reads *substernunt*, making the point
  wholly architectural. But it is personal, with a reference to the pillar
  apostles of Gal. 2:9 (*columnae* in Vulgate). The contrast here balances the
  one in the next sentence.
42 1 Cor. 10:11.   43 Luke 16:9; Acts 3:6.
44 Lev. 21:13, 17–23; 13:15; Gen. 1:28; Deut. 16:5–6; Lev. 23:23–44.
45 1 Cor. 2:13; Rom. 7:14; Ps. 119(118):18; Matt. 12:1–8.

approve the Jews as well. For we must either accept them with the gold or condemn them with it.

11. Avoid entertaining men of the world, especially those whose honours make them swell with pride. You are the priest of a crucified Lord who was poor and lived on the bread of strangers. It is a disgrace to you if the consul's lictors or soldiers keep watch before your door, and if the governor of the province has a better dinner with you than in his own palace. If you plead as an excuse your wish to intercede [46] for the unhappy and the oppressed, I reply that a secular magistrate will defer more to a clergyman who is self-denying than to one who is rich; he will pay more regard to your holiness than to your wealth. Or if he is a man who will only listen to the clergy over a glass, I will readily forego his aid and will appeal to Christ who can help more effectively than any judge. Truly "it is better to trust in the Lord than to put confidence in man. It is better to trust in the Lord than to put confidence in princes." [47]

Let your breath never smell of wine, lest the philosopher's words be said to you: "Instead of offering me a kiss you are giving me a taste of wine." Priests given to wine are both condemned by the Apostle [48] and forbidden by the old Law. Those who serve the altar, we are told, must drink neither wine nor *shechar*.[49] Now every intoxicating drink is in Hebrew called *shechar* whether it is made with yeast or of the juice of apples, whether you distil from the honeycomb a rude kind of mead or make a liquor by squeezing dates or strain a thick syrup from a decoction of corn. Whatever intoxicates and disturbs the balance of the mind, avoid as you would wine. I do not say that we are to condemn what is a creature of God.[50] The Lord himself was called a "wine-bibber" and wine in moderation was allowed to Timothy because of his weak stomach.[51] I only require that drinkers should observe that limit which their age, their health, or their constitution requires. But if without drinking wine at all I am aglow with youth and am inflamed by the heat of my blood and am of a strong and lusty habit of body, I will readily forgo the cup in which I cannot but suspect poison. The Greeks have an excellent saying rather difficult to translate,

"Fat bellies never breed fine thoughts." [52]

46 Cf. p. 237.   47 Ps. 118 (117): 8, 9.   48 I Tim. 3:3.
49 Lev. 10:9. *Shekar* (Latin, *sicera*) is translated "strong drink" in the English versions. In Luke 1:15 the word is retained in the Greek text (*sikera*).
50 I Tim. 4:4.   51 Matt. 11:19; I Tim. 5:23.
52 The Greek is extant, Kock, *Com. Att. Frag.*, III, 1234.

12. Lay upon yourself only as much fasting as you can bear, and let your fasts be pure, chaste, simple, moderate, and not superstitious. What good is it to use no oil if you seek after the most troublesome and out-of-the-way kinds of food, dried figs, pepper, nuts, dates, fine flour, honey, pistachios? All the resources of gardening are strained to save us from eating ordinary bread. There are some, I am told, who reverse the laws of nature and the human race; for they neither eat bread nor drink water but imbibe fancy decoctions of crushed herbs and beet-juice—not from a cup but from a shell. Shame on us that we have no blushes for such follies and that we feel no disgust at such superstition! To crown all, by means of our dainties we seek a reputation for abstinence. The strictest fast is bread and water. But because it brings with it no glory and because we all of us live on bread and water, it is reckoned no fast at all but an ordinary and common matter.

13. Do not angle for compliments, lest, while you win the popular applause, you do despite to God. "If I yet pleased men," says the Apostle, "I should not be the servant of Christ." [53] He ceased to please men when he became Christ's servant. Christ's soldier marches on through good report and evil report, [54] the one on the right hand and the other on the left. No praise elates him, no reproaches crush him. He is not puffed up by riches, nor depressed by poverty. Joy and sorrow he alike despises. The sun will not burn him by day nor the moon by night. [55] Do not pray at the corners of the streets, lest the applause of men interrupt the straight course of your prayers. Do not broaden your fringes and for show wear phylacteries, or, in despite of conscience, wrap yourself in the ostentation of the Pharisee. [56] It is better to wear this in your heart than on your body, to win God's approval rather than men's regard. Would you know what mode of apparel the Lord requires? Have prudence, justice, temperance, fortitude. [57] Let these be the four cardinal points of your horizon, let them be a four-horse team to bear you, Christ's charioteer, at full speed to your goal. No necklace can be more precious than these; no gems can form a brighter galaxy. By them you are decorated, you are girt about, you are protected on every side.

53 Gal. 1:10.
54 II Cor. 6:8.
55 Ps. 121 (120): 6.   56 Matt. 6:5; 23:5.
57 The four cardinal virtues of Greek philosophy. Cf. Wisdom 8:7 and Ambrose, *De Officiis.*

They are your defence as well as your glory; for every gem is turned into a shield.

14. Beware also of a blabbing tongue and of itching ears. Neither detract from others nor listen to detractors. "Thou satest," says the psalmist, "and spakest against thy brother; thou slanderedst thine own mother's son. These things hast thou done and I kept silence; thou thoughtest wickedly that I shall be such an one as thyself, but I will reprove thee and set them before thine eyes." [58] Set what? It means your words, all that you have said about others, so that you may be judged by your own sentence and found guilty yourself of the faults which you blamed in others. It is no excuse to say: "If others tell me things, I cannot be rude to them." No one cares to speak to an unwilling listener. An arrow never lodges in a stone; often it recoils and wounds the shooter. Let the detractor learn from your unwillingness to listen not to be so ready to detract. Solomon says: "Meddle not with them that are given to detraction: for their calamity shall rise suddenly; and who knoweth the destruction of them both?" [59]—of the detractor, that is, and of the person who lends an ear to his detraction.

15. It is your duty to visit the sick, to know people's homes, ladies and their children, and to be trusted with the secrets of the great. Count it your duty, therefore, to keep your tongue chaste as well as your eyes. Never discuss a woman's looks nor let one house know what is going on in another. Hippocrates,[60] before he will teach his pupils, makes them take an oath and compels them to swear to his words. He binds them over to silence, and prescribes for them their language, their gait, their dress, their manners. How much more reason have we, to whom the medicine of the soul has been committed, to love the homes of all Christians as though they were our own. Let them know us as comforters in sorrow rather than as guests in time of joy. A clergyman soon becomes an object of contempt if, however often he is asked out to dinner, he never refuses.

16. Let us never seek for presents and rarely accept them when we are asked to do so. Somehow or other the very man who begs leave to offer you a gift holds you the cheaper for your acceptance of it; while, if you refuse it, it is wonderful how much more he will come to respect you. The preacher of

---

58 Ps. 50 (49):20–21.   59 Prov. 24:21–22.
60 The great physician of the fifth century B.C. The oath may be found in the Loeb Hippocrates, I, 291 ff.

continence must not be a maker of marriages. Why does he who reads the Apostle's words, "it remaineth that they that have wives be as though they had none" [61]—why does he press a virgin to marry? Why does a priest who must be a monogamist, urge a widow to be a digamist? [62] How can the clergy be managers and stewards of other men's households and estates, when they are bidden to disregard even their own interests? [63] To wrest a thing from a friend is theft but to cheat the Church is sacrilege. When you have received money to be doled out to the poor, to be cautious or to hesitate while crowds are starving, or—and everyone can see how criminal this is— to subtract a portion for yourself, is to be more cruel than any robber. I am tortured with hunger, and are you to judge how much will satisfy my cravings? Either divide immediately what you have received, or, if you are a timid almoner, send the donor off to distribute his own gifts. Your purse ought not to be full while I remain in need. No one can look after what is mine better than I can. He is the best almoner who keeps nothing for himself.

17. You have compelled me, my dear Nepotian, in spite of the castigation which my treatise on *Virginity* has had to endure —the one which I wrote for the saintly Eustochium at Rome— you have compelled me after ten years have passed once more to open my mouth at Bethlehem and to expose myself to the stabs of every tongue. I could either escape from criticism by writing nothing, a course made impossible by your request; or else I knew that when I took up my pen all the shafts of calumny would be launched against me. I beg my opponents to hold their peace and to desist from calumny, for I have written not as an enemy but as a friend. I have not inveighed against sinners; I have but warned them to sin no more. My judgment of myself has been as strict as my judgment of them. When I wished to remove the mote from my neighbour's eye, I have first cast out the beam in my own. [64] I have injured no one. Not a name has been hinted at. My words have not been aimed at individuals and my criticism of short-comings has been quite general. If any one insists on being angry with me, he will have first to own that he himself suits my description.

---

[61] I Cor. 7:29.
[62] I Tim. 3:2. Monogamist, digamist (not bigamist), marrying once only or twice successively. See Ambrose, *Letter* 63:62–4 (p. 274) and notes there.
[63] There is much early canon law against this practice, often based on II Tim. 2:4.   [64] Matt. 7:3–5.

Letter 107 : To Laeta

INTRODUCTION

LAETA BELONGED TO THE GROUP OF HIGH-BORN
Roman ladies to whom Jerome acted as a spiritual
director and whom he encouraged to practise a life of
asceticism, whether at home or in a monastery. She was the
daughter of a pagan, Albinus, but had married the Christian
Toxotius, son of the elder Paula. She was also the cousin of
Marcella, one of Jerome's closest friends.

While very little can be said of Laeta herself, her daughter
Paula appears quite often in Jerome's correspondence. The
present letter was successful in its plea that she should be sent to
Bethlehem as a consecrated virgin, to be trained in the monastery of her grandmother Paula and her aunt Eustochium.
But—or so it would seem—Laeta was too affectionate or too
prudent a mother to send her there in infancy or early girl-
hood. There is no mention of the elder Paula ever seeing her,
and the first evidence of her presence in Bethlehem comes from
Letter 134 (written in 415–416), where Eustochium and Paula
send their greetings through Jerome to Augustine, and where
we hear of a presbyter, Firmus, who is travelling to Ravenna,
Africa and Sicily *ob rem earum*, that is, presumably, on business
concerning their estates. With Eustochium she went through
the raids made by the Pelagian party upon her monastery
(*Letters* 134–7), and on her aunt's death in 418–419 she took
charge of it, though still very young. In one of Jerome's last
letters, written in 419 to Augustine and his friend Alypius, she
is described as *neptis vestra* (grand-daughter), spiritually, of
course, but in contrast to Eustochium, *filia vestra*.

The date of her birth cannot be determined with absolute
certainty, but when this letter was written she was still unweaned (§13). The letter unquestionably precedes the death of
the elder Paula in A.D. 404, and Cavallera argues reasonably

enough that it also precedes her long illness of 402–403, which would otherwise have been mentioned in §13. He places it in 400, concluding from §2 that it ante-dates the destruction of the Temple of Marnas at Gaza in 401; though one might rather infer that Jerome is speaking rhetorically of an event which has recently occurred or at a time when the doom of the temple is known and imminent, and thus in 401 or 402.[1] Wright puts Paula's birth in 397 and the letter in 403, but without discussion.

With the substance of the letter we can compare Jerome's letter (128) to Gaudentius, on the education of his daughter. Written in A.D. 413, it is shorter, but similar. Jerome's ideas may then be compared with the almost contemporary tract of John Chrysostom, *On the Education of Children*[2] (the Golden Book), whose authenticity seems now, after some questioning, to be generally admitted. There is an amusing combination of the three documents in J. G. Davies, *Social Life of Early Christians*, Chapter 5, where it is justly pointed out that, whatever Christian parents decided to do about sending their sons to the public schools, there were none for girls.

[1] Cavallera dates the destruction to 401, without discussion. According to Mark the Deacon, it would be 402. See note on §2 below.

[2] M. L. W. Laistner, *Christianity and Pagan Culture in the Later Roman Empire*, 1951, contains a translation of Chrysostom's tract.

Letter 107 : To Laeta

THE TEXT

1. The blessed apostle Paul, writing to the Corinthians and instructing in sacred discipline a church still untaught in Christ, has among other commandments laid down also this: "The woman which hath an husband that believeth not, and if he be pleased to dwell with her, let her not leave him. For the unbelieving husband is sanctified by the believing wife, and the unbelieving wife is sanctified by the brother; else were your children unclean, but now are they holy."[1] Should any person have supposed hitherto that the bonds of discipline are too far relaxed and that too great indulgence is conceded by the teacher, let him look at the house of your father, a man of the highest rank and learning, but one still walking in darkness; and he will perceive, as the result of the Apostle's counsel, sweet fruit growing from a bitter stock and precious balsams exhaled from common canes. You yourself are the offspring of a mixed marriage; but you and my friend Toxotius are the parents of Paula. Who could have believed that to the pontiff[2] Albinus a granddaughter should be born in answer to a mother's vows; that a delighted grandfather should hear from the little one's faltering lips the song of *Alleluia*, and that in his old age he should nurse in his arms one of Christ's own virgins? Our expectations have been fully gratified. The one unbeliever is sanctified by his holy and believing family. For, when a man is surrounded by a believing crowd of children and grandchildren, he is a candidate for the faith. (I for my part think that, had he possessed such kinsfolk, even Jove himself might have come to believe in Christ!) For though he may spit upon my letter and laugh at it, and though he may call

[1] I Cor. 7:13–4.
[2] *Pontifex*, one of the State priesthoods, indicative rather of social status than religion. The college of pontiffs advised the State on all matters of cultus.

332

me a fool or a madman, his son-in-law did the same before he came to believe. Christians are not born but made. For all its gilding the Capitol is beginning to look dingy. Every temple in Rome is covered with soot and cobwebs.[3] The city is shaken to its foundations and the people pour past their half-ruined shrines to visit the tombs of the martyrs. The faith which has not been accorded to knowledge may come to be extorted by very shame.

2. I speak thus to you, Laeta, my most devout daughter in Christ, to teach you not to despair of your father's salvation. My hope is that the same faith which has gained you your daughter may win your father too, and that so you may be able to rejoice over blessings bestowed upon your entire family. You know the Lord's promise: "The things which are impossible with men are possible with God."[4] It is never too late to mend. The robber passed from the cross to paradise. Nebuchadnezzar also, the King of Babylon, recovered his reason, even after he had been made like the beasts in body and in heart, and had lived with the brutes in the wilderness. And to pass over such old stories which to unbelievers may well seem incredible, did not your own kinsman Gracchus, whose name betokens his patrician origin, when a few years back he held the Prefecture of the City, overthrow, break in pieces, and set on fire the grotto of Mithras and all the dreadful images therein? Those I mean by which the worshippers were initiated as Raven, Bridegroom, Soldier, Lion, Persian, Sun-runner, and Father? Did he not send them before him as hostages, to obtain for himself Christian baptism?[5]

Even in Rome itself paganism is left in solitude. They who once were the gods of the nations remain under their lonely roofs with owls and birds of night. The standards of the military are emblazoned with the sign of the cross. The emperor's

[3] This letter was written after the legislation of Theodosius against pagan worship. Jerome of course exaggerates.

[4] Luke 18:27.

[5] Furius Maecius Gracchus is mentioned in the *Codex Theodosianus* as Prefect of Rome in A.D. 376 and 377. His destruction of the cave of Mithras is also alluded to by Prudentius, *Contra Symmachum*, I, 562. Platner and Ashby, *Topographical Dictionary of Ancient Rome* (1929), list eight known Mithraea in Rome, with another doubtful. This passage is important for the seven degrees of initiation into Mithraism, but the text is not wholly certain. The Latin words are:—*corax, nymphius, miles, leo, Perses, heliodromus, pater*; Hilberg substitutes *cryphius* for *nymphius* on the basis of inscriptions, but this is against the manuscripts. For the family connexions of Gracchus compare *Letter* 108:1.

robes of purple and his diadem sparkling with jewels are orna-
mented with representations of the shameful yet saving gibbet.
Already the Egyptian Serapis has been made a Christian;
while at Gaza Marnas mourns in prison and every moment
expects to see his temple over-turned.[6] From India, from
Persian, from Ethiopia we daily welcome monks in crowds. The
Armenian bowman has laid aside his quiver, the Huns learn
the psalter, the chilly Scythians are warmed with the glow of
the faith. The Getae, ruddy and yellow-haired, carry tent-
churches about with their armies:[7] and perhaps their success
in fighting against us may be due to the fact that they believe
in the same religion.

3. I have nearly wandered into a new subject, and while I
have kept my wheel going, my hands have been moulding a
flagon when I meant to make a jug.[8] For, in answer to your
prayers and those of the saintly Marcella, it was my intention
to address you as a mother and to instruct you how to bring
up our little Paula, who was consecrated to Christ before her
birth, and vowed to his service before her conception. Thus in
our own day we have seen repeated the story told us in the
Prophets, of Hannah, who though at first barren, afterwards
became fruitful. You have exchanged a fertility bound up with
sorrow for offspring which shall never die. For I am confident
that, having given to the Lord your first-born, you will be the
mother of sons. It is the first-born that is offered under the Law.
Samuel and Samson are both instances of this, as is also John
the Baptist who when Mary came in leaped for joy. For he
heard the Lord thundering by the mouth of the Virgin and
desired to break from his mother's womb to meet him. As then
Paula has been born in answer to a promise, her parents should

---

[6] The Serapeum at Alexandria was destroyed in 391. Marnas was the chief
god of Gaza, sometimes said to be of Syrian or Philistine origin, sometimes to be equivalent to the Cretan Zeus (cf. the name Minos). Jerome
refers to him in *V. Hilarionis*, 20, and in his *Commentary on Isaiah* (vii, 17).
The full story of the destruction of the Marneion is told in Mark's
Life of Porphyry of Gaza, who went to Constantinople, as Bishop of Gaza,
in 398 to get an order for the destruction of the temple. He obtained it,
but it was not enforced. He went again, and obtained a fresh decree early
in 402. The temple took ten days to pull down in May, 402. Mark's
details cannot all be trusted, but the main facts seem secure. Jerome
(*Isaiah*, as above) says that churches were built instead of the Serapeum
and Marneion.

[7] Cf. Ambrose, *Letter* 20:12, and note (p. 211). The Latin here is *ecclesiarum
circumfert tentoria*; in Ambrose, *ecclesia plaustrum. Getae* = Goths.

[8] Horace, *Ars Poetica*, 21.

give her a training suitable to her birth. Samuel, as you know, was nurtured in the temple, and John was trained in the wilderness. The first was venerated for his long hair, drank neither wine nor strong drink, and even in his childhood talked with God. The second shunned cities, wore a leathern girdle, and had for his meat locusts and wild honey. Moreover, to typify repentance, he preached clothed in the spoils of the hump-backed camel.[9]

4. Thus must a soul be educated which is to be a temple of God. It must learn to hear nothing and to say nothing but what belongs to the fear of God. It must have no understanding of unclean words, and no knowledge of the world's songs. Its tongue must be steeped while still tender in the sweetness of the psalms. Boys with their wanton play must be kept far from Paula: even her maids and female attendants must be separated from worldly associates. For if they have learned some mischief, they may teach more. Get for her a set of letters made of boxwood or of ivory and called each by its proper name. Let her play with these, so that even her play may teach her something. And not only make her grasp the right order of the letters and remember their names by a rhyme, but constantly disarrange their order and put the last letters in the middle and the middle ones at the beginning, that she may know them all by sight as well as by sound. Moreover, so soon as she begins to use the style upon the wax, and her hand is still faltering, either guide her soft fingers by laying your hand upon hers, or else have the characters cut upon a tablet; so that her efforts, confined within these limits, may keep to the lines traced out for her and not stray outside of these. Offer prizes for good spelling and draw her onwards with little gifts such as children of her age delight in. And let her have companions in her lessons to excite emulation in her, that she may be stimulated when she sees them praised. You must not scold her if she is slow to learn, but must employ praise to excite her mind; let her be glad when she excels others and sorry when she is excelled by them. Above all you must take care not to make her lessons distasteful to her, lest a dislike for them conceived in childhood may continue into her maturer years. The very words which she tries bit by bit to put together ought not to be chance ones, but names specially fixed upon and heaped together for the purpose,

9 *Tortuossimi animalis*, perhaps with a reference to the writhings of penitence. Fremantle, however, compares *Letter* 79:3, *animal tortuosum*, the camel and the eye of the needle; that is, penitence is just as difficult.

those for example of the prophets or the apostles or the list of patriarchs from Adam downwards as it is given by Matthew and Luke. In this way, while she is doing something else, her memory will be stored for the future. Again, you must choose for her a master of approved years, life, and learning. A man of culture will not, I think, blush to do for a kinswoman or a highborn virgin what Aristotle did for Philip's son when, descending to the level of an usher, he consented to teach him his letters.[10] Things must not be despised as of small account if without them great results cannot be achieved. The very rudiments and first beginnings of knowledge sound differently in the mouth of an educated man and of an uneducated. Accordingly you must see that the child is not led away by the silly coaxing of women to form a habit of shortening long words or of decking herself with gold and purple. Of these habits one will spoil her conversation and the other her character. She must not therefore learn as a child what afterwards she will have to unlearn. The eloquence of the Gracchi is said to have been largely due to the way in which from their earliest years their mother spoke to them. Hortensia became an orator at her father's knee. Early impressions are hard to eradicate from the mind. When once wool has been dyed purple who can restore it to its previous whiteness? An unused jar long retains the taste and smell of that with which it is first filled.[11] Grecian history tells us that the imperious Alexander who was lord of the whole world could not rid himself of the faults of manner and gait which in his childhood he had caught from his governor Leonides. We are always ready to imitate what is evil; and faults are quickly copied where virtues appear unattainable. Paula's nurse must not be intemperate, or loose, or given to gossip. Her nursemaid must be respectable, and her foster-father of grave demeanour. When she sees her grandfather, she must leap upon his breast, put her arms round his neck, and, whether he likes it or not, sing *Alleluia* in his ears. She may be fondled by her grandmother, may smile at her father to shew that she recognizes him,[12] and may so endear herself to everyone as to make the whole family rejoice in the possession of such a rosebud. She should be told at once whom she has for her other grandmother and

10 Alexander. This and the following classical reminiscences are taken from Quintilian, *Instit. Orat.*, I. So is the advice about teaching letters.
11 Horace, *Epistles*, I, ii, 70.
12 Verg. *Buc.*, IV, 60.

whom for her aunt, who is her captain and for what army she is being trained as a recruit. Let her long to be with the absent ones, and threaten to leave you for them.

5. Let her very dress and garb remind her to whom she is promised. Do not pierce her ears or paint her face, consecrated to Christ, with white lead or rouge. Do not hang gold or pearls about her neck or load her head with jewels, or by dyeing her hair red make it suggest the fires of gehenna. Let her pearls be of another kind and such that she may sell them hereafter and buy in their place the pearl that is "of great price". In days gone by a lady of rank, Praetextata by name, at the bidding of her husband Hymettius, the uncle of Eustochia, altered that virgin's dress and appearance and waved her neglected hair, desiring to overcome the resolution of the virgin herself and the wishes of her mother. But lo! in the same night it befell her that an angel came to her in her dreams. With terrible looks he menaced punishment and broke silence with these words: "Have you presumed to put your husband's commands before those of Christ? Have you presumed to lay sacrilegious hands upon the head of one who is God's virgin? Those hands shall wither this very hour, that you may know by torment what you have done, and at the end of five months you shall be carried off to hell. And if you persist in your wickedness, you shall be bereaved both of your husband and of your children." All of which came to pass in due time, a speedy death marking the unhappy woman's too long delayed repentance. So terribly does Christ punish those who violate his temple, and so jealously does he defend his precious jewels. I have related this story here not from any desire to exult over the misfortunes of the unhappy, but to warn you that you must with much fear and carefulness keep the vow which you have made to the Lord.

6. We read of Eli the priest that he became displeasing to God on account of the sins of his children; and we are told that a man may not be made a bishop if his sons are loose and disorderly. On the other hand it is written of the woman that "she shall be saved in childbearing, if they continue in faith and charity and holiness with chastity."[13] If then parents are responsible for their children when these are of ripe age and independent, how much more must they be responsible for them when, still unweaned and weak, they cannot, in the Lord's words, "discern between their right hand and their left,"[14]

13 I Sam. 2:27ff.; I Tim. 3:4; 2:15.   14 Jonah 4:11.

338   JEROME

when, that is to say, they cannot yet distinguish good from evil?
If you take precautions to save your daughter from the bite
of a viper, why are you not equally careful to shield her from
"the hammer of the whole earth"?[15] to prevent her from drinking of the golden cup of Babylon? to keep her from going out
with Dinah to see the daughters of a strange land?[16] to save her
from the tripping dance and from the trailing robe? No one
administers poison till he has rubbed the rim of the cup with
honey;[17] so the better to deceive us, vice puts on the mien and
the semblance of virtue. Why then, you will say, do we read:
"the son shall not bear the iniquity of the father, neither
shall the father bear the iniquity of the son," but "the soul that
sinneth it shall die"? The passage, I answer, refers to those who
have discretion, such as he of whom his parents said in the Gospel: "He is of age, let him speak for himself."[18] While the son
is a child and thinks as a child, and until he comes to years of
discretion to choose between the two roads to which the letter
of Pythagoras points,[19] his parents are responsible for his
actions, whether these be good or bad. But perhaps you imagine
that, if they are not baptized, the children of Christians are alone
liable for their own sins; and that no guilt attaches to parents
who withhold from baptism those who by reason of their tender
age can offer no objection to it. The truth is that, as baptism
ensures the salvation of the child, this in turn brings advantage
to the parents. Whether you would offer your child or not lay
within your choice, but now that you have offered her, you
neglect her at your peril. Though in your case you had no
discretion, having vowed your child even before her conception.
He who offers a victim that is lame or maimed or marked with
any blemish is held guilty of sacrilege.[20] How much more
then shall she be punished who makes ready for the embraces
of the King a portion of her own body and the purity of a stain-
less soul, and then proves negligent of this her offering?

7. When she comes to be a little older and to increase like her
Spouse in wisdom and stature and in favour with God and man,
let her go with her parents to the temple of her true Father,
but let her not come out of the temple with them. Let them seek
her upon the world's highway amid the crowds and the throng

15 Babylon, Jer. 50:23.   16 Gen. 34.
17 Lucretius, I, 936.   18 Ezek. 18:20; John 9:21.
19 The Greek *hypsilon* (Y), the stem being the time of childhood, cf. Persius,
    III, 56.
20 Deut. 15:21.

of their kinsfolk, and let them find her nowhere but in the shrine of the Scriptures, questioning the prophets and the apostles on the meaning of her spiritual marriage. Let her imitate Mary, whom Gabriel found alone in her chamber and who was frightened, it would appear, by seeing a man there. Let the child emulate her of whom it is written that "the king's daughter is all glorious within." Wounded with love's arrow let her say to her beloved: "The king hath brought me into his chamber." At no time let her go abroad; lest the watchmen that go about the city find her, lest they smite and wound her and take away from her the veil of her chastity, and leave her naked in her blood. Nay rather when one knocketh at her door let her say: "I am a wall and my breasts like towers. I have washed my feet; I cannot defile them." [21]

8. Let her not take her food with others, that is, at her parents' guest-table; lest she see dishes she may long for. Some, I know, hold it a greater virtue to disdain a pleasure which is actually before them, but I think it a safer self-restraint not to know what would attract you. Once as a boy at school I met the words: "It is ill blaming what you allow to become a habit." [22] Let her learn even now not to drink wine "wherein is excess." [23] But as, before they come to their full strength, strict abstinence is dangerous to young children, let her go to the baths if she must, and let her take a little wine for her stomach's sake. [24] Let her also be supported on a flesh diet, lest her feet fail her before they commence to run their course. But I say this by way of concession, not by way of command; [25] because I fear to weaken her, not because I wish to teach her self-indulgence. Besides, why should not a Christian virgin do wholly what others do in part? The superstitious Jews reject certain animals and products as articles of food, while among the Indians the Brahmans and among the Egyptians the gymnosophists subsist altogether on porridge, rice and fruit. [26] If mere glass is worth so much, is not a pearl worth more? [27] Paula has been born in response to a vow. Let her life be as the lives of those who were born under the same conditions. If the grace accorded is in both cases the same, the pains bestowed

21 Luke 2:52, 43–46; 1:29; Ps. 45 (44) 13; S. of Sol. 1:4; 5:7, 2; 8:10; 5:3.
22 Publilius Syrus, *Sententiae*, 180.
23 Eph. 5:18.   24 I Tim. 5:23.   25 I Cor. 7:6.
26 Cf. Tertullian, *Apology*, 42: We [Christians] are not Brahmans or Indian gymnosophists, living in the woods, exiles from life . . . We repudiate no creature of God.
27 Here, and in *Epp.* 79:7, 130:9, from Tert., *Ad Martyras*, 4.

ought to be so too. Let her be deaf to the sound of the organ, and not know even why the pipe, the lyre, and the harp are made.

9. And let it be her task daily to repeat to you a fixed portion of Scripture. Let her learn by heart so many verses in the Greek, but let her be at once instructed in the Latin also. For, if the tender lips are not from the first shaped to this, the tongue is spoiled by a foreign accent and its native speech debased by alien elements. You must yourself be her teacher, a model on which she may form her childish conduct. Never let her see either in you or in her father what she cannot imitate without sin. Remember that you are the parents of a consecrated virgin, and that your example will teach her more than your precepts. Flowers are quick to fade, and a baleful wind soon withers the violet, the lily, and the crocus. Let her never appear in public without you. Let her never visit a church or a martyr's shrine unless with her mother. Let no young man, no dandy with curled hair, ogle her. If our little virgin goes to keep solemn eves and all-night vigils, let her not stir a hair's breadth from her mother's side. She must not single out one of her maids to make her a special favourite or a confidante. What she says to one all ought to know. Let her choose for a companion not a handsome well-dressed girl, able to warble a song with liquid notes, but one pale and serious, sombrely attired and inclined to melancholy. Let her take as her model some aged virgin of approved faith, character, and chastity, who can instruct her by word and by example to rise at night to recite prayers and psalms, to sing hymns in the morning, at the third, sixth, and ninth hours to take her place in the line to do battle for Christ, to kindle her lamp and offer her evening sacrifice.[28] In these occupations let her pass the day, and when night comes, let it find her still engaged in them. Let reading follow prayer and prayer again succeed to reading. Time will seem short when employed on tasks so many and so varied.

10. Let her learn too how to spin wool, to hold the distaff, to put the basket in her lap, to turn the spinning wheel and to shape the yarn with her thumb. Let her put away with disdain silken fabrics, Chinese fleeces, and gold brocades: the clothing which she makes for herself should keep out the cold and not expose the body which it professes to cover. Let her food be vegetables and wheaten bread with now and then one or two

[28] That is, six of the seven "canonical" hours of prayer: Nocturns, Mattins, Terce, Sext, None, Vespers. Cf. *Epp.* 22:37; 108:20; 130:15.

small fishes. And that I may not waste more time in giving precepts for the regulation of appetite (a subject I have treated more at length elsewhere),[29] let her meals always leave her hungry and able on the moment to begin reading or praying or chanting. I strongly disapprove—especially for those of tender years—of long and immoderate fasts in which week is added to week and even oil and fruit are forbidden as food. I have learned by experience that the ass toiling along the highway makes for an inn when it is weary. Leave that to the worshippers of Isis and Cybele who gobble up pheasants and turtle-doves piping hot, that their teeth may not violate the gifts of Ceres![30] If an unbroken fast is intended, it must be so regulated that those who have a long journey before them may hold out all through; and we must take care that we do not, after running the first lap, fall halfway. However in Lent, as I have written before now, those who practise self-denial should spread every stitch of canvas, and the charioteer should for once slacken the reins and increase the speed of his horses. Yet there will be one rule for those who live in the world and another for virgins and monks. The layman in Lent consumes the coats of his stomach, and, living like a snail on his own juice,[31] gets his paunch ready for rich foods and feasting to come. But with the virgin and the monk the case is different; for, when these give the rein to their steeds in Lent, they have to remember that for them the race knows of no intermission. An effort made only for a limited time may well be severe, but one that has no such limit must be more moderate. For whereas in the first case we can recover our breath when the race is over, in the last we have to go on continually and without stopping.

11. When you go into the country, do not leave your daughter behind at home. Leave her no power or capacity of living without you, and let her feel frightened when she is left to herself. Let her not converse with people of the world or associate with virgins indifferent to their vows. Let her not be present at the weddings of your slaves and let her take no part in the noisy games of the household. As regards the use of the bath, I know that some are content with saying that a Christian virgin should not bathe along with eunuchs or with married women, with the former because they are still men at heart, and with the latter because women with child are a revolting

[29] *Ep.* 54:9–10 and/or *Contra Jovin.*, II.
[30] Having vowed not to eat bread, they eat luxuries. Cf. p. 326.
[31] Plautus, *Captivi*, 80.

spectacle. For myself, however, I wholly disapprove of baths for
a virgin of full age. Such an one should blush and feel overcome
at the idea of seeing herself naked. By vigils and fasts she morti-
fies her body and brings it into subjection. By a cold chastity
she seeks to put out the flame of lust and to quench the hot
desires of youth. And by a deliberate squalor she makes haste
to spoil her natural good looks. Why, then, should she add fuel
to a sleeping fire by taking baths?

12. Let her treasures be not silks or gems but manuscripts
of the holy Scriptures; and in these let her think less of gilding,
and Babylonian parchment, and arabesque patterns, than of
correctness and accurate punctuation. Let her begin by learning
the Psalter and distract herself with these songs, and then let
her gather rules of life out of the Proverbs of Solomon. From
Ecclesiastes let her gain the habit of despising the world and
its vanities.[32] Let her follow the example set in Job of virtue and
of patience. Then let her pass on to the Gospels, never to be laid
aside when once they have been taken in hand. Let her also
drink in with a willing heart the Acts of the Apostles and the
Epistles. As soon as she has enriched the storehouse of her mind
with these treasures, let her commit to memory the Prophets,
the Heptateuch, the books of Kings and of Chronicles, the rolls
also of Ezra and Esther. When she has done all this, she may
safely read the Song of Songs; but not before. For, were she to
read it at the beginning, she would fail to perceive that, though
it is written in fleshly words, it is a marriage song of a spiritual
bridal; and not understanding this she would suffer hurt from
it. Let her avoid all apocryphal writings, and if she is led to
read them not by truth of the doctrines which they contain
but out of respect for the miracles contained in them; let her
understand that they are not really written by those to whom
they are ascribed, that many faulty elements have been introduced into them, and that it requires discretion to look for
gold in the midst of dirt.[33] Cyprian's writings let her have
always in her hands. The letters of Athanasius and the treatises
of Hilary[34] she may go through without fear of stumbling.
Let her take pleasure in the works and wits of all writers in

---

[32] In the preface to his *Commentary on Ecclesiastes*, Jerome relates that he
read the book with Blesilla in Rome, to induce her to despise the world.
[33] In the "Helmeted Preface" Jerome rejected all books outside the Hebrew
Canon of the Old Testament as apocryphal, though he was inconsistent
in his practice. He might be referring here to the so-called "New Testament Apocrypha"; many of these books were Gnostic.
[34] Of Poitiers.

whose books a due regard for the faith is not neglected. But if she reads the works of others, let it be rather to judge them than to follow them.

13. You will answer: "How shall I, a woman of the world, living at Rome, surrounded by a crowd, be able to observe all these injunctions?" In that case do not undertake a burthen to which you are not equal. When you have weaned Paula as Isaac was weaned, and when you have clothed her as Samuel was clothed, send her to her grandmother and aunt; set this most precious of gems in Mary's chamber and put her in the cradle where Jesus cried. Let her be brought up in a monastery, let her be among companies of virgins, let her learn to avoid swearing, let her regard lying as sacrilege, let her be ignorant of the world, let her live like the angels; while in the flesh let her be without the flesh, and let her suppose that all human beings are like herself. To say nothing of its other advantages, this course will free you from the difficult task of minding her, and from the responsibility of guardianship. It is better for you to regret her absence than to be for ever trembling for her, watching what she says and to whom she says it, to whom she bows and whom she likes best to see. Hand her over to Eustochium while she is still but an infant and her every cry is a prayer for you. She will thus become her companion in holiness now as well as her successor hereafter. Let her gaze upon and love, let her "from her earliest years admire",[35] one whose language and gait and dress are an education in virtue. Let her grandmother take her on her lap and repeat to her granddaughter the lessons that she once bestowed upon her own child. Long experience has shewn her how to rear, instruct and watch over virgins; and daily inwoven in her crown is the mystic hundred[36] which betokens the highest chastity. O happy virgin! happy Paula, daughter of Toxotius, who through the virtues of her grandmother and aunt is nobler in holiness than she is in lineage! Yes, were it possible for you with your own eyes to see your mother-in-law and your sister, and to realize the mighty souls which animate their small bodies; such is your innate chastity that I cannot doubt but that you would go to them even before your daughter, and would exchange God's first decree

---

[35] Verg., *Aen.*, VIII, 517.
[36] The parable of the sower (Matt. 13) was used to suggest that chastity in marriage is rewarded thirty-fold, faithful widowhood sixty-fold, virginity a hundredfold. Virginity is therefore *intrinsically* superior to marriage. Cf. *Ep.* 48 and Ambrose, *Letter* 63:7, 10.

for his second law of the Gospel.[37] You would count as nothing your desire for other children and would offer up yourself to the service of God. But because "there is a time to embrace, and a time to refrain from embracing", and because "the wife hath not power of her own body," and because every man should "abide in the same calling wherein he was called" in the Lord, and because he that is under the yoke ought so to run as not to leave his companion in the mire, pay back to the full in your offspring what meantime you defer paying in your own person.[38] When Hannah had once offered in the tabernacle the son whom she had vowed to God, she never took him back; for she thought it unbecoming that one who was to be a prophet should grow up in the same house with her who still desired to have other sons. Accordingly after she had conceived him and given him birth, she did not venture to come to the temple alone or to appear before the Lord empty, but first paid to him what she owed, and then, when she had offered up that great sacrifice, she returned home; and because she had borne her first-born for God, she was given five children for herself.[39] Do you marvel at the happiness of that holy woman? Imitate her faith. Moreover, if you will only send Paula, I promise to be myself both a tutor and a foster-father to her. Old as I am, I will carry her on my shoulders and train her stammering lips; and my charge will be a far prouder one than that of the worldly philosopher; for while he only taught a King of Macedon who was one day to die of Babylonian poison,[40] I shall instruct the handmaid and bride of Christ who will one day be offered in the Kingdom of heaven.

[37] Gen. 1:28 (Be fruitful, and multiply) for 1 Cor. 7:1.
[38] Eccl. 3:5; 1 Cor. 7:4, 20.
[39] I Sam. 2.
[40] Aristotle and Alexander the Great.

Letter 108 : To Eustochium

INTRODUCTION

SEVERAL OF JEROME'S LETTERS WERE WRITTEN TO console his friends for the death of their loved ones. In some the note of consolation and exhortation predominates, while others are obituary notices of historical value. Such are the letters about Blesilla (38-39), Nepotian (60), Paulina (66), Fabiola (77), Marcella (127) and, longest and most valuable of all, the present letter to Eustochium about her mother, Paula the elder.

I

Paula came of a patrician family in Rome, and was born in A.D. 347, the daughter of Rogatus and Blesilla. She was a member of the group of Christian ladies who frequented the house of Marcella, and when her husband, Toxotius, died, she gave herself to the life of religion. This was in A.D. 379 or 380, before Jerome was in Rome. She had borne four daughters, Blesilla, Paulina, Eustochium, and Rufina, and one son, Toxotius, still a baby. Jerome affords us an unusual glimpse of the unofficial side of ecclesiastical assemblies when he relates how she "put up" Epiphanius, Bishop of Salamis, during the Council of Rome in A.D. 382. Jerome, who also went to Rome for the Council, did not meet her at once, for he says that he was well known in the city before he became acquainted with her family (*Letter* 45:3). But they soon became such intimate friends that he had eventually to defend himself from slander and make a calumniator retract his words. Paula was an enthusiastic student of the Bible, eager for a mystical interpretation of it, while her friend Marcella had a taste for textual and historical studies. During these years in Rome, Jerome addressed to her *Letter* 30, on the alphabetical Psalms and the

345

mystical significance of the Hebrew alphabet; *Letter* 33, which contains an important catalogue of the writings of Origen; and *Letter* 39, on the death of her eldest daughter, Blesilla. There is also a note thanking the girl Eustochium for her St. Peter's day presents to Jerome. Blesilla had married, only to lose her husband after but seven months of marriage. Very soon afterwards she was "converted" to the ascetic life, but died three months later. Jerome, though genuinely sympathetic, found it necessary to chide Paula for giving way to excessive grief. But was there something of a bad conscience in this excess? For it was rumoured that Blesilla had died of fasting, and her death seems to have been one of the incidents which helped to drive Jerome out of the capital. "When shall we drive these detestable monks out of Rome? Why not throw them into the Tiber?"

Jerome left the city in 385, and Paula soon followed him, taking Eustochium with her. Their journey to Antioch, with a visit to Epiphanius on the way, and their pilgrimages in the Holy Land and in Egypt, are told at some length in the present letter. By autumn 386 they had settled in Bethlehem, where Paula spent the rest of her life as head of the monastery for women which she founded. Again, many of the details of her life in it are related in this letter. Bible studies still held her attention, and besides what the letter has to say, there is something to be gleaned from the numerous prefaces to the translations and commentaries on the books of the Bible. It was at Paula's request that Jerome revised his first Psalter, producing the so-called Gallican Psalter, and that he translated Origen's *Homilies on St. Luke's Gospel.* Paula and Eustochium received the dedication of a good many of his biblical works, and it was to them that the celebrated "Helmeted" Preface to the Books of Kings was addressed, with its brief introduction to the Hebrew Bible and its rejection of the Apocrypha from the Canon. Paula supervised the Bethlehem convent until her death on the 26th of January, A.D. 404 at the age of fifty-six. She was succeeded by her daughter, Eustochium, to whom Jerome dedicated several of his later works; and Eustochium was succeeded by the younger Paula, daughter of the Toxotius whom his mother had left some twenty years before her death "stretching forth his hand in entreaty" on the shore at Ostia.

II

The description of the pilgrimage (§§8–14) is of special interest, not so much philologically and topographically as psychologically and spiritually. It has not been found practicable to annotate it adequately in this volume, or even to give the hundred and more biblical references which these sections alone require. They can all be found in Hilberg's edition in the Vienna *Corpus*, or through the full-scale concordances and dictionaries of the Bible. To a large extent Jerome's comments on the places are taken from his own translation of a work of Eusebius of Caesarea on the place-names of Palestine, the references to which are also given by Hilberg. The derivations are frequently fanciful, but the topographical information is of some value, at least for the pilgrim routes. With Paula's pilgrimage one should compare that of Egeria, dating from much the same time. Her travel journey has come down in a mutilated form, beginning at her visit to Sinai and ending with a detailed account of the rites of Holy Week at Jerusalem. Translations of both these pilgrimages and of other early ones will be found in the first volume of the Palestine Pilgrims Text Society.

III

There is another part of this letter which calls for special notice. It is the digression against heresy in §§ 23–26, a digression curious in itself and in the circumstances in very poor taste. The heresy is, of course, Origenism, and even in a letter of consolation Jerome cannot restrain himself from snatching at an opportunity to attack it and to exhibit his own cleverness. To affirm Paula's orthodoxy the detail is quite unnecessary; as so often, he lets his impetuous pen run away with him. We are not told who the "cunning knave" was who approached Paula with his awkward questions, some of which might have been put by any Origenist. There are points of detail, however, which appear also in Jerome's tract against John of Jerusalem, written in A.D. 396. It is perhaps unlikely that the bishop is being directly attacked here; that would have been in execrable taste, for he attended Paula's funeral, as Jerome himself records. More probably it was one of his circle. Jerome's principal onslaught upon the Origenists, the three books against Rufinus, had also been written before the death of Paula. In the present passage he is able to appeal to the letter of Scripture and to everyday orthodox beliefs, but, though he makes some sound points, he reveals no sympathy whatsoever for those who struggle with profound and difficult problems, nor does he say positively what he thought Paul meant by a spiritual body.

Letter 108 : To Eustochium

THE TEXT

1. If all the members of my body were to be converted into tongues, and if each of my limbs were to be gifted with a human voice, I could still do no justice to the virtues of the holy and venerable Paula. Noble in family, she was nobler still in holiness; rich formerly in this world's goods, she is now more distinguished by the poverty that she has embraced for Christ. Of the stock of the Gracchi and descended from the Scipios, the heir and representative of that Paulus whose name she bore, the true and legitimate daughter of that Maecia Papiria who was mother to Africanus, she yet preferred Bethlehem to Rome, and left her palace glittering with gold to dwell in a mud cabin. We do not grieve that we have lost this perfect woman; rather we thank God that we have had her, nay that we have her still. For all live unto God, and they who are given back to the Lord are still to be reckoned members of the family. We have lost her, it is true, but the heavenly mansions have gained her; for as long as she was in the body she was absent from the Lord, and would constantly complain with tears: "Woe is me that my sojourning is prolonged; I have dwelt with the inhabitants of Kedar; my soul hath been this long time a sojourner." [1] It was no wonder that she sobbed out that she was in darkness (for this is the meaning of the word Kedar) seeing that "the world lieth in the evil one;" and that, "as its darkness is, so is its light;" and that "the light shineth in the darkness and the darkness apprehended it not." [2] Therefore she would frequently exclaim: "I am a stranger with thee and a sojourner as all my fathers were," and again, I desire "to depart and to be with Christ." As often too as she was troubled with bodily weakness (brought on by incredible abstinence and by redoubled fastings), she would be heard to say: "I keep under my body and

[1] Ps. 120 (119):5, 6.   [2] I John 5:19; Ps. 139 (138):12; John 1:5.

348

bring it into subjection; lest, when I have preached to others, I myself should be found a castaway;" and: "It is good neither to eat flesh nor to drink wine;" and: "I humbled my soul with fasting;" and: "Thou hast turned all my bed in my sickness;" and: "I am turned in my anguish, while the thorn is fastened upon me." And when the pain which she bore with such wonderful patience darted through her, as if she saw the heavens opened she would say: "Oh that I had wings like a dove! for then would I fly away and be at rest."[3]

2. I call Jesus and his holy angels, yes and the particular angel who was the guardian and the companion of this admirable woman, to bear witness that these are no words of adulation and flattery but sworn testimony, every one of them, borne to her character. They are, indeed, inadequate to the virtues of one whose praises are sung by the whole world, who is admired by bishops, regretted by bands of virgins, and wept for by crowds of monks and poor. Would you know all her virtues, reader, in short? She has left those dependent on her poor, but not so poor as she was herself. In dealing thus with her relatives and the men and women of her small household—her brothers and sisters rather than her servants—she has done nothing strange; for she has left her daughter Eustochium—a virgin consecrated to Christ, for whose comfort this sketch is made— far from her noble family and rich only in faith and grace.

3. Let me then begin my narrative. Others may go back a long way even to Paula's cradle and, if I may say so, to her rattle, and may speak of her mother Blesilla and her father Rogatus. Of these the former was a descendant of the Scipios and the Gracchi; whilst the latter came of a line wealthy and distinguished throughout Greece down to the present day. He is said there to have in his veins the blood of Agamemnon who destroyed Troy after a ten years' siege. But I shall praise only what belongs to herself, what wells forth from the pure spring of her holy mind. When in the Gospel the apostles ask their Lord and Saviour what he will give to those who have left all for his sake, he tells them that they shall receive an hundredfold now in this time and in the world to come eternal life.[4] From which we see that it is not the possession of riches that is praiseworthy but the rejection of them for Christ's sake; that, instead of glorying in our privileges, we should make them of

[3] Ps. 39 (38):12; Phil. 1:23; I Cor. 9:27; Rom. 14:21; Ps. 35 (34):13; Ps. 41:3 (40:4); Ps. 32 (31):4; Ps. 55 (54):6.
[4] Mark 10:28–30.

small account as compared with faith in the Lord. Truly the Saviour has now in this present time made good his promise to his servants and handmaidens. For one who despised the glory of a single city is to-day famous throughout the world; and one who while she lived at Rome was known by no one outside it, has by hiding herself at Bethlehem become the admiration of all lands Roman and barbarian. For what race of men is there which does not send pilgrims to the holy places? And who could find there a greater marvel than Paula? As among many jewels the most precious shines most brightly, and as the sun with its beams obscures and puts out the paler fires of the stars; so by her lowliness she surpassed all others in virtue and influence and, while she was least among all, was greater than all. The more she cast herself down, the more she was lifted up by Christ. She was hidden and yet she was not hidden. By shunning glory she earned glory; for glory follows virtue as its shadow; and deserting those who seek it, it seeks those who despise it.[5] But I must not neglect to proceed with my narrative or dwell too long on a single point, forgetful of the rules of writing.

4. Being then of such parentage, Paula married Toxotius in whose veins ran the noble blood of Aeneas and the Julii. Accordingly his daughter, Christ's virgin Eustochium, is called Julia, as he Julius,

"A name from great Iulus handed down."[6]

I speak of these things not as of importance to those who have them, but as worthy of remark in those who despise them. Men of the world look up to persons who are rich in such privileges. We, on the other hand, praise those who for the Saviour's sake despise them; and strangely depreciating all who keep them, we eulogize those who are unwilling to do so. Thus nobly born, Paula through her fruitfulness and her chastity alike won approval from all, from her husband first, then from her relatives, and lastly from the whole city. She bore five children: Blesilla, for whose death I consoled her while at Rome;[7] Paulina, who has left the reverend and admirable Pammachius to inherit both her vows and property, to whom also I addressed a little book on her death;[8] Eustochium, who is now in the holy places, a precious necklace of virginity and of

[5] Cic., *Tusc. Disp.*, I, 109; Seneca, *Ep.* 79:13; Pliny, *Ep.* I:8, 14.
[6] Verg., *Aen.*, I, 288.
[7] *Ep.* 39.   [8] *Ep.* 66.

the Church;[9] Rufina, whose untimely end overcame the affectionate heart of her mother; and Toxotius, after whom she had no more children. You can thus see that it was not her wish to continue to fulfil a wife's duty, but that she only complied with her husband's longing to have male offspring.

5. When he died, her grief was so great that she nearly died herself; yet so completely did she then give herself to the service of the Lord, that it might have seemed that she had desired his death. In what terms shall I speak of her distinguished, and noble, and formerly wealthy house, almost all the riches of which she spent upon the poor? How can I describe the great consideration she shewed to all and her far-reaching kindness even to those whom she had never seen? What poor man, as he lay dying, was not wrapped in blankets given by her? What bedridden person was not supported with money from her purse? She would seek out such with the greatest diligence throughout the city, and would think it her loss were any hungry or sick person to be supported by another's food. She robbed her children; and, when her relatives remonstrated with her for doing so, she declared that she was leaving to them a better inheritance in the mercy of Christ.

6. Nor was she long able to endure the visits and crowded receptions, which her high position in the world and her exalted family entailed upon her. She received the homage paid to her sadly, and made all the speed she could to shun and to escape those who wished to pay her compliments. It so happened that at that time the bishops of the East and West had been summoned to Rome by letter from the emperors to deal with certain dissensions between the churches, and in this way she saw two most admirable men and Christian prelates, Paulinus, Bishop of Antioch, and Epiphanius, Bishop of Salamis or, as it is now called, Constantia, in Cyprus.[10] Epiphanius, indeed, she received as her guest; and, although Paulinus was staying in another person's house, in the warmth of her heart she treated him as if he too were lodged with her. Inflamed by their virtues, she thought every moment of forsaking her country. Disregarding her home, her children, her servants, her property, and in a word everything connected with the world, she was

9 *Ep.* 22.
10 The Council of Rome, A.D. 382, met to consider the Western attitude to the Council of Constantinople, A.D. 381. Paulinus was accepted in the West as the true Bishop of Antioch. See the Introduction to *Letter* 15 (p. 304).

eager—alone and unaccompanied (if ever it could be said that she was so)—to go to the desert made famous by its Pauls and by its Antonys.[11] And at last when the winter was over and the sea was open, and when the bishops were returning to their churches, she also sailed with them in her prayers and desires. Not to prolong the story, she went down to the harbour accompanied by her brother, her kinsfolk and, above all, her own children [eager by their demonstrations of affection to overcome their loving mother].[12] At last the sails were set and the strokes of the oars carried the vessel into the deep. On the shore the little Toxotius stretched forth his hands in entreaty, while Rufina, now grown up,[13] with silent sobs besought her mother to wait till she should be married. But still Paula's eyes were dry as she turned them heavenwards; and she overcame her love for her children by her love for God. She knew herself no more as a mother, that she might prove herself a handmaid of Christ. Yet her heart was rent within her, and she wrestled with her grief, as though she were being torn away from part of herself. The greatness of the affection she had to overcome made all admire her victory the more. Among the cruel hardships which attend prisoners of war in the hands of their enemies, there is none severer than the separation of parents from their children. Though it is against the laws of nature, she endured this trial with unabated faith; nay more she sought it with a joyful heart; and spurning her love for her children by her greater love for God, she concentrated herself quietly upon Eustochium alone, the partner alike of her vows and of her voyage. Meantime the vessel ploughed onwards and all her fellow-passengers looked back to the shore. But she turned away her eyes that she might not see what she could not behold without agony. No mother, it must be confessed, ever loved her children so dearly. Before setting out she gave them all that she had, disinheriting herself upon earth that she might find an inheritance in heaven.

7. The vessel touched at the island of Pontia, ennobled long since as the place of exile of the illustrious lady Flavia Domitilla,[14] who under the Emperor Domitian was banished because

---

11 Paul, the supposed first hermit, whose "Life" was written by Jerome; Anthony, the real leader of anchoretic monasticism, whose life was written by Athanasius.

12 Hilberg excludes this clause; but it hardly seems to be an invention.

13 *nubilis.*

14 Wife of Flavius Clemens and niece of Domitian. According to Dio Cassius (67, 14) he was executed and she banished to Pandateria for

she confessed herself a Christian; and Paula, when she saw the cells in which this lady passed the years of her martyrdom, longed to take wing and see Jerusalem and the holy places. The strongest winds seemed weak and the greatest speed slow. After passing between Scylla and Charybdis she committed herself to the Adriatic sea and had a calm passage to Methone. Stopping here for a short time to recruit her wearied frame,

> "She stretched her dripping limbs upon the shore;
> Then sailed past Malea and Cythera's isle,
> The scattered Cyclades, and all the lands
> That narrow in the seas on every side." [15]

Then leaving Rhodes and Lycia behind her, she at last came in sight of Cyprus, where falling at the feet of the holy and venerable Epiphanius, she was by him detained ten days; though this was not, as he supposed, to restore her strength but, as the facts proved, that she might do God's work.[16] For she visited all the monasteries in the island, and left, so far as her means allowed, substantial relief for the brothers whom love of the holy man had brought thither from all parts of the world. Then crossing the narrow sea she landed at Seleucia, and going up thence to Antioch allowed herself to be detained for a little time by the affection of the reverend confessor Paulinus. Then, such was the ardour of her faith that she, a noble lady who had always previously been carried by eunuchs, went her way—and that in midwinter—riding upon an ass.

8. I say nothing of her journey through Coele-Syria and Phoenicia (for it is not my purpose to give you a complete itinerary of her wanderings); I shall only name such places as are mentioned in the sacred books. After leaving the Roman colony of Berytus and the ancient city of Zidon she entered Elijah's little tower on the shore at Zarephath and therein adored her Lord and Saviour. Next passing over the sands of Tyre, on which Paul had once knelt, she came to Accho or, as it is now called, Ptolemais, rode over the plains of Megiddo which had once witnessed the slaying of Josiah, and entered the land of the Philistines. Here she wondered at the ruins of

atheism. Pontia is twenty-five miles from Pandateria. Eusebius (*H.E.*, III, 18), who believed that she was a Christian, also gives Pontia. Her Christianity is not quite proved, but her connexion with the Catacomb of Domitilla adds to the probability.

[15] Verg., *Aen.*, I, 173+III, 126–127.
[16] The friendship between Epiphanius and Paula played its part in the Origenistic controversy.

Dor, once a most powerful city; and Strato's Tower, which though at one time insignificant was rebuilt by Herod, King of Judaea, and named Caesarea in honour of Caesar Augustus.[17] Here she saw the house of Cornelius now turned into a Christian church, and the humble abode of Philip, and the chamber of his daughters, the four virgins "which did prophesy." She arrived next at Antipatris, a small town half in ruins, named by Herod after his father Antipater, and at Lydda, now become Diospolis, a place made famous by the raising again of Dorcas and the restoration to health of Aeneas. Not far from this are Arimathaea, the village of Joseph who buried the Lord, and Nob, once a city of priests but now the tomb in which their slain bodies rest. Joppa too is hard by, the port of Jonah's flight; which also—if I may introduce a poetic fable—saw Andromeda bound to the rock. Again resuming her journey, she came to Nicopolis, once called Emmaus, where the Lord became known in the breaking of bread; an action by which he dedicated the house of Cleopas as a church. Starting thence she made her way up lower and higher Bethhoron, cities founded by Solomon but subsequently destroyed by several devastating wars; seeing on her right Ajalon and Gibeon, where Joshua, the son of Nun, when fighting against the five kings, gave commandments to the sun and moon, where also he condemned the Gibeonites (who by a crafty stratagem had obtained a treaty) to be hewers of wood and drawers of water. At Gibeah also, now a complete ruin, she stopped for a little while remembering its sin, and the cutting of the concubine into pieces and how twice three hundred men of the tribe of Benjamin were saved, that in after days Paul might be called a Benjamite.

9. To make a long story short, leaving on her left the mausoleum of Helena, Queen of Adiabene,[18] who in time of famine had sent corn to the Jewish people, she entered Jerusalem, Jebus, or Salem, that city of three names which, after it had sunk to ashes and decay, was by Aelius Hadrianus restored as Aelia. And although the Proconsul of Palestine, who was an intimate friend of her house, sent forward his apparitors and gave orders to have his official residence placed at her disposal, she chose a humble cell in preference to it.

---

[17] At this time Caesarea was the civil and ecclesiastical metropolis of Palestine. The Bishop of Jerusalem was a suffragan of its bishop until the Council of Ephesus, A.D. 431, which assigned a small patriarchate to Jerusalem.

[18] Josephus, *Ant. Jud.*, XX, 2, 6.

Moreover, in visiting the holy places so great was the passion
and the enthusiasm she exhibited for each, that she could never
have been torn away from one had she not been eager to
visit the rest. Before the Cross she threw herself down in adora-
tion as though she beheld the Lord hanging upon it; and when
she entered the tomb which was the scene of the Resurrection,
she kissed the stone which the angel had rolled away from the
door of the sepulchre. Indeed so ardent was her faith that she
even licked with her mouth the very spot on which the Lord's
body had lain, like one athirst for the river which he had longed
for.[19] What tears she shed there, what groans she uttered, and
what grief she poured forth, all Jerusalem knows; the Lord also,
to whom she prayed, knows it well. Going out thence she made
the ascent of Zion, a name which signifies either "citadel"
or "watch-tower." This formed the city which David formerly
stormed and afterwards rebuilt. Of its storming it is written:
"Woe to thee, Ariel"—that is, God's lion, (and indeed in those
days it was extremely strong)—"the city which David
stormed:" and of its building it is said: "His foundation is in
the holy mountains: the Lord loveth the gates of Zion more
than all the dwellings of Jacob." He does not mean the gates
which we see to-day in dust and ashes; the gates he means are
those against which hell prevails not, and through which the
multitude of those who believe enter in to Christ. There was
shewn to her, upholding the portico of a church, the blood-
stained column to which our Lord is said to have been bound
when he suffered his scourging. There was shewn to her also
the spot where the Holy Spirit came down upon one hundred
and twenty souls, thus fulfilling the prophecy of Joel.

10. Then, after distributing money to the poor and her
fellow-servants so far as her small means allowed, she
proceeded to Bethlehem stopping on the right side of the road
to visit Rachel's tomb. (Here it was that she gave birth to her
son, destined to be not what his dying mother called him,
Benoni, that is the "Son of my pangs" but, as his father in
the spirit prophetically named him, Benjamin, that is "the Son
of the right hand"). After this she entered into the cave where
the Saviour was born. Here, when she looked upon the inn
made sacred by the virgin and the stall where "the ox knew
his owner and the ass his master's crib," that the words of the

---

[19] Reading *fide et ore* or *fidei ore*. With Hilberg's *fide, ore* the meaning will
presumably be "which faith longed for," with perhaps a reference to
John 4 as in §13.

same prophet might be fulfilled: "Blessed is he that soweth upon the waters where the ox and the ass trample"; when she looked upon these things, I say, she protested in my hearing that she could behold with the eyes of faith the infant Lord wrapped in swaddling clothes and crying in the manger, the wise men worshipping God, the star shining overhead, the virgin mother, the attentive foster-father, the shepherds coming by night to see "the word that was come to pass" and thus even then to consecrate those opening phrases of the evangelist John: "In the beginning was the word" and "the word was made flesh." She declared that she could see the slaughtered innocents, the raging Herod, Joseph and Mary fleeing into Egypt; and with a mixture of tears and joy she cried: "Hail Bethlehem, house of bread, wherein was born that Bread that came down from heaven. Hail Ephratah, land of fruitfulness and fertility, whose fruit is God himself. Concerning thee has Micah prophesied of old, 'Thou, Bethlehem, house of Ephratah, art thou not the least among the thousands of Judah? Out of thee shall he come forth unto me that is to be ruler in Israel; whose goings forth are from the beginning, from days everlasting. Therefore wilt thou give them up, until the time of her that travaileth. She shall bring forth, and the remnant of his brethren shall turn unto the children of Israel.' [20] For in thee was born the prince begotten before Lucifer, whose birth from the Father is before all time; and the cradle of David's race continued in thee, until the virgin brought forth her son and the remnant of the people that believed in Christ turned unto the children of Israel and preached freely to them: 'It was necessary that the word of God should first have been spoken to you; but seeing ye put it from you and judged yourselves unworthy of everlasting life, we turn to the Gentiles.' For the Lord had said: 'I am not come but unto the lost sheep of the house of Israel.' At that time also the words of Jacob were fulfilled concerning him: 'A prince shall not fail from Judah nor a ruler from his thighs, until he come for whom it is laid up, and he shall be the expectation of the nations.' Well did David swear, well did he make a vow saying: 'Surely I will not come into the tabernacle of my house nor climb up into my bed: I will not give sleep to mine eyes, or slumber to my eyelids, or rest to the temples of my head, until I find out a place for the Lord, an habitation for the God of Jacob.' And

[20] Micah 5:2–3. Jerome translates the very awkward text of the LXX literally.

immediately he explained the object of his desire, seeing with prophetic eyes that he would come whom we now believe to have come. 'Lo we heard of him at Ephratah: we found him in the fields of the wood.' The Hebrew word *zoth*, as I have learned from your lessons,[21] means not αὐτήν (*her*), that is Mary the Lord's mother, but αὐτόν, himself. Therefore he says boldly: 'We will go into his tabernacle: we will adore in the place where his feet stood.' I too, miserable sinner though I am, have been accounted worthy to kiss the manger in which the Lord cried as a babe, and to pray in the cave in which the travailing virgin gave birth to the infant Lord. 'This is my rest' for it is my Lord's native place; 'here will I dwell' for this spot has my Saviour chosen. 'I have prepared a lamp for my Christ'. 'My soul shall live unto him and my seed shall serve him'."

After this Paula went a short distance down the hill to the tower of Edar, that is "of the flock", near which Jacob fed his flocks, and where the shepherds keeping watch by night were privileged to hear the words: "Glory to God in the highest and on earth peace to men of goodwill." While they were keeping their sheep they found the Lamb of God; whose bright and clean fleece was made wet with the dew of heaven when it was dry upon all the earth beside, and whose blood, when sprinkled on the doorposts, drove off the destroyer of Egypt and took away the sins of the world.

11. Then immediately quickening her pace she began to move along the old road which leads to Gaza, that is to the "power" or "wealth" of God, silently meditating on that type of the Gentiles, the Ethiopian eunuch, who did change his skin, and whilst he read the Old Testament, found the fountain of the Gospel.[22] Next turning to the right she passed from Beth-zur to Eshcol which means "a cluster of grapes." It was hence that the spies brought back that marvellous cluster which was the proof of the fertility of the land and a type of him who says of himself: "I have trodden the wine press alone; and of the people there was none with me." Shortly afterwards she entered the humble home of Sarah and beheld the cradle of Isaac and the traces of Abraham's oak, under which he saw Christ's day and was glad. And rising up from thence, she went up to Hebron, that is Kirjath-Arba, or "the City of the Four Men". These are Abraham, Isaac, Jacob, and the great Adam whom

21 Paula is still speaking. Jerome taught her Hebrew.
22 Jer. 13:23, "Can the Ethiopian change his skin?" Acts 8:27-39.

the Hebrews suppose (from the book of Joshua) to be buried there.[23] But many are of opinion that Caleb is the fourth, and a monument at one side is pointed out as his. After seeing these places she did not care to go on to Kirjath-sepher, that is "the village of letters;" because, despising the letter that killeth, she had found the spirit that giveth life. She admired more the upper springs and the nether springs which Othniel, the son of Kenaz, the son of Jephunneh, received for his south land and his waterless possession, and by the conducting of which he watered the dry fields of the old covenant. For thus did he typify the redemption which the sinner finds for his old sins in the waters of baptism. On the next day, soon after sunrise, she stood upon the brow of Caphar-barucha, that is, "the town of blessing," the point to which Abraham accompanied the Lord. And here, as she looked down upon the wide solitude and upon the country once belonging to Sodom and Gomorrah, to Admah and Zeboim, she beheld the balsam vines of Engedi and Segor, the "heifer of three years old" which was formerly called Bela and in Syriac is rendered Zoar that is "little". She called to mind Lot's cave, and with tears in her eyes warned the virgins, her companions, to beware of "wine wherein is excess;" for it was to this that the Moabites and Ammonites owe their origin.

12. I linger long in the land of the midday sun, for it was there and then that the spouse found her bridegroom at rest and Joseph drank wine with his brothers once more. I will return to Jerusalem and, passing by Tekoa and Amos, I will look upon the glistening cross of Mount Olivet, from which the Saviour made his ascension to the Father. Here year by year a red heifer was burned as a holocaust to the Lord, and its ashes were used to purify the children of Israel. Here also, according to Ezekiel, the Cherubim, after leaving the temple, founded the church of the Lord.

After this she visited the tomb of Lazarus and beheld the home of Mary and Martha, as well as Bethphage, "the town of the priestly jaws." Here it was that a restive foal, typical of the Gentiles, received the bridle of the Lord, and, covered with the garments of the apostles, offered its easy back for him to sit on. From this she went straight on down the hill to Jericho, thinking of the wounded man in the Gospel, of the savagery of the priests and Levites who passed him by, and of the

23 Josh. 14:15, with a confusion between Adam as a proper name and as "man."

kindness of the Samaritan, that is, the guardian, who placed the half-dead man upon his own beast and brought him down to the inn of the Church.[24] She noticed the place called Adomim or "the Place of Blood", so-called because much blood was shed there in the frequent incursions of marauders. She beheld also the sycamore tree of Zacchaeus, by which is signified the good works of repentance whereby he trod under foot his former sins of bloodshed and rapine, and from which he saw the Most High as from a pinnacle of virtue. She was shewn too the spot by the wayside where the blind men sat who, receiving their sight from the Lord, became types of the two peoples who should believe upon him. Then entering Jericho she saw the city which Hiel founded in Abiram his firstborn, and of which he set up the gates in his youngest son Segub. She looked upon the camp of Gilgal and the mound of the foreskins suggestive of the mystery of the second circumcision; and the twelve stones brought thither out of the bed of Jordan, which established the foundations of the twelve apostles.[25] She saw also that fountain of the Law once most bitter and barren, which the true Elisha seasoned with his wisdom, changing it into a well sweet and fertilizing. Scarcely had the night passed away, when, in burning heat, she hastened to the Jordan, stood by the brink of the river, and as the sun rose recalled to mind the rising of the sun of righteousness; how the priests' feet stood dry in the middle of the river-bed; how afterwards at the command of Elijah and Elisha the waters were divided hither and thither and made way for them to pass; and again how the Lord had cleansed by his baptism waters which the deluge had polluted and the destruction of mankind had defiled.

13. It would be tedious were I to tell of the valley of Achor, that is, of "trouble and crowds," where theft and covetousness were condemned; and of Bethel, "the house of God", where Jacob poor and destitute slept upon the bare ground. Here it was that, having set beneath his head a stone, which in Zechariah is described as having seven eyes and in Isaiah is spoken of as a corner-stone, he beheld a ladder reaching up to heaven; yes, and the Lord standing high above it, holding out his hand to such as were ascending and hurling from on high such as were careless. Also when she was in Mount Ephraim she made pilgrimages to the tombs of Joshua, the son of Nun, and of

24 The inn, namely the Church. Spiritual exegesis of all the details of this parable is common in the Fathers. The Good Samaritan is Christ.
25 Rev. 21:14; cf. Eph. 2:20.

Eleazar, the son of Aaron the priest, exactly opposite the one
to the other: that of Joshua being built at Timnath-serah "on
the north side of the hill of Gaash," and that of Eleazar "in
Gabaath that pertained to Phinehas his son." She was somewhat surprised to find that he who had had the distribution
of the land in his own hands had selected for himself portions
uneven and rocky. What shall I say about Shiloh, where a
ruined altar is still shewn today, and where the tribe of Benjamin anticipated Romulus in the rape of the Sabine women?
Passing by Shechem (not Sychar as many wrongly read) or as
it is now called Neapolis, she entered the church built upon
the side of Mount Gerizim around Jacob's well; that well
where the Lord was sitting when, hungry and thirsty, he was
refreshed by the faith of the woman of Samaria. Forsaking
her five husbands, by whom are intended the five books of
Moses, and that sixth, not a husband, of whom she boasted,
to wit the false teacher Dositheus,[26] she found the true Messiah
and the true Saviour. Turning away thence she saw the tombs
of the twelve patriarchs, and Samaria which, in honour of
Augustus, Herod renamed Augusta or in Greek Sebaste. There
lie the prophets Elisha and Obadiah and he than whom there
is not a greater among those that are born of women, John the
Baptist. And here she was filled with terror by the marvels
she beheld; for she saw demons screaming under different
tortures and men howling like wolves before the tombs of the
saints, baying like dogs, roaring like lions, hissing like serpents
and bellowing like bulls. They twisted their heads and bent
them backwards until they touched the ground; women too
were suspended by the feet and their clothes did not fall to
their faces.[27] She pitied them all, and shedding tears over them,
prayed Christ to have mercy on them. And weak as she was, she
climbed the mountain on foot; for in two of its caves Obadiah,
in a time of persecution and famine, had fed a hundred prophets
with bread and water. Then she passed quickly through Nazareth, the nursery of the Lord; Cana and Capernaum, familiar
with the signs wrought by him; the lake of Tiberias, sanctified
by his voyages upon it; the wilderness where countless Gentiles
were satisfied with a few loaves, while the twelve baskets of the
tribes of Israel were filled with the fragments left by them that
had eaten. She made the ascent of mount Tabor, whereon the

[26] A Samaritan, pre-Christian, heretic mentioned by Hippolytus and
Eusebius.
[27] Cf. Hilary, *Contra Const.*, 8.

Lord was transfigured. In the distance she beheld the range of
Hermon; and the wide stretching plains of Galilee, where
Sisera and all his host had once been overcome by Barak; and
the torrent Kishon separating the level ground into two parts.
Hard by also the town of Nain was pointed out to her, where
the widow's son was raised. Time would fail me sooner than
speech were I to recount all the places to which the revered
Paula was carried by her incredible faith.

14. I will now pass on to Egypt, pausing for a while on the
way at Socoh, and at Samson's well which he drew out from the
great tooth in the jaw. Here I will lave my parched lips and
refresh myself before visiting Moresheth; in old days famed for
the tomb of the prophet Micah, and now for its church. Then
skirting the country of the Horites and Gittites, Mareshah,
Edom, and Lachish, and traversing the lonely wastes of the
desert where the tracks of the traveller are lost in the yielding
sand, I will come to the river of Egypt called Sihor, that is "the
muddy river," and go through the five cities of Egypt which
speak the language of Canaan, and through the land of
Goshen and the plains of Zoan, on which God wrought his
marvellous works. And I will visit the city of No, which has
since become Alexandria; and Nitria, the town of the Lord,
where day by day the filth of multitudes is washed away with
the pure nitre of virtue. No sooner did she come in sight of it
than there came to meet her the reverend and estimable
bishop, the confessor Isidore, accompanied by countless multitudes of monks, many of whom were dignified by priestly or
Levitical rank. On seeing these she rejoiced to behold the
glory of the Lord; but protested that she had no claim to be
received with such honour. Need I speak of the Macarii,
Arsetes, Serapions, or other pillars of Christ? [28] Was there any
cell that she did not enter? Or any man at whose feet she did
not throw herself? In each of his saints she believed that she
saw Christ himself; and whatever she bestowed upon them,
she rejoiced to feel that she had bestowed it upon the Lord.
Her enthusiasm was wonderful and her endurance scarcely
credible in a woman. Forgetful of her sex and of her weakness,
she even desired to make her abode, together with the girls
who accompanied her, among these thousands of monks. And,

[28] Cf. Palladius, *Lausiac Hist.*, 46, where Melania "went to the mountain
of Nitria, where she met . . . Arsisius, Sarapion the great, . . . Isidore
the confessor, Bishop of Hermopolis." Three hermits named Macarius,
two of them eminent, are described by Palladius, op. cit., 15, 17, 18.

as they were all willing to welcome her, she might perhaps have
sought and obtained permission to do so, had she not been
drawn away by a still greater passion for the holy places.
Coming by sea from Pelusium to Maiuma on account of the
great heat, she returned so rapidly that you would have thought
her a bird. Not long afterwards, making up her mind to dwell
permanently in holy Bethlehem, she took up her abode for three
years [29] in a miserable hostelry; till she could build the requisite
cells and monastic buildings, to say nothing of a guest house
for passing travellers, where they might find the welcome which
Mary and Joseph had missed. At this point I conclude my
narrative of the journeys that she made, accompanied by
her daughter and many other virgins.

15. I am now free to describe at greater length the virtue
which was her peculiar charm; and in setting forth this I call
God to witness that I am no flatterer. I add nothing. I exaggerate nothing. On the contrary I tone down much, that I may
not appear to relate incredibilities. My carping critics, for ever
biting me as hard as they can, need not insinuate that I am
drawing on my imagination or decking Paula, like Aesop's
crow, with the fine feathers of other birds. Humility is the first
of Christian graces, and hers was so pronounced that one who
had never seen her, and who on account of her celebrity had
desired to see her, would have believed that he saw not her but
the lowest of her maids. When she was surrounded by companies of virgins she was always the least remarkable in dress,
in speech, in gesture, and in gait. From the time that her husband died until she fell asleep herself, she never sat at meat with
a man, even though she might know him to be holy and standing upon the pinnacle of the episcopate. She never entered a
bath except when dangerously ill. Even in the severest fever
she rested not on an ordinary soft bed but on the hard ground,
covered only with a mat of goat's hair; if that can be called
rest which made day and night alike a time of almost unbroken
prayer. Well did she fulfil the words of the psalter: "Every
night I shall wash my bed; I shall water my couch with my
tears"![30] Her tears welled forth as it were from fountains, and
she lamented her slightest faults as if they were sins of the deepest dye. Constantly did I warn her to spare her eyes and to keep
them for the reading of the gospel; but she only said: "I must
disfigure that face which, contrary to God's commandment,
I have painted with rouge, white lead, and antimony. I must

29 A.D. 386–389.   30 Ps. 6:6.

mortify that body which has been given up to many pleasures. I must make up for my long laughter by constant weeping. I must exchange my soft linen and costly silks for rough goat's hair. I who have pleased my husband and the world, desire now to please Christ." Were I, among her great and signal virtues, to select her chastity as a subject of praise, my words would seem superfluous; for, even when she was still in the world, she set an example to all the matrons of Rome, and bore herself so admirably that the most slanderous never ventured to couple scandal with her name. No mind could be more considerate than hers, or none kinder towards the lowly. She did not court the powerful; at the same time she did not turn from them with a proud and vainglorious disdain. If she saw a poor man, she supported him: and if she saw a rich one, she urged him to do good. Her liberality alone knew no bounds. Indeed, so anxious was she to turn no applicant away that she borrowed money at interest and often contracted new loans to pay off old ones. I was wrong, I admit; but when I saw her so profuse in giving, I reproved her, alleging the Apostle's words: "I mean not that other men be eased and ye burthened; but by an equality that now at this time your abundance may be a supply for their want, that their abundance also may be a supply for your want."[31] I quoted from the Gospel the Saviour's words: "He that hath two coats, let him impart one of them to him that hath none";[32] and I warned her that she might not always have means to do as she would wish. Other arguments I adduced to the same purpose; but with admirable modesty and brevity she overruled them all. "God is my witness," she said, "that what I do I do for his sake. My prayer is that I may die a beggar, not leaving a penny to my daughter and indebted to strangers for my winding-sheet." She then concluded with these words: "I, if I beg, shall find many to give to me; but if this beggar does not obtain help from me who by borrowing can give it to him, and dies, of whom will his soul be required?" I wished to be more careful in managing our concerns, but she, with a faith more glowing than mine, clave to the Saviour with her whole heart, and, poor in spirit, followed the Lord in his poverty, giving back to him what she had received and becoming poor for his sake. She obtained her wish at last and died leaving her daughter overwhelmed with a mass of debt. This she still owes and

[31] II Cor. 8:13-14.
[32] Luke 3:11, reading "*alteram*", one of the two, only.

indeed cannot hope to pay off by her own exertions, but only by the faith and mercy of Christ.

16. Many ladies like to confer their gifts upon those who will blow their trumpet for them, and while they are extremely profuse to a few, withhold help from the many. From this fault Paula was altogether free. She gave her money to each according as each had need, not ministering to self-indulgence, but relieving want. No poor person went away from her empty-handed. And all this she was enabled to do not by the greatness of her wealth but by her careful management of it. She constantly had on her lips such phrases as these: "Blessed are the merciful, for they shall obtain mercy": and "As water quenches a fire, so alms quencheth sins;" and "make to yourselves friends of the mammon of unrighteousness that they may receive you into everlasting habitations;" and "give alms, and behold all things are clean;" and Daniel's words to King Nebuchadnezzar in which he admonished him to redeem his sins by almsgiving. She wished to spend her money not upon these stones, that shall pass away with the earth and this age, but upon those living stones which roll over the earth; of which, in the Apocalypse of John, the city of the great king is built; of which also the scripture tells us that they shall be changed into sapphire and emerald and jasper and other gems.[33]

17. But these qualities she may well share with not a few others, and the devil knows that it is not in these that the highest virtue consists. For, when Job has lost his substance and when his house has been overthrown and his children destroyed, Satan says to the Lord: "Skin for skin, all that a man hath will he give for his life. But put forth thine hand and touch his bone and his flesh, and he will curse thee to thy face."[34] We know that many persons, while they have given alms, have yet given nothing which touches their bodily comfort; and while they have held out a helping hand to those in need, are themselves overcome with sensual indulgences; they whitewash the outside, but within they are "full of dead men's bones."[35] Paula was not one of these. Her self-restraint was so great as to be immoderate; and her fasts and labours were so severe as to weaken her constitution. Except on feast days she would scarcely ever take oil with her food; a fact from which may be judged what she thought of wine, sauce, fish, honey, milk, eggs, and

33 Matt. 5:7; Ecclus. 3:30; Luke 16:9; 11:41; Dan. 4:27 (24); Zech. 9:16; Rev. 21:14, 19–21.
34 Job 2:4, 5.   35 Matt. 23:27.

other things agreeable to the palate. Some persons believe that in taking these they are extremely frugal; and, even if they surfeit themselves with them, they still fancy their chastity safe.

18. Envy always follows in the track of virtue; "it is ever the mountain top that is smitten by the lightning."[36] It is not surprising that I declare this of men, when the jealousy of the Pharisees succeeded in crucifying our Lord himself. All the saints have had illwishers, and even Paradise was not free from the serpent, through whose envy death came into the world.[37] So the Lord stirred up against Paula Hadad the Edomite, to buffet her that she might not exalt herself, and warned her frequently by the thorn in her flesh not to be elated by the greatness of her own virtues or to fancy that, compared with the faults of other women, she had attained the summit of perfection.[38] For my part I used to say that it was best to give in to rancour and to retire before madness. So Jacob dealt with his brother Esau; so David met the unrelenting persecution of Saul. I reminded her how the first of these fled into Mesopotamia; and how the second surrendered himself to men of another race, and chose to submit to foreign foes rather than to enmity at home.[39] She, however, replied as follows: "Your suggestion would be a wise one if the devil did not everywhere fight against God's servants and handmaidens, and did he not always precede the fugitives to their chosen refuges. Moreover, I am deterred from accepting it by my love for the holy places; and I cannot find another Bethlehem anywhere else in the world. Why may I not by my patience conquer this rancour? Why may I not by my humility break down this pride, and when I am smitten on the one cheek offer to the smiter the other? Surely the apostle Paul says 'Overcome evil with good.' Did not the apostles glory when they suffered reproach for the Lord's sake? Did not even the Saviour humble himself, taking the form of a servant and being made obedient to the Father unto death, even the death of the cross, that he might save us by his passion? If Job had not fought the battle and won the victory, he would never have received the crown of righteousness, or have heard the Lord say: 'Thinkest thou that I have spoken unto thee for aught else than this, that thou mightest appear righteous.' In the gospel those only are said to be

[36] Hor., *Odes*, II, 10, 11.   [37] Wisdom, 2:24.
[38] I Kings 11:14, Solomon's adversary. But who does he stand for? Thorn, cf. II Cor. 12:7.
[39] Gen. 27:41 ff.; I Sam. 21:10, to Achish of Gath.

blessed who suffer persecution for righteousness' sake.[40] If conscience is at rest, and we know that it is not from any fault of our own that we are suffering, affliction in this world is a ground for reward." When the enemy was more than usually forward and ventured to strive with her in argument, she used to chant the words of the Psalter: "While the sinner stood against me, I was dumb and humbled myself; I kept silence even from good words;" and again, "I, as a deaf man, heard not; and I was as a dumb man that openeth not his mouth;" and "I was as a man that heareth not, and in whose mouth are no reproofs."[41] When she felt herself tempted, she dwelt upon the words in Deuteronomy: "The Lord your God proveth you, to know whether ye love the Lord your God with all your heart and with all your soul."[42] In tribulations and afflictions she turned to the splendid language of Isaiah: "Ye that are weaned from the milk and drawn away from the breasts, look for tribulation upon tribulation, for hope upon hope: here a little, there a little, must these things be by reason of the malice of the lips and by reason of a strange tongue."[43] This passage of Scripture she explained for her own consolation as meaning that the weaned, that is, those who have come to full age, must endure tribulation upon tribulation, that they may be accounted worthy to receive hope upon hope, "knowing that tribulation worketh patience, and patience probation, and probation hope: and hope maketh not ashamed" and "though our outward man perish, yet the inward man is renewed"; and "our light affliction which is but for a moment worketh in us an eternal weight of glory; while we look not at the things which are seen but at the things which are not seen: for the things which are seen are temporal but the things which are not seen are eternal."[44] She used to say that, although to human impatience the time might seem slow in coming, yet that it would not be long but that presently help would come from God who says: "In an acceptable time have I heard thee, and in a day of salvation have I helped thee."[45] We ought not, she declared, to dread the deceitful lips and tongues of the wicked, for we rejoice in the aid of the Lord and we ought to listen to his warning [by his prophet: "Fear ye not the reproach of men, neither be ye afraid of their

---

[40] Matt. 5:39; Rom. 12:21; Phil. 2:7–8; Job 40:8; Matt. 5:10.
[41] Ps. 39:1, 2 (38:2, 3); Ps. 38 (37):12–14.
[42] Deut. 13:3. [43] Isa. 28:9–11.
[44] Rom. 5:3–5; II Cor. 4:16–18. [45] Isa. 49:8.

revilings; for the moth shall eat them up like a garment, and the worm shall eat them like wool"]: [46] "In your patience ye shall win your souls": and "the sufferings of this present time are not worthy to be compared with the glory which shall be revealed in us"; and in another place, that we may be patient in all things that befall us, "he that is patient is of great under- standing: but he that is little of spirit exalteth folly." [47]

19. In her frequent sicknesses and infirmities she used to say: "When I am weak, then am I strong;" "We have this treasure in earthen vessels" until "this corruptible shall have put on incorruption and this mortal shall have put on immortality," and again: "as the sufferings of Christ abound in us, so our consolation also aboundeth by Christ;" and then "as ye are partakers of the sufferings, so shall ye be also of the consola- tion." [48] In sorrow she used to sing: "Why art thou cast down, O my soul? and why art thou disquieted within me? hope thou in God, for I shall yet praise him, who is the health of my counten- ance and my God." In the hour of danger she used to say: "If any man will come after me, let him deny himself and take up his cross and follow me;" and again: "Whosoever will save his life shall lose it," and "whosoever will lose his life for my sake, shall save it." [49] When the exhaustion of her substance and the ruin of her property were announced to her, she said: "What is a man profited, if he shall gain the whole world and lose his own soul? or what shall a man give in exchange for his soul;" and, "Naked came I out of my mother's womb, and naked shall I return thither. As it pleased the Lord, so hath it come to pass; blessed be the name of the Lord;" and these words: "Love not the world neither the things that are in the world. For all that is in the world is the desire of the flesh and the lust of the eyes and the pride of this life, which is not of the Father, but is of the world. And the world passeth away and the lust thereof." [50] I know that when word was sent to her of the serious illnesses of her children and particularly of Toxotius whom she most dearly loved, she first by her self- control fulfilled the saying: "I was troubled and I did not speak," and then cried out in these words: "He that loveth son or daughter more than me is not worthy of me." And she

[46] Isa. 51:7–8, rejected by Hilberg.
[47] Luke 21:19; Rom. 8:18; Prov. 14:29.
[48] II Cor. 12:10; 4:7; I Cor. 15:54; II Cor. 1:5, 7.
[49] Ps. 42:11 (41:12); Luke 9:23–24.
[50] Matt. 16:26; Job 1:21; I John 2:15–17.

prayed to the Lord and said: "Possess thou the children of those that have been put to death," who for thy sake every day put their own bodies to death.[51] I am aware that a talebearer —a class of persons who do a great deal of harm—once told her as a kindness that, owing to her great fervour in virtue, some people thought her mad and declared that something should be done for her head. She replied: "We are made a spectacle unto the world and to angels and to men; we are fools for Christ's sake", but "the foolishness of God is wiser than men." It is for this reason that even the Saviour says to the Father: "Thou knowest my foolishness[," and again "I am as a wonder unto many, but thou art my strong refuge." "I was as a beast before thee; nevertheless I am continually with thee]."[52] In the Gospel we read that even his kinsfolk desired to bind him as one of weak mind. His opponents also reviled him saying: "He has a devil and is a Samaritan," and "he casteth out devils by Beelzebub the chief of the devils."[53] But let us listen to the exhortation of the Apostle: "Our rejoicing is this, the testimony of our conscience that in holiness and sincerity and by the grace of God, we have had our conversation in the world." And let us hear the Lord when he says to his apostles: "Because ye are not of the world, therefore the world hateth you; if ye were of the world the world would love his own." And then she turned her words to the Lord himself, saying: "Thou knowest the secrets of the heart," and "all this is come upon us; yet have we not forgotten thee, neither have we dealt falsely against thy covenant; our heart is not turned back. For thy sake are we killed all the day long; we are counted as sheep for the slaughter." But "the Lord is on my side: I will not fear what man doeth unto me." For I have read: "My son, honour the Lord, and thou shalt be made strong; and beside him fear thou no man."[54] These passages and others like them she used as Christ's armour against all vices in general, and particularly to defend herself against the furious onslaughts of envy; and thus, patiently enduring wrongs, she stilled the fury of a heart ready to burst. Down to the very day of her death two things were conspicuous in her life, one, her own great patience

---

51 Ps. 77:4 (76:5); Matt. 10:37; Ps. 79 (78):11.
52 I Cor. 4:9–10; 1:25; Ps. 69:5 (68:6); Ps. 71 (70):7; Ps. 73 (72):22–23. The passage in brackets is excluded by Hilberg.
53 Mark 3:21; John 8:48; Luke 11:15.
54 II Cor. 1:12; John 15:18–19; Ps. 44 (43):21; *ibid.*, 17–18, 22; Ps. 118 (117):6; Prov. 7:1a (LXX).

and the other, the jealousy which was manifested towards her.
Now jealousy gnaws the heart of him who harbours it: and while
it strives to injure its rival, raves with all the force of its fury
against itself.

20. I shall now describe the order of her monastery and the
method by which she turned the continence of saintly souls to
her own profit. She sowed carnal things that she might reap
spiritual things; [55] she gave earthly things that she might receive
heavenly things; she forewent things temporal that she might
in their stead obtain things eternal. Besides establishing a monastery for men, the charge of which she left to men, she divided
into three companies and monasteries the numerous virgins
whom she had gathered out of different provinces, some of
whom are of noble birth while others belonged to the middle
or lower classes. [56] But, although they worked and had their
meals separately from each other, these three companies met
together for psalm-singing and prayer. After the chanting of
the Alleluia—the signal by which they were summoned to the
Collect [57]—no one was permitted to remain behind. But
coming either first or among the first, she used to await the
arrival of the rest, urging them to diligence rather by her own
modest example than by motives of fear. At dawn, at the third,
sixth, and ninth hours, at evening, and at midnight they recited
the Psalter each in turn. [58] No sister was allowed to be ignorant
of the psalms, and all had every day to learn a certain portion
of the holy Scriptures. On the Lord's day only, they proceeded
to the church beside which they lived, each company following
its own mother-superior. [59] Returning home in the same order,
they then devoted themselves to their allotted tasks, and made
garments either for themselves or else for others. If any was
of noble birth, she was not allowed to have an attendant from
home lest her maid, having her mind full of the doings of
old days and of the licence of childhood, might by constant
converse open old wounds and renew former errors. All the
sisters were clothed alike. Linen was not used except for drying
the hands. So strictly did she separate them from men that she
would not allow even eunuchs to approach them, lest she should

[55] I Cor. 9:11.
[56] The Latin does not say quite unambiguously that the three companies
were determined by social status, but that is what it seems to mean.
[57] *Collecta*, assembly, cf. *Ep.* 51:1.
[58] Cf. note 28 on *Letter* 107:9 (p. 340).
[59] The Church of the Nativity at Bethlehem.

give any occasion to slanderous tongues, always ready to cavil
at the religious, to console themselves for their own misdoing.
When anyone was backward in coming to the recitation of the
psalms or shewed herself remiss in her work, she used to
approach her in different ways. Was she quick-tempered?
Paula coaxed her. Was she phlegmatic? Paula chid her, copying
the example of the Apostle who said: "What will ye? Shall I
come to you with a rod or in the spirit of gentleness and of
meekness?" [60] Apart from food and raiment she allowed no
one to have anything she could call her own, for Paul had said:
"Having food and raiment we are therewith content." [61]:
She was afraid lest the custom of having more should breed
covetousness in them; an appetite which no wealth can satisfy, for the more it has, the more it requires, and neither opu-
lence nor indigence is able to diminish it. When the sisters
quarrelled one with another, she reconciled them with soothing
words. If the young girls were troubled with fleshly desires, she
broke their force by imposing frequent and redoubled fasts;
for she wished them to be ill in body rather than to suffer in
soul. If she chanced to notice any sister too attentive to her
dress, she reproved her for her error with knitted brows and
severe looks, saying: "A clean body and a clean dress mean an
unclean soul; a virgin's lips should never utter an improper or
an impure word, for such indicate a lascivious mind, and by
the outward man the faults of the inward are made manifest."
When she saw a sister verbose and talkative or forward and
taking pleasure in quarrels, and when she found after frequent
admonitions that the offender shewed no signs of improvement,
she placed her among the lowest of the sisters and outside their
society, ordering her to pray at the door of the refectory and
take her food by herself, in the hope that where rebuke had
failed, shame might bring about a reformation. The sin of theft
she loathed as if it were sacrilege; and that which among men
of the world is counted little or nothing, she declared to be
a crime of the deepest dye in a monastery. How shall I describe
her kindness and attention towards the sick or the wonderful
care and devotion with which she nursed them? Yet, although
when others were sick she freely gave them every indulgence,
and even allowed them to eat meat, whenever she fell ill herself,
she made no concessions to her own weakness, and seemed unfair
in this respect, that in her own case she exchanged for harshness
the kindness which she was always ready to shew to others.

[60] I Cor. 4:21.   [61] I Tim. 6:8.

21. No young girl of sound and vigorous constitution ever delivered herself up to a regimen so rigid as that imposed upon herself by Paula, whose physical powers age had impaired and enfeebled. I admit that in this she was too determined, refusing to spare herself or to listen to advice. I will relate something in my own experience. In the extreme heat of the month of July she was once attacked by a violent fever, and we despaired of her life. However by God's mercy she rallied and the doctors urged upon her the necessity of taking a little light wine to accelerate her recovery; saying that if she continued to drink water they feared that she might become dropsical. I secretly appealed to the blessed pope Epiphanius[62] to admonish, nay even to compel her, to take the wine. But she, with her usual sagacity and quickness, at once perceived the stratagem, and with a smile told him that his advice came from me. Not to waste more words, the blessed prelate after many exhortations left her chamber; and, when I asked him what he had accomplished, replied: "Only that, old as I am, I have been almost persuaded to drink no more wine." I relate this story not because I approve of persons rashly taking upon themselves burthens beyond their strength (for does not the Scripture say: "Burden not thyself"?[63]) but because I wish, from this quality of perseverance in her, to shew the passion of her mind and the yearning of her believing soul, as she says: "My soul thirsteth for thee, and my flesh, in how many ways!"[64] Difficult as it is always to avoid extremes, the philosophers are quite right in their opinion that virtue is a mean and vice an excess,[65] or as we may express it in one short sentence "In nothing too much."[66] While thus unyielding in her contempt for food, she was easily moved to sorrow and felt crushed by the deaths of her kinsfolk, especially those of her children. When, one after another, her husband and her daughters fell asleep, on each occasion the shock of their loss endangered her life. And although she signed her mouth and her breast with the sign of the cross, and endeavoured thus to alleviate a mother's grief, her feelings overpowered her, and her maternal instincts were too much for her confiding mind. Thus while her intellect retained its mastery, she was overcome by sheer physical

[62] Epiphanius, Bishop of Salamis (§§6–7), who was in Palestine on his campaign against Origenism. Bishops were often called *papa*.
[63] Ecclus. 13:2.   [64] Ps. 63 (62):1.
[65] Jerome gives the terms in Greek. Cf. Aristotle, *Nic. Eth.*, II, 6.
[66] *Ne quid nimis*, Terence, *Andria*, 61, from the Greek proverb, *meden agan*.

weakness. For when sickness once seized her, it clung to her so long that it brought anxiety to us and danger to herself. Yet even then she was full of joy and repeated every moment: "O wretched man that I am! who shall deliver me from the body of this death?" [67] The careful reader may say that my words are an invective rather than an eulogy. I call that Jesus whom she served, and whom I desire to serve, to be my witness, that so far from unduly eulogizing her or depreciating her, I tell the truth about her as one Christian writing of another; that I am writing a memoir and not a panegyric, and that what were faults in her might well be virtues in others less saintly. I speak thus of her faults to satisfy my own feelings and the passionate regret of us her brothers and sisters, who all of us love her still and all of us deplore her loss.

22. However, she has finished her course, she has kept the faith, and now she enjoys the crown of righteousness. She follows the Lamb whithersoever he goes. She is filled now because once she was hungry. With joy does she sing: "As we have heard, so have we seen in the city of the Lord of hosts, in the city of our God." O blessed change! Once she wept but now laughs for evermore. Once she despised the broken cisterns; but now she has found the Lord a fountain. [68] [Once she wore haircloth but now she is clothed in white raiment, and can say: "Thou hast cut off my sackcloth, and girded me with gladness." Once she ate ashes like bread and mingled her drink with weeping; saying: "My tears have been my meat day and night;" but now for all time she eats the bread of angels and sings: "O taste and see that the Lord is gracious;" and "my heart hath uttered a good word; I speak the things which I have made for the king." She sees fulfilled in herself Isaiah's words, or rather those of the Lord speaking through Isaiah: "Behold, my servants shall eat, but ye shall be hungry: behold, my servants shall drink, but ye shall be thirsty: behold, my servants shall rejoice, but ye shall be ashamed: behold, my servants shall sing for joy, but ye shall cry for sorrow of heart, and shall howl for vexation of spirit." I have said that she always shunned the broken cisterns; she did so that she might

---

67 Rom. 7:24.
68 II Tim. 4:7, 8; Rev. 14:4; Luke 6:21; Ps. 48 (47): 8; Jer. 2:13; John 4:14. The bracketed passage which follows is so marked by Hilberg as being the addition of some learned reader. The repetition of the last words is certainly awkward. The passage contains Ps. 30:11; 102:9; 42:3; 78:25; 34:8; 45:1; Isa. 65:13–14.

find the Lord a fountain, and] that she might rejoice and sing: "As the hart desireth the waterbrooks, so longeth my soul after thee, O God. My soul is athirst for the strong God, the living God. When shall I come and appear before the presence of God?" [69]

23. [70] I must briefly mention the manner in which she avoided the foul cisterns of the heretics whom she regarded as no better than heathen. A certain cunning knave, in his own estimation both learned and clever, began without my knowledge to put to her such questions as these: "What sin has an infant committed that it should be seized by the devil? Shall we be young or old when we rise again? If we die young and rise young, we shall after the resurrection require to have nurses. If however, we die young and rise old, the dead will not rise again at all: they will be transformed into new beings. Will there be a distinction of sexes in the next world? Or will there be no such distinction? If the distinction continues, there will be wedlock and sexual intercourse and procreation of children. If it does not continue, the bodies that rise again will not be the same." For, he argued: "the earthy tabernacle weigheth down the mind that museth upon many things," but the bodies that we shall have in heaven will be subtle and spiritual according to the words of the Apostle: "it is sown a natural body: it is raised a spiritual body." [71] From all of which considerations he sought to prove that rational creatures have through their faults and previous sins fallen to bodily conditions; and that according to the nature and guilt of their transgression, they are born in this or that state of life. Some, he said, rejoice in sound bodies and wealthy and noble parents; others have for their portion diseased frames and poverty-stricken homes, and by imprisonment in the present world and in bodies pay the penalty of their former sins. She listened and reported what she heard to me, at the same time pointing out the man. Thus upon me was laid the task of opposing this most noxious viper and deadly pest. It is of such that the Psalmist speaks when he writes: "Deliver not the soul that confesseth thee unto the wild beasts," and "Rebuke, Lord, the wild beast of the reeds:" creatures who write iniquity and speak lies against the Lord and lift up their mouths against the Most High. [72] As the fellow had

[69] Ps. 42:1-2.
[70] For §§ 23-26 see the literature on Origenism, and compare Jerome's letter against John of Jerusalem, especially cc. 7, 16, 23-36.
[71] Wisdom 9:15; I Cor. 15:44.   [72] Ps. 74 (73):19; 68 (67):30.

tried to deceive Paula, I went to him at her request, and by asking him a few questions involved him in a dilemma. Do you believe, said I, that there will be a resurrection of the dead or not? He replied, I believe. I went on: Will the bodies that rise again be the same or different? He said, The same. Then I asked: What of their sex? Will that remain unaltered or will it be changed? At this question he became silent and swayed his head this way and that as a serpent does to avoid being struck. Accordingly I continued, As you have nothing to say I will answer for you and will draw the conclusion from your premises. If the woman shall not rise again as a woman nor the man as a man, there will be no resurrection of the dead. For sex has its members, and the members make up the whole body. But if there shall be no sex and no members, what will become of the resurrection of the body, which cannot exist without sex and members? And if there shall be no resurrection of the body, there can be no resurrection of the dead. But as to your objection taken from marriage, that, if the members shall remain the same, marriage follows, that is disposed of by the Saviour's words: "Ye do err, not knowing the Scriptures nor the power of God. For in the resurrection of the dead they shall neither marry nor be given in marriage, but are as the angels." [73] When it is said that they neither marry nor are given in marriage, the distinction of sex is shewn to persist. For no one says of things which have no capacity for marriage, such as a stick or a stone, that they neither marry nor are given in marriage; but this may well be said of those who, while they can marry, yet abstain from doing so by their own virtue and by the grace of Christ. But if you will cavil at this and say, how shall we in that case be like the angels with whom there is neither male nor female, hear my answer in brief as follows. What the Lord promises to us is not the nature of angels, but their mode of life and their bliss. And therefore John the Baptist was called an angel [74] even before he was beheaded, and all God's holy men and virgins manifest in themselves, even in this world, the life of angels. When it is said: "Ye shall be like the angels," likeness only is promised and not a change of nature.

24. And now do you in your turn answer me these questions. How do you explain the fact that Thomas felt the hands of the risen Lord and beheld his side pierced by the spear? And the fact that Peter saw the Lord standing on the shore and eating

73 Matt. 22:29, 30.   74 Luke 7:27. Greek 'angelos' means messenger.

a piece of a roasted fish and a honeycomb. If he stood, he must certainly have had feet. If he pointed to his wounded side, he must have also had chest and belly, for to these the sides are attached and without them they cannot be. If he spoke, he must have used a tongue and palate and teeth. For as the bow strikes the strings, so does the tongue come in contact with the teeth to produce vocal sounds. If his hands were felt, it follows that he must have had arms as well. Since therefore it is admitted that he had all the members which go to make up the body, he must have also had the whole body formed of them, and that not a woman's, but a man's; that is to say, it rose again in the sex in which it died. And if you cavil further and say: We shall eat then, I suppose, after the resurrection? or, How can a solid and material body enter in, contrary to its nature, through closed doors? you shall receive this reply. Do not for this matter of food find fault with belief in the resurrection. For our Lord, after raising the daughter of the ruler of the synagogue, commanded food to be given her; and Lazarus, who had been dead four days, is described as sitting at meat with him, the object in both cases being to shew that the resurrection was not merely apparent. And if from his entering in through closed doors you strive to prove that his body was spiritual and ethereal, he must have had a spiritual body even before he suffered, since —contrary to the nature of heavy bodies—he was able to walk upon the sea. The apostle Peter also must be believed to have had a spiritual body, for he also walked upon the waters with hesitant step. The true explanation is that when anything is done against nature, it is a manifestation of God's might and power. And to shew plainly that in these great signs our attention is asked not to a change in nature but to the almighty power of God, he who by faith had walked on water, began to sink for the want of faith, and would have done so, had not the hand of the Lord lifted him up with the words: "O thou of little faith, wherefore didst thou doubt?" I wonder that you can display such effrontery when the Lord said: "Reach hither thy finger, and behold my hands; and reach hither thy hand and thrust it into my side: and be not faithless but believing," and in another place: "Behold my hands and my feet that it is I myself: handle me and see; for a spirit hath not flesh and bones as ye see me have. And when he had thus spoken he shewed them his hands and his feet." [75] You hear him speak of bones and flesh, of feet and hands; and yet you want to palm

[75] Matt. 14:31; John 20:27; Luke 24:39–40.

off on me the bubbles and airy nothings of which the Stoics rave![76]

25. Moreover, if you ask how it is that a mere infant which has never sinned is seized by the devil, or at what age we shall rise again seeing that we die at different ages; my only answer —an unwelcome one, I fancy—will be in the words of Scripture: "The judgments of the Lord are a great deep," and "O the depth of the riches both of the wisdom and knowledge of God! how unsearchable are his judgments, and his ways past finding out! For who hath known the mind of the Lord? or who hath been his counsellor?"[77] No difference of age can affect the reality of the body. Although our frames are in a perpetual flux and lose or gain daily, these changes do not make of us different individuals every day. I was not one person at ten years old, another at thirty and another at fifty; nor am I another now when all my head is grey. According to the traditions of the churches and the teaching of the apostle Paul, the answer must be this: that we shall rise as perfect men in the measure of the age of the fulness of Christ.[78] At this age the Jews suppose Adam to have been created, and at this age we read that the Lord and Saviour rose again. Many other arguments did I adduce from both testaments to stifle the outcry of this heretic.

26. From that day forward so profoundly did she commence to loathe the man—and all who agreed with him in his doctrine —that she publicly proclaimed them as enemies of the Lord. I have related this incident less with the design of confuting in a few words a heresy which would require volumes to confute it, than with the object of shewing the great faith of this saintly woman who preferred to subject herself to perpetual hostility from men, rather than by friendships hurtful to herself to provoke or to offend God.

[76] *Globos Stoicorum atque aeria quaedam deliramenta.* The Stoic Chrysippus said that souls are spherical after their separation from the body (Arnim, *Frag. Stoic.*, 815). Since to the Stoic soul is a substance (*corpus*), however tenuous, it must have shape, and, being soul, the perfect shape. See Plato, *Timaeus*, 33b, 63a, for the sphere. Again, it must have colour, and so that of the pure air (cf. Tertullian, *De Anima*, 9). I leave the version "airy nothings," as a familiar phrase. Strictly, the shape and colour are necessary because they are "somethings." On Stoic and early Christian notions of the soul, J. H. Waszink's commentary on Tertullian, *De Anima*, is of very great value. For the Origenistic notion of the spherical resurrection body see Lib. Christ. Class. II (*Alexandrian Christianity*), pp. 191, 232, 381–382.

[77] Ps. 36 (35):6; Rom. 11:33–34.   [78] Eph. 4:13.

26 (27). To revert then to that description of her character which I began a little time ago; no mind was ever more docile than was hers. She was slow to speak and swift to hear, remembering the precept: "Keep silence and hearken, O Israel." [79] The holy Scriptures she knew by heart, and said of the history contained in them that it was the foundation of the truth; but, though she loved even this, she still preferred to seek for the underlying spiritual meaning and made this the keystone of the spiritual building raised within her soul. She asked leave that she and her daughter might read through the Old and New Testaments under my guidance. Out of modesty I at first refused compliance, but as she persisted in her demand and frequently urged me to consent to it, I at last did so and taught her what I had learned not from myself—self-confidence is the worst of teachers—but from the Church's most famous writers. Wherever I stuck fast and honestly confessed myself at fault, she would by no means rest content, but would force me by fresh questions to point out to her which of many possible solutions seemed to me the most probable. I will mention here another fact which to those who are envious may well seem incredible. While I myself, beginning as a young man, have with much toil and effort partially acquired the Hebrew tongue, and study it now unceasingly lest if I leave it, it also may leave me, Paula, on making up her mind that she too would learn it, succeeded so well that she could chant the psalms in Hebrew and could speak the language without a trace of the pronunciation peculiar to Latin. The same accomplishment can be seen to this day in her daughter Eustochium, who always kept close to her mother's side, obeyed all her commands, never slept apart from her, never walked abroad or took a meal without her, never had a penny that she could call her own, rejoiced when her mother gave to the poor her little patrimony, and fully believed that in filial affection she had the best heritage and the truest riches. I must not pass over in silence the joy which she felt when she heard her granddaughter, Paula, the child of Laeta and Toxotius—who was born, and I may even say conceived, in answer to a vow of her parents, dedicating her to virginity—when, I say, she heard the little one in her cradle, still playing with a rattle, still stammering, sing "alleluia" and falter out the words "grandmother" and "aunt". [80] One wish alone made her long to see her native land again; that she might know her son and his

[79] James 1:19; Deut. 27:9.   [80] See *Letter* 107.

wife and child to have renounced the world and to be serving Christ. And it has been granted to her in part. For while her granddaughter is destined to take the veil, her daughter-in-law has vowed herself to perpetual chastity, and by faith and alms emulates the example that her mother has set her. She strives to exhibit at Rome the virtues which Paula set forth in all their fulness at Jerusalem.

27 (28). What ails thee, my soul? Why dost thou shudder to approach her death? I have made my treatise longer than it should be already; dreading to come to the end and vainly supposing that by saying nothing of it and by occupying myself with her praises, I could postpone the evil day. Hitherto the wind has been all in my favour and my keel has smoothly ploughed through the heaving waves. But now my speech is running upon the rocks, the billows are mountain high, and imminent shipwreck awaits both monasteries.[81] We must needs cry out: "Master, save us, we perish;" and "awake, why sleepest thou, O Lord?"[82] For who could tell the tale of Paula's dying with dry eyes? She fell into a most serious illness, and thus gained what she most desired, to leave us and to be joined more fully to the Lord. Eustochium's affection for her mother, always true and tried, in this time of sickness approved itself still more to all. She sat by her bedside, she fanned her, she supported her head, she arranged her pillows, she chafed her feet, she rubbed her stomach, she smoothed down the bedclothes, she heated hot water, she brought towels. In fact she anticipated the servants in all their duties, and when one of them did anything, she regarded it as so much taken away from her own gain. How unceasingly she prayed, how copiously she wept, how constantly she ran to and fro between her prostrate mother and the cave of the Lord, imploring God that she might not be deprived of a companion so dear, that if Paula was to die she might herself no longer live, and that one bier might carry them both to burial! Alas for the frailty and perishableness of human nature! Except that our belief in Christ raises us up to heaven and promises eternity to our souls, the physical conditions of life are the same for us as for the brutes. "There is one event to the righteous and to the wicked; to the good and to the evil; to the clean and to the unclean; to him that sacrificeth and to him that sacrificeth not: as is the good, so is the

---

[81] Not *nostrum*, both of us, as Fremantle's text read, but *monasterii* (Hilberg), the two monasteries for men and women at Bethlehem.
[82] Luke 8:24; Ps. 44:23.

sinner; and he that sweareth as he that feareth an oath." [83]
Man and beast alike are dissolved into dust and ashes.

28 (29). Why do I still linger, and prolong my suffering by
postponing it? Paula's intelligence shewed her that her death
was near. Her body and limbs grew cold, and only in her holy
breast did the warm beat of the living soul continue. Yet, as
though she were leaving strangers to go home to her own people,
she whispered the verses of the psalmist: "Lord, I have loved
the beauty of thy house and the place where thine honour
dwelleth," and "How amiable are thy tabernacles, O Lord
of hosts! My soul longeth, yea, even fainteth, for the courts
of the Lord," and "I had rather be an outcast in the house of
my God than to dwell in the tents of the wicked." When I asked
her why she remained silent, refusing to answer my call,
whether she was in pain, she replied in Greek that she had no
suffering and that all things were to her eyes calm and tranquil.
After this she said no more, but closed her eyes as though she
already despised all mortal things, and kept repeating the same
verses down to the moment at which she breathed out her soul,
but in a tone so low that I could scarcely hear what she said.
Raising her finger also to her mouth, she made the sign of the
cross upon her lips. Then her breath failed her and she gasped
for death; yet even when her soul was eager to break free, she
turned the death-rattle (which comes at last to all) into the
praise of the Lord. The Bishop of Jerusalem and some from
other cities were present, also a great number of the inferior
clergy, both priests and levites. The entire monastery was
filled with companies of virgins and monks. As soon as she
heard the bridegroom saying: "Rise up, my love, my fair one,
my dove, and come away: for, lo, the winter is past, the rain
is over and gone," she answered joyfully "the flowers appear
on the earth; the time to cut them has come" and "I believe
that I shall see the good things of the Lord in the land of the
living." [84]

29 (30). No weeping or lamentation followed her death,
such as are the custom of the world; the swarms of monks
united in chanting the psalms in their several tongues. The
bishops lifted up the dead woman with their own hands,
and some of them put their shoulders to the bier, carried her
to the church in the cave of the Saviour, and laid her down in

[83] Eccl. 9:2.
[84] Ps. 26 (25):8; 84:1, 2, 10; S. of Sol. 2:10–12; Ps. 27 (26):13. Priests and
levites are presbyters and deacons.

the centre of it. Other bishops meantime carried torches and tapers in the procession, and yet others led the singing of the choirs. The whole population of the cities of Palestine came to her funeral. Not a single monk lurked in the desert or lingered in his cell. Not a single virgin remained shut up in the seclusion of her chamber. To each and all it would have seemed sacrilege to have withheld the last tokens of respect from a woman so saintly. As in the case of Dorcas,[85] the widows and the poor shewed the garments Paula had given them; while the destitute cried aloud that they had lost in her a mother and a nurse. Strange to say, the paleness of death had not altered her expression; only a certain solemnity and seriousness had overspread her features. You would have thought her not dead but asleep.

One after another they chanted the psalms, now in Greek, now in Latin, now in Syriac; and this not merely for the three days which elapsed before she was buried beneath the church and close to the cave of the Lord, but throughout the remainder of the week. All who were assembled felt that it was their own funeral, and shed tears as if for themselves. Her daughter, the revered virgin Eustochium, "as a child that is weaned of its mother,"[86] could not be torn away from her parent. She kissed her eyes, pressed her lips upon her brow, embraced her frame, and wanted to be buried with her mother.

30 (31). Jesus is witness that Paula has left not a single penny to her daughter, but, as I said before, a large mass of debt; and, worse even than this, a crowd of brothers and sisters whom it is hard for her to support, but whom it would be undutiful to cast off. Could there be a more admirable instance of virtue than that of this noble lady who in the fervour of her faith gave away so much of her great wealth that she reduced herself to well-nigh the last degree of poverty? Others may boast, if they will, of money spent in charity, of large sums heaped upon God's treasury,[87] of votive offerings hung up with cords of gold. None of them has given more to the poor than she, for she kept nothing for herself. But now she enjoys the true riches and those good things "which eye hath not seen nor ear heard, neither have they entered into the heart of man."[88] If we mourn, it is for ourselves and not for her; yet

[85] Acts 9:39.   [86] Ps. 131 (130):2.
[87] *In corban Dei*, cf. Matt. 27:6; Mark 7:11. "Brothers and sisters" (above) means monks and nuns.
[88] I Cor. 2:9.

even so, if we persist in weeping for one who reigns with Christ, we shall seem to envy her her glory.

31 (32). Be not anxious, Eustochium: you are endowed with a splendid heritage. The Lord is your portion; and, to increase your joy, your mother has now after a long martyrdom won her crown. It is not only the shedding of blood that is accounted a confession; the spotless service of a devout mind is itself a daily martyrdom. Both alike are crowned; with roses and violets in the one case, with lilies in the other. Thus in the Song of Songs it is written: "My cousin is white and ruddy;"[89] for whether the victory be won in peace or war, God gives the same guerdon to those who win it. Like Abraham, your mother heard the words: "Get thee out of thy country, and from thy kindred, and come unto a land that I will shew thee;" and the Lord's command given through Jeremiah: "Flee out of the midst of Babylon, and save your souls." To the day of her death she never returned to Chaldaea, or regretted the flesh-pots of Egypt and its savoury meats. Accompanied by her virgin bands, she became a fellow-citizen of the Saviour; and now that she has ascended from her little Bethlehem to the heavenly realms, she can say to the true Naomi: "Thy people shall be my people and thy God my God."[90]

32 (33). I have spent the labour of two nights in dictating for you this treatise; and in doing so I have felt a grief as deep as your own. I say in "dictating" for I have not been able to write it myself. As often as I have taken up my pen and have tried to fulfil my promise, my fingers have stiffened, my hand has fallen, and my power over it has vanished. The rudeness of the diction, devoid as it is of all elegance or charm, bears witness only to the wishes of the writer.

33 (34). And now, Paula, farewell, and aid with your prayers the old age of your votary. Your faith and your works unite you to Christ; thus standing in his presence you will the more readily gain what you ask. "I have built a monument more lasting than bronze,"[91] which no lapse of time will be able to destroy. And I have cut an inscription on your tomb, which I here subjoin; that, wherever my narrative may go, the reader may learn that you are buried at Bethlehem and not uncommemorated there.

[89] S. of Sol. 5:10, with *fratruelis*, cousin, following LXX. In the Vulgate, Jerome has the familiar "beloved."
[90] Gen. 12:1; Jer. 51:6; Ex. 16:3; Ruth 1:16.
[91] Horace, *Odes*, III, 30, 1.

THE INSCRIPTION ON THE TOMB

Within this tomb a child of Scipio lies,
A daughter of the far-famed Pauline house,
A scion of the Gracchi, of the stock
Of Agamemnon's self, illustrious:
Here rests the lady Paula, well-beloved
Of both her parents, with Eustochium
For daughter; she the first of Roman dames
Who hardship chose and Bethlehem for Christ.

In front of the cavern there is another inscription as follows:—

Seest thou here hollowed in the rock a grave?
'Tis Paula's tomb; high heaven has her soul.
Who Rome and friends, riches and home, forsook,
Here in this lonely spot to find her rest.
For here Christ's manger was, and here the kings
To him, both God and man, their offerings made.

34 (35). The holy and blessed Paula fell asleep on the 26th of January on the third day of the week, after the sun had set. She was buried on the 28th of January, in the sixth consulship of the Emperor Honorius and the first of Aristaenetus.[92] She lived in the vows of religion five years at Rome and twenty years at Bethlehem. The whole duration of her life was fifty-six years, eight months, and twenty-one days.

[92] A.D. 404.

Letter 146 : To Evangelus

INTRODUCTION

I

IT IS NOW GENERALLY TAKEN AS AN ESTABLISHED
fact that the author of the earliest Latin commentary on
the Epistles of Paul, once attributed to Ambrose, and the
author of the *Quaestiones Veteris et Novi Testamenti*, once ascribed
to Augustine, was one and the same person; and that person
is commonly spoken of as "Ambrosiaster."[1] Who he was we
do not know, though he certainly lived in Rome under Pope
Damasus (366–384). The identification of him with Isaac the
Jew, an opponent of Damasus, is no more than a clever guess,
with not much to be said for it.

When Jerome wrote his commentaries on some of the Pauline
epistles, including Titus (not later than 392, and probably
about 388), he showed no knowledge of Ambrosiaster's work.
But in his *Letter 73* (which can fortunately be dated to A.D. 398)
he is replying to one of the *Quaestiones* (109), sent to him for
comment by the same Evangelus who received the present
letter. It is a brief tract suggesting that Melchizedek should be
thought of as the Holy Spirit, sent to bless Abraham. Jerome
dismisses this anonymous pamphlet with extracts from "standard commentators". He is obliged to admit that Origen and
Didymus of Alexandria had taken the same line; but Hippolytus, Irenaeus, Eusebius, Eustathius of Antioch and others
had agreed in believing Melchizedek to have been a real man.

---

[1] For the Commentaries see A. Souter, *The Earliest Latin Commentaries
on the Epistles of St. Paul*, 1927; the *Quaestiones* were edited by Souter for
the Vienna *Corpus* (C.S.E.L., 50, 1908, called *Pseudo-Augustinus*); and on
Ambrosiaster see Souter, *A Study of Ambrosiaster* (Texts and Studies,
vol. VII, 4), 1905. I have not seen C. Martini, *Ambrosiaster*, Rome,
1944.

There is nothing to determine the date of *Letter* 146, except
that it must be later than the Pauline commentaries, nor to
explain what Evangelus had to do with the issue under discussion. It is evidently based on another of the *Quaestiones*, no.
101, and this time Jerome finds Ambrosiaster more to his taste.
Ambrosiaster is refuting the folly which supposes that deacons
—particularly at Rome—are equal to presbyters. It was true,
as a matter of fact, that the deacons in many dioceses were
more prominent and, in a sense, more important than the
presbyters, and this was notably the case at Rome where the
deacons administered large funds and great estates. Ambrosiaster insists on their lower rank in the Church in that they are
not priests, cannot celebrate the eucharist, and must serve
those who do, whether bishops or presbyters; for these are both
sacerdotes. He goes on to support his point by showing that in
the New Testament (he argues from I Timothy 3) *presbyter*
and *episcopus*, "bishop," mean the same thing. With this
Quaestio may be compared his commentaries on I Timothy and
Ephesians.

II

Jerome uses many of the same instances and arguments.
But he very much develops the scriptural proofs of the equivalence of presbyter and bishop. Thus he appears to change the
emphasis from an attack on diaconal pride, vis-à-vis the presbyter, to an assertion of presbyteral dignity, vis-à-vis the bishop.
One remembers that he wanted to be as independent as possible
of Bishop John of Jerusalem. The points of New Testament
scholarship were not new to him; they appear in his *Commentary
on Titus*. Today the original equivalence of *presbyter* and *episcopus* is widely accepted on much the same evidence. The
wider implications of Jerome's remarks cannot be discussed
here. Briefly, while he maintains their original equivalence, he
does not deny that, by later church order, ordination is reserved to the bishop. Otherwise, he seems to think, the presbyter is as good as the bishop. Nor does he deny that there is
some sense in which the bishops are successors of the apostles.
But he does hold that individual presbyters were elevated to
rule over others at a date *subsequent* to the New Testament
documents which he quotes. There is a fairly full discussion
of Jerome's views and some similar ones by Dr. T. G. Jalland
in *The Apostolic Ministry*, ed. K. E. Kirk, pp. 314–340.

III

The passage about Alexandria has to be linked with the different, but related, assertion of Ambrosiaster: "In Alexandria and throughout Egypt, in the absence of a bishop, the presbyter seals" (*consignat*, part of baptism), and with a few other well-known statements regarding special traditions at Alexandria. These have been studied recently by Dr. W. Telfer in *Journal of Ecclesiastical History*, Vol. III, (1952), pp. 1–2. He goes so far as to say that "It is probable that a majority of scholars hold the opinion that the early bishops of Alexandria received their episcopal office at the hands of their fellow-presbyters." The question of the Alexandrian succession, and in particular Origen's evidence, is carefully examined by Dr. A. Ehrhardt in his book, *The Apostolic Succession* (1953), chapter 6.

Letter 146 : To Evangelus

THE TEXT

1. We read in Isaiah the words: "the fool will speak folly,"[1] and I am told that some one has been mad enough to put deacons before[2] presbyters, that is, before bishops. For when the Apostle clearly teaches that presbyters are the same as bishops, must not a mere server of tables and of widows be insane to set himself up arrogantly over men through whose prayers the body and blood of Christ are made?[3] Do you ask for proof of what I say? Listen to this passage: "Paul and Timotheus, the servants of Christ Jesus, to all the saints in Christ Jesus which are at Philippi, with the bishops and deacons." Do you wish for another instance? In the *Acts of the Apostles* Paul thus speaks to the priests of a single church: "Take heed unto yourselves and to all the flock, in the which the Holy Ghost hath made you bishops, to rule the church of the Lord which he purchased with his own blood". And lest any should in a spirit of contention argue that there must then have been more bishops than one in a single church, there is the following passage which clearly proves a bishop and a presbyter to be the same. Writing to Titus the Apostle says: "For this cause left I thee in Crete, that thou shouldest set in order the things that are wanting, and appoint presybters in every city, as I had instructed thee: if any be blameless, the husband of one wife, having believing children not accused of wantonness or unruly. For a bishop must be blameless as the steward of God." And to Timothy he says: "Neglect not the gift of prophecy that is in thee, which was given thee through the laying on of the hands of the presbytery."[4] Peter also

---

[1] Isa. 32:6.
[2] *Anteferret*. Ambrosiaster says *coaequare, non dicam praeferre (Quaestio, 2)*.
[3] *Conficitur*.
[4] Phil. 1:1; Acts 20:28; Titus 1:5–7; I Tim. 4:14.

says in his first epistle: "The presbyters which are among
you I exhort, who am your fellow-presbyter and a witness of
the sufferings of Christ and also a partaker of the glory that
shall be revealed: rule the flock of Christ, inspecting it not by
constraint but willingly, according unto God." [5] In the Greek
the meaning is still plainer, for the word used is ἐπισκοπεύοντες,
that is to say, "overseeing", and this is the origin of the name
"bishop". But perhaps the testimony of these great men seems
to you insufficient. If so, then listen to the blast of the Gospel
trumpet, that son of thunder, the disciple whom Jesus loved and
who, reclining on the Saviour's breast, drank in the waters of
sound doctrine. "The presbyter unto the elect lady and her
children, whom I love in the truth;" and in another letter: "The
presbyter unto the well-beloved Gaius, whom I love in the
truth." [6] When subsequently one was chosen to preside over
the rest, this was done to remedy schism [7] and to prevent
each individual from rending the Church of Christ by
drawing it to himself. For even at Alexandria, from the time
of Mark the Evangelist until the episcopates of Heraclas and
Dionysius, the presbyters always used to choose one of their
own number and set him in a more exalted rank and call him
"bishop", like an army making an emperor, or deacons
choosing one of themselves whom they know to be diligent and
calling him archdeacon. [8] For what function, excepting ordination, belongs to a bishop that does not also belong to a presbyter? It is not the case that there is one church at Rome and
another in all the world beside. Gaul and Britain, Africa and
Persia, India and the East, and all the barbarian tribes worship
one Christ and observe one rule of truth. If you ask for authority, the world outweighs its capital. Wherever there is a bishop,
whether it be at Rome or at Eugubium, whether it be at
Constantinople or at Rhegium, whether it be at Alexandria or
at Tanis, his dignity is the same and his priesthood is the same.
Neither the command of wealth nor the lowliness of poverty

---

[5] I Peter 5:1–2, with *inspicere* as a literal rendering of *episkopein*, oversee.
[6] II John 1:1; III John 1:1.
[7] The passage is very close to his commentary on Titus.
[8] Heraclas, 231–246; Dionysius, 246–264. The Latin is *presbyteri . . . elec-
tum . . . conlocatum episcopum nominabant*, which naturally means "*they*
elected and *they* set and they called him bishop." The word translated
rank is *gradus*. For the implications see the literature quoted in the introduction to this letter, and in general the books on the Ministry of the
Church. Jerome obscures his argument by accepting the tradition about
St. Mark!

makes him a higher or a lower bishop. All alike are successors
of the apostles.[9]

2. But you will say: "How comes it then that at Rome a presbyter is ordained on the recommendation of a deacon?"[10]
Why do you bring forward a custom which exists in one city
only? Why do you maintain, in opposition to the laws of the
Church, a paucity which has given rise to arrogance? The
rarer anything is, the more it is sought after. In India penny-
royal is more costly than pepper. Their paucity makes deacons
persons of consequence, while presbyters are less thought of
owing to their great numbers.[11] But even in the church of Rome
the deacons stand while the presbyters seat themselves, although
bad habits have by degrees so far crept in that I have seen a
deacon, in the absence of the bishop, seat himself among the
presbyters, and at social gatherings give his blessing to them.[12]
Those who act thus must learn that they are wrong and must
give heed to the apostles' words: "It is not fit that we should
leave the word of God and serve tables."[13] They must consider
the reasons which led to the appointment of deacons at the
beginning. They must read the Acts of the Apostles and bear
in mind their true position.

Of the names "presbyter" and "bishop" the first denotes
age, the second rank. In writing both to Titus and to Timothy,
the Apostle speaks of the ordination of a bishop and of deacons,
but says not a word of the presbyters; for the fact is that the
word "bishop" includes presbyter also.[14] Again when a man is
promoted it is from a lower place to a higher.[15] Either then a

9 In the appeal from *urbs* to *orbis* and in the following sentences Jerome
seems to be returning to a second or third century position, with the
regula veritatis or *fidei* in each apostolic church as the *auctoritas* for doctrine
and bishops all equal. Any one would allow, of course, that the importance of a man's see does not affect his *sacerdotium*, the fact that he is a
bishop. Jerome appears to go further and say that it does not affect his
dignity (*meritum*) or make him "higher" than another bishop (*subli-
miorem*). But the passage is rhetorical, and he does not say enough to
define his views precisely.

10 From Q. 9, but Ambrosiaster gives a different answer. In effect, he says
why not? Laymen give testimony to deacons, etc.

11 Under Pope Cornelius (*c.* 253) there were seven deacons to forty-six
presbyters at Rome (Eus., *H.E.*, VI, 43, 11). The deacons remained
seven for a long time.

12 Both points from Ambrosiaster, Q. 3 and 7. Compare Nicaea, canon 18.

13 Acts 6:2.

14 Cf. Q. 4 *ad fin.*, *Maior ordo intra se et apud se habet et minorem.*

15 Cf. Q. 4 *ad init.*, *Quasi ex presbiteris diaconi et non ex diaconibus presbiteri
ordinentur.*

presbyter should be ordained deacon, from the lesser office, that is, to the more important, to prove that a presbyter is inferior to a deacon; or if on the other hand it is the deacon that is ordained presbyter, this latter should recognize that, although he may be less highly paid than a deacon, he is superior to him in virtue of his priesthood. In fact as if to tell us that the traditions handed down by the apostles were taken by them from the Old Testament, bishops, presbyters and deacons occupy in the Church the same positions as those which were occupied by Aaron, his sons, and the Levites in the temple.

SELECT BIBLIOGRAPHY

A. GENERAL HISTORIES OF THE EARLY CHURCH

Duchesne, L.: *The Early History of the Christian Church.* English translation in three volumes, Murray, London 1909–1924.

Fliche, A. and Martin, V. edd.: *Histoire de l'Eglise*, vols. 1–4. Bloud et Gay, Paris 1934–1937.
>The first two volumes have been translated by E. C. Messenger and published as J. Lebreton and J. Zeiller, *The History of the Primitive Church*, 4 vols., Burns, Oates and Washbourne, London 1942–1948; and the third as J. R. Palanque (etc.), *The Church in the Christian Roman Empire*, 2 vols., 1949–1952.

Gwatkin, H. M.: *Early Church History to* A.D. 313, 2 vols., Macmillan, London 1909.

Kidd, B. J.: *A History of the Church to* A.D. 461, 3 vols., Oxford 1922.

Lietzmann, H.: *Geschichte der Alten Kirche*, 4 vols., Berlin 1932–1944.
>This has been translated by B. L. Woolf and published as:
>1. *The Beginnings of the Christian Church*, Nicholson and Watson, London 1937.
>2. *The Founding of the Church Universal*, Nicholson and Watson, London 1938.
>3. *From Constantine to Julian*, Lutterworth Press, London 1950.
>4. *The Era of the Church Fathers*, Lutterworth Press, London 1951.

B. PATROLOGY AND THE HISTORY OF PATRISTIC DOCTRINE

Altaner, B.: *Patrologie*, ed. 3, Freiburg, 1951.

Bardenhewer, O.: *Geschichte der altkirchlichen Literatur*, 5 vols., Freiburg 1912–1932.

Bethune-Baker, J. F.: *An Introduction to the Early History of Christian Doctrine.* Methuen, London 1903, and subsequent revisions.

Harnack, A.: *History of Dogma*, 7 vols. Williams and Norgate, London 1894–1899.

Labriolle, P. de: *Histoire de la Littérature Latine Chrétienne*, 3rd ed., revised by G. Bardy, Paris 1947.
>There is an English translation of the first edition, Kegan Paul, London 1924.

Loofs, F.: *Leitfaden zum Studium der Dogmengeschichte*, ed. 4, Halle 1906.
>A revised edition, by K. Aland, is in progress. Parts 1 and 2 were published by Niemeyer, Halle 1950, 1953.

Quasten, J.: *Patrology*, 2 vols. (so far), Utrecht 1950, 1953.

Seeberg, R.: *Lehrbuch der Dogmengeschichte*, I–II, ed. 3, Leipzig 1922.

Tixeront, J.: *History of Dogmas*, 3 vols. Herder, U.S.A. 1930.

C. THE PATRISTIC DOCTRINE OF THE CHURCH AND THE MINISTRY

Bardy, G.: *La Théologie de l'Eglise de saint Clément de Rome à saint Irenée*.

—— *La Théologie de l'Eglise de saint Irenée au concile de Nicée*. Les Editions du Cerf, Paris 1945 and 1947.

Burn-Murdoch, H.: *Church, Continuity and Unity*. Cambridge University Press: 1945.

Lubac, H. de: *Catholicism*. Burns, Oates and Washbourne, London 1950.

Gore, C.: *The Church and the Ministry*, 1886, revised by C. H. Turner, 1919, and published with an appendix, S.P.C.K., London 1936.

Greenslade, S. L.: *Schism in the Early Church*. S.C.M. Press, London 1953.

Headlam, A. C.: *The Doctrine of the Church and Christian Reunion*. John Murray, London 1920.

Jalland, T. G.: *The Origin and Evolution of the Christian Church*. Hutchinson, London n.d. (Preface, 1948).

Kirk, K. E., ed.: *The Apostolic Ministry*. Hodder and Stoughton, London 1946. Especially c. IV, "The Ministry in the Early Church," by Dom Gregory Dix.

Mersch, E.: *Le Corps Mystique du Christ*, ed. 2, 2 vols. Paris 1936.

Swete, H. B., ed.: *Essays on the Early History of the Church and the Ministry*. Macmillan, London 1918, 1921. Especially c. III, "Apostolic Succession," by C. H. Turner.

D. TERTULLIAN

(i) *Editions and Translations*

Q. S Fl. *Tertulliani quae supersunt omnia*, ed. F. Oehler, Leipzig 1853–1854, in 3 vols., the third containing dissertations. Long the standard complete edition, with valuable notes.

Tertulliani Opera, Vienna 1890–1942 (C.S.E.L. vols. XX, XLVII, LXIX, LXX), edited by A. Reifferscheid, G. Wissowa, A. Kroymann, H. Hoppe, and to be completed by one more volume.

Q. S. Fl. *Tertulliani Opera*, Turnhout 1954 (*Corpus Christianorum*, Series Latina, I–II). A complete text; some works are reprints of the Vienna and other texts, some are newly edited. Volume I contains a valuable bibliography.

The Writings of Tertullian, translated by S. Thelwall and P. Holmes, 4 vols. Edinburgh 1868–1870. Complete.

Tertullian: Apologetic and Practical Treatises, translated by C. Dodgson, Oxford 1842, 2nd ed. 1854. 14 works.

There is a German translation by K. Kellner and G. Esser in the *Bibliothek der Kirchenväter*, Kempten 1912, 1916. This is much more reliable than the above English versions.

The S.P.C.K. has published more modern translations of the following works: *The Testimony of the Soul, The Prescription of Heretics* (T. H. Bindley, 1914); *Against Praxeas, Concerning Prayer, Concerning Baptism, Concerning the Resurrection of the Flesh* (A. Souter, 1919–1922); *Against Praxeas* (E. Evans, 1948); *On the Prayer* (E. Evans, 1953), the last two as part of commentaries. T. R. Glover translated the *Apology* and *De Spectaculis* for the *Loeb Library*, Heinemann, 1931.

Of commentaries on individual works, the following are particularly noteworthy: E. Evans, *Tertullian's Treatise against Praxeas*, S.P.C.K., 1948, J. E. B. Mayor, *Tertullian's Apology*, Cambridge 1917 (valuable for patristic Latin), J. P. Waltzing, *Tertullien: Apologétique*, Paris 1931, J. H. Waszink, *Tertulliani De Anima*, Amsterdam 1947.

(ii) *Language*

Hoppe, H.: *Syntax und Stil des Tertullian*. Leipzig 1903.
Löfstedt, E.: *Zur Sprache Tertullians*. Lund 1920.
Thörnell, G.: *Studia Tertullianea*, I–IV. Uppsala 1918–1926.

See also the 100-page *Index Rerum et Locutionum* in vol. II of the *Corpus Christianorum*.

(iii) *General and Biographical*

D'Alès, A.: *La Théologie de Tertullien*. Paris 1905.
Dekkers, E.: *Tertullianus en de geschiedenis der Liturgie*. Brussels 1947.
Glover, T. R.: *The Conflict of Religions in the Early Roman Empire*. London 1909.
Lortz, J.: *Tertullian als Apologet*, 2 vols. Münster 1927–1928.
Monceaux, P.: *Histoire littéraire de l'Afrique chrétienne, I, Les origines*. Paris 1901.
Nisters, B.: *Tertullian. Sein Persönlichkeit und sein Schicksal*. Münster 1950.
Nöldechen, E.: *Tertullian*. Gotha 1890.
Roberts, R.: *The Theology of Tertullian*. London 1924.
Rolffs, E.: *Tertullian, der Vater des abendländischen Christentums*. Berlin 1930.
Rönsch, H.: *Das neue Testament Tertullians*. Leipzig 1871.

(iv) *De Praescriptionibus Haereticorum*

(a) Separate editions, commentaries and translations
Brink, J. N. Bakhuizen van den: *De Praescriptione Haereticorum*. Hague 1946, with a few improvements to the text, but no notes.

Bindley, T. H.: *De Praescriptione Haereticorum.* Oxford 1893, with commentary.
——, *The "Prescription" of the Heretics.* English translation with some notes, S.P.C.K., 1914.
Labriolle, P. de: *De Praescriptione Haereticorum,* with French translation and some notes. Paris 1907.
Preuschen, E.: *De Praescriptione Haereticorum.* Friburg 1892, 1910.
Rauschen, G.: *Liber De Praescriptione Haereticorum.* Bonn 1906, with brief commentary in Latin. Revised by J. Martin, Bonn 1930.

(b) *Studies*
Adam, K.: *Der Kirchenbegriff Tertullians.* Paderborn 1907.
Stirnimann, J.: *Die Praescriptio Tertullians im Lichte des römischen Rechtes und der Theologie.* Freiburg 1949.
Turner, H. E. W.: *The Pattern of Christian Truth,* especially chapter 1. London 1954.
Also the books listed in section C of this bibliography.

(v) *De Idololatria*

Cadoux, C. J.: *The Early Church and the World.* Edinburgh 1925.
Greenslade, S. L.: *The Church and the Social Order.* S.C.M. Press, 1948.
Guignebert, C.: *Tertullien: Etude sur ses Sentiments à l'égard de l'Empire et de la Société civile.* Paris 1901.
Troeltsch, E.: *The Social Teaching of the Christian Churches,* translated by Olive Wyon. London 1931 (chapter one).

E. CYPRIAN

(i) *Editions and Translations*

S. Thasci Caecili Cypriani Opera Omnia, ed. W. Hartel. (C.S.E.L., vol. III, 1, 2, 3), Vienna 1868–1871.
Saint Cyprien: Correspondance, ed. L. Bayard, 2 vols. Paris (Collection Budé) 1925. Text, better than Hartel's, and French translation.
The Genuine Works of St. Cyprian, translated by Nathaniel Marshall. London 1717.
The Treatises of S. Caecilius Cyprian, translated [by Charles Thornton]. Oxford 1839 (*Library of the Fathers*). This volume includes the *Life* by Pontius the Deacon and the *Martyrdom.*
The Epistles of S. Cyprian, translated by H. Carey. Oxford 1844 (*Library of the Fathers*).
The Writings of Cyprian, translated by R. E. Wallis, 2 vols. Edinburgh 1868–1869 (*Ante-Nicene Christian Library*).
Select Epistles of St. Cyprian treating of the Episcopate, edited with introduction and a few notes by T. A. Lacey, S.P.C.K. n.d. The translation is a revision of Marshall's.
     There is a German version by Julius Baer in the *Bibliothek der Kirchenväter,* 2 vols. Kempten 1918, 1928.

(ii) *Language*

Bayard, L.: *Le Latin de Saint Cyprien*. Paris, 1902.
Janssen, H.: *Kultur und Sprache . . . von Tertullian bis Cyprian*. Nijmegen 1938 (*Latinitas Christianorum Primaeva*, VIII).
Merkx, P. J.: *Zur Syntax der Casus und Tempora in den Traktaten des hl. Cyprians*. Nijmegen 1939 (L.C.P. IX).
Schrijnen, J. and Mohrmann, C.: *Studien zur Syntax der Briefe des hl. Cyprian*, 2 vols. Nijmegen 1936–1937 (L.C.P. V, VI).
Watson, E. W.: *The Style and Language of St. Cyprian* (*Studia Biblica et Ecclesiastica*, vol. IV). Oxford 1896.

(iii) *General and Biographical*

There is a brief life of Cyprian by his own deacon, Pontius. The text is in Hartel, vol. iii, and a translation in the *Library of the Fathers* (see above). See also A. Harnack, *Das Leben Cyprians von Pontius*, Leipzig 1913 (T.U., xxxix, 3). The official *Acta* of his martyrdom are extant; text in Hartel, iii, and in many collections of *Acta*, translation in *Lib. Fathers*, as above, and in E. C. E. Owen, *Some Authentic Acts of the Early Martyrs*, Oxford 1927.
Benson, E. W.: *Cyprian*. London 1897.
D'Alès, A.: *La Théologie de Saint Cyprien*. Paris 1922.
—— *Novatien*, Paris 1925.
Koch, H.: *Cyprianische Untersuchungen*. Bonn 1926.
Monceaux, P.: *Saint Cyprien et son temps* (=*Hist. litt. de l'Afrique chrétienne*, t. II. Paris 1902).
Soden, H. von: *Die Cyprianische Briefsammlung*. Leipzig 1904 (T.U., xxv, 3).
—— *Das lateinische Neue Testament in Afrika zur Zeit Cyprians* (T.U., xxxiii). Leipzig 1909.

(iv) *De Unitate*

(a) Separate editions and translations
Blakeney, E. H.: *Cyprian: De Unitate Ecclesiae*. Text, English translation, and a few notes. S.P.C.K., 1928 (*Texts for Students*, 43).
Labriolle, P. de: *Saint Cyprien, de l'Unité de l'Eglise catholique*. Text, introduction, French translation and notes. Paris 1942.
Wright, F. A.: *Fathers of the Church*, London 1928. This contains an English translation of *De Unitate*.

(b) *The Problem of the text of cc. iv–v*
(P.T. =Primacy text, T.R. =Textus Receptus)
Bévenot, M.: *"Primatus Petro Datur": St. Cyprian on the Papacy*, and *"Hi qui sacrificaverunt"* (J. Theol. Studies, N.S. vol. V (1954)) pp. 19–35, 68–72. B. replies to Le Moyne, re-affirms his previous conclusions, and claims to have found a demonstrative argument in favour of them.

Bévenot, M.: *St. Cyprian's De unitate chap. 4 in the light of the manuscripts.* (Analecta Gregoriana XI) Rome 1937. P.T. first, T.R. from Baptismal controversy; much fuller study of MSS.

Chapman, Dom John: *Les interpolations dans le traité de S. Cyprien sur l'unité de l'Eglise.* Revue Benedictine, vol. 19 (1902), pp. 246–254, 357–373; vol. 20, 26–51. Both texts Cyprianic; P.T. second against Novatianism at Rome. Later Chapman put P.T. first, with T.R. a revision in the context of the Baptismal controversy (as Bévenot, etc.).

Eynde, D. van den: *La double édition du "De Unitate" de S. Cyprien.* Rev. Hist Ecclés. vol. 29 (1933), pp. 5–24. P.T. first, T.R. revision during Baptismal controversy.

Ludwig, J.: *Die Primatworte Mt. 16. 18–19, in der altkirchlichen Exegese.* Münster 1952. P.T. lone Cyprianic; T.R. by one of his supporters in the Baptismal controversy.

Le Moyne, J.: *Saint Cyprien est-il bien l'auteur de la rédaction brève du "De Unitate" chapitre 4?* Rev. Ben. vol. 63 (1953), pp. 70–115. T.R. against Novatian and alone Cyprianic. P.T. fourth century against Donatism.

Perler, O.: *Zur Datierung (Unit 4)* and *Die ursprünglichen Texte (Unit. 5).* Römische Quartalschrift, vol. 44 (1936), pp. 1–44, 151–168. P.T. first, T.R. 255–256.

(c) Cyprian's Doctrine of the Church

Besides the general books mentioned in sections C and E (iii), the following should be noted:

Bévenot, M.: *"A Bishop is responsible to God alone,"* in *Mélanges Jules Lebreton* I, 397–415. Paris 1951.

Butler, Abbot C.: *St. Cyprian on the Church, I, II, III.* Downside Review, vol. 70 (1952–1953), pp. 1–13, 119–134; vol. 71, pp. 258–272.

Koch, H.: *Cathedra Petri.* Giessen 1930.

—— *Cyprian und der römische Primat.* Leipzig 1910 (T.U., xxxv, 1).

Poschmann, B.: *Ecclesia principalis.* Breslau 1933.

Consult also the books on the history of the Papacy, e.g. E. Caspar: *Geschichte des Papsttums*, I, 58–102 (Tübingen 1930); T. G. Jalland: *The Church and the Papacy*, 155–178 (S.P.C.K., 1944); J. Chapman: *Studies on the Early Papacy*, c. 2: St. Cyprian on the Church, London 1928; and P. Batiffol: *L'Eglise naissante et le Catholicisme* (ed. 5, Paris 1911; ed. 9, 1927) c.8.

F. AMBROSE

(i) Editions and Translations

The standard edition is still that of the Benedictine scholars, J. Du Frische and N. Le Nourry, 2 vols., Paris 1686, 1690. This is better than that of P. A. Ballerini, Milan 1875–1883, though his variant readings are valuable. The Benedictine text is reproduced in Migne, P.L. XIV–XVII. Several works, but not yet the letters, have been published in C.S.E.L.

Letters 17, 18, and 57 are well edited by J. Wytzes (see below), with German translations. Letter 51 is included, with an English version, in Mannix, *De Obitu Theodosii* (see below).

There is a complete English version of the letters in the Library of the Fathers, made anonymously and revised by H. Walford (Oxford 1881). Vol. X of the *Nicene and Post-Nicene Fathers, St. Ambrose: Select Works and Letters*, translated by H. de Romestin, Oxford and New York 1896, contains the *De Officiis* and eight other treatises, with a dozen letters, including eight of those in the present volume.

(ii) *Biographical and General*

The life of St. Ambrose was written briefly by his secretary, the deacon Paulinus, about A.D. 422. The text is included in the editions of Ambrose. There is an edition with English translation and notes by M. S. Kaniecka, Washington 1928, and a translation is included in *The Western Fathers*, translated and edited by F. R. Hoare, London 1954. The accounts of Ambrose in the early Greek historians, Socrates, Sozomen and Theodoret, are not very trustworthy.

Adams, M. A.: *The Latinity of the Letters of Saint Ambrose*. Washington 1927. Sometimes useful, but not authoritative.

Ambrosiana, Milan 1897. A collection of studies.

Ambrosiana, Milan 1942. A second collection.

Boissier, G.: *La fin du paganisme*, 2 vols. Paris 1891.

Broglie, J. V. A., Duc de: *L'Eglise et l'Empire romain au IVe siècle*. Paris 1867–1868.

—— *Saint Ambroise*, Paris 1899; 4th ed. 1903, with appendix, *Les Pères Bollandistes et la pénitence de Théodose*.

Campenhausen, Hans von: *Ambrosius von Mailand als Kirchenpolitiker*. Leipzig 1929.

Labriolle, P. de: *Saint Ambroise*. Paris 1908.
    This book contains many passages from Ambrose, including some of the letters in the present volume, in a French translation. There is a (not very good) English translation of the book by H. Wilson, Herder Book Co., St. Louis 1928.

Dill, Sir Samuel: *Roman Society in the Last Century of the Western Empire*. London 1898, ed. 2, 1899.

Dudden, F. Homes: *Saint Ambrose, His Life and Times*, 2 vols. Oxford 1935.
    A very comprehensive and very readable account of his life and teaching. The most important in English.

Ensslin, W.: *Die Religionspolitik des Kaisers Theodosius d. Gr.* Munich 1953.

Förster, Th.: *Ambrosius, Bischof von Mailand*. Halle 1884.

Hodgkin, T.: *Italy and her Invaders*, vol I. Oxford 1879, ed. 2, 1892.

Ihm, M.: *Studia Ambrosiana*. Leipzig 1890.

Kauffmann, F.: *Aus der Schule des Wulfila*. Strassburg 1899. Important for Auxentius of Durostorum, Palladius and the Council of Aquileia.

Mannix, M. D.: *Sancti Ambrosii Oratio de Obitu Theodosii*. Text, translation, introduction and commentary. Washington 1925.

Ortroy, F. van: *Saint Ambroise et l'empereur Théodose* (Analecta Bollandiana, xxiii, 1904, pp. 417–426).

Palanque, J. R.: *Saint Ambroise et l'Empire Romain*. Paris 1933.
    With Campenhausen's, the most important book on Ambrose and politics. It contains also the fullest discussion of the chronology of his writings and a 20-page bibliography.

Rand, E. K.: *Founders of the Middle Ages*. Cambridge, U.S.A. 1929, chap. III.

Rauschen, G.: *Jahrbücher der christlichen Kirche unter dem Kaiser Theodosius dem Grossen*. Freiburg 1897.

Schuster, Cardinal I., *S. Ambrogio e le più antiche basiliche milanesi*. Milan 1940.

Seeck, O.: *Geschichte des Untergangs der antiken Welt*, 6 vols. with supplements, 2nd ed. Stuttgart 1921.

—— *Regesten der Kaiser und Päpste für die Jahre 311 bis 476*. Stuttgart 1919.

Stein, E.: *Geschichte des spätrömischen Reiches*, I, 284–476. Vienna 1928.

Thamin, R.: *Saint Ambroise et la morale chrétienne au IVe siècle*. Paris 1895.

Tillemont, L. de: *Mémoires pour servir a l'histoire ecclésiastique des six premiers siècles*, vol. X. Paris 1705.

Wytzes, J.: *Der Streit um den Altar der Viktoria*. Amsterdam 1936.

Zeiller, J.: *Les origines chrétiennes dans les provinces danubiennes de l'Empire romain*. Paris 1918.

G. JEROME

(i) *Editions and Translations*

The standard complete edition of Jerome is that of D. Vallarsi, ed. 2, Venice 1766–1772, which is reprinted in Migne, P.L., XXII–XXX. The Letters have been edited by Hilberg in C.S.E.L., 54, 55, 56, Vienna 1910, 1912, 1918. He died without producing the volume of prolegomena and indices, but the text is complete. There is an excellent edition of the letters, with French translation and some notes, by J. Labourt, Paris (*Collection Budé*), 5 vols., 1949–1955; these volumes cover Letters 1–109.

Most of the letters, a number of the treatises and many of the prefaces to his works or translations are included in the Jerome volume of the *Nicene and Post-Nicene Fathers* (vol. 6), edited by W. H. Fremantle, Oxford and New York 1893. Another volume of this series (3) contains the *De Viris Illustribus* with its continuation by Gennadius.

A selection of the letters was translated (from Hilberg's text) by F. A. Wright for the Loeb Library, London 1933.

(ii) *Biographical and General*

Antin, P.: *Essai sur Saint Jérôme*. Paris 1951.

Brochet, J.: *Saint Jérôme et ses ennemis*. Paris 1906.

Cavallera, F.: *Saint Jérôme: Sa Vie et son Œuvre*, 2 vols. Paris and Louvain 1922. This work was not finished. It is the chief factual biography, but does not discuss Jerome's thought, as had been planned.

—— *Le Schisme d'Antioche*. Paris 1905.

Génier, R.: *Sainte Paule*. Paris 1917.

Goelzer, H.: *Etude lexicographique et grammaticale de la Latinité de Saint Jérome*. Paris 1884.

Grützmacher, G.: *Hieronymus*, 3 vols. Berlin 1901, 1906, 1908.

Haller, W.: *Iovinianus*. Leipzig 1897 (T.U., xvii, 2).

Miscellanea Geronimiana. Rome 1920. Sixteen essays.

Monceaux, P.: *Saint Jérome: sa jeunesse, l'étudiant, l'ermite*. Paris 1932.

—— *St. Jerome: the Early Years*. London 1933. A translation of the above book by F. J. Sheed.

Murphy, F. X.: *Rufinus of Aquileia*. Washington 1945.

Rand, E. K.: *Founders of the Middle Ages*. Cambridge, U.S.A. 1929, chap. IV.

Tillemont, L. de: *Mémoires pour servir à l'histoire ecclésiastique des six premiers siècles*, vol. XII. Paris 1707.

Villain, M.: *Rufin d'Aquilée, la querelle autour d'Origène*, in Recherches de science religieuse, XXVII (1937), pp. 5–37, 165–195.

INDEXES

GENERAL INDEX

(Biblical names are not normally included. For references to early Christian writers consult also Index II. The Bibliography is not included in the Index.)

Abodah Zara, 79, 94, 95, 99
Academy, 36
Achaea, 56
Acholius, 206
Acolyte, 320
Actium, 190
Adiabene, 354
Adoptianism, 189
Adrianople, 188, 248
Adriatic, 353
Aelia (Jerusalem), 354
Aemilia-Liguria, 175, 268
Aeneas, 350
Aesop, 362
Africa, 57, 113–116, 119, 121, 123, 147–148, 158–159, 179, 182, 330, 387
    See also Carthage, Curubis, Donatism, Numidia
Agamemnon, 349, 382
Agrippinus, 147, 159
Alans, 223
Albina, 283
Albinus, 330, 332
Alemanni, 223
Alexander the Great, 336, 344
Alexander, Bishop of Alexandria, 186
Alexandria, 51, 183, 186, 192, 234, 265, 284–285, 303, 304, 308, 309, 334, 361, 385, 387
Altar of Victory, 176, 190–199, 259–264
Altinum, 282, 290, 312, 313
Alypius, 330
Ambrose, 15, 16, 91, 174–278, 283, 288, 305, 310, 313, 321, 383
Ambrosiaster, 176, 383–389
Ammianus Marcellinus, 233
Anacletus, 53
Anastasius, 286

Ancyra, *see* Basil, Marcellus.
Andragathias, 224, 236
Andromeda, 354
Anicetus, 70
Antelii, 100
Anthony, 281, 352
Anthropians, 160
Antioch, 51, 183, 239, 251, 263, 282–284, 290, 302–306, 308, 309, 346, 351, 353
Antipater, 354
Antipatris, 354
Antoninus Pius, 50, 51
Apelles, 22, 35, 38, 51, 54, 55, 58, 160
Apollinariys, 308
Apollo, 100
Apostles, 26, 37, 43–49, 52, 53, 55–58, 63–73, 75, 76, 91, 109, 120, 126, 139–142, 162, 164–167, 169
Apostolic Succession, 26–29, 43, 52–53, 65, 68–70, 72, 73, 75, 76, 115, 120, 152–153, 297, 299, 385, 387
Aquileia, 175, 182–189, 219, 226, 228, 232, 237, 240, 265, 281, 282, 284, 290
Arbogast, 192, 259
Arcadius, 236, 239, 258
Archdeacon, 387
Arethusa, *see* Mark
Arianism, Arius, 49, 175–178, 182–189, 199–201, 206–207, 210–211, 214, 248, 265, 283, 302–304, 307–311
Ariminum, 185, 200, 206, 207, 283
Aristaenetus, 382
Aristotle, 35, 300, 336, 344, 371
Ark, 109, 110, 128, 151, 307, 308
Arles, 149, 207
Armenia, 334
Arnim, H. von, 376
Arnobius, 313

BIBLICAL REFERENCES

OLD TESTAMENT

NEW TESTAMENT

PATRISTIC REFERENCES

[For references to authors apart from their works consult the General Index]